# TAKING EUROPE FOR JESUS

# TAKING EUROPE FOR JESUS

BY JOSHUA SCHWISOW

Generations
PASSING ON THE FAITH

Copyright © 2022 by Generations

All rights reserved.
Printed in the United States of America.
1st Printing, 2022

ISBN: 978-1-954745-29-2

Unless otherwise noted, Scripture taken from the New King James Version®. Copyright © 1982 by Thomas Nelson. Used by permission. All rights reserved.

Cover Design: Justin Turley
Cover Image: Lake Geneva, iStock.com
Interior Layout Design: Sarah Lee Bryant

Published by:
Generations
19039 Plaza Drive Ste 210
Parker, Colorado 80134
www.generations.org

For more information on this and
other titles from Generations,
visit www.generations.org or call 888-389-9080.

# CONTENTS

INTRODUCTION .................................................................................................. 9

## UNIT 1 ............................................................................................................... 13

PROLOGUE ....................................................................................................... 15

**CHAPTER 1**
Introduction to Europe ..................................................................................... 17

**CHAPTER 2**
Rome: A Republic Turned into an Empire ...................................................... 33

**CHAPTER 3**
The Birth of Christianity in the Fullness of Time ............................................ 43

**CHAPTER 4**
Roman Culture and Religion ............................................................................ 51

**CHAPTER 5**
Rome's Persecution of Christ's People ............................................................ 59

**CHAPTER 6**
Irenaeus of Lyons: Fighting for the Faith Once Delivered .............................. 65

**CHAPTER 7**
Ambrose of Milan: Shepherd of God's People ................................................ 75

**CHAPTER 8**
How Christianity Came to Great Britain ......................................................... 85

**CHAPTER 9**
Patrick: Missionary to the Irish ........................................................................ 93

## UNIT 2 ............................................................................................................. 103

**CHAPTER 10**
Columba and the Monastery of Iona ............................................................. 107

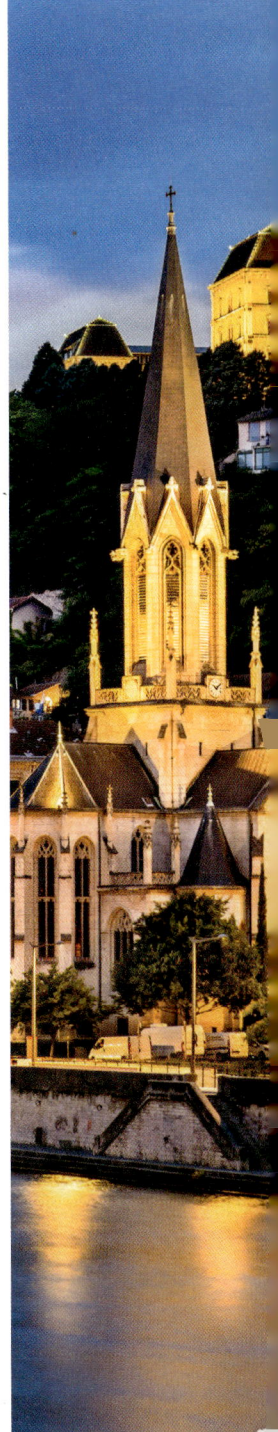

**CHAPTER 11**
Church and Community Life in the British Isles ........................................................ 115

**CHAPTER 12**
Bede: Historian of the English Church ........................................................ 121

**CHAPTER 13**
Alcuin: Court Adviser to Charlemagne ........................................................ 129

**CHAPTER 14**
Anskar: Missionary to Denmark and Sweden ........................................................ 139

**CHAPTER 15**
Cyril and Methodius: Reaching the Slavs for Christ ........................................................ 149

**CHAPTER 16**
Alfred the Great: Christian King of Wessex ........................................................ 161

**CHAPTER 17**
Athelstan: First King of England ........................................................ 169

# UNIT 3 ........................................................ 175

**CHAPTER 18**
The Crusade Against the Cathars ........................................................ 179

**CHAPTER 19**
The Waldensian Movement ........................................................ 187

**CHAPTER 20**
The Black Death ........................................................ 195

**CHAPTER 21**
John Wycliffe and the Lollards ........................................................ 201

**CHAPTER 22**
John Huss: The Preacher of Prague ........................................................ 211

**CHAPTER 23**
Girolamo Savonarola: Reformer of Florence ........................................................ 223

# UNIT 4 ........................................................ 235

CHAPTER 24
The Reformation in France.................................................................................. 239

CHAPTER 25
Pierre Viret: Evangelist to France ........................................................................ 247

CHAPTER 26
The Sufferings of the Huguenots ......................................................................... 253

CHAPTER 27
Lady Jane Grey: Nine Day Queen of England ...................................................... 261

CHAPTER 28
Count Zinzendorf and the Moravian Brethren ................................................... 273

CHAPTER 29
The Great Awakening........................................................................................... 285

CHAPTER 30
John Newton: God's Amazing Grace to a Wretched Sinner ............................... 293

CHAPTER 31
Charles Simeon: Perseverance in Suffering......................................................... 307

CHAPTER 32
Brownlow North: Evangelist to the British Isles...................................................317

CHAPTER 33
Charles and Susannah Spurgeon: A Spiritual Harvest in London ...................... 329

CHAPTER 34
Dr. Martyn Lloyd-Jones: Preaching the Whole Counsel of God.......................... 343

CHAPTER 35
Diet Eman: Faithful Christian of the Dutch Resistance ...................................... 353

BIBLIOGRAPHY .................................................................................................... 365

LIST OF IMAGES ................................................................................................... 367

# INTRODUCTION FOR PARENTS AND TEACHERS

Dear Parents and Teachers,

Thank you for choosing *Taking Europe for Jesus* for your student's history studies. Before your student gets started, here is some introductory information so you can make the best use of this course.

*Taking Europe for Jesus* contains thirty-five chapters retelling some of the most significant stories from European Christian history. Because this course is designed for sixth grade readers, it is necessarily limited in its scope. We've selected some of our favorite stories, but many stories that could be told were not included. We hope this book will whet you and your student's appetite to delve more deeply into the many wonderful works of God in Europe.

For a more comprehensive look at world history (including Europe) you will find more detail provided in two other works published by Generations:

- *Preparing the World for Jesus* by Kevin Swanson (covers the BC period)
- *Taking the World for Jesus* by Kevin Swanson (covers the AD period)

Many of the chapters in this book are biographical in nature. We use biography to teach history for a few reasons. First, a biographical approach immerses the reader into a particular place and time with living color. The student gets to "see the sights" and "hear the sounds" by reading stories of real people. We also use biography because God accomplishes His purposes through faithful messengers. The gospel of Jesus Christ is spread throughout the world by His servants.

*Taking Europe for Jesus* is part of a larger series. In 2017, Generations published a high school textbook called *Taking the World for Jesus*. In that book, author Kevin Swanson recounted the history of Christian missions from Jerusalem to the ends of the earth. In our *Taking the World* series, it is our desire to retell that same history, continent by continent for younger children as well. These stories cover the history of Jesus Christ's rule being recognized throughout the world. The Bible says He is ruler over all kings on earth (Rev. 1:5). The stories in this series of history books recount how Jesus' rule was both further established and recognized all over the world.

*Taking Europe for Jesus* begins with an introductory chapter focused on European geography. This chapter is intended to orient the reader to the locations and sights they will encounter in the stories that follow. Chapters 2-5 focus on the birth of Christianity in the world of the Roman Empire. These chapters include some review of key biblical events in order to connect these redemptive events into the flow of history. Chapters 6-35 include a mix of biography, regional history, and key movements or events in European history from a Christian perspective.

In order to make this course visually engaging, we have included maps, historical artwork, and photography. Taking time to examine the maps will help the student gain a grasp of the geography of Europe. Each chapter also contains Prayer Points. These are suggested topics to guide the reader into a time of prayer. We should give thanks and praise to God for His great works done in the past. And we should pray that God's kingdom would come and His will be done in the future. It is recommended that the parent/teacher and student take time to pray together after each chapter is read.

We have included numerous quotations within the chapters. In some cases, original quotations have been simplified to be more understandable for readers at a sixth grade level. However, every effort has been made to accurately communicate the meaning of the original quotations.

The bibliography at the end of the book contains a list of primary and secondary sources consulted in the research and writing of this book.

An accompanying workbook for this textbook is also available. It contains a lesson schedule, written assignments, and enrichment projects to further reinforce what is learned in the reading of this book.

We offer this resource to Christian families around the world with the prayer that Jesus Christ, our great King and Savior, would be glorified in our humble efforts.

For Christ's Kingdom,
Joshua Schwisow
*The Generations Curriculum Team*
*December 2021*

ANCIENT ROMAN AMPITHEATRE IN ARLES, FRANCE

# UNIT 1

# AD 33-500

At that time a great persecution arose against the church which was at Jerusalem; and they were all scattered throughout the regions of Judea and Samaria, except the apostles... Therefore those who were scattered went everywhere preaching the word. (Acts 8:1, 4)

After our Lord's death and resurrection, He ascended into heaven. From that place of authority, Jesus rules over all things. Before He left earth, He gave His disciples a mission. It was a mission impossible to achieve by human strength. This was the mission: disciple all the nations by baptizing them and by teaching them the commands of King Jesus (Matt. 28:18-20). This mission was unachievable by human power alone.

However, the early Christians were not alone. The Holy Spirit empowered them. The Book of Acts tells us what happened. Jesus Christ continued his work from heaven. The Holy Spirit was poured out on the disciples. With this power, the Apostles and early Christians began to execute the mission. They took the faith all over the Roman world.

Christianity expanded rapidly into Palestine, Asia Minor, and into Europe. But it was not easy. Difficulty and danger came with every opportunity. The first three centuries of Christianity's expansion can be summarized in two words: **persecution** and **growth**. **Tertullian** was an early church father in Africa. He wisely observed "the blood of the martyrs is the seed of the church." The blood of Christians was not shed in vain. It seeded the faith all over Europe. Through seven major persecutions, the seed was scattered. Eventually, however, the Roman persecutions ended. In God's providence, the **Emperor Constantine** (reigned AD 306-337) confessed the name of Christ. This brought about a period of peace for the Lord's people.

The Roman Empire reached its largest size around AD 117. But within 300 years, it collapsed. In AD 409, the Romans withdrew from the island of Great Britain. A year later, another monumental event occurred. The **Visigoths**, a Germanic people, attacked the great city of Rome. The city was plundered and burned. News of this event shook the world. It was a sign of Rome's weakening grip over Europe. **Jerome**, a Christian leader alive at that time, understood how times had changed. He wrote, "the city which had taken the whole world was *taken itself*." Then, in AD 476, the Roman Empire dissolved. The mighty empire was no more. But Christ's church marched on. It continued its expansion into every corner of Europe.

This period of European history was a dangerous time. Even after the Roman persecutions died down, this did not mean the end of obstacles or enemies for Christ's people. Early Christian missionaries in Europe did not wrestle against flesh and blood. They battled against the demonic hordes. It was these "principalities and powers" that had for centuries reigned supreme over much of Europe. Thankfully, the power of Jesus Christ is greater than all the forces of darkness. By one word, Jesus, in his earthly ministry, expelled the demons. And where the Holy Spirit empowered Christ's servants, the forces of darkness also had to flee.

By the AD 400s, there were numerous signs of how far Christianity had expanded. One good example is the missionary we know as **Patrick**. It was Patrick of Ireland who was called by God to take the gospel to the pagan peoples of Ireland. Great Britain and Ireland were considered "the ends of the earth." Even there, the church was established. These once idol-worshipping peoples turned from idols to serve the living God. It was the power of Christ's gospel that transformed Europe.

## Timeline of Key Events

| | |
|---|---|
| AD 33 | Jesus Christ's Death and Resurrection |
| AD 52 | First Christian convert in Europe (Lydia in Philippi) |
| AD 64-68 | Persecution under Nero |
| AD 89-96 | Persecution under Domitian |
| AD 156 | Death of Polycarp of Smyrna |
| AD 177 | Persecution of Christians in Gaul |
| AD 303-311 | "Great Persecution" under Diocletian |
| AD 325 | Council of Nicaea |
| AD 354 | Birth of Augustine of Hippo |
| AD 390 | Birth of Patrick of Ireland |
| AD 404 | Roman gladiatorial games come to an end |
| AD 409 | Withdrawal of the Romans from Great Britain |
| AD 429 | Germanus opposes Pelagianism in Great Britain |
| AD 476 | Fall of the Roman Empire |

# PROLOGUE

One Saturday, in the ancient city of Philippi, a few men went down to the river. It was customary on the Jewish Sabbath for citizens of the city to pray at the river. A number of women gathered at the banks of the river to pour out their hearts in prayer to God. Among the women who gathered that day was a woman named Lydia. She was a seller of purple fabrics.

That day, a few men happened to attend the prayer meeting as well. Among them was the Apostle Paul. He, with his fellow companions, went down to the river because they knew it was a place of prayer. Perhaps on those riverbanks in Philippi they would find hearts ready to receive the good news about Jesus the Christ.

Paul and his companions met Lydia. Then they started up a conversation. Paul told Lydia about Jesus the Messiah. He explained how Jesus fulfilled the Old Covenant Scriptures. He explained Jesus' death and resurrection. During that conversation, God showed His grace to Lydia. "The Lord opened her heart to heed the things spoken by Paul" (Acts 16:14). After receiving the good news, the Bible tells us, "she and her household were baptized" (Acts 16:15).

What is so significant about Lydia's conversion? Why recount her conversion at the beginning of this book?

According to the Book of Acts, Lydia may be the very first Christian from the continent we know today as Europe. Jesus Christ, the King of kings and Lord of lords, began His saving work in Europe starting with the salvation of Lydia and her household.

From the first century to the present, Europe has been shaped by the Christian faith. What started with one woman and her household would spread to every people group and nation in Europe.

This book is about that story: the story of how Jesus Christ transformed Europe.

LAUTERBRUNNEN VALLEY, SWISS ALPS

# INTRODUCTION TO EUROPE 1

O Lord, how manifold are Your works!
In wisdom You have made them all.
The earth is full of Your possessions.
(Ps. 104:24)

Welcome to Europe! In this book, you will embark on a journey through the history of this part of the world. Spanning from the time of Christ's ascension all the way until the present, you will learn of many of God's mighty acts of salvation and judgment in Europe. In story after story, you will see how Jesus Christ is Savior of the world and King over all things. The Bible says that Jesus Christ is the "Lamb of God who takes away the sins of the world" (John 1:29). He is also ruler of all the kings of this earth (Rev. 1:5). In the chapters that follow, you will find these two truths about Jesus Christ demonstrated in European history.

Before we begin that historical exploration, let's first learn more about this important part of God's world. This brief geographical survey of Europe will help prepare you for the people, places, and events in the chapters that follow.

## REGIONS OF EUROPE

Europe is the western portion of the landmass we call **Eurasia**. (Eurasia is the largest landmass in the world. It contains all of Europe and all of Asia.) Europe has different regions, and each region contains nations with various languages, unique histories, and distinct cultures. Take a look at the map and table below to see some of the different regions of Europe.

There are about fifty separate sovereign nations in Europe today. Many of these nations are members of a multi-national union called the European Union (EU). This union was formed in 1993.

## MOUNTAINS

Give the king Your judgments, O God,
And Your righteousness to the king's Son.
He will judge Your people with righteousness,

MT. ELBRUS, RUSSIA

# TAKING EUROPE FOR JESUS

## Four Major Regions of Europe

| | |
|---|---|
| Northern Europe | Sweden, Norway, Iceland |
| Western Europe | United Kingdom, France, Belgium |
| Southern Europe | Spain, Portugal, Italy, Greece |
| Central and Eastern Europe | Russia, Ukraine, Hungary, Czech Republic |

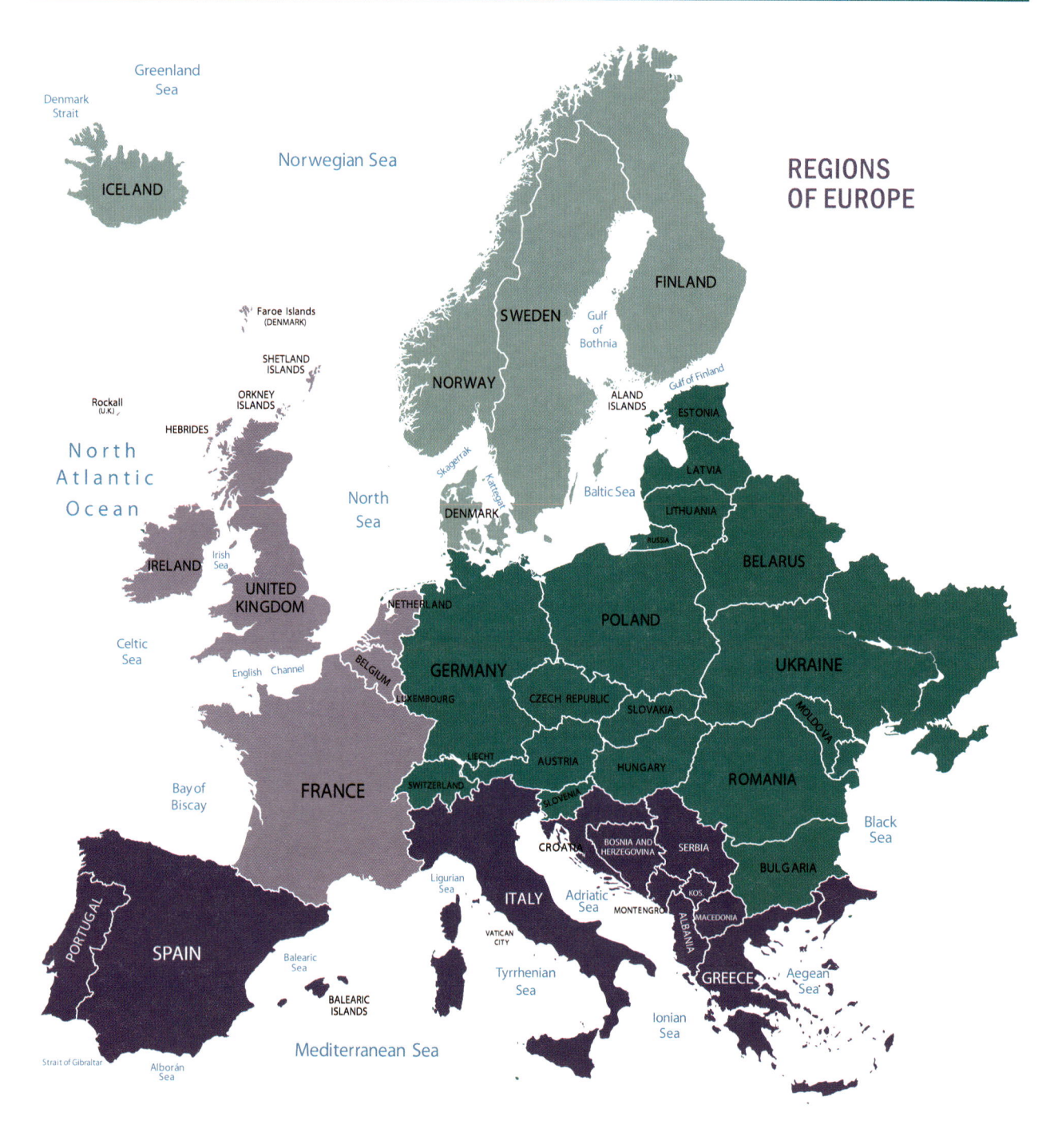

REGIONS OF EUROPE

# 1. INTRODUCTION TO EUROPE

And Your poor with justice.
The mountains will bring peace to the people,
And the little hills, by righteousness. (Ps. 72:1-3)

Europe contains a number of mountain ranges including the beautiful Alps. The tallest mountain in Europe is located in Russia. **Mt. Elbrus** stands at 18,510 feet (5,642m) above sea level. It is part of the mountain range known as the Caucasus Mountains. It is very close to the border of the country of Georgia. Mt. Elbrus is a currently dormant volcano. Because of its great height, temperatures at the peak can reach -50° Fahrenheit (-46° Celsius). Mt. Elbrus is a popular location for mountain climbers because it holds the title of "tallest mountain in Europe."

One of the most beautiful natural landmarks in Europe is the **Matterhorn**. It sits on the border of Italy and Switzerland in the Alps. At its peak, it stands at 14,692 feet (4,478m) above sea level. The Matterhorn is particularly noteworthy for its perfectly pointed peak. It is also shaped in such a way that it is very steep. The first known successful climb to the top was completed on July 14, 1865. The Matterhorn is an Alpine treasure in Europe, showing forth the power and beauty of our great God who made the mountains rise.

The tallest mountain in the Alps is **Mont Blanc**. It stands at 15,774 feet (4,808m) above sea level. It is located on the border of France and Italy. Because of its remarkable beauty, Mont Blanc and its surrounding landscape attracts many climbers, hikers, skiers, and snowboarders. As human beings, we are drawn

MATTERHORN, SWITZERLAND

MONT BLANC, FRANCE AND ITALY

### Select Mountains in Europe

| Mountain | Elevation | Location |
| --- | --- | --- |
| Mt. Elbrus | 18,510 ft. (5,642m) | Russia |
| The Matterhorn | 14,692 ft. (4,478m) | Switzerland/Italy |
| Mont Blanc | 15,774 ft. (4,808m) | France/Italy |
| Ben Nevis | 4,413 ft. (1,345m) | Scotland |
| Mount Olympus | 9,570 ft. (2,917m) | Greece |
| Mt. Radhošť | 3,704 ft. (1,129m) | Czech Republic |

to the grandeur of these mountains. Yet it is important that we as God's people give Him the glory for creating these anchors of the European landscape.

The island of Great Britain is also considered part of Europe. It does not contain mountains of such great height as the European mainland. However, there are mountain ranges in Great Britain. In particular, the northern region of Scotland is called the **Scottish High-**

CHURCH ON MT. RADHOŠŤ

**lands.** It is known as the Highlands because of its hilly terrain and numerous mountains. In the Grampian Mountain Range, you will find the tallest mountain in Great Britain. The peak of **Ben Nevis** is 4,413 feet (1,345m) above sea level.

One important European mountain of historical significance is **Mount Olympus**. It is located in Greece. Mount Olympus (9,570 feet, or 2,917m above sea level) is the tallest mountain in Greece. It figured heavily in Greek mythology as the home of the twelve

BEN NEVIS, SCOTLAND

Olympian gods. Pagan religions often associate various parts of God's creation with false gods. False religions often worship different parts of God's creation. However, we as Christians know that this mountain belongs to the one true and living God. It is the God and Father of our Lord Jesus Christ who created this mountain. It is God who rules over this mountain.

Finally, we'll look at one more mountain. This mountain is not nearly as well known as the others. But it is an important mountain for Christians. Among the beautiful mountains of the Czech Republic, there is one known as **Mt. Radhošť** (3,704 feet, or 1,129m above sea level). For centuries, it was a mountain associated with the worship of a god known to the Slavs as Radegast. This god was just one of many false gods worshiped by the Slavs. But one day, the statue of Radegast sitting upon the mountain was destroyed. It is believed that when missionary brothers Cyril and Methodius visited the mountain, they had the idol torn down. Today, there is a church on the top of Mt. Radhošť. In a later chapter, you will learn more about what happened on this mountain.

## RIVERS

But My faithfulness and My mercy shall be with him,
And in My name his horn shall be exalted.
Also I will set his hand over the sea,
And his right hand over the rivers. (Ps. 89:24-25)

Water is essential for life. Without water, human beings cannot survive. That is why we see God's mercy in providing such an abundance of water to the nations of Europe. Our God is kind and merciful by giving rivers and sending rain even to those who are ungrateful (Matt. 5:45). Ever since people settled in Europe after Noah's flood, rivers have provided an important source of water. The rivers have also served as a means of transportation. They continue to be used to transport goods and services to this day.

**VOLGA RIVER, RUSSIA**

RHINE RIVER, SWITZERLAND

## Major Rivers in Europe

| River | Length | Location |
| --- | --- | --- |
| Volga River | 2,194 miles (3,531km) | Russia |
| Rhine River | 760 miles (1,230km) | Switzerland, Austria, France, Germany, etc. |
| Danube River | 1,770 miles (2,850km) | Germany, Slovakia, Hungary, Romania, etc. |
| Seine River | 482 miles (775km) | France |

    The longest river in Europe is the **Volga River**. It is 2,194 miles long (3,531km). The entirety of the Volga River is found in the largest country in the world: Russia. The Volga is considered by many in Russia to be their "national river." Because of its importance for transportation and commerce, many cities in Russia have been built along the banks of the Volga. One of the largest cities built along the river is the city named after the river: Volgograd.

    In western Europe, passing through Switzerland, Austria, Germany, France, and other nations is the **Rhine River**. The Rhine is about 760 miles in length (1,230km). During the Middle Ages, the Rhine was important for the Holy Roman Empire. Because of this, many

**SEINE RIVER, PARIS, FRANCE**

castles from the Middle Ages were built along the Rhine River. One city that was important during the period of the Protestant Reformation is Strasbourg, France. Strasbourg is near the border of modern-day Germany and is built on the banks of the Rhine. Many Reformers such as Martin Bucer and John Calvin either lived in or visited Strasbourg.

The second longest river in Europe is the **Danube River**. It begins in Germany and flows all the way into the Black Sea in eastern Europe. It is 1,770 miles long (2,850km). A river tour on the Danube will take you to many different places in Europe from west to east. There is also a bike trail that takes you all the way from Germany to the Danube Delta, where the river empties into the Black Sea. If you cycled at fifteen miles per hour for eight hours per day, it would take you over two weeks to bike the length of the Danube. You would surely burn a lot of calories, and in the process, you would have seen a good portion of Europe!

One of France's longest rivers is the **Seine River**. Though not nearly as long as the Volga, the Seine is quite a large river in France (482 miles long, 775km). It is a well-known river because it passes through Paris, the capital and largest city in France. The average depth of the Seine as it passes through the city is 31 feet (9.5m). Because the Seine flows through such a large city as Paris, people have built over thirty-seven bridges over the river inside the city.

## CLIMATE REGIONS IN EUROPE

He sends out His command to the earth;
His word runs very swiftly.
He gives snow like wool;
He scatters the frost like ashes;
He casts out His hail like morsels;
Who can stand before His cold?
He sends out His word and melts them;
He causes His wind to blow, and the waters flow.
(Ps. 147:15-18)

Much of Europe is located at a high latitude. For example, much of it is at a higher latitude than the United States. But in general, much of Europe has a milder climate than other parts of the world at a similar latitude. For example, the weather in northern portions of Canada gets much colder than areas in Europe at a similar latitude. Scientists believe part of the reason for this is the **Gulf Stream**. The Gulf Stream is a warm ocean current that begins in the Gulf of Mexico and pushes northeast across the Atlantic Ocean up into the waters around Europe. This keeps much of Europe warmer than other countries. However, Europe still has a diversity of climate regions. Temperatures in these regions range from the extremely hot to the extremely cold. The warmest temperature on record in Europe was recorded in July 1977 in Athens, Greece. The temperature reached 118° Fahrenheit (48° Celsius). The coldest temperature on record was recorded in December 1978. The temperature dropped to -78° Fahrenheit (-58° Celsius) in a remote region of northern Russia (Komi Republic, Russia). What is the weather like in different regions of Europe? Using the list of regions above, here are a few examples of the different climates found in Europe.

In Northern Europe, particularly in the countries known as **Scandinavia** (Denmark, Norway, Sweden, Finland, Iceland), extremely cold temperatures and tundra can be found. The southern portions of Scandinavia benefit from the warming effects of the Gulf Stream. But

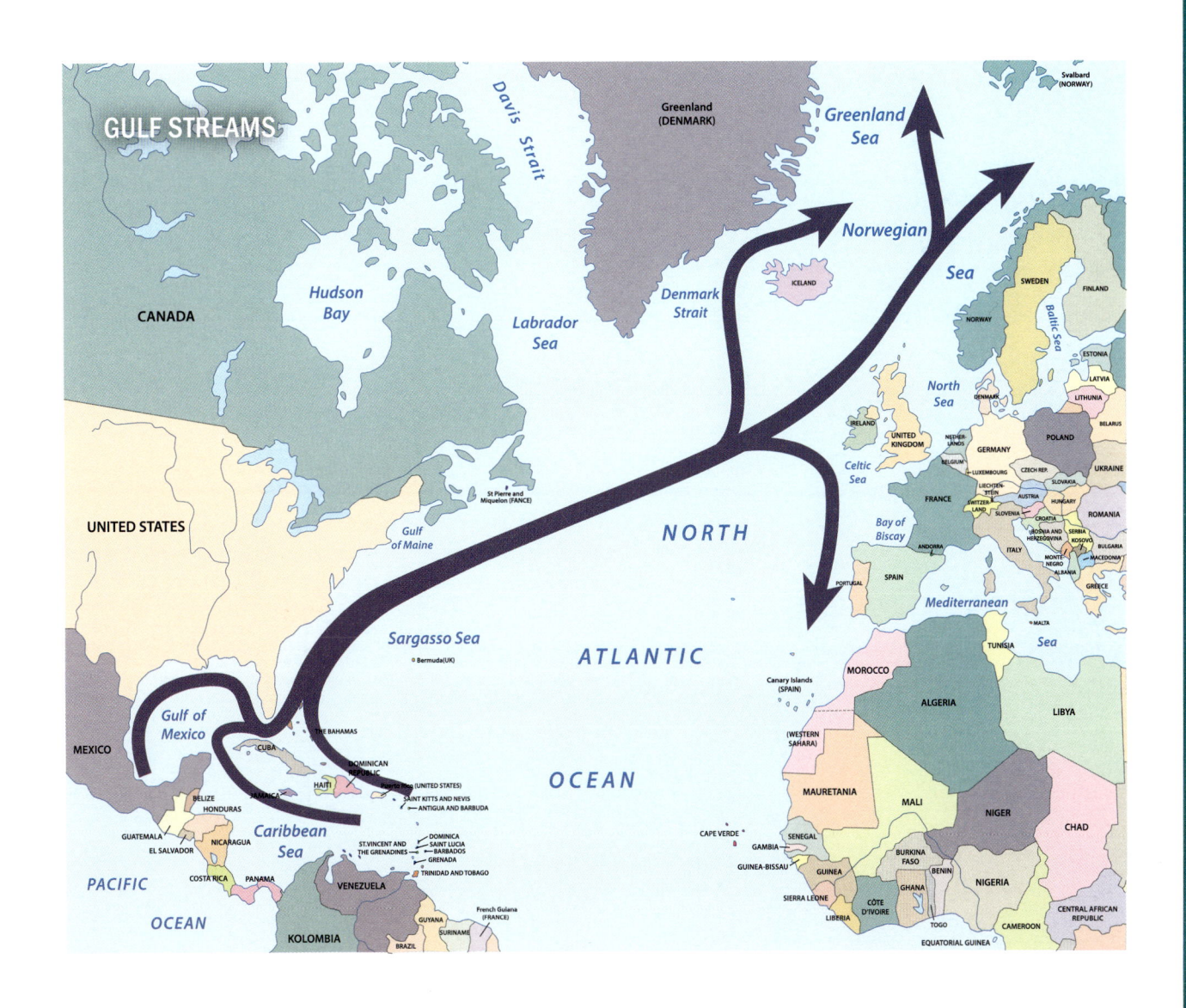

26 TAKING EUROPE FOR JESUS

AURORA BOREALIS AS SEEN IN NORWAY

ARDENNES FOREST, BELGIUM

as you travel further north, the temperatures become much more extreme. At such high latitudes, daylight is very limited in the winter. This makes for a frigid, icy, and snowy environment. A city like Kautokeino, Norway is in the far north of Norway in an inland region. The average high in January is 14° Fahrenheit (-10° Celsius). However, the temperatures are still not as extreme as inland regions of northern Canada, for example.

In Western Europe, off the coast of the mainland, are the islands of Great Britain and Ireland. The warm Gulf Stream in the ocean keeps the climates of these two islands much milder than parts of mainland Europe.

Western Europe also contains many beautiful forests such as the **Ardennes Forest** in Belgium and Luxembourg. This region of Europe is a dense green in the summer and as the season turns to fall, a dazzling array of colors emerge as the leaves turn colors and begin to fall.

Southern Europe contains some of Europe's warmest weather. The nations of southern Europe such as Spain, Italy, and Greece have extensive coastline on the Mediterranean Sea. The proximity of the sea to these nations produces a unique climate region characterized by dry summers and warm, wet winters. One of the warmest spots on the coast of the Mediterranean is the city of **Marseilles** (pronounced Mar-say), France. It is considered the sunniest city in France. It also receives many dry winds coming up from the Sahara Desert in Africa. This makes Marseilles have very dry, very hot summers. One of the driest places in all of Europe is the **Bardenas Reales**. It is a desert region in southeast Spain. Because of how dry and hot this region is, some of the ground will actually crack apart. It looks very much like a dry and parched desert.

Portions of central and eastern Europe

UKRAINE COUNTRYSIDE

contain some of the most fertile land in all of Europe. Ukraine in particular is known as the "breadbasket of Europe" because it contains some of the best farmland in all of Europe. Western Ukraine receives abundant rainfall, and most of Ukraine has a temperate climate that is good for growing food. Ukraine contains about one fourth of the world's most fertile soil called "black soil." Ukraine is one of the poorest nations in Europe, but it has abundant agricultural potential because of its soil and climate.

## FASCINATING CREATURES OF EUROPE

Sing to the LORD with thanksgiving;
Sing praises on the harp to our God,
Who covers the heavens with clouds,
Who prepares rain for the earth,
Who makes grass to grow on the mountains.
He gives to the beast its food,
And to the young ravens that cry. (Ps. 147:7-9)

God's glory is not only displayed in the mountains, forests, hills, and rivers of Europe. It is also seen in the diversity, complexity, and beauty of the animals, birds, and fish of Europe. Here are just a few of the fascinating animals of Europe God has made to show forth His glory.

Children living in the far north of Scandinavia have to deal with the drastic shifts of sunlight from winter to summer. While summer brings very long days to this northern part of the world, winter means just a few hours of sunlight a day. But Scandinavian children may get a chance to see beautiful **reindeer** walking the forests near their home. In Siberia, Russia, and in Scandinavia, the beautiful **arctic fox** may also be spotted. **Polar bears** can be found in the arctic regions of Europe. In the Carpathian Mountains of central Europe, **brown bears** can be seen in the forests.

Near the **Iberian Peninsula**, a population of **Iberian lynx** can be found. This lynx is a wild cat that lives in Spain and Portugal. Its primary food source is rabbits.

Many of the European nations benefit from long coastlines. This makes fish an important source of food as well as an important part of trade and commerce. Common fish in the northern waters of Europe include **cod, herring, halibut**, and **haddock**. In the Mediterranean Sea, such beautiful creatures as **whales, dolphins**, and **seals** are common.

One of the most impressive birds found in Europe is the **Great Grey Owl**. It can be found in northern regions of Europe such as Finland. This owl is considered the world's largest owl by wing length. The wingspan of this marvelous bird can reach up to 5 feet (152cm).

On a hike through the Scottish Highlands, you might have the chance to see a **European pine marten**. It is a small mammal similar to a weasel or badger. These little creatures can grow

IBERIAN LYNX

PINE MARTEN

REINDEER IN NORWAY

**GREAT GREY OWL**

up to 21 inches in length (53cm) and typically weigh around 3 pounds (1.36kg).

Europe, like the rest of this world, awaits Jesus' return at the last day. When our Lord returns, He will bring about a new heavens and a new earth (Rev. 21-22). The creation groans, waiting for the revealing of the sons of God (Rom. 8:19-22). One day, death and corruption will come to an end. One day, Jesus Christ will return. And there will no longer be death anymore. Animals that once fought and ate each other will lie down together in peace. ■

---

"It shall come to pass
That before they call, I will answer;
And while they are still speaking, I will hear.
The wolf and the lamb shall feed together,
The lion shall eat straw like the ox,
And dust shall be the serpent's food.
They shall not hurt nor destroy in all My holy mountain,"
Says the LORD. (Isa. 65:24-25)

# PRAYER POINTS: EUROPE

You've now gotten a small glimpse into the continent of Europe. Now, our response should be to praise God for His great power and majesty displayed in the beauty of His creation. Take time now to pray a prayer of praise and adoration to our great God!

- **Praise God for His Power:** We learn how powerful our God is when we look at the great mountain peaks of the Alps. Our God spoke the mountains into existence. The God who established the great mountains and stretched out the ocean and sea around Europe is worthy of our worship. Praise the God who made all things by the Word of His power!

- **Praise God for His Wisdom:** The diversity and creativity of creation is all around us. The climates, the animals, and the plants of Europe all show God's creativity. They also show how orderly creation is. Despite the fact that this is a sin-cursed world, the Lord has made His creatures with exactly what they need to survive and thrive.

- **Praise God for His Goodness:** Though we live in a fallen world, wounded by the fall into sin, God is still good to His creation. He continues to provide the sun to give us warmth. He sends rain to the peoples of Europe so they can eat. He gives them rivers to grow their crops. He provides food for His creation. He providentially cares for every creature and plant in Europe. Not a sparrow falls apart from the will of our Heavenly Father. Behold the goodness of God.

## Basic Facts about Europe

| | |
|---|---|
| **Total Estimated Population** | 746 million |
| **Total Area** | 3,930,000 square miles (10,180,000km) |
| **Number of Countries** | 50 |
| **Number of Languages** | 50+ |
| **Largest Country** | Russia |
| **Smallest Country** | Vatican City (in Rome) |

ANCIENT ROMAN FORUM, ROME ITALY

# ROME: A REPUBLIC TURNED INTO AN EMPIRE

Look to Me, and be saved,
All you ends of the earth!
For I am God, and there is no other. (Isa. 45:22)

About 750 years before the birth of our Lord Jesus, a city was founded. What began as a small settlement on the Italian peninsula eventually became one of the largest human empires. The settlement known as Rome would become the Roman Empire. At its height, this empire ruled over the area all around the Mediterranean Sea, including parts of Europe, modern-day Iraq, and Iran. It was during the time of this Empire that the Lord Jesus Christ was born (Luke 2:1). The Roman Empire was vast for a time. But like all human kingdoms, it did not last. Nevertheless, the Roman Empire left its stamp upon Europe in the centuries that followed its collapse. How did this Empire grow to such large proportions?

Small settlements are found in all times and places in human history. Wherever people settle, they build dwelling places, they raise food, and they care for animals. Humans dwell together and build villages, towns, and cities. God created man to take dominion of the earth. This is natural to human existence. But massive empires do not form through peaceful dominion work. Instead, the colossal empires of men are usually formed through war and conquest.

It shouldn't surprise us that the seeds of the Roman Empire were built on a brotherly feud. According to Roman legend, Rome began when two young men, Romulus and Remus, set out to build a new city. The two brothers fought each other over who would be the leader of this settlement. It was a battle for pre-

RUINS OF THE DOMUS FLAVIA PALACE IN ROME

**LOCATION OF ROME**

eminence and power. In order to end the feud, Romulus killed Remus. Now, nothing stood in Romulus' way. He then made himself ruler of the new settlement. Romulus named the city in his own honor: Rome. Murder became the pattern for future leaders of this empire. The history of the Roman Republic and the Roman Empire is a long tale of many wars, political murders, and violence. Evidence of these corrupt foundations can be seen in the gladiator games of Rome. Many of the peoples of Rome found delight in watching real human blood shed for sport.

What a difference there is between the kingdom of Jesus and the kingdom of Rome! The kingdom of Jesus Christ is built on the sacrificial self-giving of its own King. King Jesus came from heaven to earth to save His own people. Human empires are never built in this way. Human lives are taken in order to secure power for those rulers at the top. In the chapters that follow, you will learn more about the confrontation between these rival kingdoms. Jesus' kingdom, a kingdom of righteousness, peace, and joy in the Holy Spirit (Rom. 14:17), came into conflict with the Roman kingdom.

Both the Bible and the records of history record this: Jesus' kingdom overcame the Roman Empire. As the Bible foretold, Jesus' kingdom would become the greatest kingdom in the world. That is what God revealed to Daniel. God told Daniel about a kingdom as strong as iron. This was a kingdom made by men. But Jesus' kingdom is stronger than all manmade kingdoms, and Daniel learned that Jesus' kingdom would destroy all others and would last forever:

> And the fourth kingdom shall be as strong as iron, inasmuch as iron breaks in pieces and shatters everything; and like iron that crushes, that kingdom will break in pieces and crush all the others. . . . And in the days of these kings the God of heaven will set up a kingdom which shall never be destroyed; and the kingdom shall not be left to other people; it shall break in pieces and consume all these kingdoms, and it shall stand forever. (Dan. 2:40, 44)

The kingdom of Jesus Christ is a kingdom that can never be destroyed. Christ rules over the world. All the kingdoms of the world have become the kingdom of our Lord (Rev. 11:15). Jesus Christ is "ruler over the kings of the earth" (Rev. 1:5). This is the perspective Christians bring to history. It is the perspective we must have as we learn more about the Roman Empire.

## THE HISTORY OF THE ROMAN REPUBLIC

From 750 BC to 509 BC, Rome was a small city-state led by a king. Around 509 BC, Rome's **monarchy** came to an end. This marked the beginning of the Roman **Republic**. Under their new form of government, Rome was ruled by members of the Senate. The people of Rome also elected Roman citizens to serve in legislative assemblies. This republic would last until 27 BC. At that time the republic became an empire. Shortly before the birth of our Lord Jesus Christ, a man named Augustus became the first emperor of the Roman Empire.

Before Rome became an empire, it progressively gained control throughout the Mediterranean world. Through various wars and conquests, Rome became the dominant power in this part of the world. But Rome faced a competitor. Another contender for power arose on the coast of North Africa. That rival was another city-state known as **Carthage**. Founded some seventy-five years before Rome, Carthage also gained territory through conquest. As Rome expanded its power, Carthage vied for control of the Mediterranean. Rome's struggle for dominance in the Mediterranean led to three major wars against Carthage. These wars are called the **Punic Wars**. Most historians divide these wars into three.

- The First Punic War (264-241 BC)
- The Second Punic War (218-201 BC)
- The Third Punic War (149-146 BC)

Among the most famous events of ancient history is the daring military attack led by the Carthaginian general **Hannibal** (247-c. 183 BC). This took place during the Second Punic War (218-201 BC). Hannibal led a massive army over the treach-

**DANIEL INTERPRETS NEBUCHADNEZZAR'S DREAM**

**HANNIBAL**

---

**Monarchy** ▪ A monarchy is a form of government in which a single monarch (either a king or a queen) rules over the people.

**Republic** ▪ A republic is a state in which supreme power is held by the people and their elected representatives. A republic has an elected or nominated president/leader rather than a king. The government of the United States of America is a republic as defined by the Constitution of the United States.

**THE ROMAN EMPIRE AT ITS LARGEST (AD 117)**

eral almost brought Rome to its knees. In battle after battle, Hannibal defeated the Romans until he was within six miles of the great city of Rome itself. At that point, Hannibal's advance was stopped by the Romans.

As Hannibal invaded the Italian mainland, the Romans responded with another strategy. The Roman armies led an attack against Carthage. This forced Hannibal to return home to protect his own city. The Romans then successfully conquered Carthage. By the end of the Third Punic War (149-146 BC), Carthage was destroyed. This final victory insured Rome's place as the greatest military power in the ancient Western world. Rome faced no other major rivals in the Mediterranean.

Rome continued its advance elsewhere. The might of the Roman Republic grew decade after decade. The Republic reached its largest size under the leadership of **Julius Caesar** (100-44 BC). In the last years of the Republic, Rome held control of a vast territory. Rome's government ruled over North Africa as well as modern-day Spain, France, Germany, Italy, Greece, Turkey, Israel, Egypt, and the Netherlands. Shortly after the birth of Christ, the Roman Empire would also conquer the British Isles.

Rome's conquests were often cruel. Peoples of other lands were subjugated by violent force. In most cases,

erous Alps into northern Italy. Instead of approaching Rome from the sea, Hannibal had an ambitious plan. His strategy was to attack the city of Rome from the north. With some 26,000 men, this mighty Carthaginian gen-

# 2. ROME: A REPUBLIC TURNED INTO AN EMPIRE 37

**JULIUS CAESAR (100-44 BC)**

Rome had little interest in the cultures of the peoples they conquered. Romans believed their culture, their government, and their religion were the greatest on earth.

## ROMAN AND GREEK CULTURE
However, there was one notable exception to this pattern. The Romans had an appreciation for Greek culture. Before Rome's dominance, Greece became a large empire through the military conquests of **Alexander the Great** (356-323 BC). Alexander's kingdom was short-lived. But his military conquests had a significant effect on the ancient world. Through Alexander's conquests, the Greek language spread. Eventually, the Greek language became one of the most popular languages in the Mediterranean world. As God purposed it, the New Testament was written in Greek. It was the common language of Jesus' time. This enabled many people in many lands to receive the good news about Jesus Christ.

Alexander's kingdom was enormous. It came into his possession in a short period of years. But it also rapidly dissolved. When Alexander the Great died in 323 BC, the empire was split up into smaller kingdoms. Greek dominance faded. Yet Greek philosophy, Greek politics, and Greek language remained influential. Rome eventually conquered Greece as well.

**ALEXANDER THE GREAT (356-323 BC)**

**EMPIRE OF ALEXANDER THE GREAT**

Rome began to adopt Greek ideas, Greek education, the Greek fables, and the Greek false gods. They would re-name the gods to give them a Roman flavor. For example, the Greek god Zeus was re-named Jupiter, Ares became Mars, and Hera became Juno. To the Romans, Greece was the great example of cultural development in art, literature, philosophy, and government.

---

For all the gods of the peoples are idols, but the LORD made the heavens. (Ps. 96:5)

---

The Romans and Greeks worshiped many false gods. The Roman gods were much like sinful men and women. They were gods made in the image of man. The Bible teaches that man is made in God's image. But false religion reverses this order. False gods are always made to be more like human beings than like the true God. This reveals something important about Roman religion. The Romans were most impressed with the glory of man. That's why their gods were so much like themselves.

## THE END OF THE REPUBLIC

In the Book of Daniel, the proud Babylonian king Nebuchadnezzar appears. Nebuchadnezzar was impressed with all the works he had done. He exalted himself as he reflected on the glories of his vast empire. But God judged him for his pride.

---

The king spoke, saying, "Is not this great Babylon, that I have built for a royal dwelling by my mighty power and for the honor of my majesty?" While the word was still in the king's mouth, a voice fell from heaven: "King Nebuchadnezzar, to you it is spoken: the kingdom has departed from you!" (Dan. 4:30-31)

---

Like Nebuchadnezzar, Rome was proud of its achievements. There was nothing in the history of the kingdoms of men like the great city of Rome and its "glorious" empire. God's Word warns against this pride. "God resists the proud, but gives grace to the humble" (Jas. 4:6). The Lord always brings proud nations down. This is what happened to Nebuchadnezzar in Daniel 4.

Rome's republican form of government did not last. The strain of governing so large an empire was too great for it. Internal wrangling for power weakened the Republic. The character of the nation was corrupted. Rome was incapable of handling such a big empire. For centuries, Roman society prided itself on respecting the rights of the people. Rome valued equality in government.

But the Romans failed to realize that man is sinful and proud by nature. Sinful men always seek more power. Leaders in the Roman government were not satisfied with limiting their own power. The lust for power and glory even-

**STATUE OF ZEUS**

tually led to the end of the Roman Republic. About thirty years before the birth of Jesus Christ, Rome became an empire led by an emperor.

Octavian—who is also known by the title "Augustus Caesar"—reigned as emperor between 27 BC and AD 14. He brought in the era known as the **Pax Romana**. This Latin phrase means the "Peace of Rome." By this time, Rome had subdued most of its enemies. Apart from a few conflicts on the far perimeter of Rome's reach, the empire experienced a season of relative peace for two hundred years. When Jesus Christ, the Son of God, came into the world, Rome was ruling much of the known world. It was at its highest level of power, prosperity, peace, and pride. Was this the kingdom the world had been waiting for? Augustus Caesar himself was referred to as "the savior of the world." Was he?

A Roman philosopher named **Epictetus** (c. AD 50-135) knew that the Roman Emperor could not really save the world. He wrote,

> While the Emperor may give peace from war on land and sea, he is unable to give peace from passion, grief, and envy. He cannot give peace of heart, for which man yearns more than even for outward peace.

Epictetus was not a Christian. But what he wrote here was wise. The peace of Rome did not bring peace between God and man. Augustus Caesar could not save the Romans from their sins. The world needed another Savior.

The true Savior from God was born in a small village. One night, near Bethlehem, a lowly group of shepherds heard the good news. A multitude of angels appeared and sang the praises of God.

"Glory to God in the highest,
And on earth peace, goodwill toward men!"
(Luke 2:14)

**AUGUSTUS CAESAR**

One of the angels declared, "I bring you good tidings of great joy which will be to all people" (Luke 2:10). The good news was this: in the city of David, a Savior was born. The angels announced the birth of Christ the Lord.

That night, the King of kings and Lord of lords was born. He came and established His kingdom that will never be destroyed. Jesus Christ came to "save His people from their sins" (Matt. 1:21). Augustus Caesar's claim to be savior of the world was false. That title belongs to Jesus Christ alone.

**And it came to pass in those days that a decree went out from Caesar Augustus that all the world should be registered. This census first took place while Quirinius was governing Syria. . . . Joseph also went up from Galilee, out of the city of Nazareth, into Judea, to the city of David, which is called Bethlehem, because he was of the house and lineage of David, to be registered with Mary, his betrothed wife, who was with child. (Luke 2:1-5)**

# PRAYER POINTS

- **Praise Our God for the Kingdom of Jesus Christ:** The kingdom of our Lord and Savior Jesus is a kingdom that can never end. It is the kingdom that crushes all other previous kingdoms and then fills the whole earth. Let us praise God for His power in establishing this kingdom.

- **Thank God for Participation in the Kingdom:** Our Lord Jesus said, "it is your Father's good pleasure to give you the kingdom" (Luke 12:32). By faith, we receive this kingdom as a gift from our Heavenly Father. It is an inestimable blessing to be a member of the kingdom of Christ. To be a member of this kingdom is to experience fellowship with Jesus Christ, to receive the gift of eternal life, and to enjoy all the fruits of righteousness, peace, and joy in the Holy Spirit (Rom. 14:17).

- **Pray for the Advance of Christ's Kingdom:** Our Lord instructs us in His prayer to pray, "Your kingdom come, your will be done on earth as it is in heaven" (Matt. 6:10). Throughout the duration of this course, pray continually for the advance of Christ's kingdom throughout the world. Pray that Jesus' kingdom would come in greater measure in your own community, starting with your family.

## 2. ROME: A REPUBLIC TURNED INTO AN EMPIRE  41

BETHLEHEM

ROMAN AQUEDUCT

# THE BIRTH OF CHRISTIANITY IN THE FULLNESS OF TIME

> But when the fullness of the time had come, God sent forth His Son, born of a woman, born under the law, to redeem those who were under the law, that we might receive the adoption as sons. (Gal. 4:4-5)

The *Pax Romana* or the "Peace of Rome" brought peace and prosperity to many. It brought safer travel by land and sea. This was a blessing from God. There were new opportunities for commerce. Yet, despite Rome's achievements, a more pressing problem remained. Rome could not provide forgiveness of sins. No human emperor could protect its citizens from death and judgment.

As we learned in the last chapter, it was during the reign of Augustus Caesar that the Savior of the world was born. After Jesus' birth, Jesus grew up in the small village of Nazareth. For about thirty years, He lived in obscurity. Residents of Nazareth would pass by Joseph's carpentry shop. They knew Jesus, the son of Joseph and Mary. He was an ordinary carpenter, it seemed. But almost no one in Nazareth knew Jesus' full identity. They did not know that the Jesus they knew was the eternal Son of God. He was the Savior of the world. He was the appointed Lamb of God who would take away sin. He was the final prophet of God. He was and He is King over all.

When Jesus began His public ministry, being about thirty years old, Israel began to learn who this man was. Jesus began His public ministry after He was baptized in the river Jordan by **John the Baptist** (Matt. 3:13-17). Immediately after His baptism, the Holy Spirit led Jesus into the wilderness. As the second Adam, Jesus would do what the first Adam failed to do. Jesus overcame Satan. For forty days, our Lord was tempted in the wilderness by Satan. Adam had failed to obey God when he was tempted by Satan in the Garden (Gen. 3:1-11). But Jesus obeyed God and resisted Satan's temptation in the desert under more difficult conditions (Matt. 4:1-11). The ancient prophecy of Genesis 3:15 was finally coming to pass.

JOHN THE BAPTIST

**DESERT REGION OF ISRAEL, OUR LORD WAS TEMPTED BY THE DEVIL IN THE DESERT FOR 40 DAYS**

"And I will put enmity
Between you and the woman,
And between your seed and her Seed;
He shall bruise your head,
And you shall bruise His heel." (Gen. 3:15)

Genesis 3 foretold that the seed of the woman would destroy Satan. Jesus Christ was that seed of the woman. He came to crush the head of Satan. His temptation in the wilderness demonstrated His power to overcome the evil one.

After this time of temptation, Jesus began preaching throughout the land of Israel about the kingdom of God. He declared, "Repent and believe the gospel" (Mark 1:15). Jesus announced the wonderful news of His kingdom. He healed the sick. He raised the dead. He set free those who were captive to sin and the devil.

The demon world, led by Satan the prince of demons, unleashed a furious counterattack on Jesus and His disciples. The devil wanted to stop Jesus from fulfilling His mission. But Jesus came to do the will of His Father—to die on the cross and rise again from the dead on the third day. The effect of Christ's death and resurrection would change the world. Jesus said that the ruler of the world would be cast out. Then Jesus said "[I] will draw all peoples to Myself" (John 12:31-32).

## JESUS CHRIST'S MISSION IN JERUSALEM

At the end of His public ministry, Jesus entered Jerusalem with His disciples. There He partook of the Passover meal. That night, Jesus was betrayed by one of his disciples, Judas Iscariot. He was condemned to death under the rule of the Roman governor in Jerusalem. The governor's name was **Pontius Pilate** (governed AD 26-36). Jesus was rejected by His own people, the Jews. They demanded Jesus' execution, shouting out "Crucify Him!" All of Jesus' disciples abandoned Him as He was taken to the cross and put to death by the Romans. What they did not realize is that this was the greatest battle ever fought and won. By Jesus' death and resurrection, Satan was defeated. Forgiveness of sins was secured for all who believe. After Jesus' death, on the third day, Jesus rose again from the dead by the power of God. Death was now defeated.

### 3. THE BIRTH OF CHRISTIANITY IN THE FULLNESS OF TIME

**JESUS DIED ON THE CROSS AND ROSE AGAIN ON THE THIRD DAY**

Following His victorious resurrection, Jesus appeared to His apostles. He gave them the **Great Commission**.

**And Jesus came and spoke to them, saying, "All authority has been given to Me in heaven and on earth. Go therefore and make disciples of all the nations, baptizing them in the name of the Father and of the Son and of the Holy Spirit, teaching them to observe all things that I have commanded you; and lo, I am with you always, even to the end of the age." Amen. (Matt. 28:18-20)**

Jesus told His apostles to go into all parts of the world. They would take the gospel, "the good news," and tell the world what Jesus had done. They were to make disciples by baptizing in the name of the Father, Son, and Holy Spirit. And they were to teach these new disciples every single thing that Jesus commanded.

The apostles had good reason to be encouraged. Why? Because Jesus said that all authority in heaven and on earth belonged to Him. The apostles delivered this message in the name of the One who reigns over all things. There was another reason to be encouraged. Jesus promised the apostles that He would be with them until His return.

What do these promises mean for us?

Jesus' promise means that His mission cannot fail. Our Lord will accomplish His mission. That mission remains the most important project taking place on earth right now. That is why, in this study of Europe's history, our attention will be on Christ's kingdom.

Before Jesus ascended to heaven, He promised the apostles they would receive power for this important mission. The Book of Acts records what He said.

**Therefore, when they had come together, they asked Him, saying, "Lord, will You at this time restore the kingdom to Israel?" And He said to them, "It is not for you to know times or seasons which the Father has put in His own authority. But you shall receive power when the Holy Spirit has come upon you; and you shall be witnesses to Me in Jerusalem, and in all Judea and Samaria, and to the end of the earth." (Acts 1:6-8)**

Such a worldwide mission effort would require power. That is why the Holy Spirit

## 46 TAKING EUROPE FOR JESUS

**DAY OF PENTECOST**

came on the Day of **Pentecost**. The powerful Holy Spirit of God gave the apostles power to preach the gospel to all the nations.

About forty days after Jesus rose from the dead came the day of Pentecost. Worshipers of God from different lands gathered in Jerusalem for this festival each year. On that day, the Holy Spirit descended upon the Christian disciples. They were given the ability to proclaim "the wonderful works of God" in different languages.

The worldwide gospel mission had begun. From Jerusalem the message would spread to Judea. From Judea, the message would spread to Samaria. Eventually, the message would reach the heart of the Roman Empire: the city of Rome. And from Rome, the good news about Jesus would spread throughout all the earth.

**THE MEDITERRANEAN WORLD**

# 3. THE BIRTH OF CHRISTIANITY IN THE FULLNESS OF TIME

## THE MISSIONARY WORK OF THE APOSTLES

The first days of the Christian church are recorded in the Book of Acts. A medical doctor named **Luke** wrote Acts. Luke was a companion of **Paul the Apostle**. Acts is a remarkable record of God's mighty works. This Holy-Spirit inspired book of the New Testament is a priceless treasure. In Acts, we read of all that Jesus continued to do through His apostles.

The beginning chapters of Acts record the rapid spread of the church in Jerusalem and the surrounding cities. Acts repeatedly records how Jesus' mission was successful in its growth.

*PETER PREACHING TO CORNELIUS (ACTS 10)*

---

*Then the word of God spread, and the number of the disciples multiplied greatly in Jerusalem, and a great many of the priests were obedient to the faith. (Acts 6:7, emphasis added)*

---

Much of Acts focuses on the missionary efforts of Peter and Paul. Peter served as an apostle to the Jews. Paul was called by Jesus Christ to be an apostle to the Gentiles. After His resurrection, the Lord Jesus told Peter that he would face martyrdom (see John 21:18). Peter began ministering primarily to the Jews in Jerusalem, in Joppa (by the Mediterranean Sea), and Antioch (in Syria). His ministry included Asia Minor (modern-day Turkey) and Rome. Peter finished the work God had for him. His earthly life ended when he was killed in Rome. By order of the evil Emperor **Nero** (reigned AD 54-68), Peter was executed around AD 67 or 68. We learn from a Christian writer named Origen that Peter was crucified upside down. This was by Peter's own request. Peter did not think he was worthy to die in the same way Jesus had been crucified.

The conversion of Paul to faith in Christ is one of the most dramatic events in Acts. At first, we read that Paul (first called Saul) was responsible for the execution of some of the first Christians. Paul oversaw the execution of **Stephen**, the first witness to die in Acts (Acts 7-8). But on the road to Damascus, on his way to imprison and kill more Christians, Jesus stopped Paul. Paul was blinded by the light of Christ's glory. Jesus then commanded Paul to go to Damascus and wait. The Lord then sent His servant Ananias to minister to Paul. The Lord Jesus told Ananias:

---

*"Go, for he is a chosen vessel of Mine to bear My name before Gentiles, kings, and the children of Israel. For I will show him how many things he must suffer for My name's sake." (Acts 9:15-16)*

Paul was baptized and was then sent by Jesus to bear witness to all the nations. In many ways, Paul was an ideal evangelist. The Lord Jesus used Paul's natural gifts for God's glory. Paul was an educated man. He understood Greek philosophy, having been raised in Tarsus. He was one of the most committed Pharisees. He was a former disciple of one of the leading Jewish teachers, a man named Gamaliel. Paul would use this training in his preaching and teaching. However, it was the Holy Spirit's empowering of Paul that was the most important factor in his ministry.

Paul's life as an apostle wasn't easy, however. Few missionaries have ever suffered as much as Paul did. Paul tells us that he suffered the loss of all things in order to gain Jesus Christ (Phil. 3:7-11).

Paul's first missionary journey covered 1,400 miles (covering Cyprus and modern-day Turkey). His second missionary journey was twice as long. It spanned about 2,800 miles. He traveled through Syria, Turkey, Greece, and Jerusalem, mostly on foot. On his third missionary journey, Paul visited Turkey, Greece, Lebanon, and Israel. On this third journey, Paul logged another 2,700 miles. The Apostle Paul also wrote a large portion of the New Testament. In his letters, he wrote to churches as well as individuals (Timothy, Titus, Philemon). On his fourth missionary journey, he sailed to Rome. On this fourth journey, Paul was put under arrest by the Romans. He appealed his case to Caesar. Sometime after this fourth journey, Paul was put to death in Rome. Historical records tell us he was executed by the Emperor Nero. A likely date for Paul's execution is AD 67.

Paul's final written testimony was sent to his son in the faith, Timothy. Paul wrote,

> I have fought the good fight, I have finished the race, I have kept the faith. Finally, there is laid up for me the crown of righteousness, which the Lord, the righteous Judge, will give to me on that Day, and not to me only but also to all who have loved His appearing. (2 Tim. 4:7-8)

After Peter and Paul's deaths, the Apostle John's ministry went on. John's ministry was active particularly in Asia Minor. It is believed that John spent much of his time in Ephesus (modern-day Turkey). He wrote five New Testament books in all, including three letters (1, 2, 3 John) and the Gospel of John. He penned his fifth work, the Book of Revelation, while exiled on the island of Patmos. After his exile, John died somewhere between AD 80 and 100 and was buried at Ephesus.

The missionary labors of the other

PAUL PREACHING ON MARS HILL

## 3. THE BIRTH OF CHRISTIANITY IN THE FULLNESS OF TIME 49

EPHESUS

apostles are not all recorded in the New Testament. However, early church documents tell us that the other apostles took the gospel into Egypt, Syria, Greece, Africa, and India. The apostles were faithful in carrying out Jesus' commission.

The Romans did not intend for the gospel to spread throughout the world. However, in God's perfect providence, the Romans and Greeks prepared the way to make it happen. The Christian faith spread rapidly. This was due in part to the peace of Rome (the *Pax Romana*) which provided for safer travel. A ship could cross the Mediterranean without encountering a single pirate. Also, a vast network of well-built roads throughout the Roman Empire gave the apostles a solid path upon which they would wear out their sandals. They did exactly that as they spread the good news all over the world. These were the beginnings of Jesus Christ's mission to Europe. ∎

## PRAYER POINTS

- **Thank God for missionary work all over the world:** The work of the apostles to carry out the Great Commission has changed the world. The fact that you are reading this book is evidence that the gospel has gone out into all the world. Give thanks to God for the spread of the good news about Jesus into all parts of the world. In particular, give thanks to God for the early spread of this gospel into Europe.

- **Pray for Gospel Advance in Europe:** Europe has changed in many ways over the last 300 years. There are not nearly as many Christians in Europe as there once were. Let us pray that the Lord Jesus would revive His church in Europe once again.

ANCIENT ROMAN ROAD IN OSTIA, ANTICA

# ROMAN CULTURE AND RELIGION

They shall be ashamed
And also disgraced, all of them;
They shall go in confusion together,
Who are makers of idols.
But Israel shall be saved by the LORD
With an everlasting salvation;
You shall not be ashamed or disgraced
Forever and ever. (Isa. 45:16-17)

Roman citizens prided themselves on the greatness of their civilization. Rome was powerful. Rome was rich. Rome was glorious. Or so it seemed. The Bible teaches that those who commit sin are slaves to sin (John 8:34). Even if the richest Roman thought they were free, in reality they were in bondage to sin. The people of Rome didn't need larger homes or more servants. They didn't need more entertainment. What they needed most was a Savior. A look at Roman society will make this clear.

Men in Roman society were taught from their youth to seek *dignitas* (personal and family dignity or honor). This was the highest personal value for a Roman. They loved the glory and praise of man more than the praise and glory of God (see John 12:43). People and families were valued by how much honor they had in society. Roman men could win this honor (or *dignitas*) in a variety of ways. The two most common ways were through political office or by gaining military victories. It is no surprise then that Rome became a large empire. When power and prestige are the highest value, men will always seek after more.

In Roman society, the family was the fundamental social unit. The head of the Roman household was the oldest living male. He was known as the *paterfamilias* (pronounced payter-fa-milli-us). As the head of the home, this man had almost unlimited authority over what happened to the family. The *paterfamilias* would arrange all marriages. He could decide whether infants would be allowed to live. He even had the ability to have older children killed or sold as slaves.

A PATRICIAN'S FAMILY IN ANCIENT ROME

## A ROMAN FAMILY AT DINNER

Human life was cheap in Roman culture. Sometimes, families abandoned their infants to die. If a baby was not desired, it was not kept. It is heartbreaking to read how infants and young children were treated in Roman society. Roman law stated that a "dreadfully deformed child shall be quickly killed." Sometimes Roman fishermen would find babies in their nets while fishing.

Sadly, Rome was in the grip of the devil. Spiritual darkness and gross immorality were everywhere. The Romans did not submit to God's law. God's law requires us to respect the lives of children as well as adults. According to biblical law, a husband and father only has limited authority in his home. A husband and a father is subject to Christ's authority. He can only do what Jesus commands. In a Christian home, the life of every single person should be protected, cherished, and nurtured.

In the first few centuries of Christian history, many in the Roman Empire converted to the faith. In turning to Christ, these former Gentiles had to put off old ways of thinking and sinful ways of life.

---

This I say, therefore, and testify in the Lord, that you should no longer walk as the rest of the Gentiles walk, in the futility of their mind, having their understanding darkened, being alienated from the life of God, because of the ignorance that is in them, because of the blindness of their heart; who being past feeling, have given themselves over to lewdness, to work all uncleanness with greediness. But you have not so learned Christ. (Eph. 4:17-20)

---

When they became Christians, people could no longer live for their own selfish desires. Instead, in following Jesus Christ, a new pattern of family life was to emerge in the home. Paul describes what the Christian community was to look like:

> Let all bitterness, wrath, anger, clamor, and evil speaking be put away from you, with all malice. And be kind to one another, tenderhearted, forgiving one another, even as God in Christ forgave you. (Eph. 4:31-32)

## THE CORRUPT LIVES OF ROMAN LEADERS

As we learned in a previous chapter, Rome began when Romulus murdered his brother. This pattern of violating God's commandments was common among Rome's leaders. Corrupt emperors like Nero (reigned AD 54-68), Hadrian (reigned AD 117-138), Elagabalus (reigned AD 218-222), and Carus (reigned AD 282-283) were especially known for their immoral lifestyles. They were not content to marry a woman and be faithful to her in marriage. These powerful emperors regularly broke God's seventh commandment in some of the most heinous ways. Their transgressions of God's law provoked God's wrath.

> You shall not commit adultery. (Ex. 20:14)

It was common for Roman emperors to murder their own family members so they could secure their own positions in power. These were terrible violations of God's sixth commandment. Tiberius (reigned AD 14-37) killed his stepson Agrippa. Nero murdered his own mother and his wife.

What did the Roman rulers teach by their murderous behavior? They taught their citizens to act just like they did. Human life was easily disposed of.

**NERO (AD 54-68)**

> You shall not murder. (Ex. 20:13)

## THE ENTERTAINMENT OF ROME

The gladiatorial "games" were a big part of Roman life. Here is another grisly example of what the world looks like without the saving work of Jesus. Human blood was shed. For the citizens of Rome, killing was a mere sport. The **Colosseum** in Rome was the most well-known location for such games. Battle re-enactments would often take place in the Colosseum. However, these re-enactments are far different from what you might see today. In the Colosseum, real blood was shed as battles were replayed. Often, criminals were executed by being cast to wild beasts.

It wasn't just the Colosseum in Rome that conducted the games. At least 230 amphitheaters have been discovered in ancient cities around the old Roman world. The great Colosseum in Rome

**HADRIAN (AD 117-138)**

COLOSSEUM IN ROME

was just one of many amphitheaters. This wicked type of entertainment demonstrates how corrupt Roman culture was at the time.

In the next chapter, you will learn how the Roman games came to an end.

## ROMAN RELIGION

> Therefore, if you died with Christ from the basic principles of the world, why, as though living in the world, do you subject yourselves to regulations—'Do not touch, do not taste, do not handle,' which all concern things which perish with the using—according to the commandments and doctrines of men? These things indeed have an appearance of wisdom in self-imposed religion, false humility, and neglect of the body, but are of no value against the indulgence of the flesh. (Col. 2:20-23)

Roman people believed in many gods. The highest gods and goddesses of Rome were the Olympians. Chief among the Roman gods was **Jupiter**. Every time the Romans would conquer an enemy, they would add additional gods to the list. The mixing of various gods and various religions is called **syncretism**. The Romans believed in treating all the gods equally. However, even though all gods were accepted, the Romans believed their emperor should be worshiped above all other gods. The Romans were **polytheists**.

**Syncretism** ▪ Syncretism is the attempt to mix different religions together and make them one.

**Polytheism** ▪ The belief in or worship of many gods. Polytheism is different than monotheism, the belief in and worship of only one God.

**ROMAN GLADIATORS**

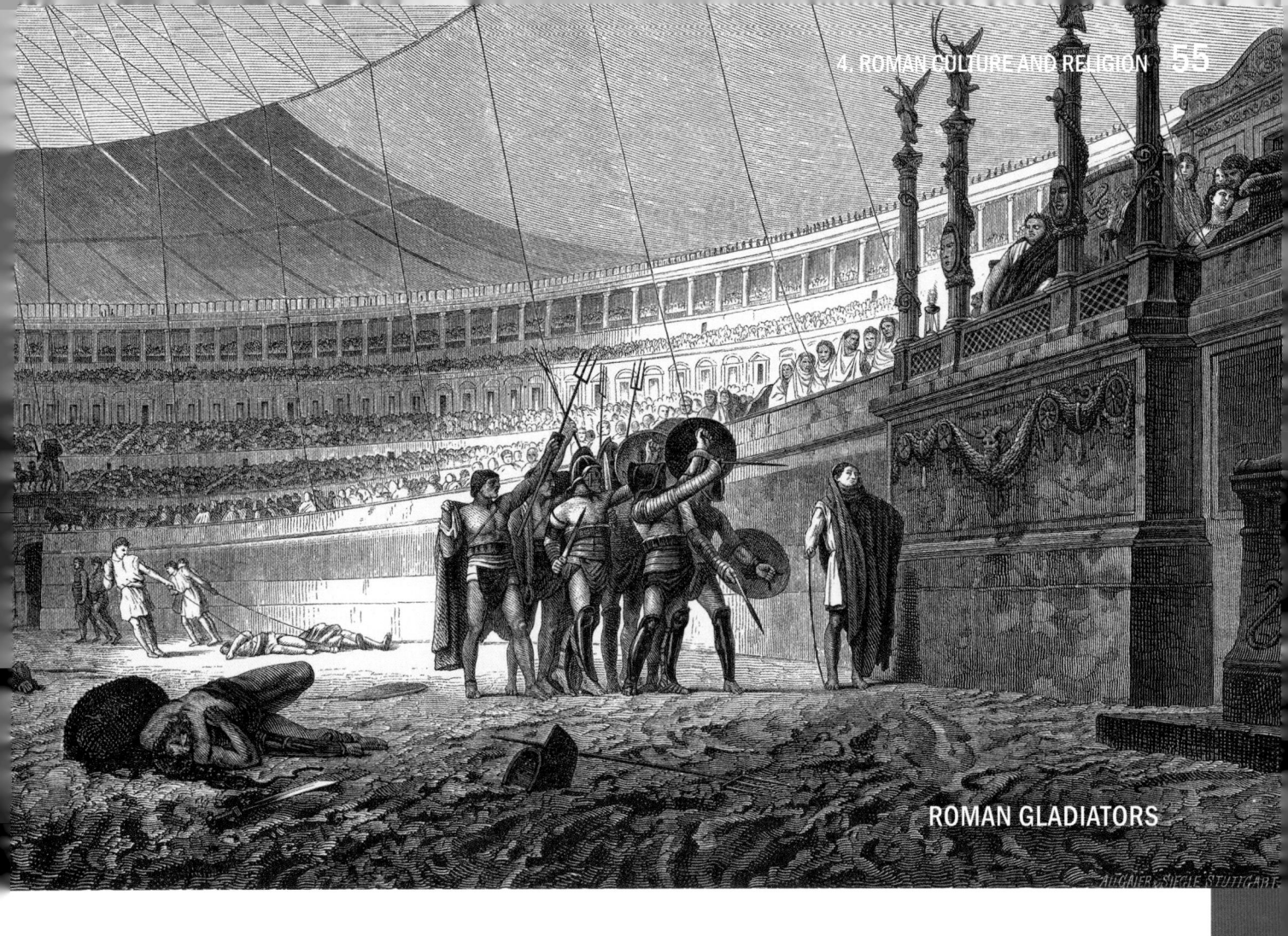

When Christianity began to spread across the Empire, the Romans were shocked by how exclusive Christian beliefs were. The Christians taught there was only one true God. Christians refused to worship any other god. Additionally, Christians refused to worship the emperor. Because of this, the term "atheist" (one who does not believe in God) was applied to the Christians. Of course, Christians are not atheists. But the Romans thought they were because Christians refused to worship the gods of Rome.

Roman religion involved many strange rituals. The people used these rituals in an attempt to gain favor from the gods. All non-Christian religions try to gain favor from their gods through external rituals.

For the Romans, right belief or right doctrine was not important. What mattered most was ritual (what you did and how you did it). Romans felt free to change their beliefs as the occasion demanded. It was right ritual that mattered most to them. Animals were to be sacrificed in just the right way. Prayers were to be said in the correct manner. Through these rituals, the Romans thought they could control the gods. They thought the gods existed to serve them.

The peoples of the Roman Empire were very religious. But they worshiped in ignorance. Without the knowledge of Jesus Christ, they did not know the one true and living God. When the Apostle Paul walked through Athens, he found an idol dedicated to "the unknown God." Seeing an opportunity to witness about Christ, Paul proclaimed the truth in Athens. ■

**A ROMAN TEMPLE CALLED THE "PANTHEON"**

## 4. ROMAN CULTURE AND RELIGION 57

"Therefore, the One whom you worship without knowing, Him I proclaim to you: . . . Truly, these times of ignorance God overlooked, but now commands all men everywhere to repent, because He has appointed a day on which He will judge the world in righteousness by the Man whom He has ordained. He has given assurance of this to all by raising Him from the dead." (Acts 17:23, 30-31)

ROMAN TEMPLE WORSHIP

# PRAYER POINTS

- **Praise God for the Destruction of False Religion in Europe:** As Jesus' gospel advanced into the Roman Empire, many turned from idols to serve the living God. This is the work of God. Praise the Lord for bringing down evil practices and false religions in the Roman Empire!

- **Pray for Godly Family Life in Your Home:** Families in ancient Rome did not live according to God's Word. There was much cruelty toward women and children. Give thanks for God's grace in your family. Ask God to further bring the "aroma of Christ" to your home by an abundant manifestation of the fruit of the Spirit.

- **Pray Against Modern Idols:** Discuss with your parents or siblings some examples of modern idols in your nation. Ask God to open the eyes of those who are following false gods or worldly idols. Ask the Lord to bring a spiritual awakening to your nation so that people would see that their idols cannot save them from sin.

INTERIOR OF THE ROMAN COLOSSEUM

# ROME'S PERSECUTION OF CHRIST'S PEOPLE

And they overcame [the dragon] by the blood of the Lamb and by the word of their testimony, and they did not love their lives to the death. (Rev. 12:11)

Before Christ's coming to earth, the Jewish people had spread throughout the Mediterranean world. Jews would return to visit their homeland in Israel. But they found new homes in many different lands. This was known as the *Diaspora* (the dispersion). Like Christians, the Jews were unique in refusing to worship the gods of Rome. They would not worship the emperor either. The Romans carved out a religious exemption for the Jews. They did not require Jews to participate in Roman religion.

As Christianity spread throughout the Empire, Romans thought Christianity was part of Judaism. To the Romans, Christianity seemed to be a variation of Jewish belief. Christians were sometimes called members of the sect of the **Nazarenes**. They earned this title because they followed Jesus of Nazareth. Of course, Jesus and His disciples were Jews. And Christians claimed the Old Testament Scriptures as their own. Because of this, the Romans didn't persecute the Christians because they thought they were just like the Jews. For a time, Christians had freedom to worship God. But this changed during the reign of Emperor **Nero** (reigned AD 54-68).

As the kingdom of Jesus Christ takes root in a country, persecution almost always follows. The evil one will not allow the work of Christ to go on without opposition. Wherever the church is growing, persecution comes with it. This is what happened in Korea and China in the 1900s. The same thing is happening in the Middle East today. Muslims are becoming Christians by the thousands. As the church grows, persecution is also increasing. Such was the case during the early years of Christianity. As the early Church increased throughout the Roman Empire, intense seasons of persecution followed.

CHRISTIAN MARTYRS IN ANCIENT ROME

**NERO (REIGNED AD 54-68)**

It is estimated that over 100,000 Christians were killed in the Roman Empire. This happened during ten major persecutions between AD 64 and 313. Here is a list of the Caesars (or emperors) who persecuted the Church, with the years of their persecutions:

- **Nero** — AD 64-68
- **Domitian** — AD 89-96
- **Trajan** — AD 107-117
- **Marcus Aurelius** — AD 161-180
- **Severus** — AD 193-211
- **Maximinus** — AD 235-238
- **Decius** — AD 249-251
- **Valerian** — AD 257-259
- **Aurelian** — AD 274-275
- **Diocletian** — AD 303-311

In some cases, Christians were publicly executed in the Roman games in the large amphitheaters. Thousands of people would watch and cheer. Christians were subjected to brutal acts of violence. The church historian **Eusebius** recorded many of the horrible sufferings of God's people. Some descriptions are almost too difficult to read. Here are two notable stories of courageous martyrs for Christ.

There was a young man who lived in Lyons. His name was **Sanctus**. He was a deacon in the early Church. When the authorities came to arrest Sanctus' pastor, Sanctus was arrested with him. When asked to give away his name, his birthplace, and the names of his fellow believers, Sanctus refused. His only answer to every question was, "I am a Christian." For many days, the Romans inflicted harm on his body, but he did not back down. Sanctus would only continue to cry out, "I am a Christian!" until he died. To the end, he never denied his Lord. To the end, Sanctus would only say, "I am a Christian!"

A young woman named **Blandina** was also arrested during the same persecution in Lyons. This was around the year AD 177. The Roman

**BLANDINA**

government leaders subjected this Christian lady to violent harm for many days. Over and over again, they pressed her to worship their gods. But she would not give in to them. When a young Christian boy of fifteen years of age was thrown into the arena with her, Blandina encouraged him to stand strong for Christ. The boy did just that. Finally, after many weeks of suffering, Blandina was killed after being thrown to a wild bull. She fought the good fight of faith, and she conquered through the blood of the Lamb (Rev. 12:11). These early martyrs were ordinary Christians with extraordinary faith in Jesus. Though they are now dead, their lives still speak.

The last of the Roman persecutions was the worst of all. It is called the **Great Persecution** (AD 303-311). It happened during Emperor **Diocletian**'s reign. Not only were many believers killed, but Christian books (including the Scriptures) and church buildings were burned. The emperor issued a total of four edicts, ordering an attack on the Christian faith all over the Empire.

- **The First Edict of Diocletian:** All church buildings were to be destroyed. All Bibles were to be burned, and all Christian worship was forbidden.
- **The Second Edict of Diocletian:** All pastors and church leaders were to be arrested and imprisoned.
- **The Third Edict:** All pastors and church leaders were to offer sacrifice to the gods, or they were to be tortured.
- **The Fourth Edict of Diocletian:** All citizens throughout the Empire were commanded to sacrifice to the gods. If any refused, they were to be killed.[1]

There were times of peace for the Christians during the first three centuries of the church. But Christians in the Roman Empire *always* dealt with some opposition from the world. Our Lord Jesus warned us of this when He said:

DIOCLETIAN
(REIGNED AD 284-305)

---

"If you were of the world, the world would love its own. Yet because you are not of the world, but I chose you out of the world, therefore the world hates you." (John 15:19)

---

Though the Roman emperors wanted to stamp out the Christian faith, it kept growing through these trials and tribulations. What Rome meant for evil, God was going to use for good—for the salvation of many throughout the Empire.

In the end, Jesus won His battles over the Roman Empire. In AD 313, the Emperor **Constantine** put an end to the persecutions. Christians built the first hospitals and began to care for the orphans abandoned by their parents. Christians changed the government laws to make it harder to kill babies. The laws of the land began to align more with God's law found in the Scriptures.

One notable example of Christian transformation is the end of the gladiatorial games. The story of how the games ended is also a profile in Christian courage. The church histo-

---

[1] N. R. Needham, *2000 Years of Christ's Power: Volume 1, The Age of the Early Church Fathers* (Fearn, Ross-Shire: Christian Focus, 2016), 162-163.

TELEMACHUS STOPS THE GAMES

the hateful spectacle of the games was taking place, Telemachus went into the stadium, stepped down into the arena, and tried to stop the men who were fighting each other. The spectators of the bloody match were outraged. Inspired by the mad fury of the demons who delight in deeds of violence, they stoned to death Telemachus the peacemaker. But when the admirable emperor heard of this, he numbered Telemachus among the army of victorious martyrs, and put an end to that ungodly spectacle of the games.

Roman Emperor Honorius (reigned AD 393-423) was so impressed with the man's faith that he put a final end to the games on January 1, 404. Telemachus gave his life to stop the games. He is one outstanding example of courage found among the early Christians. ∎

---

**The wicked flee when no one pursues, But the righteous are bold as a lion. (Prov. 28:1)**

---

rian **Theodoret** recorded how the end of the Roman games finally came about. According to him, a Christian monk named **Telemachus** was grieved by the terrible killings in the coliseums. He journeyed from the East all the way to Rome. He then descended into the arena in the middle of the games. Then, Telemachus preached against the bloody games. Theodoret wrote:

> A man named Telemachus, who had become a monk, set out from the Eastern Empire and entered Rome. There, when

## 5. ROME'S PERSECUTION OF CHRIST'S PEOPLE 63

ROMAN AMPITHEATER

# PRAYER POINTS

- **Pray for a nation where persecution is severe:** Using online resources such as *Operation World* or Open Doors, choose one nation where persecution against Christians is severe today. Begin to pray for that nation. Ask the Lord Jesus to protect His people, to strengthen the church there, and to stop evildoers.

ANCIENT THEATER OF FOURVIERE IN LYONS, FRANCE

# IRENAEUS OF LYONS: FIGHTING FOR THE FAITH ONCE DELIVERED

> Beloved, while I was very diligent to write to you concerning our common salvation, I found it necessary to write to you exhorting you to contend earnestly for the faith which was once for all delivered to the saints. For certain men have crept in unnoticed, who long ago were marked out for this condemnation, ungodly men, who turn the grace of our God into lewdness and deny the only Lord God and our Lord Jesus Christ. (Jude 3-4)

As **Polycarp** entered the stadium in Smyrna, the crowds jeered. Polycarp was led before the Roman governor and was pressed to deny his faith in Jesus Christ. To this he answered, "Eighty and six years I have served Jesus, and He never did me any wrong. How then can I blaspheme my King and Savior?"

The governor threatened Polycarp, saying, "I have wild beasts at hand. I will give you to them unless you repent."

Polycarp boldly replied, "Call them then. For we are not accustomed to repent of what is good in order to adopt what is evil."

The governor intensified his threats. "If you refuse to repent, I will cause you to be consumed by fire since you despise the wild beasts."

Polycarp remained unmoved. "You threaten me with fire which burns for an hour, and after a little while is extinguished. But you are ignorant of the fire of the coming judgment and of eternal punishment reserved for the ungodly. But why do you wait? Bring forth what you will."

Polycarp was then bound and killed at the stake. His last words were words of faith offered up in prayer to God.

The date of Polycarp's death was around AD 156. On the coast of the Aegean Sea, in the city of **Smyrna**, a faithful Christian pastor was martyred for his faith. He is known to history as Polycarp, the bishop of Smyrna. His story is told in the ancient document known as

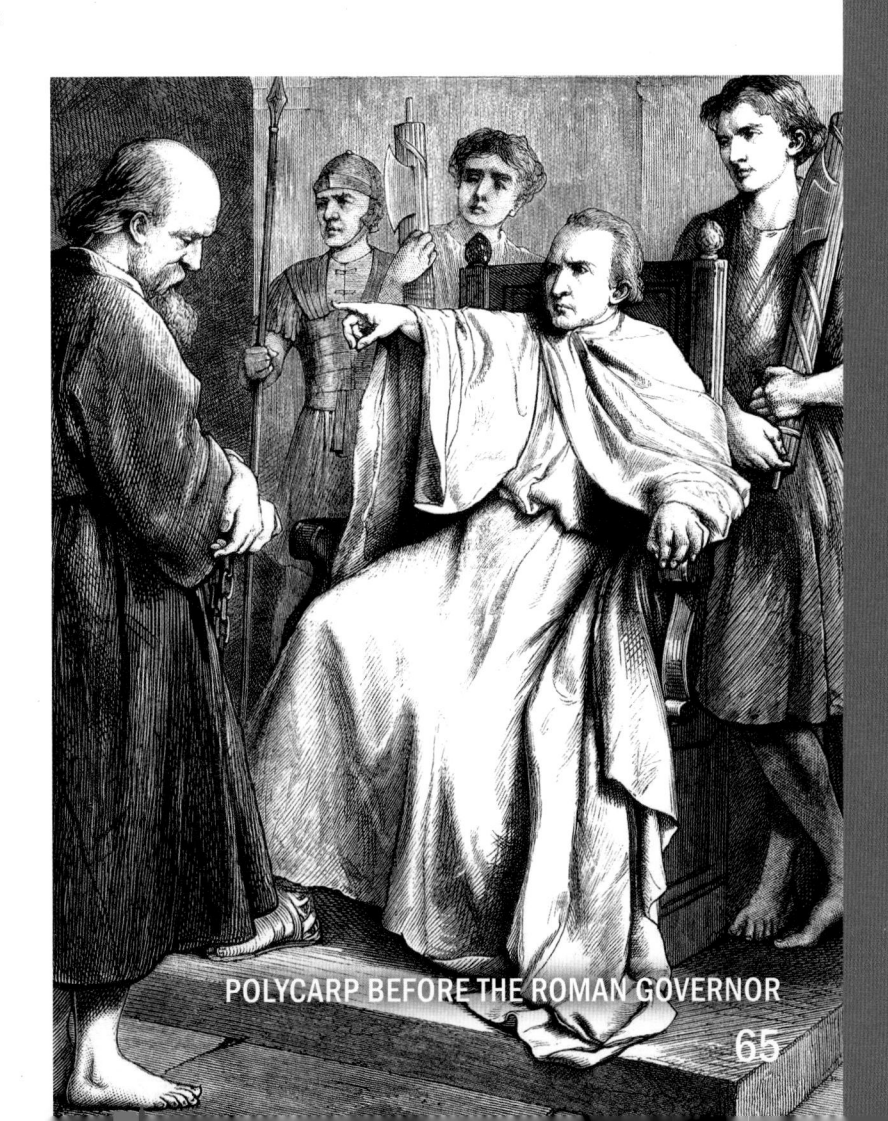

**POLYCARP BEFORE THE ROMAN GOVERNOR**

***The Martyrdom of Polycarp.*** Polycarp's faithful stand for Jesus Christ is one of the most well-known martyrdoms in Christian history. His testimony continues to inspire courage in Christians today. For those who knew Polycarp, his stand for Jesus was even more impactful.

**LOCATION OF LYONS, FRANCE**

One who knew Polycarp personally was **Irenaeus of Lyons**, a disciple of Polycarp's. The older man's teaching and example was particularly valuable to Irenaeus. One reason why Polycarp's instruction was so valued is because he was discipled by the Apostle John. That means Irenaeus was discipled by Polycarp who was discipled by John. And John was an actual eyewitness of the resurrected Lord Jesus Christ.

Irenaeus remembered with fondness the time he spent with Polycarp. He wrote of his experience with Polycarp:

> I can remember the place where the blessed Polycarp used to sit when he preached his sermons. I remember how he came in and went out. I remember the manner of his life. I remember what he looked like. I can recall the sermons he delivered to the people, and how he used to report his association with John and the others who had seen the Lord. Polycarp would relate their words, and the things concerning the Lord he had heard from them, about His miracles and teachings. Polycarp had received all this from eyewitnesses of the Word of life. I listened eagerly to these things at the time, by God's mercy which was bestowed on me. I made notes of them, not on paper, but in my heart. And now constantly, by the grace of God, I meditate on them faithfully.

There is much that we do not know about Irenaeus' life. He lived a very long time ago. For this reason, some details about his life have disappeared. However, knowing something about this godly Christian leader is important for Christians today. He was one of the earliest defenders of the Christian faith. Irenaeus defended the true faith against twisted, heretical forms of Christianity. His most important book is known as ***Against Heresies***.

A **heresy** is a belief or practice that is contrary to what the Bible teaches. The Bible warns against false prophets and false teachers who will bring heresies into the church. Peter uses the word "heresy" to describe these false teachers.

---

**But there were also false prophets among the people, even as there will be false teachers among you, who will secretly bring in destructive heresies, even denying the Lord who bought them, and bring on themselves swift destruction. (2 Pet. 2:1)**

---

Irenaeus was a man who loved God's truth. For this reason, he fought for the faith that he had received from Polycarp. Polycarp received it from the Apostle John. The Apostle John received it from Jesus Christ.

6. IRENAEUS OF LYONS: FIGHTING FOR THE FAITH ONCE DELIVERED    67

SENANQUE ABBEY, PROVENCE FRANCE

## IRENAEUS CALLED TO GAUL

> But you must continue in the things which you have learned and been assured of, knowing from whom you have learned them, and that from childhood you have known the Holy Scriptures, which are able to make you wise for salvation through faith which is in Christ Jesus. (2 Tim. 3:14-15)

Sometime after Polycarp's death, Irenaeus moved to the city of Lyons (pronounced "lee-awn"). Lyons is located in a region of Europe once called **Gaul**. Much of Gaul is now modern-day France. Sometime after arriving in Lyons, a severe persecution broke out against the church. The year was AD 177. This persecution happened during the reign of Emperor **Marcus Aurelius** (reigned AD 161-180). Pothinus was bishop of Lyons at the time. This elderly man was imprisoned. Pothinus was about ninety years old. He likely had been one of the founding members of the Christian church in Lyons.

Pothinus was soon martyred along with other Christians such as Sanctus, Blandina, Ponticus, a fifteen-year-old boy, and a man named Attalus. Each of them gave their lives up for the sake of Jesus Christ. They would not bow to any idol. They would not deny the Lord Jesus who had redeemed them. It is estimated that around forty-eight Christians died in this persecution.

In God's providence, Irenaeus was spared. Now that the church in Lyons was without a pastor, Irenaeus was called to replace Pothinus. As a pastor, it was important for Irenaeus to comfort and strengthen the suffering saints in Lyons who had lost many of their fellow brothers and sisters.

The persecution died down. But the devil, the foe of Christ and His people, has other strategies. After the persecution ended, the evil one set about to twist the truth of the gospel through false teaching.

## IRENAEUS CONTENDS AGAINST HERESY

> Now I urge you, brethren, note those who cause divisions and offenses, contrary to the doctrine which you learned, and avoid them. For those who are such do not serve our Lord Jesus Christ, but their own belly, and by smooth words and flattering speech deceive the hearts of the simple. (Rom. 16:17-18)

At this time, a dangerous heresy sprang up. This root of false teaching deceived many people and caused division in the church. The heresy was called **Gnosticism**. The meaning of this word comes from the Greek word for knowledge (*gnosis*). It was called Gnosticism because its followers claimed to have a secret, special knowledge that others did not have. Only those with this secret knowledge could attain to the greatest heights of salvation.

Gnostics despised the physical creation. They believed that physical things like the ocean, plants, dirt, and animals were created by a lower god. They called this god the **demiurge**. They believed Jesus came to give us the knowledge necessary to escape this physical creation and become "pure spirits." Gnostics believed that a person's body was a "prison house" from which we need to escape.

This is contrary to what the Bible teaches.

**PAGES FROM A GNOSTIC WRITING**

God calls His creation "good." God is redeeming all things through Jesus Christ. As human beings, we have both a body and soul. One day, when Jesus returns, there will be a resurrection of the dead. Both our bodies and our souls will be resurrected. Physical things are not evil. It is the fall into sin that damaged the creation. But God will restore all things.

Because of their unbiblical beliefs, the Gnostics also lived in ungodly ways. Some Gnostics abstained from many foods and drinks. They believed the body and its pleasures were evil. They would abstain from marriage. Paul warned that false teachers like them would come to deceive the church (1 Tim. 4:1-3). Other Gnostics didn't think it mattered what they did with their bodies. They reasoned, "We are leaving these bodies behind anyway." These Gnostics thought they could do whatever they wanted. As a result, they broke God's commandments by sinning with their bodies.

Irenaeus was deeply concerned about this

---

[1] The word "catholic" means "universal." When we confess that we believe in "the holy catholic church" we mean that we believe that the Lord Jesus Christ has established a church all over the world. This church includes peoples from every tribe, tongue, and nation.

false teaching. He began studying what the Gnostics were saying. Over many years, he wrote several books against the Gnostics. These books were collected into one larger work called *Against Heresies*.

In this very large work, Irenaeus explains all the strange, silly, and unbiblical teachings of the Gnostics. But he didn't only expose false teaching. He also taught people the truth. He compared the Gnostic teaching with what the Bible actually teaches. He argued that the Gnostics were separating from the faith delivered by the Apostles. Irenaeus also showed how all the Christian churches in different places held to the same basic core convictions. The churches held to what was called the **Rule of Faith**. There were different written summaries of early Christian beliefs. One of the earliest Christian creeds is called the **Apostles Creed**. The creed was probably not written by the twelve apostles, but it states what the apostles believed. It is a good summary of what the New Testament teaches.

Here is one version of the Apostles Creed in English.

> I believe in God, the Father almighty, creator of heaven and earth.
> I believe in Jesus Christ, his only Son, our Lord,
> who was conceived by the Holy Spirit
> and born of the virgin Mary.
> He suffered under Pontius Pilate,
> was crucified, died, and was buried;
> he descended to hell.
> The third day he rose again from the dead.
> He ascended to heaven
> and is seated at the right hand of God the Father almighty.
> From there he will come to judge the living and the dead.
> I believe in the Holy Spirit,
> the holy catholic church,[1]
> the communion of saints,
> the forgiveness of sins,
> the resurrection of the body,
> and the life everlasting. Amen.

Statements of faith like the Apostles Creed were helpful. They helped Christians distinguish false teaching from what the Bible taught and what Christians confessed. As Irenaeus combatted Gnostic teaching, he did not just rely on the Rule of Faith. He believed that the Bible is God's Word. The Bible was the final and only perfect standard to use in judging the Gnostics. For this reason, throughout his book, Irenaeus quotes thousands of Bible passages. He saw the Bible as a unified whole. The Bible is inspired by God and is therefore without any error. Irenaeus explained the importance of rooting our beliefs in the Bible. He wrote, "The tradition from the apostles does exist in the Church. That tradition is preserved among us. Let us, therefore, prove our doctrine from the Scriptures provided by those apostles who wrote the Gospel."

Irenaeus also knew that heresies are evidence of a spiritual problem in the heart of false teachers. False teachers are proud men whom Irenaeus described as "puffed up with pride" and are men who do not "place the fear of God supreme in their hearts." This is an important insight. When we are proud about our knowledge, we open ourselves up to the devil's temptations. We must fear God and not be wise in our own eyes. The Apostle Paul warns us:

**Knowledge puffs up, but love edifies. And if anyone thinks that he knows anything, he knows nothing yet as he ought to know. (1 Cor. 8:1-2)**

THE NEW TESTAMENT IN GREEK

## IRENAEUS PROTECTS CHRIST'S FLOCK

**I am the good shepherd. The good shepherd gives His life for the sheep. But a hireling, he who is not the shepherd, one who does not own the sheep, sees the wolf coming and leaves the sheep and flees; and the wolf catches the sheep and scatters them. (John 10:11-12)**

Irenaeus was a pastor of souls. He knew that there was more at stake than just words and ideas. The lives of real people were affected by false teaching. Some ideas and words can be deadly to souls. Many of the Gnostic leaders persuaded Christians to leave the true church and join them. One dangerous false teacher was named Marcus. Many people left the churches near Lyons to follow Marcus.

Not only did Marcus teach Gnostic ideas. He also did magic tricks with water and wine to gain followers. He would tell the women who joined his group to prophesy. He would puff these women up with pride, declaring that they could give people a message from God. Sometimes the women told Marcus they didn't know what to say. Marcus said, "Just say whatever comes into your mind." After saying whatever came into their minds, Marcus declared the women to be prophetesses.

In God's mercy, the Lord preserved some women from Marcus' lies. Women returned to Irenaeus and the other pastors and reported what Marcus was doing. But others were deceived. Some women even left their husbands to follow Marcus. Many Gnostics like Marcus also used magic to trick and to gain converts. This was very disturbing to Irenaeus.

## 6. IRENAEUS OF LYONS: FIGHTING FOR THE FAITH ONCE DELIVERED

He warned the flock in Lyons to stay away from the dangerous and heretical Gnostic teachers like Marcus.

As Irenaeus grew older, he continued to exhort the flock in Lyons to stand strong for Jesus. He reminded his fellow Christians that following the Lord comes at a cost. Though violent persecutions were not constant, Christians always faced some degree of opposition from the world. Then, in 202, another persecution arose. This persecution happened during the reign of Emperor Septimius Severus (193-211). It is believed that Irenaeus died somewhere around this time. Whether or not he was martyred, we do not know. Whatever the circumstances, we know that Irenaeus dedicated his life to the truth of the gospel. We are all indebted to his labors to contend for the faith once delivered to us, the saints. ■

**CHURCH OF SAINT-BRUNO DES CHARTREUX, LYONS, FRANCE**

# PRAYER POINTS: FRANCE

- **Pray for dead hearts to be awakened to the things of God:** Since the radically secular French Revolution of 1789, France has been one of the most secular nations in Europe. Yet, like most nations in Europe, it has a Christian heritage that goes back almost to the beginning of Christianity. Only about six percent of the population in France attend church on a weekly basis. Most French people are "without God and without hope in the world" (Eph. 2:12). Ask the Lord to awaken dead hearts to the things of God. Pray that God would send forth faithful Christians who would share God's Word with the unbelievers of France.

- **Pray in light of changing demographics:** The population of France is changing. Many immigrants, especially from Muslim backgrounds, are now living in France in greater numbers than ever before. The birth rate among French families is falling. This means that in the future, more people in France will likely be born with a heritage from a nation elsewhere in the world, especially from Muslim nations. Pray that God would use this change in France as an opportunity for the gospel to penetrate both into the French people as well as the foreign immigrants now in France.

## Basic Facts about France (French Republic)

| | |
|---|---|
| Total population: | 67 million |
| Total area: | 247,000 square miles |
| Capital: | Paris |
| Official language: | French |
| Primary religions: | Roman Catholic, Atheist, Islam |

PEACE ARCH, MILAN, ITALY

# AMBROSE OF MILAN: SHEPHERD OF GOD'S PEOPLE

> And I will give you shepherds according to My heart, who will feed you with knowledge and understanding. (Jer. 3:15)

The church of Milan was now without a pastor. It was AD 374 and Bishop Auxentius was dead. At this time, controversy over Jesus Christ's nature continued to trouble the church. The **Council of Nicaea** (AD 325) declared that Jesus Christ was the eternal Son of God. It declared that the Son of God was of the same nature with God the Father. Just as the Father was eternally God, so the Son was also eternally God.

But not everyone agreed with the decision reached at Nicaea. Some still followed the teaching of **Arius**. It was Arius who argued that the Son of God was a created being. In response, Nicaea declared Arius' teaching to be in error. Nicaea did not end the arguments over this important question.

Auxentius had taken the side of Arius. For this reason, he was opposed by many and supported by others. Now that Auxentius was gone, the question was, who would replace him as the new bishop? And what would the new pastor believe about Jesus Christ?

Fierce debates raged among the citizens of Milan. Without someone intervening, soon there would be a riot.

**Ambrose** (AD 340-397) was governor of the region. Sensing the need to intervene, Ambrose tried to calm the citizens of Milan. He urged them to seek peace. As he spoke to the people, many were impressed by his wise words. As Ambrose spoke, a young boy in the crowd cried out, "Let Ambrose be bishop!"

Ambrose was stunned by the suggestion. This was hardly his intention in speaking to the crowd. He only wanted peace while a successor for Auxentius was chosen. Soon the boy's suggestion spread like wildfire through the crowd. The crowd chanted, "Ambrose! Bishop! Ambrose! Bishop!" Ambrose, terrified, hardly felt qualified for such an important role in the church. But the crowd was convinced.

COUNCIL OF NICAEA

**LOCATION OF MILAN**

Ambrose was the right choice.

Ambrose tried numerous ways to get out of this appeal. He even fled Milan by horse one night. But then he changed his mind and returned. Eventually, he submitted to the call of Milan's citizens. At this time, Ambrose was not yet baptized. But over the period of eight days, he was baptized and then ordained bishop of Milan.

## AMBROSE BEGINS HIS MINISTRY

Looking back, it seems that the people of Milan did not take heed to Paul's instruction in 1 Timothy 3:

> A bishop then must be blameless, . . . not a novice, lest being puffed up with pride he fall into the same condemnation as the devil. (1 Tim. 3:6)

Ambrose was surely a novice in the faith. He was a young Christian. It was true that he was a skilled governor and gifted speaker. But Ambrose did not know the Bible very well.

Despite this fact, God had mercy on Ambrose and the people of Milan. Ambrose became one of the most important church leaders in the early centuries of the church. A fellow bishop in Caesarea named Basil heard the news about Ambrose. Basil was hopeful that the false Arian teaching would be corrected by Ambrose. Basil wrote to him:

> Take heart, man of God, because you have neither received nor learned the Gospel of Christ from humans. Rather, the Lord himself has taken you from among the judges of the earth to seat you on the chair of the Apostles: Fight the good fight. If there is someone affected by the curse of the Arian insanity, restore him to the ancient path of the Fathers.

When Basil referred to the "curse of the Arian insanity," he was speaking of Arian doctrine. Clearly, Basil believed Arius' view of Jesus

**MOSAIC OF AMBROSE**

MILAN CATHEDRAL

Christ was in grave error.

Ambrose was reluctant to become bishop of Milan. But after his election and ordination, he dedicated his life to ministry. He sold his great estates and gave the proceeds to the poor. He retained an allowance to provide for his unmarried sister Marcellina. Ambrose became known for his disciplined life of prayer and fasting. He was steadfast in prayer, sometimes praying through much of the night. He also zealously studied the Bible and the writings of other church leaders. Every Sunday he preached from God's Word. He taught the Christians in Milan to meditate often on the Bible. He wrote this about God's Word: "Let us procure for our minds this food that, ground and refined by long meditation, be for the heart of man like heavenly manna."

Ambrose was known by many as a loving and humble man. These are important characteristics for shepherds in Christ's church. One of Ambrose's prayers gives the reader a sense of this pastor's heart. Pastors are called to restore wayward sinners. This restoration work must be done in humility and gentleness (Gal. 6:1). Ambrose wrote, "Every time I seek to restore someone who has fallen into sin, I must show compassion. I should not be proud. Instead, I should groan and weep, so that, as often as I weep for another, I weep for myself." Ambrose knew that he was a sinner too. He also needed to weep over his own sins.

For over twenty years (374-397), Ambrose continued as bishop of Milan. He left behind a significant legacy for the church in Europe. Now, let's learn more about Ambrose's legacy.

## AMBROSE'S HYMNS

**Let the word of Christ dwell in you richly in all wisdom, teaching and admonishing one another in psalms and hymns and spiritual songs, singing with grace in your hearts to the Lord. (Col. 3:16)**

Ambrose is remembered for his contribu-

BASILICA OF SAINT AMBROSE, THE CHURCH WHERE
AMBROSE SERVED AS BISHOP

tions to church music. For example, in many eastern churches, it was common to practice **antiphonal singing**. This means that one verse would be sung by half of the congregation. Then, on the next verse, the other half of the congregation would sing. This would repeat as the verses of the psalm or hymn were completed. Ambrose introduced this eastern practice of antiphonal singing in Milan. From Milan, it spread to other churches in the West.

Ambrose also wrote hymns. We don't know exactly how many he wrote, but it is believed to be around a dozen. Ambrose wrote hymns of praise to teach sound doctrine. A good example is the hymn *Come, Redeemer of the Nations*. In this hymn, Ambrose writes about Jesus Christ's incarnation.

> Come, thou Redeemer of the earth,
> and manifest thy virgin-birth:
> let every age adoring fall;
> such birth befits the God of all.
>
> Begotten of no human will,
> but of the Spirit, thou art still
> the Word of God, in flesh arrayed,
> the Saviour, now to us displayed.
>
> From God the Father he proceeds,
> to God the Father back he speeds,
> runs out his course to death and hell,
> returns on God's high throne to dwell.
>
> O equal to thy Father, thou!
> Gird on thy fleshly mantle now,
> the weakness of our mortal state
> with deathless might invigorate.
>
> Thy cradle here shall glitter bright,
> and darkness glow with new-born light,
> no more shall night extinguish day,
> where love's bright beams their power display.
>
> O Jesus, virgin-born, to thee
> eternal praise and glory be,
> whom with the Father we adore

and Holy Spirit, evermore. Amen.

Many important biblical doctrines are taught in this hymn. Ambrose mentions the virgin birth. He teaches that Jesus Christ is God. And he describes Jesus the Son as equal with the Father. The hymn ends on a note of praise to Father, Son, and Holy Spirit.

Ambrose's hymn-writing and emphasis on congregational singing had a lasting effect on the church in Europe.

## AMBROSE AND CIVIL RULERS

> Now therefore, be wise, O kings;
> Be instructed, you judges of the earth.
> Serve the LORD with fear,
> And rejoice with trembling.
> Kiss the Son, lest He be angry,
> And you perish in the way,
> When His wrath is kindled but a little.
> Blessed are all those who put their trust in Him.
> (Ps. 2:10-12)

Bishops in the Roman world played an important role in society. They often interacted with emperors, empresses, and governors. Milan was a prominent city in the Roman Empire. Because Ambrose was bishop of Milan, he was an influential man. Through Ambrose's preaching, the church in Milan returned to the Nicene doctrine that Jesus Christ was eternally God. But not everyone agreed with Ambrose. The Arians continued to press for their views.

One significant person who held to Arian views was the Empress Justina. The Empress requested that a separate church be established for those with Arian views. But Ambrose maintained that the authority of the church was independent of civil authorities. As a minister in Christ's church, Ambrose was not bound to do whatever the emperor or empress said. He once wrote, "The Church belongs to God,

# TAKING EUROPE FOR JESUS

**AMBROSE AND THEODOSIUS**

therefore it cannot be assigned to Caesar. The emperor is *within* the church, not *above* it." The Empress was refused.

Ambrose's words were put to the test in 390. That year, in the city of Thessalonica, a riot broke out. A murderous, rampaging mob killed the governor Botherich. Along with Botherich, the mob killed other officials of the province as well. Word of the riot soon reached Emperor **Theodosius**. The news was not calmly received. Theodosius had a well-known weakness. He was easily angered. Even Theodosius' wife and children would hide when he fell into a rage. When Theodosius received the news of the riot, he was furious and sent soldiers to Thessalonica. Their order was to massacre the Thessalonians. When Theodosius calmed down, he realized his order was unjust. But he changed his mind too late. Around 7,000 people died as a result of Theodosius' orders.

Ancient Roman emperors could often get away with anything. But the influence of Christ's church had grown since the time of Emperor **Constantine**. Now, the emperor was subject to the discipline of Christ's church. When Ambrose heard about the Thessalonian massacre, he promptly excommunicated Theodosius from the church. Such heinous crimes called for Theodosius to be barred from the church until he repented. Ambrose then wrote a letter to the emperor. In the letter, he exhorted Theodosius to deep, heart-felt, and public repentance.

Here is a portion of the letter Ambrose sent to Theodosius:

> I cannot deny that you are zealous for the faith and that you fear God. But you have a naturally passionate spirit. And while you easily yield to love when that spirit is subdued, yet when it is stirred up you become a raging beast. I would gladly have left you to the workings of your own heart, but I dare not remain silent or gloss over your sin. No one in all human history has ever before heard of such a bloody scene as the one at Thessalonica! I warned you against it. I pleaded with you. You yourself realized its horror and tried to cancel your decree. And now I call you to repent. Remember how King David repented of his crime. Will you be ashamed to do what David did? You can wash away your sins only be tears, by repentance, by humbling your soul before God. You are a man. You have sinned as a man. You must repent as a man. No angel, no archangel can forgive you. God alone can forgive you. And He forgives those who repent. . . . I love you. I honor you from my heart. I pray for you. If you believe this,

accept what I say. But if you do not believe it, forgive me for preferring God to you.

The following Sunday, Emperor Theodosius tried to enter the church for worship. But he found his way barred. There stood Ambrose, blocking the doors of the church. Ambrose told the emperor he would not be allowed to attend public worship for a time. For the next eight months, Theodosius was barred from church. Remarkably, Theodosius did submit to the church's discipline. He repented publicly in the streets. Upon his return to the church, he kneeled before the whole congregation and asked God for forgiveness.

This was a first in the Roman Empire. For a Christian bishop to confront an emperor with his sin showed the significant impact the church was making on Roman society.

## INFLUENCE ON AUGUSTINE

In 384, a newly appointed teacher of rhetoric came to Milan. His name was **Augustine**. When he arrived in Milan, he was not a Christian. His mother Monica had long prayed for Augustine's conversion to Christ. After many years had passed, Augustine was still living for himself. But during his time in Milan he would repent and turn back to the Lord.

Monica joined Augustine in Milan. Together, they would attend the worship services in Milan. Monica loved Ambrose and often spoke to him about Augustine. Augustine, for his part, attended church to hear the often-praised speaking abilities of Ambrose. At first, Augustine listened to Ambrose merely because he was interested in the pastor's style of preaching. Yet, in time, Augustine began to be affected by God's Word itself. Ambrose was also a loving man. He reached out to Augustine and established a relationship with him. Augustine described Ambrose as a "friendly

**AUGUSTINE AND HIS MOTHER MONICA**

man" and said, "that man of God received me as a father would and welcomed my coming." During those years at Milan, the Lord opened Augustine's heart to the truth. Upon reading the Scriptures one day, Augustine believed. In 387, he was baptized by Ambrose in Milan. In the years that followed, Augustine served as a bishop in Africa. His time under Ambrose's teaching was instrumental. It equipped Augustine for his own ministry.

## AMBROSE'S LAST YEARS

In the early months of 397, Ambrose became ill. He was confined to his bedroom. After decades of ministry, the people of Milan cared deeply for their pastor. They sent letters to Ambrose, asking him to pray to God that his life would be lengthened. Ambrose responded, "I have so lived among you that I cannot be ashamed to live longer; but neither do I fear to die; for we have a good Lord."

By the end of his life, Ambrose was known

by people in places far from Milan. His faithful preaching and holy life were a testimony to the world. Even a distant tribe in the region of Germany learned of Ambrose. This tribe was known as the "Marcomanni." They lived between the Elbe and Oder rivers. Queen Fritigil heard "of the fame of a holy man from the words of a Christian in Italy who happened to be among them." Queen Fritigil wanted to know more about Ambrose and the Christian faith. She sent ambassadors to Ambrose, asking for a book from which she could learn the Christian faith. Ambrose gave a letter to the ambassadors for Queen Fritigil. In the letter, he explained what it meant to be a Christian. He also urged Queen Fritigil to convince her husband the king to keep the peace with Rome. In this way, Ambrose's ministry extended beyond the church in Milan.

At the beginning of April, Ambrose knew that his death was approaching. He spent his last hours in prayer. On Saturday, April 4th, 397, Ambrose finished his earthly race. He lived for fifty-seven years. Though his life was short in light of eternity, his legacy endures. ∎

## PRAYER POINTS: ITALY

- **Thank God for the Christian heritage of Italy:** Godly pastors and faithful churches were planted here in the first centuries of the church. Thank the Lord for what He has done in the past in Italy. It was to Rome that Paul wrote his inspired letter (Romans) that continues to change the world. From Italy, the message of the gospel went forth into other parts of Europe.

- **Pray for biblical reformation in Italy:** The seat of the Roman Catholic Church is in Rome, the capital city of Italy. For this reason, Italy has long been dominated by the Roman Catholic Church. Today, about 85% of Italians profess some kind of connection to the Roman Church. In contrast, only about half of one percent of the Italian population describes itself as Protestant. Italy never experienced the fruits of the Protestant Reformation like other parts of Europe. But if God so wills, that Reformation could come to Italy in our generation. Let us pray that the church would be reformed in Italy.

- **Pray for the light of the gospel to overcome secularism:** Like many nations in modern Europe, Italy is becoming more secular. This means that increasingly, many citizens of Italy do not believe in any religion. They may be atheists (those who do not believe in the existence of any God) or agnostics (those who don't know or care about God's existence). A godless view of the world is one of the strategies Satan uses to send people to hell. A secular worldview among many in Europe makes them indifferent to the things of God. Pray that Christ would send His light into Europe once again and awaken dead hearts.

## Basic Facts about Italy (Italian Republic)

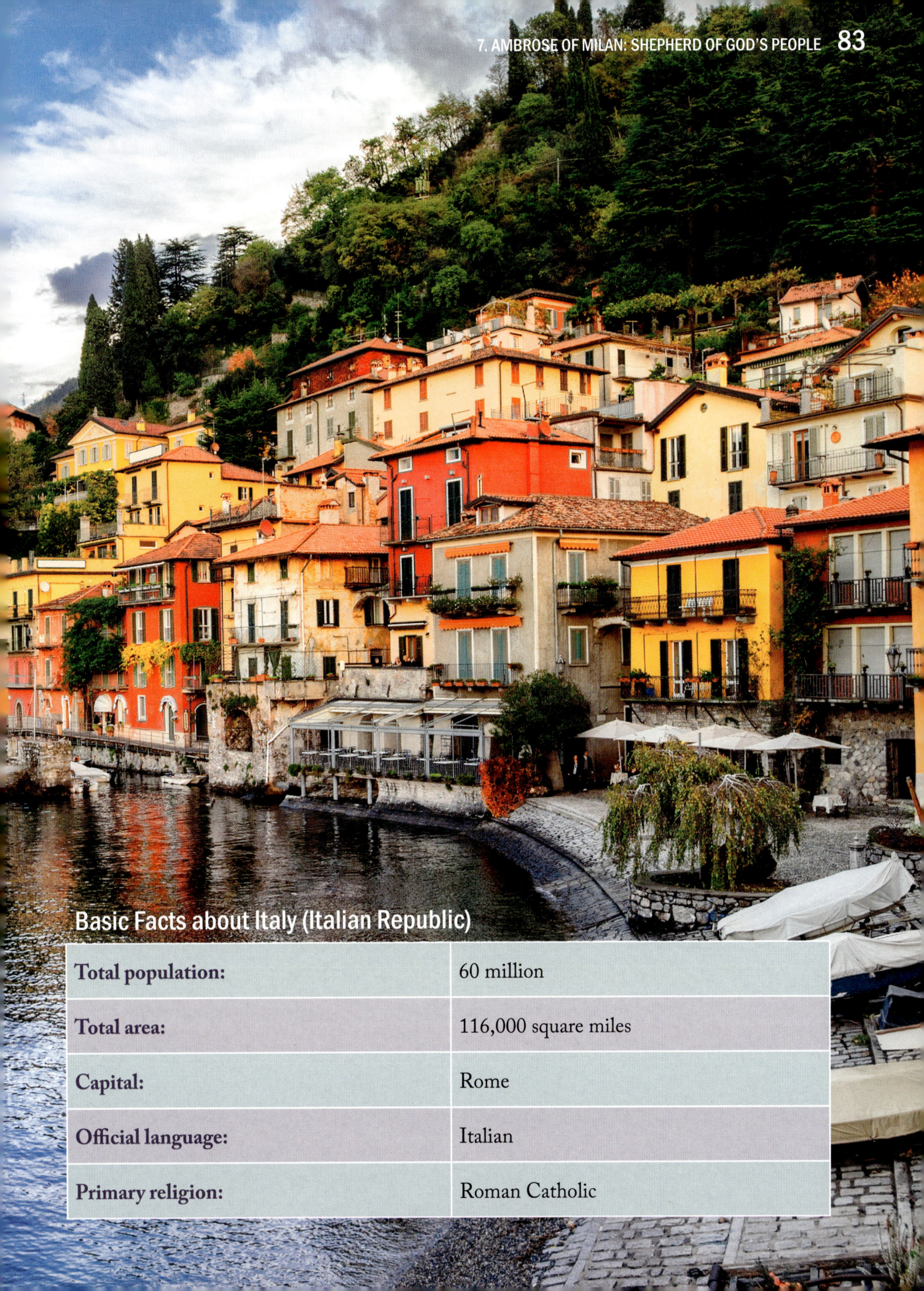

| | |
|---|---|
| Total population: | 60 million |
| Total area: | 116,000 square miles |
| Capital: | Rome |
| Official language: | Italian |
| Primary religion: | Roman Catholic |

WHITE CLIFFS OF DOVER, ENGLAND

# HOW CHRISTIANITY CAME TO GREAT BRITAIN

"Indeed" He says,
"It is too small a thing that You should be My Servant
To raise up the tribes of Jacob,
And to restore the preserved ones of Israel;
I will also give You as a light to the Gentiles,
That You should be My salvation to the ends of the earth." (Isa. 49:6)

In the early years of the Roman Empire, before Jesus was born, the island of Great Britain was a mysterious place. To people in Rome, Great Britain seemed like the end of the earth. Much like we think of traveling to Antarctica today, Roman people viewed Great Britain as a faraway and dangerous land. The Roman poet Virgil described Britain as "a whole world away, as it were." In a speech praising the Emperor Constantius I, somebody declared that, "beyond Ocean there is only Britain." However, in time Britain also became part of the Roman Empire.

Julius Caesar was the first to reach Britain in the early years of the Roman Republic. We think he first landed in Britain in 55 BC. As the Roman Empire grew in power, Rome brought the various tribes of Britain under its rule. These tribes were forced to pay tribute (or taxes) to Rome. The Roman people thought the native peoples of Britain were wild and unruly. Rome found it difficult to control them. To protect the Roman portion of Britain, Emperor Hadrian (reigned AD 117-138) built a wall across Great Britain known as **Hadrian's Wall**. This wall separated the southern Roman-controlled portion of Britain from the northern British tribes. Large sections of Hadrian's Wall remain to this day. If you visit England, you can see the ruins of the wall.

Those tribes south of Hadrian's Wall stayed under Rome's control until the end of the 300s. But it is hard work to keep an empire together. Britain proved to be somewhat of a headache for Rome. At the turn of the 5th century, the Roman Empire built on human pride was crumbling. Barbarian tribes attacked the empire on all sides. Many of these tribes drew near to Rome itself. While Jesus' kingdom was spreading over the whole world, the kingdoms of men were falling. By AD 410, Rome was no longer willing to send its military forces into Britain. Soon the Empire lost control of the British Isles.

## FIRST MISSIONARIES TO BRITAIN

The kings of Tarshish and of the isles will bring presents; the kings of Sheba and Seba will offer gifts. Yes, all kings shall fall down before Him; all nations shall serve Him. (Ps. 72:10-11)

A Christian historian named **Bede** (pronounced "bead") provides us the earliest history of the British Isles. Bede also records the first missionary efforts in Britain. Once, Great Britain was a pagan land. But later it would become a missionary-sending center itself. In later centuries, the Christian faith spread from England and Ireland into Germany, Sweden, Iceland, America, Africa, and Asia. For this reason, the history of the Christian faith in England is important for every Christian in the world to know. Bede tells of this critical history.

## TAKING EUROPE FOR JESUS

**HADRIAN'S WALL**

He wrote a book that told what happened in Britain from the time of the Roman occupation in the 1st century through the 8th century. Bede published his *Ecclesiastical History of the English People* around AD 731.

Bede's first record of the Christian faith in Britain takes place in AD 167. A British king named Lucius wrote to Eleutherus, the bishop of Rome. King Lucius asked the bishop how he might become a Christian. Some time after this, the Britons received the faith. They remained faithful to this profession until the major persecution of Christians in AD 311. This persecution is known as the **Diocletian persecution**. It happened during the reign of the Emperor Diocletian.

Bede also tells of the first martyr in Britain under that terrible persecution. A Christian missionary or teacher was hiding from the local Roman authorities who had been given orders to hunt down and kill

**BEDE**

## 8. HOW CHRISTIANITY CAME TO GREAT BRITAIN

receive the everlasting fires of hell."

Alban was beaten and then led off to be executed. He was the first of many other martyrs in Britain to die for Jesus. Others hid in the woods and caves until the persecution ended. When they emerged, these brave souls began the task of rebuilding the churches which had been destroyed by the Roman authorities.

**Germanus** was another important Chris-

**MAP OF THE UNITED KINGDOM**

**STAINED GLASS DEPICTION OF ALBAN'S MARTYRDOM**

Christians. He found refuge in the home of a man named **Alban**. While the Christian stayed with him, Alban was impressed by the man's faith and continual prayers. Eventually, Alban also accepted the gospel and trusted in Christ. Somehow, word reached the Roman powers that there was a Christian staying at Alban's home. When the soldiers arrived, Alban quickly put on the coat belonging to his guest. Thinking Alban was the missionary, the soldiers arrested Alban instead.

The soldiers brought Alban before the pagan judge while the official was offering sacrifices to demon gods. The judge invited Alban to join him in the idolatrous service, but Alban flatly refused. He boldly informed the judge, "I am now a Christian. These sacrifices you are offering to devils can't help you. Nor can these devils answer your prayers or give you what you ask. Instead, whoever sacrifices to them will

tian in the early history of Britain. This man was born into a rich and powerful family in Gaul (modern-day France). He was born around AD 378. At first, Germanus served as a governor or duke in charge of the Gallic Provinces. When the pastor of the local church in Auserre died, Germanus took his place. He was forty years old at the time.

About that time, a well-educated Briton named **Pelagius** was spreading false teaching in the churches. He taught that children are not born with the problem of sin. Children were born without sin, he said. They only became sinful by imitating the sinful activity around them. Pelagius believed that it was possible for people to obey God's law and to save themselves. Pelagius misunderstood what the Bible teaches about the fallen human condition (see Rom. 5:12-21). As a result of Pelagius' view, people began to misunderstand the gospel. If we can save ourselves by our own righteous deeds, then why did Jesus Christ have to die and rise again? As Paul says in Galatians, "if righteousness comes through the law, then Christ died in vain" (Gal. 2:21). Pelagius' teachings were very harmful, and they damaged the churches in Britain. Germanus was selected to lead a group of pastors from Gaul (France) to address this crisis across the English Channel. He was thrust into the front lines of battle. The conflict would end up being more than just a theological disagreement.

After the Romans pulled out of the British Isles, the Britons were not strong enough to defend themselves from invasion. The Scottish Picts would attack them from the north, and the Saxons were crossing over from northern Germany, taking over land in the south and east. The native peoples in Southern Britain had been weakened militarily because they had been ruled by Rome for the past 400 years. More and more, the Britons found themselves squeezed into the western side of the island, while the Saxons dominated the eastern side.

When Pastor Germanus made it to Britain, he found himself in the middle of a war between the Britons and the invading Picts and Saxons. The Britons were desperate, afraid they would be wiped out by these pagan tribes. Somewhere in the mountains of Wales, however, Germanus took charge of the armies of the Christian Britons. As the enemy drew near in a valley between two mountains, Germanus cried out "Alleluia" three times. The entire British army joined him in the shouting. As Bede tells the story, the sound disturbed the enemy so much that they dropped all their weapons and gear and fled the battlefield.

While he ministered in Britain, Germanus prayed for the healing of the son of an important chieftain. God granted his request. This encouraged the faith of the tribes. He also spent a great deal of time discipling the Britons in the Christian faith. The church was in dire need of missionary work. This was especially the case due to Pelagius' false teaching. Germanus entered into long debates with the Pelagians before large audiences throughout Britain. It is believed that he won many hearts to believe in the truth of God's grace.

---

For by grace you have been saved through faith, and that not of yourselves; it is the gift of God. (Eph. 2:8)

---

While God was humbling proud Rome in the 5th century, He raised up a beacon of gospel hope on these distant isles—a light that

**PELAGIUS**

would continue to shine brightly for centuries to come. ∎

---

So [Simeon] came by the Spirit into the temple. And when the parents brought in the Child Jesus, to do for Him according to the custom of the law, he took Him up in his arms and blessed God and said:
"Lord, now You are letting Your servant depart in peace,
According to Your word;
For my eyes have seen Your salvation
Which You have prepared before the face of all peoples,
A light to bring revelation to the Gentiles,
And the glory of Your people Israel."
(Luke 2:27-32)

---

## PRAYER POINTS: UNITED KINGDOM

- **Praise God for a rich Christian heritage:** The nations of England, Wales, Scotland, and Northern Ireland form the United Kingdom. These nations have received an abundant inheritance of the Christian world and life view. And from the nations constituting the UK, many missionaries have gone out all over the world. Additionally, Bible translations such as the King James Version were produced in England and have influenced Christians all over the world. Give thanks to God for this precious heritage.

- **Pray that God would revive the United Kingdom:** Church attendance used to be almost universal in the nations of the UK. But today, church attendance is very low. It is estimated that less than five percent of people in the UK attend church on a weekly basis. This means that most people in the UK do not worship God and do not know Jesus Christ. The UK is in desperate need of the visitation of God's Holy Spirit. Pray that God would revive the UK for His glory.

## 8. HOW CHRISTIANITY CAME TO GREAT BRITAIN

### Basic Facts about United Kingdom of Great Britain and Northern Ireland

| | |
|---|---|
| **Total population:** | 67 million |
| **Total area:** | 93,628 square miles |
| **Capital:** | London |
| **Official language:** | English |
| **Major religions:** | Protestant Christianity, Atheist or Agnostic |

GLOUCESTERSHIRE, ENGLAND

CLIFFS OF MOHER, IRELAND

# PATRICK: MISSIONARY TO THE IRISH

And again, Isaiah says:
"There shall be a root of Jesse;
And He who shall rise to reign over the Gentiles,
In Him the Gentiles shall hope." (Rom. 15:12)

Time and time again, history shows how God uses for good what man intends for evil (Gen. 50:20). It was Joseph who told his brothers this in the Book of Genesis. Joseph's brothers had one plan. They meant to get rid of Joseph once and for all. But God used the brothers' evil actions to preserve God's people in the famine that was to come. What Joseph said thousands of years ago is also true in the life of St. Patrick. It was the kidnapping of a young man that would ultimately lead to the evangelization of Ireland, for the glory of God. The story of Ireland's Christianization begins with the kidnapping of **Patrick** at age sixteen.

## CAPTIVITY IN IRELAND

Offer to God thanksgiving,
And pay your vows to the Most High.
Call upon Me in the day of trouble;
I will deliver you, and you shall glorify Me.
(Ps. 50:14-15)

Patrick grew up in a Christian home on the shores of Great Britain. His exact birthplace is not known, but it was likely near the western coast of Great Britain. As with his birthplace, we do not know for sure when Patrick was born. It was around the year AD 390. By this time, the Romans had ruled much of Great Britain for about 350 years.

To the west of Great Britain lies the neighboring island of Ireland. Separating Great Britain from Ireland is the Irish Sea. In Patrick's day, it was not uncommon for Irish pirates to raid settlements along the coast of Great Britain. In the providence of God, Irish raiders visited Patrick's settlement one day. With many others, Patrick was kidnapped and brought to Ireland against his will. There Patrick became a slave and lived as a shepherd.

This was a difficult trial for young Patrick. But it was not without its purpose. Though Patrick had grown up in a Christian home before he was kidnapped, he wrote in his *Confession* that he "did not know the true God."

**GREAT BRITAIN AND IRELAND**

He believed God sent him into captivity to awaken his soul. Patrick wrote:

> There the Lord opened my mind to an awareness of my unbelief, in order that, even so late, I might remember my transgressions and turn with all my heart to the Lord my God, who had regard for my insignificance and pitied my youth and ignorance. And he watched over me before I knew him, and before I learned sense or even distinguished between good and evil, and he protected me, and consoled me as a father would his son.

Patrick's life of captivity and servitude drove him to cry out to God. As it was for Patrick, so it is for each of us. Until we are humbled and see our need for a Savior, we do not call upon God. Patrick's life of prayer grew. He prayed as many as one hundred times a day. He records in his *Confession*:

> But after I reached Ireland I used to pasture the flock each day and I used to pray many times a day. More and more did the love of God, and my fear of him and faith increase, and my spirit was moved so that in a day I said from one up to a hundred prayers, and in the night a like number; besides I used to stay out in the forests and on the mountain and I would wake up before daylight to pray in the snow, in icy coldness, in rain, and I used to feel neither ill nor any slothfulness, because, as I now see, the Spirit was burning in me at that time.

The Holy Spirit brought new life to Patrick's dead heart.

While living in captivity, Patrick thought often of going home. One night, he dreamed that he was being called home. Then, after six years, the Lord provided Patrick a way of escape. He found a ship and left Ireland. Crossing the Irish Sea, Patrick found his way home. It was a difficult and dangerous journey. But he once again found his parents. Patrick's parents never wanted him to leave again. But God had other plans for Patrick.

## CALL TO IRELAND

> Then He said to them, "Thus it is written, and thus it was necessary for the Christ to suffer and to rise from the dead the third day, and that repentance and remission of sins should be preached in His name to all nations, beginning at Jerusalem. (Luke 24:46-47)

Safely back in Great Britain, the last thing on Patrick's mind was to return to Ireland. For him, Ireland was associated with kidnapping, slavery, and exile from home. Yet God had worked on Patrick's heart. He loved the Lord Jesus Christ. And with God's help, he would also come

**STAINED GLASS DEPICTION OF PATRICK**

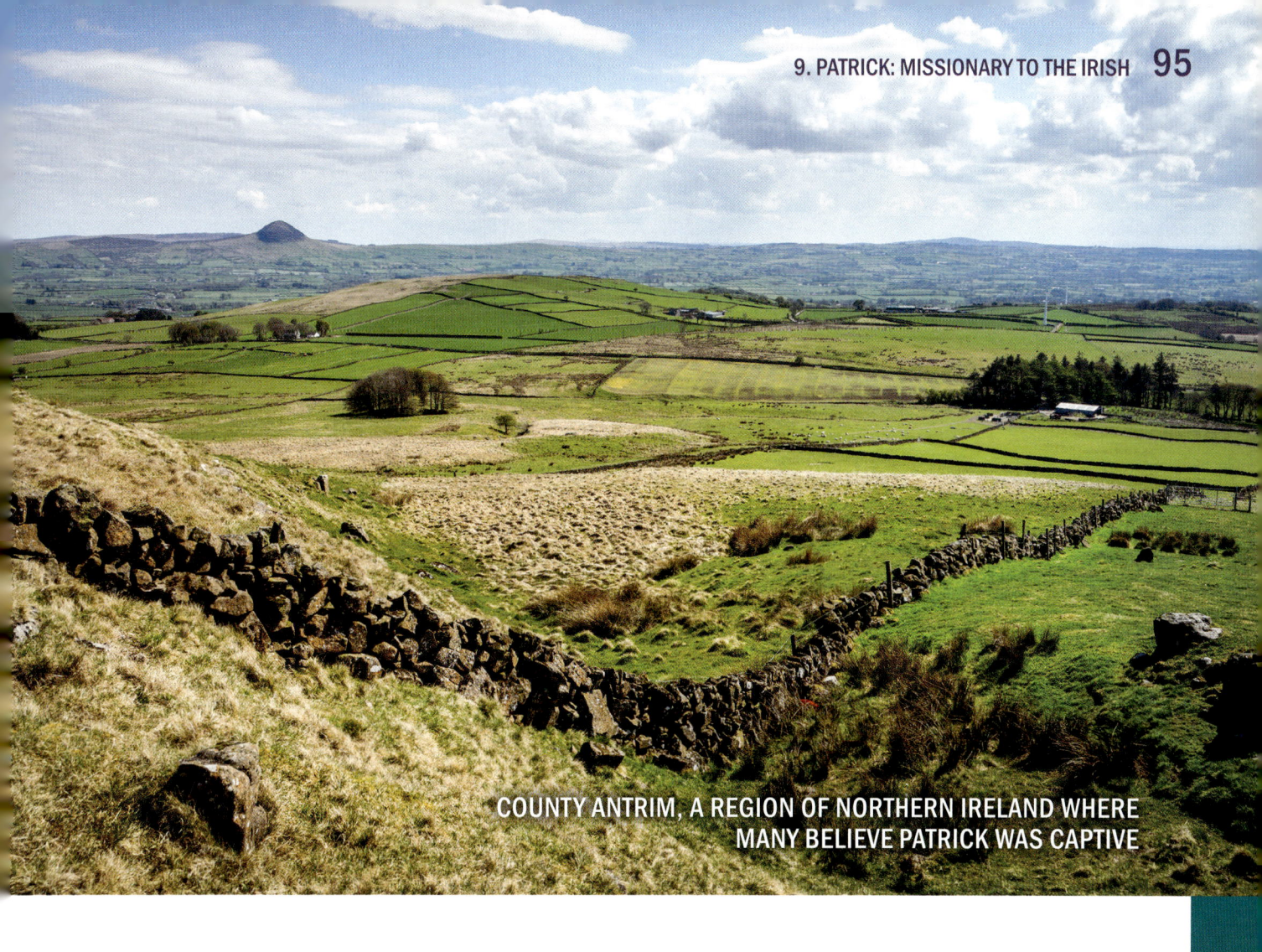

COUNTY ANTRIM, A REGION OF NORTHERN IRELAND WHERE MANY BELIEVE PATRICK WAS CAPTIVE

to love the peoples of Ireland.

One night, Patrick dreamed. In that dream, a man named Victoricus called to him. Victoricus' call was soon joined by other Irish voices calling to Patrick, saying: "We beg you, holy youth, that you shall come and shall walk again among us." It seemed that the Lord called Patrick back to the place of his captivity.

For some years, Patrick trained for the ministry and was discipled in Great Britain. Then he set out across the Irish Sea once again. This time, he went not as a slave to pirates but as a servant of the Lord Jesus Christ. He was, like Paul, under obligation to preach the gospel.

Then, from about AD 430 to 460, Patrick spent his remaining life as a pastor to the Irish. Through his faithful labors, thousands upon thousands came to saving faith in Jesus Christ. Churches were established. New ministers were raised up and sent out. And the Word of God multiplied throughout Ireland. Worshipers of the creation became worshipers of Father, Son, and Holy Spirit.

Amazing things happened in Ireland, all by God's power. But Patrick's ministry was not without opposition. Where the forces of Satan and the demons are opposed, there is sure to be a response. For thousands of years, Ireland was a haunt for demons. The peoples of Ireland worshiped many false gods. There is also evidence that human sacrifice was a common component of Irish religion.

While some embraced the gospel, others tried to attack or capture Patrick. At this time, Ireland had no central authority. Many kings and many tribes existed throughout Ireland. For this reason, travel was dangerous. Patrick never knew what the response of the next king or tribe would be. But God was with him. He went to Ireland in the powerful name of the

SAINT KEVIN'S MONASTERY IN GLENDALOUCH, IRELAND

risen Lord Jesus. For this reason, Patrick was not afraid. He wrote, "I fear none of these things because of the promises of heaven. I have cast myself into the hands of God Almighty, who rules everywhere."

As Patrick continued his ministry to the Irish, he learned what it meant to give up his life as a living sacrifice. Paul, writing in Romans 12, tells each of us to give up our bodies as a living sacrifice to the Lord (Rom. 12:1-2). Ministry to the Irish involved much sacrifice. Patrick recounted how he learned this lesson.

> I came to the people of Ireland to preach the Gospel, and to suffer insult from the unbelievers, bearing the reproach of my going abroad and many persecutions even unto bonds, and to give my free birth for the benefit of others; and, should I be worthy, I am prepared to give even my life without hesitation and most gladly for his name, and it is there that I wish to spend it until I die, if the Lord would grant it to me.

Having been enslaved himself, Patrick knew what it was like to live in bondage. He became passionate in fighting against slavery. In addition to his longest work, the *Confession*, we also have an important letter written by him. It was a letter written to a man named **Coroticus**. Patrick spared no hard words in this letter. He warned Coroticus against the wickedness of the slave trade. Patrick is just one more example of a faithful Christian seeking the emancipation of slaves.

## PATRICK'S BREASTPLATE

Finally, my brethren, be strong in the Lord and in the power of His might. Put on the whole armor of God, that you may be able to stand against the wiles of the devil. (Eph. 6:10-11)

An extended prayer, known as **"Patrick's breastplate,"** is attributed to Patrick. If he indeed wrote it, it gives us another glimpse into his Christ-centered faith. This extended prayer is an application of what Scripture tells us to do: put on the whole armor of God (Eph. 6:11). By praying this prayer, Patrick took up God's armor against the schemes of the devil. We can do the same by praying similar prayers.

If you want to know what someone believes, listen to how they pray. By looking at Patrick's prayer, we learn much about Patrick's faith. We learn that he believed in the Trinity. We also see how important Jesus Christ was to him. It also becomes clear that he believed in God's sovereignty.

Read Patrick's entire prayer below:

I arise today
Through a mighty strength, the invocation of the Trinity,
Through the belief in the threeness,
Through the confession of the oneness
Of the Creator of Creation.

I arise today
Through the strength of Christ's birth with his baptism,
Through the strength of his crucifixion with his burial,
Through the strength of his resurrection with his ascension,
Through the strength of his descent for the Judgment Day.

I arise today
Through the strength of the love of Cherubim,
In obedience of angels,
In the service of archangels,
In hope of resurrection to meet with reward,
In prayers of patriarchs,
In predictions of prophets,
In preaching of apostles,
In faith of confessors,
In innocence of holy virgins,
In deeds of righteous men.

I arise today
Through the strength of heaven:
Light of sun,
Radiance of moon,
Splendor of fire,
Speed of lightning,
Swiftness of wind,
Depth of sea,
Stability of earth,
Firmness of rock.

I arise today
Through God's strength to pilot me:
God's might to uphold me,
God's wisdom to guide me,
God's eye to look before me,
God's ear to hear me,
God's word to speak for me,
God's hand to guard me,
God's way to lie before me,
God's shield to protect me,
God's host to save me
From snares of demons,
From temptations of vices,
From everyone who shall wish me ill,
Afar and anear,
Alone and in multitude.

I summon today all these powers between me and those evils,
Against every cruel merciless power that may oppose my body and soul,
Against incantations of false prophets,
Against black laws of pagandom,
Against false laws of heretics,
Against craft of idolatry,
Against spells of witches and smiths and wizards,
Against every knowledge that corrupts man's body and soul.

Christ to shield me today
Against poison, against burning,
Against drowning, against wounding,
So that there may come to me abundance of reward.
Christ with me, Christ before me, Christ behind me,

Christ in me, Christ beneath me, Christ above me,
Christ on my right, Christ on my left,
Christ when I lie down, Christ when I sit down, Christ when I arise,
Christ in the heart of every man who thinks of me,
Christ in the mouth of everyone who speaks of me,
Christ in every eye that sees me,
Christ in every ear that hears me.

I arise today
Through a mighty strength, the invocation of the Trinity,
Through belief in the threeness,
Through confession of the oneness
Of the Creator of Creation.

## MINISTER OF THE WORD

"Is not My word like a fire?" says the LORD, "And like a hammer that breaks the rock in pieces?" (Jer. 23:29)

Patrick did not leave behind many writings. His *Confession* is a very short document. But even with the few writings he left, one thing is obvious: he loved God's Word. He frequently quotes from the Bible. When he quoted the Bible, he often said "the Lord says." This means

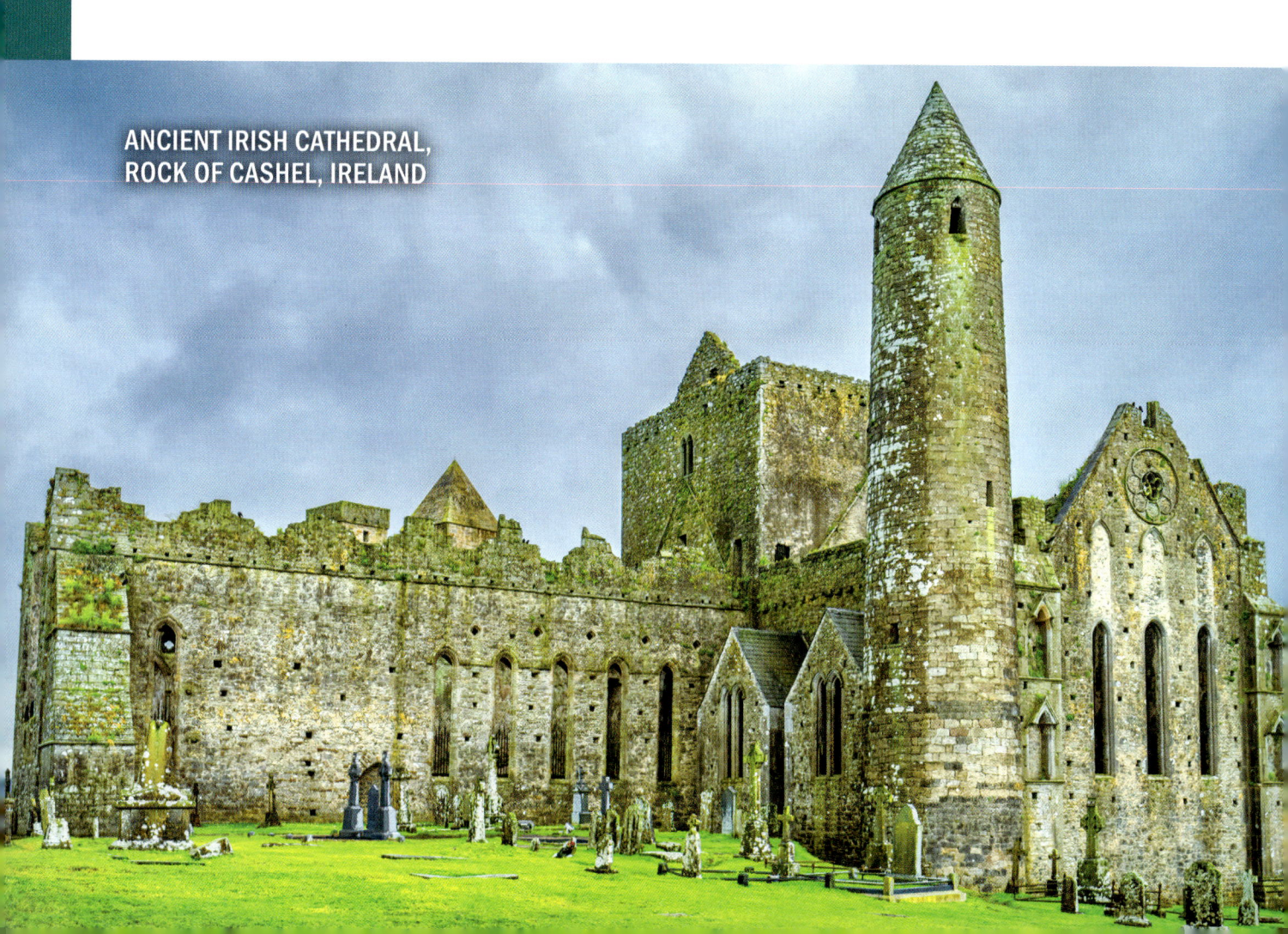

**ANCIENT IRISH CATHEDRAL, ROCK OF CASHEL, IRELAND**

that Patrick believed the Bible to be God's inspired Word. One particular quote of importance is found in his letter to Coroticus. Patrick wanted Coroticus to know that Patrick did not speak on his own authority. He spoke with the authority of God's Word backing him up. He wrote:

> It is not my words that I have set forth in Latin, but those of God and the apostles and prophets, who have never lied. "He who believes shall be saved; but he who believes not shall be condemned." "God has spoken."

Like other faithful missionaries before him, Patrick was a minister of God's Word. He did not go to Ireland to share his own ideas. He shared the everlasting truth of God. He shared the saving gospel of Jesus Christ.

## PATRICK'S HUMILITY

As one reads Patrick's *Confession*, it becomes plain that he was a humble, God-fearing man. Patrick even tells us that he hesitated to write his story. He feared that others would criticize his poor style of writing. He saw himself as unlearned and simple. But despite Patrick's feelings of insufficiency, he wrote in order that God would be glorified. He saw it as a picture of God's mercy that he, of all people, should be called to minister to the Irish. He did not deserve such an important role. But God was good to give him such an important job.

Patrick begins and ends his *Confession* with a note of humility. His last words in the *Confession* are these:

> I exhort those who believe in and fear God. Whoever seeks to examine or receive this document composed by the obviously unlearned sinner Patrick in Ireland, do not ascribe any good thing to me, but truly believe that any good thing I said or did was the gift of God. This is my confession before I die.

Patrick wants the world to know this: anything he did was because God enabled him to do it. It was God who accomplished great things. Patrick was just a humble and unlearned servant.

May we join Patrick's confession and give thanks to God for saving us from our sins and for making us servants of Jesus Christ. ∎

## Basic Facts about Republic of Ireland

| Total population: | 5 million |
| --- | --- |
| Total area: | 27,133 square miles |
| Capital: | Dublin |
| Official languages: | Irish, English |
| Primary religion: | Roman Catholic |

# PRAYER POINTS: REPUBLIC OF IRELAND

- **Praise God for the missionary work of Patrick:** The Lord used Patrick and the missionaries who followed him to transform the pagan land of Ireland into a Christian land. Since the time of Patrick, the Christian faith has had a dominant influence in Ireland. It has shaped Irish culture for some 1500 years. Even today, as Ireland becomes more secular, the Christian tradition still exercises significant influence on its people.

- **Lament the decline of Christian faith in Ireland:** In recent years, Ireland has turned against God's Word by legalizing several wicked practices. In 2015, the practice of unnatural unions (homosexuality) between two men or two women was defined as legal by Ireland. Then, in 2018, the killing of unborn children (abortion) was made legal. Sexual immorality and murder of this kind invites the judgment of God (Deut. 28). We must lament the decline of Christian faith in Ireland. Let us pray that God would turn wayward hearts back to Himself.

- **Pray for faithful shepherds and faithful churches:** Most churches in Ireland are part of the Roman Catholic Church. Ireland is in desperate need of faithful pastor/shepherds who will preach the true gospel. Let us ask the Lord to send many laborers into the harvest so that faithful churches would be established and so that Ireland would be discipled again in the commands of Jesus Christ.

COWS GRAZING IN IRELAND

ARCH BRIDGE IN KROMLAU, GERMANY

# UNIT 2

# AD 500-1000

"I will declare the decree:
The LORD has said to Me,
'You are My Son,
Today I have begotten You.
Ask of Me, and I will give You
The nations for Your inheritance,
And the ends of the earth for Your possession.'" (Ps. 2:7-8)

Jesus' mission cannot and will not fail. Rome fell in AD 476. But the servants of Christ continued in the discipleship of Europe. From AD 500 to AD 1000, the message of Christ's victory over sin and death reached new regions of Europe. Some historians of Christianity call this time the **Frontier Age**. Missionaries made their way to the frontiers of Europe. Churches were established in the northeast of Europe in Great Britain and Ireland. In the far north, Anskar carried the message to Denmark and Sweden. On the eastern edge of Europe, Cyril and Methodius reached the Slavs.

A new threat emerged in the east in AD 610. In the desert town of **Mecca**, there was a merchant named **Muhammad**. He claimed to receive direct revelation from **Allah** (the Arabic word for God). Muhammad compiled these revelations into a new holy book, the *Qur'an*. The book served as the pillar of a new religion: **Islam**. It was a religion that combined elements of Judaism and Christianity. But Islam was a new religion altogether. Judaism and Christianity were both rejected as false. Muhammad and his disciples claimed Islam was the only true religion. Muhammad also believed he was God's final prophet on earth. The devil had crafted a new lie to combat Christ's gospel.

The **Muslims** were not content to keep this new religion to themselves. By sword and conquest, the Muslims swept into North Africa, and then into Europe. First, Spain fell to the Muslims. Next, the region of France came under attack. However, the Muslim advance was stopped at a place called **Tours**. It was at the **Battle of Tours** (AD 732) that **Charles Martel** halted the Muslim conquest. This pivotal victory preserved Europe from Muslim domination.

Charles Martel's grandson, **Charlemagne** would unite much of Europe under one rule. He was a general mighty in war. Altogether, Charlemagne fought fifty-four military campaigns. At his death, Charlemagne's empire was the largest in Europe. No empire in Europe would reach such a size until Napoleon's French Empire in the 1800s. Charlemagne's dominions included the modern countries of France, Switzerland, Germany, Austria, the Czech Republic, and parts of Spain.

During this period, the popes in Rome became increasingly corrupt. The 900s marked some of the most heinous and wicked behavior among the popes in Rome. By the 900s, the popes wielded enormous power over the kings, queens, and nations of Europe. It is no surprise, then, that many of the popes lied, stole, and murdered to gain and keep such authority. Just two examples illustrate the unrighteous behavior of the popes. **Pope Sergius III** (pope from AD 904-911) ordered the murder of two previous popes. His illegitimate son then became **Pope John XI** (pope from AD 931-935). The situation only grew worse in the AD 1000s and beyond. The unbiblical institution of the papacy was not bearing good fruit.

## Timeline of Key Events

| | |
|---|---|
| AD 563 | Iona Abbey established |
| AD 731 | Bede completes his *Ecclesiastical History of the English People* |
| AD 732 | Charles Martel repels Muslim invaders at the Battle of Tours |
| AD 782 | Alcuin joins Charlemagne's royal court |
| AD 789 | First Viking invasion of Great Britain |
| AD 800 | Charlemagne crowned Emperor of the Holy Roman Empire |
| AD 829 | Anskar's mission to Sweden |
| AD 863 | Cyril's and Methodius' mission to the Slavs |
| AD 878 | Alfred the Great defeats Guthrum at the Battle of Edington |
| AD 973 | Athelstan prevails at the Battle of Brunanburh |

ST. MARTIN'S CROSS, ISLE OF IONA

# COLUMBA AND THE MONASTERY OF IONA

Sing to the LORD a new song,
And His praise from the ends of the earth,
You who go down to the sea, and all that is in it,
You coastlands and you inhabitants of them!
(Isa. 42:10)

Off the western coast of Scotland is a very small island. Three miles long by a mile and a half wide, the island of **Iona** is dwarfed by the nearby island of Mull. Iona is little. But it has earned a big place in the history of Christianity in Europe. Missionaries from Iona would spread the faith far and wide throughout the land of Scotland and other parts of Europe.

Today, if you visit Iona, you will see just how isolated it is. From Scotland, you take a ferry to the island of Mull. Then you cross the island of Mull. At the western shore of that island, you will board another ferry. After a short boat ride, you will find yourself standing on the historic island of Iona. Today, a few hundred people call Iona home. A few shops, hotels, and churches dot the landscape. Not far from the pier, just a ten-minute walk, is the ancient Iona Abbey. It was here, on this plot of ground, that the Christian faith went forth throughout Europe.

## COLUMBA FOUNDS IONA

The early story of the Iona mission begins with a man named **Columba**. Columba was born in Ireland around AD 521. By this time, Christ had already saved many people in Ireland. Columba had the privilege of being born to Christian parents. As he grew older, his parents entrusted him to the care of a Christian priest. This man instructed Columba in the Christian faith. When Columba became an adult, he also began planting churches and monasteries throughout Ireland.

When he was about forty years old, he left Ireland and crossed to Great Britain. There he would establish a Christian community on the small island of Iona. With twelve other companions, Columba founded an abbey on the island. The year was 563. From that date until 597, Columba would be the primary spiritual leader of the Iona community.

Columba also brought the gospel to the

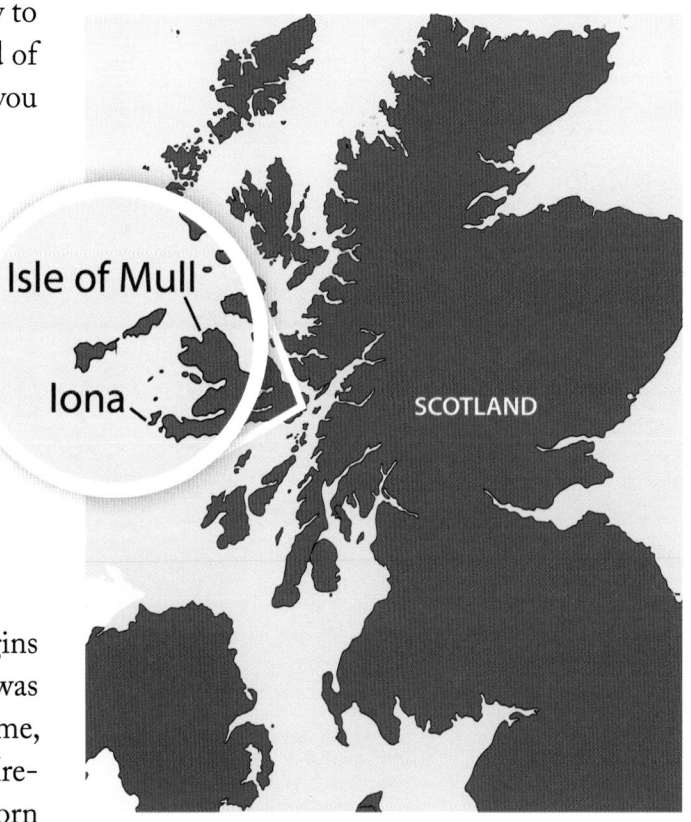

**LOCATION OF IONA**

107

people group called the **Picts**. According to Bede, the southern Picts had already embraced the true faith when Columba arrived. But Bede explained that the northern Picts were separated from the southern Picts by a large mountain range. This mountain range is called the **Grampian Mountain** range. In previous years, a man named **Ninian** proclaimed the faith to the southern Picts. The Picts then abandoned their idols and worshiped the true God.

Between 563 and 597, Iona would become one of the most important missionary-sending centers in the history of Christ's church. Over one hundred men would be trained by Columba. Many of those men set out to take the gospel all over Europe. Missionaries from Iona traveled all over Britain and journeyed to Gaul, Germany, Switzerland, and Italy.

## COMMUNITY LIFE ON IONA

Behold, how good and how pleasant it is
For brethren to dwell together in unity! (Ps. 133:1)

Like many monasteries, daily life at the abbey on Iona was a combination of worship, study, and work. All three aspects were considered essential by Columba and his disciples. As **abbot** ("father"), Columba was considered the spiritual father of the community until his death. He led by example in all these areas by his untiring labors, his steadfast devotion, and his diligent study of God's Word. The main version of the Bible available to Columba was the Latin Bible. Columba taught that all of life was to be lived in accord with biblical teaching.

One of Columba's lifelong tasks was to copy

**BEN NEVIS, ONE OF THE MOUNTAINS IN THE GRAMPIAN MOUNTAIN RANGE, AND THE TALLEST MOUNTAIN IN GREAT BRITAIN**

## 10. COLUMBA AND THE MONASTERY OF IONA

IONA ABBEY

the Scriptures. One of the most famous productions believed to have been produced by Columba and his contemporaries is the *Book of Kells*. It is a translation of the four Gospels containing uniquely Celtic calligraphy and artwork. Columba and the other men of the monastery dedicated themselves to constant study of the Bible. The book of Psalms took a special place of prominence. The psalms formed the songs and prayers of the community. **Adomnan,** Columba's early biographer, recounted that Columba sang with such volume that he could be "heard a mile's distance when singing psalms." Whether or not this is an exaggeration, it certainly shows the zeal Columba had for singing God's prayer book, the Psalms.

Worship on Iona was an every-hour, every-day experience. Far from being limited to Sunday, worship for the monks of Iona was constant. Each day, certain hours were set aside for this. At these set times, the community would gather to sing the psalms and other hymns, to read portions of Scripture, and to pray together.

**A PAGE FROM THE *BOOK OF KELLS* DISPLAYING JESUS' GENEALOGY FROM THE GOSPEL OF LUKE**

CLOISTER OF IONA ABBEY

These set hours (known as **canonical hours**) were not optional. Every monk was expected to attend. Even if a monk was far away working in the field, he was expected to gather with the rest of the community. If one of the monks was too far away, he was expected to kneel and pray right where he was at the set times.

Prayer was a central aspect of life on Iona. Columba led by example. He prayed without ceasing. The disciples of Iona knew that Columba never began any kind of work without prayer. Historian Duncan MacCallum writes, "He implored the blessing of God on everything that was useful to man. When he saw the fields of corn ripening, he thanked his Maker for His kind providence. He never entered a house without praying a blessing upon it."

Manual labor was a necessity at the abbey. After all, without hard work, there would be no food for the Iona community. Fishing, raising cattle and other animals, planting, cultivating, and harvesting were all daily practices on Iona. Numerous other works of industry were developed including metal-working, leather-making, and corn-drying. Some degree of trade developed between Iona and other communities in Ireland and Great Britain. The Christians of Iona took dominion of their little island. There was a simplicity about life on Iona. Elders in the church were taught by Columba to live lives free of extravagance. They were to be content with the basic necessities of food and clothing.

## COLUMBA'S FAITH AND CHARACTER

**Shepherd the flock of God which is among you, serving as overseers, not by compulsion but willingly, not for dishonest gain but eagerly; nor as being lords over those entrusted to you, but being examples to the flock. (1 Pet. 5:2-3)**

Through ancient writings and biographies, we know much about Columba. He was a man of great faith and holy character. His faith is demonstrated first in his courageous missionary work. Not only did he disciple God's people on Iona, but he also traveled throughout the British Isles, spreading the faith. On one occasion, a pagan leader, an archdruid named Coivi, confronted Columba. The druids believed that to travel on the third day of the week was unlucky. Coivi believed some evil would happen to Columba if he traveled on the third day of the week.

Coivi asked Columba, "Are you resolved to sail tomorrow?"

Columba told Coivi, "Yes, if God wills."

Coivi replied, "You cannot! I will raise a storm and cause contrary winds. I'll cover you all around with darkness."

Columba was not afraid of Coivi's threat. He told the druid, "The Omnipotent commands all. In His name I always undertake whatever I intend to do. Guided by His providence, I shall go and not fear."

The Lord blessed Columba with numerous opportunities to give spiritual counsel to various local rulers. Once, King Rough, the king of Ireland, asked Columba, "Will I be saved?"

Columba was not afraid of King Rough's authority. He exhorted the king to repentance, saying, "Hardly, unless you mend and change your ways and forsake your sins."

Columba also taught his disciples that the beginning of wisdom is the fear of the Lord. In his last months, he exhorted his fellow disciples to fear the Lord. As he stood with some of them, looking over the whole island of Iona, he told them that God would surely bless the community "as long as they feared God."

## THE LEGACY OF IONA

Through the centuries, missionaries from Iona and from other Celtic communities spread all over Europe. A certain missionary strategy was followed by many of these Celtic Christians. They often sent out twelve men (sometimes families) to plant new churches. They would build little churches out of rock.

**FISHING BOATS IN THE BAY OF IONA**

Then, every day the bells would sound in the morning and evening. This was a signal that the pastor (or bishop) would provide the villagers a teaching lesson from the Old and New Testaments of the Bible. Over time, the surrounding villages would gather to learn more of God's Word on a daily basis. This faithful pattern of discipleship was instrumental in the conversion of nations.

Training centers called monasteries were formed to teach the young men the Word of God as well. Sometimes the church leaders were single men, but often they were married men. In many cases, the pastorate would pass down from father to son. There are instances in which there were fifteen to twenty generations of fathers and sons that served as pastors in the same local church! This is a remarkable pattern of faithfulness.

After Columba's death, the land of Northumbria (northern England and southern Scotland) was still very much in pagan darkness. However, a king named **Oswald** turned to Christ in the middle of a battle, and he sent for missionaries from Iona. A dedicated Ionian missionary named **Aidan** (c. 590-651) answered the call and earnestly discipled the people of this pagan land. He encouraged the Christian disciples to read God's Word consistently. Aidan also freed a number of slaves. Some of these came to faith and were later ordained as ministers in the Celtic church. Aidan also founded numerous churches, schools, and monasteries throughout Northumbria. The most notable of these institutions was on the small island of **Lindisfarne**. This monastery on Lindisfarne was very similar to Iona. Aidan's discipleship center at Lindisfarne became a haven of learning and a hub for launching missionaries far and wide. ■

---

The LORD has made bare His holy arm
In the eyes of all the nations;
And all the ends of the earth shall see
    The salvation of our God.
        (Isa. 52:10)

---

**STATUE OF AIDAN IN LINDISFARNE**

## Basic Facts about Republic of Scotland

*The island of Iona is part of modern-day Scotland, one of the nations within the United Kingdom (UK).*

| | |
|---|---|
| Total population: | 5.5 million |
| Total area: | 30,000 square miles |
| Capital: | Edinburgh |
| Official languages: | English, Scots, Scottish Gaelic |
| Primary religion: | Protestant Christian, Atheist, Agnostic |

# PRAYER POINTS: SCOTLAND

- **Praise God for missionaries from Scotland:** The legacy of Scotland as a missionary-sending center goes all the way back to the time of Columba. But even in more recent centuries, numerous well-known missionaries have come from Scotland. Scottish names include David Livingstone, Mary Slessor, Robert Moffat, Eric Liddell, and others. God has graciously used many from this land to spread the good news of Jesus Christ all over the world. Give thanks to God for this heritage of faith.

- **Pray for repentance and freedom from idols:** Only about fifty percent of the population in Scotland profess any connection to Christianity. This number used to be much higher. As Scotland turns away from its Christian heritage, there has been a turning back to idols which cannot save. Alcohol and drug abuse are common in Scotland. About fifty percent of children are born to a father and mother that are not married. These sins have destructive effects on the people of Scotland. Pray that God would grant faith in Jesus and repentance to the Scottish people.

- **Pray for the Church of Scotland and other denominations in Scotland:** The official Church of Scotland has a rich Protestant, Christian heritage. During the time of the Reformation, the Church of Scotland became Protestant and Presbyterian. The church's beliefs and practices were reformed according to Scripture. But as the people of Scotland have departed from the faith, the official Church of Scotland has suffered greatly. Pray that God would revive this ailing church. Let us also pray for the many other churches in Scotland, that God would use them to advance the gospel.

KILMORIE CHAPEL, SCOTLAND

# CHURCH AND COMMUNITY LIFE IN THE BRITISH ISLES

**And they continued steadfastly in the apostles' doctrine and fellowship, in the breaking of bread, and in prayers. (Acts 2:42)**

So far, we have learned how Christianity came to Great Britain and Ireland. Now, let's explore what church life and community life was like during this time. What did life in a Christian community look like in Great Britain and Ireland? Due to the distance of time, we only know a little about this. But there are ancient records and books that help answer these questions.

## CHURCH PRACTICES IN IRELAND

**I write so that you may know how you ought to conduct yourself in the house of God, which is the church of the living God, the pillar and ground of the truth. (1 Tim. 3:15)**

From a document called *The First Synod of St. Patrick*, we learn a few interesting facts about the early churches in Ireland. This document contained official church decisions that were made sometime after the time of Patrick. Here are several examples of the teachings and practices of the Irish church:

- Pastors' wives were to wear head coverings over their hair.
- Christians who murdered, practiced witchcraft, or committed sexual sin like the pagans were encouraged to repent, and they could be restored to the church after a year's time.
- Christians convicted of stealing were encouraged to repent, and they could be restored to the church after six months' time.
- A pastor could buy a slave's freedom, but he should not free the slave by kidnapping him or her.
- The churches were to sing from the Book of Psalms found in the Old Testament.
- A pastor who involved himself in armed combat with a pagan would be excommunicated (removed from the membership of the church).

To this day, the Christian roots in Ireland run very deep. Much of this was due to the influence of Patrick. He introduced the faith to Ireland over 1,500 years ago. His pioneering labors for Christ's church in Ireland had a far-reaching effect in the centuries that followed. As representatives from Rome retreated from the British Isles, native-born Christians spread the faith in this western corner of Europe. During that time, when Rome was in steady decline, Celtic Christianity flourished.

Many of the Irish were taught to read and write so they could read the Bible. This is typical of Christian missionary work around the world. The missionaries did not use schools run by the government (as is common in many nations today). They chose teachers who feared and loved God. These were the people they wanted to teach in their schools. These schools were discipleship centers. Men and women were taught to sing the psalms and read the Gospels of Matthew, Mark, Luke, and John. These training centers were grounded in the

WHITBY ABBEY, THE LOCATION WHERE THE COUNCIL (OR SYNOD) OF WHITBY WAS HELD

teachings of the Bible. These centers would then send bold missionaries out to Scotland, Britain, and beyond. These young missionaries would in turn build more Christian discipleship centers to spread the gospel even more. This pattern of discipleship spread the Christian faith around the world.

The early Celtic (Irish) church was independent of the church in Rome. The Roman Church was led by the Pope. But the early Irish church did not recognize the Pope's authority. The Irish church didn't follow what the Roman church taught. Irish pastors and missionaries were allowed to get married, unlike the Roman monks and pastors. Churches sometimes argue over little things. The Celtic church celebrated Easter on a different day than the Roman Church, and this grew into a big argument. Eventually, a church council was held in **Whitby** (AD 664) to resolve the disagreement. The result of this meeting was that the churches in Great Britain shifted the date of their celebration of Easter to match the date that the Roman church used.

## COMMUNITY LIFE IN ENGLAND IN THE 600S AND 700S

During this time, Anglo-Saxon England was divided into several different "mini-kingdoms" led by a king. These various kingdoms included Kent, Sussex, Wessex, East Anglia, Essex, Mercia, and Northumbria. Leadership in Anglo-Saxon England was often fragile. If a king was not able to gather enough of a military force to protect his kingdom, he would be replaced.

Life under the Anglo-Saxon kings in these small kingdoms was very communal. Communities were fairly small, and every person would have known most of the other folks in the community. The "hall" or the "**mead hall**" was the place where the local community would gather with a king or another local authority. We are given a picture of life in the Mead Hall

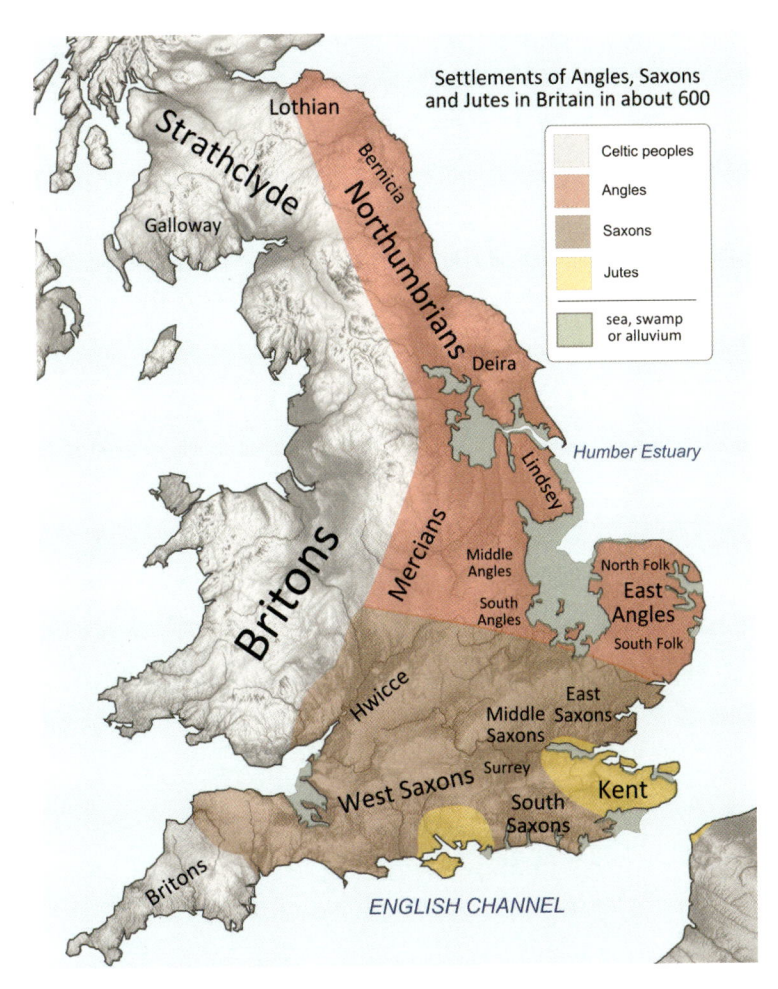

## 11. CHURCH AND COMMUNITY LIFE IN THE BRITISH ISLES 117

**KINGDOMS OF GREAT BRITAIN AROUND 600**

door and quickly flies out through the other. For the few moments it is inside, the storm and wintry tempest cannot touch it, but after the briefest moment of calm, it flits from your sight, out of the wintry storm and into it again. So this life of man appears but for a moment; what follows or indeed what went before, we know not at all.

The words of this Northumbrian Christian drew an illustration using pictures common to the Anglo-Saxon people at that time. The point of these words is plain: the Christian wants King Eadwine to understand that life is short. It is important that we deal with eternal matters and turn to God, through Jesus Christ, for our salvation.

As the Christian faith spread through Anglo-Saxon England, it brought with it many beneficial changes. There was an increase of literacy among the various tribal leaders. As in Bede's history. In his book, **Bede** records the words of a Northumbrian nobleman who asked King Eadwine to accept Christianity:

> This is how the present life on earth, King, appears to me in comparison with that time which is unknown to us. You are sitting feasting with your ealdormen and thegns [noblemen] in winter time; the fire is burning on the hearth in the middle of the hall and all inside is warm, while outside the wintry storms of rain and snow are raging; and a sparrow flies swiftly through the hall. It enters in at one

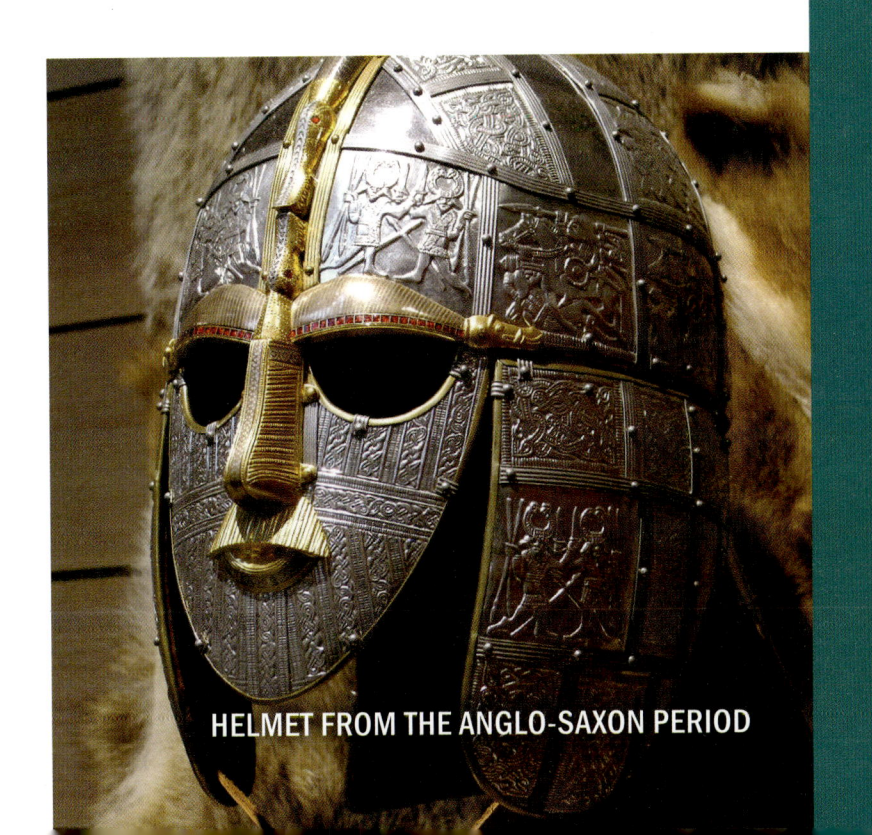

**HELMET FROM THE ANGLO-SAXON PERIOD**

kings and their subjects gained the ability to read and write, they could now draw up written law codes that would serve as a fixed standard of justice in the community. Far more stable than oral law (law which is not written down but only known by memory and transmitted verbally), the people could now read the laws for themselves. This becomes an often-repeated pattern in the development of Western history. As missionaries preach the gospel, they bring with them the Bible and other written texts. Then the community learns to read so they can read God's Word themselves. Then other areas of life are affected by this increased learning. It brings numerous benefits to the society. Wherever the Christian faith spreads, increased literacy and educational efforts always follow. ∎

## PRAYER POINTS: UNITED KINGDOM

> **Therefore I exhort first of all that supplications, prayers, intercessions, and giving of thanks be made for all men, for kings and all who are in authority, that we may lead a quiet and peaceable life in all godliness and reverence. For this is good and acceptable in the sight of God our Savior, who desires all men to be saved and to come to the knowledge of the truth. (1 Tim. 2:1-4)**

In this Prayer Points, we will pray for those in civil government in the United Kingdom.

- **Pray for the monarch of the United Kingdom:** At the time of this book's writing, the reigning monarch in the United Kingdom is Queen Elizabeth II. While the monarch of the United Kingdom has far less power than the kings and queens of the Middle Ages, the monarch is still considered the head of state in the United Kingdom. Pray for the reigning monarch of the United Kingdom: that the monarch would believe in the Lord Jesus Christ and submit to Christ's kingship. Pray that the monarch would be an example of godliness and righteousness to the citizens of the United Kingdom. Ask God to surround the monarch with godly advisers.

- **Pray for the Parliament of the United Kingdom:** The Parliament of the United Kingdom consists of two houses: the House of Lords and the House of Commons. Those members of Parliament (MPs) in the House of Commons are elected by the people of various districts of the United Kingdom. Ask God to raise up more righteous rulers in the United Kingdom. Ask the Lord to put Christians in places of government so that they can seek to apply God's standards of righteousness in the UK. Beseech the Lord to stop those in Parliament who would seek to legislate wicked laws.

## 11. CHURCH AND COMMUNITY LIFE IN THE BRITISH ISLES

### Basic Facts about England

*The United Kingdom consists of the nations of England, Wales, Scotland, and Northern Ireland. The facts below pertain to England, one of the countries within the UK.*

| | |
|---|---|
| Total population: | 56 million |
| Total area: | 50,000 square miles |
| Capital: | London |
| Official language: | English |
| Primary religions: | Protestant Christian, Atheist, Agnostic |

REPLICA OF AN ANGLO-SAXON VILLAGE

RIVER TYNE, ENGLAND

# BEDE: HISTORIAN OF THE ENGLISH CHURCH

For Ezra had prepared his heart to seek the Law of the Lord, and to do it, and to teach statutes and ordinances in Israel. (Ezra 7:10)

In northeast England, near the mouth of the River Tyne, a few miles from the English coast, is the English town of **Jarrow**. It was here and in the neighboring town of **Wearmouth** that the first great work of English history was written. The book we know today as *Ecclesiastical History of the English People* was written by a man named **Bede** (pronounced "beed").

Our knowledge of Great Britain and Ireland during the Anglo-Saxon period comes largely from Bede's book. This historian and monk lived from AD 673 to 735 in the monastery in Jarrow. His *Ecclesiastical History of the English People* was a very popular work throughout the Middle Ages. Because of his skillful historical work, Bede is known as the father of English history. Today, his *History* is still consulted by historians of England. It contains historical information from the earliest periods of English history available nowhere else. Bede wrote his history when he was about sixty years old. The accuracy of his history is quite remarkable considering that he lived in such a remote part of the world. From what we know, Bede rarely traveled. When he did travel, he did not travel very far. What he knew about kings, wars, and missionaries came primarily through written sources available to him at Jarrow and personal correspondence with others.

## BEDE'S LIFE AS A MONK

Hear, O LORD, when I cry with my voice!
Have mercy also upon me, and answer me.
When You said, "Seek My face,"
My heart said to You, "Your face, LORD, I will seek." (Ps. 27:7-8)

Bede was born in AD 673 near the monastery of Wearmouth (on the northeastern coast of England). As a boy, he began his education at seven years old under Abbot **Benedict**. He then moved a few miles north to Jarrow to continue his studies. Bede remained there for the rest of his life. He was ordained as a deacon at

**BEDE**

**LOCATION OF WEARMOUTH AND JARROW**

age nineteen and then a pastor at age thirty. He continued his work as a monk in Jarrow until he died in his early sixties in AD 735.

Life at the monastery centered around prayer, singing, study, meditation, and labor. There was a lot of work to be done on the monastery grounds. As a young man, Bede learned many practical skills. He learned gardening, cooking, and carpentry. He also loved poetry and music. Above all, he loved to study. He was a man of books. But in one sense, we could say he was a man of *one* book: the Bible. It was to the Bible that Bede gave most of his time in study.

## BEDE'S LOVE FOR GOD'S WORD

Oh, how I love Your law!
It is my meditation all the day. (Ps. 119:97)

Bede loved to read. He would read for hours upon hours each day. He read works of history, theology, biography, and science. At his disposal was an extensive library at the monastery. The abbot of the monastery, Abbot Benedict, had traveled all over Europe. During his many journeys, Benedict would hunt for rare books. When he was able to acquire one,

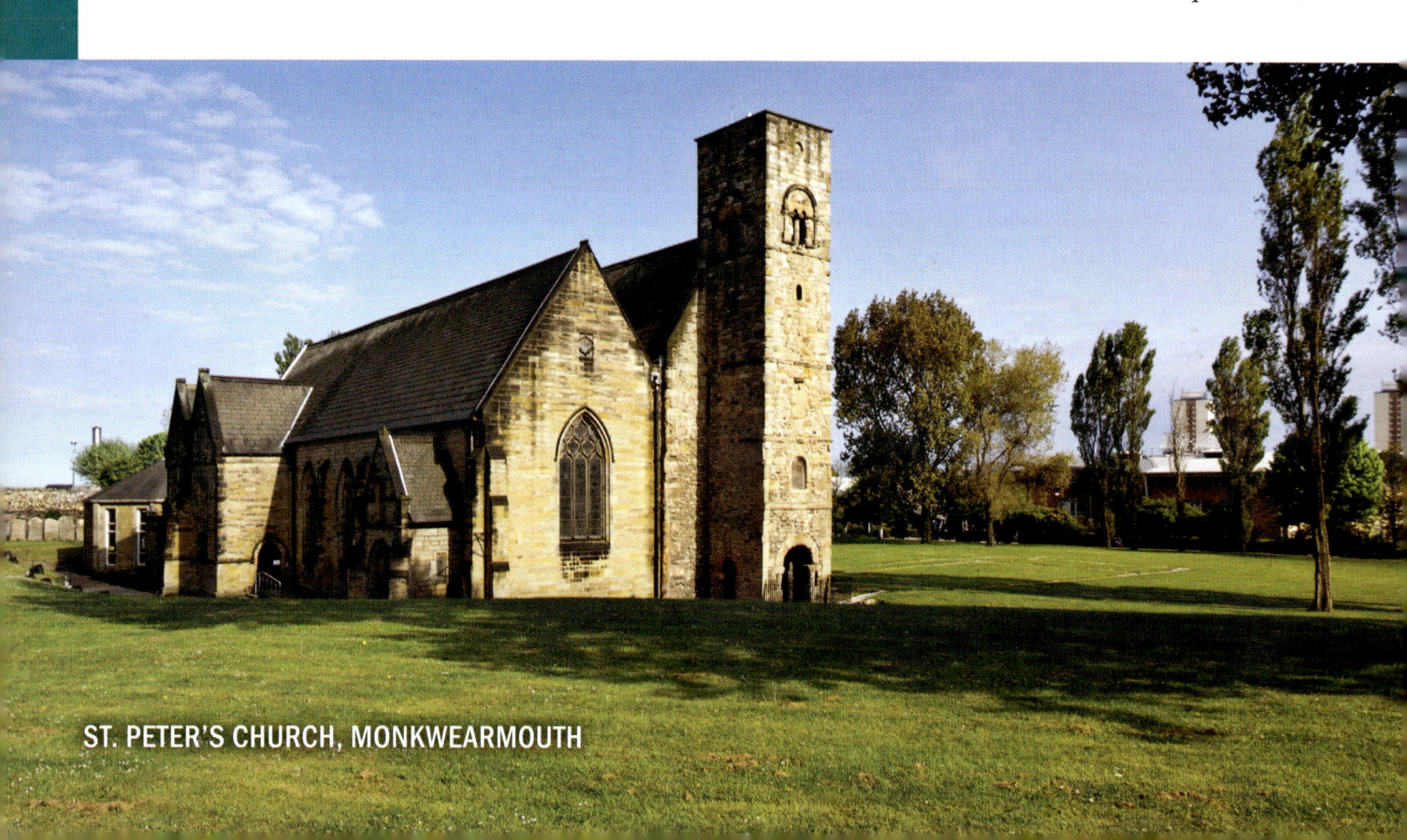

ST. PETER'S CHURCH, MONKWEARMOUTH

## 12. BEDE: HISTORIAN OF THE ENGLISH CHURCH

Benedict brought it back to Jarrow. Bede was content never to travel beyond the island of Great Britain. But he was glad that Abbot Benedict would bring back so many valuable books for his study.

Bede's studies all revolved around the study of the Bible. Every other book was secondary in importance to the Bible. Many of the books Bede studied were commentaries on the Bible. Bede diligently pored over commentary after commentary from Christians of the past. He wanted to know how faithful men in earlier times understood God's Word. He wanted to know the meaning and application of every word in the Bible.

In Bede's day, the Bible hadn't been fully translated into his native tongue of Anglo-Saxon. Bede read the Bible in a Latin translation. (Most books were written in Latin in Bede's day.) In order to better understand the Bible, he wrote his own commentaries on it. This helped Bede think through the meaning of the Bible's words as he read them. It helped him interpret the Bible, but it also taught others about what the Bible was saying. As Bede pondered on the text and wrote his comments, he also prayed. He knew that reading the Bible is not just an exercise of the mind. Reading God's Word requires us to respond in praise and worship. It is not enough for us to understand the meaning. God's Word is living and active. It requires a response from those who read.

A good example of Bede's own spiritual response to God's Word is found in his commentary on the Gospel of Luke. As he wrote his comments on chapters 10 and 11 of Luke, he realized that he too must respond to the teaching of Jesus Christ. He pondered the meaning of Luke 10:21:

**IMAGE OF BEDE WRITING HIS *HISTORY***

> In that hour Jesus rejoiced in the Spirit and said, "I thank You, Father, Lord of heaven and earth, that You have hidden these things from the wise and prudent and revealed them to babes. Even so, Father, for so it seemed good in Your sight.

Bede realized he needed to pray for humility lest he himself fall into pride. He recorded his prayer to the Lord next:

> Since the fourth section of the gospel I am explaining begins with the reading about how the spirit of pride was cast out by the finger of God, I humbly beseech your mercy, O Christ, that your good spirit may lead me in a right path . . . and having cast out evil from me, may I keep the commandments of my God and by opening the eyes of my soul may I, devout reader, begin

to behold the wondrous things of Your law.

Bede's response to God's Word is a good example of how we should approach the study of the Scriptures. We must come to the Bible in humility, asking God to instruct us (Ps. 119:18). Bede studied diligently to understand the meaning of every verse. He united strenuous labor in study with a humble and prayer-saturated approach to Bible study. Bede also knew that our knowledge of Scripture grows over time. In some cases, we may interpret a text wrongly, and we should be open to correction. In one of his commentaries, Bede admits as much:

> I beg the reader, if he sees that I have trod in the right path, to give thanks to God; and if he discovers that it is otherwise than I desired, let him pray the Lord to pardon my error.

Bede wrote commentary after commentary. Yet he realized that his countrymen outside the monastery could not read Latin. Bede hoped that one day more of the Bible would be available in Anglo-Saxon. He decided to make his own first contribution to that goal. He translated the Gospel of John into Anglo-Saxon (an early form of English). Sadly, Bede's translation has been lost to history. It is only through his disciple **Cuthbert** that we know of its existence.

## BEDE'S TEACHING

**You therefore, my son, be strong in the grace that is in Christ Jesus. And the things that you have heard from me among many witnesses, commit these to faithful men who will be able to teach others also. (2 Tim. 2:1-2)**

As a monk, Bede devoted much time to study and prayer. In addition to his own spiritual disciplines, he was responsible for discipling other young men. Bede wrote, "it was always my delight to learn and to teach." In order to pass on the faith, Bede wrote numerous

**DURHAM COAST, ENGLAND**

books, preached many sermons, and taught his fellow brothers side-by-side. For many of the young men entering the monastery at Jarrow, they first had to learn Latin. Bede knew the language well and even wrote grammatical books to help his students learn the language. The primary tool for learning Latin was the Latin Bible. The common translation of the Bible into Latin was produced by Jerome in the 4th century.

Bede's primary focus was on teaching his disciples the Bible. But he also taught other subjects. To do this, Bede would sometimes use Latin classics. However, he was careful to warn his students to be careful with non-Christian writings. He carefully distinguished the biblical writings from the non-Christian writings. He told his students:

> With much more caution must the rose be plucked from among sharp thorns than the lily from soft leaves; much more securely is sound advice sought in apostolic than in Platonic pages.

Bede provided an illustration here. It is much safer for your hand if you pluck a lily from soft leaves. This refers to the Bible. The Word of God is always safe. It contains no error. But the Latin and Greek classics (such as Plato) contain many errors, so great care has to be used in reading them. Students may find some truth in these books, but students must use great caution. If they aren't careful, they will cut their hand on the thorns of untruth and error found in the pages of these books.

In his teaching, Bede also devoted much attention to numbers. He observed that the Bible was full of numbers, and he wanted to understand why those numbers were there. Numbers were important to Bede for another reason. By numbers and dates, we understand time. With the incarnation of Jesus Christ and His death, resurrection, and ascension, history changed forever. Bede wanted his students to understand time and history. In order to compute the dates of history with more accuracy, Bede adopted a system of dating we still use today.

Bede divided history between the period before Christ's birth and the period after Christ's birth. The term "**BC**" was used to refer to that period before Christ was born ("before Christ"). And the period after Jesus' coming was termed "**AD**." These two letters stand for the Latin phrase *Anno Domini*. Translated from Latin, this means "in the year of our Lord." Bede's approach became the standard way in which dates on the Western calendar were calculated.

Bede also taught his fellow brothers through occasional sermons. A number of books still exist with Bede's sermons (also known as "homilies"). Bede often preached on significant days on the calendar such as the Christian celebrations of Easter, Pentecost, Christmas, and Palm Sunday, among others.

## BEDE'S PERSONAL CHARACTER

**The aim of our charge is love that issues from a pure heart and a good conscience and a sincere faith. (1 Tim. 1:5 ESV)**

In Bede's *Ecclesiastical History*, he provides a very brief summary about himself. But Bede did not write an autobiography. For this reason, we must learn from others who knew what he was like as a Christian man. Bede's younger disciple Cuthbert gave his own personal remembrances of Bede, written in AD 735. He testifies:

> Every day he gave lessons to us, his students; for the rest of the day he was busy singing the psalms as best he could. He would spend the whole night in prayer and thanksgiving to God unless a short sleep prevented him. When he woke again, he

immediately meditated on the accustomed chants from Scripture, not forgetting to give thanks to God with hands outstretched. In all truth I can say that I never saw nor heard any other man so diligent in giving thanks to the living God.

Bede was a man of deep emotion who loved the Lord. Cuthbert wrote about one occasion when Bede was singing to God the words, "Do not leave us orphans." Cuthbert noted that, "He burst into tears and wept copiously. After an hour he would repeat what he had left unfinished and thus he continued the whole day. And when we heard this, we shared his sorrow and wept; we wept and cried in turn; indeed we wept as we studied."

In November AD 734, a few months before his death, Bede wrote a letter to a fellow minister named Bishop Egbert. Bede speaks with the heart of a shepherd, similar to how the Apostle Paul wrote to his son in the faith, the young Timothy:

> Above all I would like to persuade you to restrain yourself from idle conversation. Restrain yourself from disparaging remarks and other pollutions of an undisciplined tongue. Devote your mind and your speech to the word of God and meditation on the Scriptures. Read especially the letters of Paul the Apostle to Timothy and Titus.

Like Paul, Bede warns Egbert about false teachers who would lead God's flock astray from the pure faith.

> I earnestly ask and entreat you in the Lord to protect . . . the flock committed to your care against the persistence of ravening wolves, and to recall that you have been appointed to be not a hireling but a shepherd, who shows his love for the supreme Shepherd by carefully feeding his sheep and by being ready, if necessary, with the blessed prince of the apostles, to lay down his life for these same sheep.

Bede's pastoral priorities are exactly in line with the teaching of Scripture. Pastors are called to "shepherd the flock" in love (1 Pet. 5:1-4), to guard the sheep against wolves (Acts 20:28-30), and to preach the Word at all times (2 Tim. 4:1-2). Through these written records, we receive an illuminating glimpse into the faith and godliness of the father of English history.

## Basic Facts about England

*The United Kingdom consists of the nations of England, Wales, Scotland, and Northern Ireland. The facts below pertain to England, one of the countries within the UK.*

| Total population: | 56 million |
| --- | --- |
| Total area: | 50,000 square miles |
| Capital: | London |
| Official language: | English |
| Primary religions: | Protestant Christian, Atheist, Agnostic |

> Shepherd the flock of God which is among you, serving as overseers, not by compulsion but willingly, not for dishonest gain but eagerly; nor as being lords over those entrusted to you, but being examples to the flock. (1 Pet. 5:2-3)

In 735, Bede was ill and near death. As he neared his entrance into glory, he adopted the words of Ambrose. It was Ambrose who had said:

> I have not so lived that life among you as would now make me ashamed; but I am not afraid to die either, for the God we serve is good.

In these last words Bede testified that he had no reason to be ashamed. He had devoted his life to the service of the Lord Jesus Christ. He pursued holiness. He lived an honest, God-fearing life. And like Paul, Bede was not afraid to die. He knew that the God he served is a good God. He could say with Paul, "to depart and be with Christ is far better" (Phil. 1:23). ∎

## PRAYER POINTS: ENGLAND

In this Prayer Points, we will pray for the churches of England.

- **Pray for the Church of England to Turn Back to God's Word:** The national church in England is called the Church of England. This national church has a rich heritage going back to the time of the Protestant Reformation. However, in recent decades, the Church of England has departed from biblical teaching in both doctrine and practice. There are some faithful pastors and church members within the Church of England. But the national church is in dire need of restoration and revival. Ask the Lord to cleanse all the churches in England of false doctrine and immoral practices.

- **Give Thanks to God for Faithful Pastors:** Church attendance in England is a mere fraction of what it once was. As the nation has turned away from God, it has become increasingly difficult to minister to a people in rebellion against God. Give thanks to God for faithful pastors that keep on laboring in discipleship despite opposition.

- **Ask God to Make the True Churches in England to Be Bold in Preaching, Prayer, and Evangelism:** As England becomes more hostile to Christianity, Christians may face additional opposition or persecution. There are recent news stories of street preachers in England being arrested for sharing the gospel. Pray that God's people in England would be faithful in proclaiming the truth, steadfast in prayer, and increasingly bold in sharing the truth with others.

VINEYARD AND CHURCH IN ALSACE, FRANCE

# ALCUIN: COURT ADVISER TO CHARLEMAGNE

Now therefore, be wise, O kings;
Be instructed, you judges of the earth.
Serve the LORD with fear,
And rejoice with trembling.
Kiss the Son, lest He be angry,
And you perish in the way,
When His wrath is kindled but a little.
Blessed are all those who put their trust in Him.
(Ps. 2:10-12)

On Christmas Day in the year 800, an important event in history occurred. It happened in St. Peter's Basilica in Rome. **Charlemagne** (pronounced "shar-le-main"), king of the Franks, was present in the church. Pope Leo III took a crown in his hand and placed it upon Charles' head. The pope said, "May God grant life to the great and pacific emperor!" Christmas Day in the year 800 was important because it marked the revival of the "**Holy Roman Empire**" in Europe.

Rome's original empire had fallen in the early 400s when Rome was sacked. Since that time, the empire had dissolved. But now, King Charles, who reigned over the Franks, had extended his empire all across Europe. Much of Europe was now under his control. (One of the few exceptions to his rule was the British Isles.) Charles' kingdom was a vast kingdom.

What made the "Holy Roman Empire" different than the first Roman Empire? This new empire under Charles was influenced by Christianity in every area of life. The Holy Roman Empire was not a perfect kingdom. But by the year 800, Jesus Christ had transformed much in Europe. Now, in the reign of Charles (or Charlemagne, as he is known to history), Christi-

CORONATION OF CHARLEMAGNE

**MEDIEVAL ARTWORK DEPICTING ALCUIN**

Jesus. In this chapter, we will learn how Alcuin used his knowledge of God's Word to influence powerful men such as Charlemagne. We will also learn how Alcuin shaped Christian education.

Long before Alcuin resided in Charles' court, he spent his early years in Great Britain. He was born in York around 735. At that time, York was part of the Anglo-Saxon kingdom of Northumbria. Alcuin lost his parents at a young age. As a boy, he was cared for by ministers of the church. His upbringing in the church was a great blessing. It laid the foundation for his work as a minister, scholar, and court adviser. He often spoke fondly of the men who became his fathers and brothers in York. Alcuin wrote, "O beloved fathers and brethren, remember me: I will be yours, whether in life or in death!"

Shortly before Alcuin's birth, the historian and churchman **Bede** died. As we learned in a previous chapter, Bede shaped the English church in many ways. His writings were read widely, and Alcuin was trained in Bede's thought. Alcuin took on many of Bede's own convictions. Bede taught Alcuin what godly kingship looked like. Alcuin and Bede both believed that a good king was a king who feared God. A godly king would love God. A faithful Christian king would serve under the reign of King Jesus. And a godly king would administer true justice in his realm.

anity and the kingdoms of Europe were thoroughly intertwined. Though Charles' reign was not without its sins, and though the church had its corruptions, clearly the influence of Christ had become pervasive throughout Europe. Charlemagne did make it his effort to rule over a Christian kingdom. He wanted to make the Bible the foundation for law, education, government, church, and all other aspects of life. In order to lead this kingdom as a king under God, Charlemagne called for Christian leaders to advise him.

Within Charlemagne's court was a godly man who had a significant influence upon the king. His name was **Alcuin of York** (735-804). Surprisingly, Alcuin was not a Frank. He was a foreigner who came from the British Isles. He served in Charlemagne's court for some time, giving the king godly advice. Though the king did not always listen to Alcuin's advice, Alcuin was faithful in shepherding King Charles and urging him to obey the greater King: King

As a Christian man and scholar, Alcuin's influence grew as he traveled between various royal courts in Europe. Most of what we know about Alcuin is found in his many letters. He was a diligent letter writer. Through his correspondence, he wrote to kings, exhorting them to obey the Lord. Alcuin also wrote to his fellow ministers to encourage them to pious devotion to the Lord.

## ALCUIN'S INFLUENCE IN CHARLEMAGNE'S COURT

*The king establishes the land by justice,*
*But he who receives bribes overthrows it.*
*(Prov. 29:4)*

Some time around the year 782, Alcuin was invited to join Charlemagne's court. Alcuin joined a number of other Christian advisers to the king. He would serve both as a teacher of Charlemagne and his sons as well as an adviser when it came to public policy. Charlemagne viewed himself much like one of the kings of Israel and Judah. Just as King Josiah reformed his kingdom to bring it into conformity to God's law, Charlemagne wished to do the same for the Holy Roman Empire.

Charlemagne extended his kingdom through numerous battles of conquest. He subdued many of the surrounding kingdoms. Charlemagne believed he could bring conversion to these kingdoms by forced conversion through baptism. Additionally, he required the conquered peoples to make tribute by forced tithes. These were two mistakes he made. By forcing baptism upon the subjugated peoples, Charlemagne did not realize the gospel does not advance by the sword. The gospel advances through the preaching of the gospel. The gospel moves forward through the Great Commission: baptizing and teaching the new disciples to obey what Jesus has commanded (Matt. 28:18-20).

Alcuin used his influence in Charlemagne's court to rebuke the king for this policy. Alcuin, having grown up in Great Britain, was more familiar with the pattern of evangelism among his own people. Forced conversions were rare. Evangelism and education went together in Great Britain. The pattern was to preach, to baptize, and then to train in godliness. Alcuin was, of course, thankful that many had come to a knowledge of the truth even through Charlemagne's conquests. Nevertheless, he argued that compulsory baptisms were inappropriate.

**ILLUSTRATION OF CHARLEMAGNE**

## CHARLEMAGNE'S CONQUESTS

Alcuin explained to King Charlemagne that faith could not be forced. He quoted Augustine who said, "Faith is something voluntary, never compelled." Here is what Augustine meant. If you have to force someone to become a Christian under threat of violence, they clearly do not have saving faith. If they had true faith, they would freely embrace the truth. Alcuin also argued that God's ministers were to be "preachers and not predators." Alcuin urged King Charles to send faithful pastors into the kingdoms he conquered. Alcuin wanted to send men who could teach the people about Jesus Christ and His ways. He wrote to the king:

> Seek for the new nation preachers of upright conduct, who are well taught in the faith, who follow the example of the Apostles in preaching the Gospel; in the beginning feeding their hearers with the milk of faith.

Alcuin was bold to correct the king. This counsel was needful for King Charlemagne, and it may have had some influence in Charlemagne's later years. Alcuin is a good example of a pastor directing a civil leader to obey God's Word. We need more men like Alcuin who are willing to speak boldly and truthfully to presidents, governors, representatives, and mayors.

Alcuin's influence in Charlemagne's court can also be found in a document called the *Admonitio Generalis* ("General Admonition"). This was a document created in 789. It contained royal policy for Charlemagne's kingdom. It covered such topics as law and justice, church, education, and charity. Alcuin wrote portions of this document. In it we find much biblical wisdom. A series of chapters contains the Ten Commandments applied to the kingdom. God's law was the foundation of all justice in Charlemagne's realm. Alcuin also urged church ministers to dedicate themselves to preaching and teaching. He exhorted judges to keep the peace and to become educated so they could wisely administer justice. Throughout the document, the Bible is constantly referenced.

However, not all of Alcuin's teachings were biblical. He taught in some of his writings that the pope in Rome was above all other human authorities. Like most in his day, Alcuin believed that the pope represented Christ's authority on earth. Alcuin did not recognize that the office of the pope is not a biblical office. Due to these views of the pope's power, Alcuin did believe that the pope was the one who should make men emperors, as Leo III had done with Charlemagne. This unbiblical perspective would not be remedied until later reformers like John Wycliffe and John Huss.

## ABBOT OF TOURS

**You therefore, my son, be strong in the grace that is in Christ Jesus. And the things that you have heard from me among many witnesses, commit these to faithful men who will be able to teach others also. (2 Tim. 2:1-2)**

In 796, Alcuin took on an important new office. He was appointed the abbot of Tours. This meant that he was the head of the monastery in the town of **Tours**. Tours is located in modern-day France. Alcuin was the leader of a large monastery containing over 200 monks. In this new role, he was the chief spiritual leader at Tours. Additionally, he was responsible for other aspects of the monastery's work. This included overseeing the landholdings owned by the monastery.

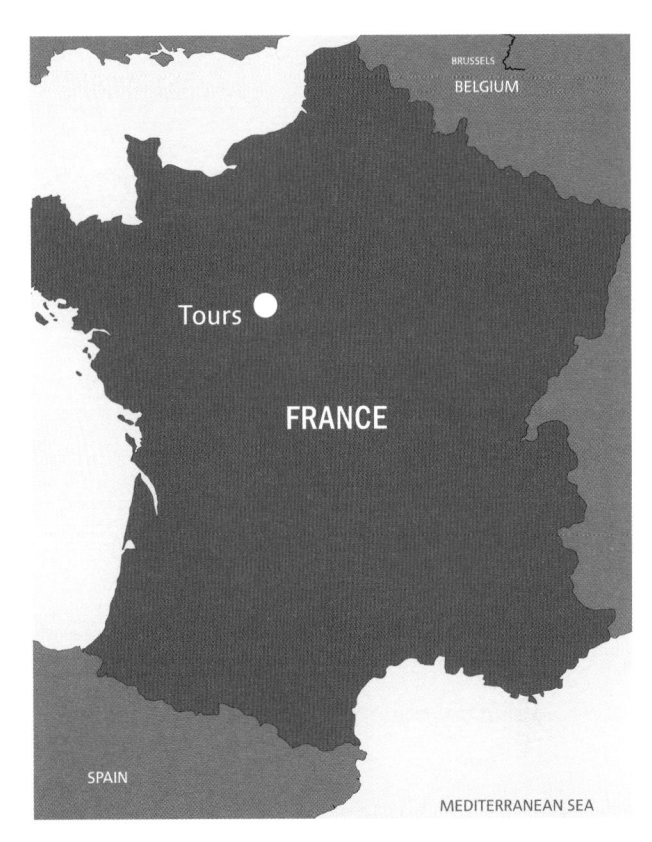

**LOCATION OF TOURS**

Alcuin oversaw the work of the **Scriptorium**. This was a part of the monastery where copies of God's Word were copied by hand. In Alcuin's day, the printing press was not yet invented. For this reason, every copy of the Bible was produced carefully by hand. To get a sense of the monk's daily work as a scribe, Alcuin wrote a poem that summarized this work. This poem was inscribed at the monastery in Tours. Here is a portion of what he wrote:

> Here sit those who copy the words of the holy law,
> And also the sacred sayings of the holy fathers.
> These guard lest they sow frivolity among their words,
> Or commit folly because of the error of their hands.
>
> They seek out with the utmost care correct versions of books,

So that their pens may fly along the right paths.
They distinguish proper grammar and sense with colons,
Placing points each in their proper places:
Lest the reader in church reads falsely,
Or suddenly falls silent before his devout brethren.

For it is a noble task to write out holy books,
Nor does the scribe wish for any reward himself.
It is better to copy out books than to till vines,
For one serves the stomach, but the other the mind.
The master can offer many volumes, old and new.
To a person who can read the holy sayings of the fathers.

In this inscription, Alcuin explains that the scribes' work was to copy first the words of Holy Scripture. The scribes were also making copies of books written by church fathers from the past. The scribe was to work diligently and carefully lest mistakes be introduced into new copies. Alcuin also calls the work of the scribe a "noble task." The scribe was one who served his fellow brethren in Christ by feeding their minds with truth.

## EDUCATION IN THE MONASTERY OF TOURS

**The fear of the LORD is the beginning of wisdom; A good understanding have all those who do His commandments. His praise endures forever. (Ps. 111:10)**

Alcuin was a committed teacher. And as the abbot of Tours, he shaped the life of devotion, learning, and work in the monastery. Daily life at the monastery was full of learning in numerous subjects. A particular emphasis was laid upon learning the psalms, memorizing the psalms, and singing the psalms. Alcuin also taught his disciples that all subjects must be studied in light of Christ's incarnation. The study of grammar, arithmetic, geometry, astronomy, and music were all just tools to better know and serve God.

A series of "monastic proverbs" are found in the poem "Let the Devotee Read These Precepts." Among the proverbs, likely written by Alcuin, we find such exhortations as:

- "It is best for the mind to be vested in the love of Christ."
- "Do not love yourself, nor the world, but only Christ."
- "A good mind excels all other treasures."
- "The teacher will be truly great who in his deeds fulfills what he teaches."
- "The root of wisdom is to fear the Lord with the mind."

For Alcuin, education must have a God-centered goal. The purpose of education was not to gain worldly treasures or to become proud. Rather, the goal of education was to know Christ and to serve Christ in all of life.

Alcuin also frequently exhorted his students to be on guard against false philosophies. He warned his disciples against some of the pagan writings. Referencing the Roman writer Virgil, Alcuin wrote that wisdom "will not be found in the lies of Virgil, but in abundance within the truth of the Gospel." Alcuin taught his students that biblical wisdom was far superior to the Greeks and urged his students to find wisdom in God-inspired books such as Proverbs and Ecclesiastes.

## ALCUIN'S WISDOM PRESERVED IN LETTERS

**A man has joy by the answer of his mouth,**

MARMOUTIER ABBEY, TOURS

**And a word spoken in due season, how good it is! (Prov. 15:23)**

We don't know much about Alcuin's personal life. However, many of his letters are preserved. These letters give us a glimpse into his love for the Lord and his love for others. We also find much godly wisdom contained in these writings.

Toward the end of his life, Alcuin wrote a letter to one of his disciples. The man's name was Hrabanus. Alcuin deeply loved this man. Some of his last words to Hrabanus urged this man to study the Bible, "seeking out how Christ was predicted in the prophets and shown forth in the gospels; and when you have found him, do not lose him, but lead him into the dwelling-place of your heart, and possess him there as the ruler of your life." Alcuin exhorted Hrabanus to love Christ and regard the Lord as "his redeemer, ruler and the benefactor of all good things." This is good counsel for every young Christian to take to heart. Read the Bible. Seek Christ in its pages. Love Christ. Submit to His kingly reign.

Another letter, written around June 800, shows the depth of relationship Alcuin had with King Charlemagne. That year, Queen Liudgard died. Alcuin wrote as a loving pastor to King Charles, seeking to comfort the king with the words of Jesus Christ. In his letter, Alcuin quoted Jesus' words, "Come to Me, all you who labor and are heavy laden, and I will give you rest" (Matt. 11:28). Alcuin also reminded the king of God's promise in Romans 8: nothing can separate us from the love of Christ. He explained to the king that we are all subject to death because of Adam's sin. "We are born in order to die, but we die in order that we may live," Alcuin wrote.

Alcuin's last years were lived out in Tours. As he grew older, he suffered from blindness. While physical weakness slowed him down, he continued steadfastly in his devotions. Then, on May 19, 804, Alcuin died. He left behind a legacy of courageous faith and devotion to the Lord. He must be remembered for his faithful counsel and leadership in the court of Charlemagne. Additionally, his work in furthering education set a pattern for the Western church for centuries to come. ∎

# PRAYER POINTS: FRANCE

- **Pray for dead hearts to be awakened to the things of God:** Since the radically secular French Revolution of 1789, France has been one of the most secular nations in Europe. Yet, like most nations in Europe, it has a Christian heritage that goes back almost to the beginning of Christianity. It is estimated that only six percent of the population in France attend church on a weekly basis. Most French people are "without God and without hope in the world" (Eph. 2:12). Ask the Lord to awaken dead hearts to the things of God. Pray that God would send forth faithful Christians who would share God's Word with the unbelievers of France.

- **Pray in light of changing demographics:** The population of France is changing. Many immigrants, especially from Muslim backgrounds, are now living in France in greater numbers than ever before. The birth rate among French families is falling. This likely means that in the future, more people in France will be born with a heritage from a nation elsewhere in the world, especially from Muslim nations. Pray that God would use this change in France as an opportunity for the gospel to penetrate both into the French people as well as the foreign immigrants now in France.

- **Pray against the forces of darkness in France:** *Operation World* reports that there are ten times more people earning a living by occult practices (witchcraft and sorcery) than there are evangelical pastors in France. This means that for every ten people actively practicing occultic rituals, there is just one Bible-believing pastor. Pray against the demonic forces that are bringing destruction to the people of France. Pray that God would raise up more faithful missionaries and pastors in France.

### 13. ALCUIN: COURT ADVISER TO CHARLEMAGNE

MEDIEVAL SQUARE IN MODERN-DAY TOURS, FRANCE

## Basic Facts about France (French Republic)

| | |
|---|---|
| **Total population:** | 67 million |
| **Total area:** | 247,000 square miles |
| **Capital:** | Paris |
| **Official language:** | French |
| **Primary religions:** | Roman Catholic, Atheist, Islam |

LIGHTHOUSE ON THE COAST OF DENMARK

# ANSKAR: MISSIONARY TO DENMARK AND SWEDEN

**Then Jesus spoke to them again, saying, "I am the light of the world. He who follows Me shall not walk in darkness, but have the light of life." (John 8:12)**

On the morning of January 28, AD 814, the king of the Carolingian Empire passed into eternity. Charles the Great, also known as **Charlemagne**, was gone. In the days that followed, much of Europe mourned. One unnamed monk recorded something of the sadness and grief felt at that time:

> From the lands where the sun rises to western shores, people are crying and wailing.... the Franks, the Romans, all Christians, are stung with mourning and great worry.... the young and old, glorious nobles, all lament the loss of their Caesar.... the world laments the death of Charles.... O Christ, you who govern the heavenly host, grant a peaceful place to Charles in your kingdom. Alas for miserable me.

Charlemagne established a mighty empire. By 814, much of Western Europe was subservient to Charlemagne. Through numerous campaigns, Charlemagne subjugated many people groups including the Saxons. As he conquered, he also forced Christianity upon his new subjects. The choice was simple: baptism or death. One way or another, Charlemagne wanted a Christian empire. But for many of those forced into baptism, it would be a Christian empire in name only. Yes, Charlemagne's forced conversions were efficient. But where true conversion did not take place, the Lord Jesus was not honored and served.

It was in Aachen (now part of Germany) that Charlemagne drew his last breath. About 200 miles west lived a young man thirteen years old. He lived at **Corbey Abbey** in Picardy. His

ILLUSTRATION OF ANSKAR

name was **Anskar**. Within a decade of Charlemagne's death, Anskar would carry on the work of Christ's Great Commission. Anskar would become known as "the Apostle of the North." He has achieved this title because he was the first Christian missionary to Denmark and Sweden.

Instead of converting by sword and force, Anskar would preach the gospel. He used the sword of God's Word, that mighty spiritual weapon. Instead of forcing baptisms by threat of violence, Anskar sought to persuade through preaching and discipleship. To use the words of a later missionary to North Africa, **Raymond Lull** (1232-1315), "They think they can conquer by force of arms. It seems to me that the victory can be won in no other way than as You, O Lord Christ, did seek to win it, by love and prayer and self-sacrifice." Anskar did exactly that. He loved the Danes and the Swedes. He prayed for their salvation. He sacrificially served them. And the Lord blessed that sacrifice.

The early 800s marked a new chapter in the Christianization of Europe. It was through the sacrificial work of a faithful band of brothers that the faith became rooted in Scandinavia. Anskar is the best-known among a group of devoted missionaries to Denmark and Sweden. Through his story, we get a window into the progress of the gospel in the 800s.

Anskar's friend and successor, Bishop Rimbert, left to following generations a written account of Anskar's life. It is called *Vita Anskarii* (*The Life of Anskar*). It contains a firsthand testimony concerning Anskar's life and contributions. Rimbert's admiration for Anskar is evident on every page. Let's learn about this godly missionary through Rimbert's account.

## CALLING TO MISSIONARY SERVICE

Born in 801, Anskar grew up at Corbey Abbey. Having lost his mother at a young age, he was raised in the monastery. As a boy, he was tempted by other children to engage in foolish talk and aimless behavior. But through a series of dreams, Anskar was awakened to spiritual things. He grew into a sober young man. Like others in January 814, he was grieved by the news of Charlemagne's death. During this time in his youth, he devoted himself to prayer and fasting.

**CORBEY ABBEY**

In one dream, Anskar believed God promised him the "crown of martyrdom." From then on, he believed he would die serving Jesus Christ. When Anskar later died of natural causes, he would experience a crisis of faith. Yet this dream made a significant impact on him. He was always ready to give everything for the sake of Christ. Anskar considered it an honor to serve and die for Jesus.

In 822, Anskar joined other brothers in forming a new monastery on the River Weser. It was located in the region of Westphalia (in modern-day Germany). The monastery was called "New Corbey." There, Anskar served as a teacher to children. He also preached in the church. Anskar was beloved at New Corbey.

At the same time, civil war erupted among the Danes. **King Harald** was exiled from Denmark. He went south and took refuge in the Carolingian Empire. While there, he was persuaded to become a Christian. He was baptized. King Harald then wished to bring the message of Christ to his own people. He also wanted to restore his dominions. At a public assembly, Harald beseeched men of the church to send a preacher. Rimbert records it in this way:

> When King Harald wished to return to seek to recover his dominions, he began to make a diligent inquiry. He wanted to find a holy and devoted man who could go and continue with him, and who might strengthen him and his people, and by teaching the doctrine of salvation might persuade them to receive the faith of the Lord.

Wala, an abbot from the monastery, told King Harald he knew a man who would go. Wala described Anskar as a man who "burned with zeal for true religion" and a man "eager to endure suffering for the name of God." Anskar was then summoned to appear before the king of the Danes. The king asked Anskar to come to his kingdom with him. Anskar replied that he was ready to serve God among the Danes.

**DENMARK**

## GOSPEL WORK AMONG THE DANES

> And everyone who has left houses or brothers or sisters or father or mother or wife or children or lands, for My name's sake, shall receive a hundredfold, and inherit eternal life. (Matt. 19:29)

Anskar made preparations to depart with King Harald. Bringing the faith to a hostile people is not an easy endeavor. Some were shocked that Anskar would be so bold as to preach the faith to a barbarous people. Others were dismayed that he would leave his fellow brothers and sisters behind. One brother, Autbertus, asked Anskar whether he was really going to leave.

Anskar replied, "I am asked whether I am willing on God's behalf to go to pagan nations in order to preach the gospel. So far from daring to oppose this suggestion I desire, with all my strength, that the opportunity for going may be granted to me, and that no one may be able to divert me from this design." Hearing

SKANDERBORG, JUTLAND, DENMARK

Anskar's reply, Autbertus decided to throw in his lot with him. Autbertus said, "I will never suffer you to go alone, but I desire, for the love of God, to go with you, provided only that you can obtain the consent of the lord abbot." The abbot consented. Anskar and Autbertus were off to Denmark, the land of the Danes. Together, they would bring the light of Christ's Word to the dark lands of the north.

Anskar and Autbertus journeyed north with King Harald. They traveled into the land of the Danes, located on the Jutland Peninsula. Soon, Anskar established a school for boys. Around twelve boys became part of the school. Some of King Harald's sons were also pupils at the school. Two years passed as Anskar and Autbertus taught the Christian faith. After two years, Autbertus became sick. He returned to New Corbey, hoping to recover. But it was not to be. Shortly after his return, Autbertus went to be with the Lord.

Two years of work among the Danes seemed to produce little effect. Autbertus was gone. Harald was unable to retake his former dominions. Anskar returned to New Corbey.

## GOSPEL WORK AMONG THE SWEDES

*My brethren, count it all joy when you fall into various trials, knowing that the testing of your faith produces patience. But let patience have its perfect work, that you may be perfect and complete, lacking nothing. (Jas. 1:2-4)*

In 829, the king of the Swedes, Bjorn II, visited the emperor of the Carolingian Empire. This emperor was the son of Charlemagne. His name was Louis. He is often referred to as Louis the Pious. Bjorn asked Louis to send missionaries to Sweden. He was eager for the Christian faith to be propagated among his people. Louis knew of Anskar's earnest labors among the Danes. So he summoned Anskar and appointed him to proclaim the holy faith among the Swedes.

Anskar, with a fellow brother named Witmar, set out for Sweden. They boarded a ship with merchants and crossed the ocean. But they were soon waylaid by pirates. The merchants were quickly defeated. Anskar and Witmar were robbed of almost all their possessions. Pirates stole the royal gifts meant for the Swedish rulers. They also took around forty books meant for the instruction of the Swedes.

This was a grievous trial for Anskar and Witmar. But they would not be stopped. They decided to go on. Together, they pressed on. Over land and sea, they made their way to Sweden. In time, they arrived at a port called **Birka**. They were welcomed by King Bjorn II. He gave the missionaries permission to freely preach the gospel to everyone in his kingdom. Anskar and Witmar began to publish the message of Christ's salvation to the Swedes. The chief leader of the town received Christ and was baptized. His name was Herigar. He then constructed a church on his own property and served the Lord.

After six months, Anskar and Witmar returned to Emperor Louis. They recounted the amazing works that God was doing. Overjoyed, the emperor gave thanks to God for the reception of the faith among the Swedes. After this, Anskar was appointed as archbishop over Hamburg and Bremen. From here, he would

"ANSKAR'S CROSS" IN BIRKA, SWEDEN

REPLICA OF VIKING-ERA BOATS IN BIRKA, SWEDEN

oversee the sending of missionaries to the Danes and the Swedes.

A man named Gautbert was then sent to minister to the Swedish people. Rimbert recounts the progress of the faith in these words:

> This Gautbert ... went to Sweden, and was honorably received by the king and the people; and he began amidst general goodwill and approval, to build a church there and to preach the faith of the gospel, and there was great rejoicing amongst the Christians who were living there, and the number of those who believed increased daily.

Missionaries continued to be sent to the Danes and Swedes. Anskar continued as a pastor over these outreach efforts. He returned to Denmark and continued the work. He also began to redeem boys from slavery. In particular, he focused on Danish and Slav boys who had been forced into slavery. Anskar redeemed them and then began teaching them the Christian faith.

Gospel advance continued in Denmark and Sweden. The churches were growing. However, attacks of the evil one persisted. During this time, while Anskar was in Denmark, the city of **Hamburg** was attacked. Sitting on the River Elbe, Hamburg today is a major port in Europe. For Anskar and the other missionaries, it was home base. One day, a group of pirates launched a surprise attack upon the town. So quickly did the attack occur that the people of Hamburg were unprepared. Many fled the town with anything they could carry.

Over two days, pirates burned and destroyed much of the city. Many residents of Hamburg died in the attack. The church and the monastery were both burned to the ground. A copy of the Bible, gifted from Emperor Louis to Anskar, was also destroyed. When Anskar returned and saw the devastation, he humbly submitted to God's providence. He repeated the words of Job: "The Lord gave, the Lord has taken away. Blessed be the name of the Lord." Though all his earthly possessions were gone, Anskar put his hope in God.

Shortly after the pirate attack on Hamburg, Gautbert in Sweden also faced the fury of Satan. A group of Swedes who opposed Gautbert's preaching attacked his home and drove him out. Because of this, the Swedes were without a Christian pastor for seven years. This grieved Anskar deeply. Eventually, he sent another brother named Ardgar into Sweden. Ardgar returned to minister to Herigar. The work continued.

Some received the Word of God, but others rejected it. Herigar continued steadfast in the faith and had many opportunities to witness to his fellow Swedes. On one occasion, he suffered a terrible injury to his leg. For a time, he had to be carried everywhere he went. He was not able to walk on his own. Some Swedes used this injury as an opportunity to mock him. Some said, "It is because you have no god that you are not healed!" Others urged Herigar to sacrifice to the pagan gods in order to regain his health.

Herigar rejected such suggestions. He would "not seek aid from vain images but from his Lord Jesus Christ who, if He wished, could cure him in a moment of his sickness." Then Herigar asked his servants to carry him to the church. Having been laid upon the floor of the church, Herigar cried out to God for healing. Rimbert records Herigar's prayer:

My Lord Jesus Christ, grant to me your servant now my former health in order that these unhappy men may know that You are the only God and that there is none beside You, and in order that my enemies may behold the great things that You do, and may turn in confusion from their errors and be converted to the knowledge of Your name. Accomplish, I beseech You, that which I ask for the sake of Your holy name, which is blessed for evermore, that they who believe in You may not be confounded, O Lord.

Rimbert records that after Herigar prayed, he was healed. The unbelievers in the town were put to shame.

Wherever the gospel is preached, opposition will come. But the Word of God and the Spirit of God is greater than the forces of darkness. Anskar's early labors, along with his brothers, began to yield fruit in Denmark and Sweden.

## ANSKAR'S FAITH AND CHARACTER

Bishop Rimbert knew Anskar personally. In *The Life of Anskar*, he recounts what Anskar was like as a man. We are told that Anskar dressed in a very plain manner. He was not a wealthy man. He did not care for earthly possessions. Rimbert also says that Anskar was dedicated to preaching God's Word to the people. He was a

**HAMBURG, GERMANY IN THE 1100S**

pastor to God's people. But he also loved to be alone. He would spend much time in meditation and prayer.

One of Anskar's frequent temptations was pride and selfish ambition. Whenever this sin showed itself, he was sad. Rimbert tells us that Anskar frequently prayed that the Lord would deliver him from this sin. One of the ways that Anskar fought against pride was to dedicate himself to serving others. He gave away many of his possessions. He also continued to spend his money redeeming boys from slavery. Having freed these boys, Anskar then taught them the Bible and prepared them for ministry.

Anskar also founded a hospital for the poor in **Bremen**. The tithes from churches in the surrounding area were directed to support the hospital. The poor and sick now had a place to rest and recover without needing to pay for care. When people were sick, Anskar would frequently go and pray over them. Many were healed. Some attributed miracles to Anskar, but he humbly replied in the following way:

> Were I worthy of such a favour from my God, I would ask that He would grant to me this one miracle, that by His grace He would make of me a good man.

When Anskar turned sixty-four, his health declined, and he neared the time of death. Even then, Rimbert records, he daily gave thanks to God. Anskar repeated the words of Job, "If we have received good at the Lord's hand, why should we not endure evil?" But as he neared death, Anskar remembered the dream of his youth. He believed that he would die by martyrdom rather than from growing old. His brothers reminded him that his entire life was one of sacrifice and suffering. They told Anskar that it was the Lord's will that he receive the crown of righteousness in this way.

Rimbert records something of Anskar's last day on earth. After receiving communion, Anskar prayed, asking God to forgive him for his sins. He repeated the words of Psalm 25, Psalm 51, and Psalm 22: "According to your mercy think upon me, according to Your goodness, O Lord. God be merciful to me a sinner. Into your hands, O Lord, I commend my spirit." Sometime after this, Anskar breathed his last. The "Apostle of the north" had worked diligently to see the gospel brought to the Danes and Swedes. Anskar was gone, but the church of Jesus Christ marched onward. This is the legacy of Anskar. ∎

## Basic Facts about Denmark

| Total population: | 5.8 million |
| --- | --- |
| Total area: | 16,577 square miles |
| Capital: | Copenhagen |
| Official language: | Danish |
| Primary religions: | Protestant Christian, Atheist, Agnostic |

## 14. ANSKAR: MISSIONARY TO DENMARK AND SWEDEN

# PRAYER POINTS: DENMARK

- **Pray that many in Denmark would come to believe in and know the one true God:** Approximately 81% of the Danish people are affiliated with the national Danish church: the Church of Denmark. But only 33% of Danes believe that a personal God exists. Weekly church attendance is around 2%. This means that the national church is a husk of what it used to be. It no longer has much influence in people's lives. For many, being a member of the Church of Denmark is only part of tradition. It is not a living faith. Let us pray that God would reveal Himself through the Holy Spirit to the Danish people. Pray that God would awaken the Danes out of their spiritual slumber so that they would see their sinful condition and their need for Jesus Christ.

- **Pray that the Lord of the Harvest would send more laborers into the field of Denmark:** Because the churches are so sparsely attended in Denmark, there are not many godly and Bible-believing pastors in Denmark. Let us remember that Jesus is the Lord of the harvest (Matt. 9:38). Let us ask Him to send more laborers into this field for gospel work. Denmark, though once a missionary-sending nation, needs missionaries! Pray for new Anskars to visit Denmark!

BREMEN, GERMANY

STATUE OF CYRIL AND METHODIUS ON MOUNT RADHOŠŤ

# CYRIL AND METHODIUS: REACHING THE SLAVS FOR CHRIST

I, the LORD, have called You in righteousness,
And will hold Your hand;
I will keep You and give You as a covenant to the people,
As a light to the Gentiles,
To open blind eyes,
To bring out prisoners from the prison,
Those who sit in darkness from the prison house.
I am the LORD, that is My name;
And My glory I will not give to another,
Nor My praise to carved images. (Isa. 42:6-8)

Among the beautiful mountains of the Czech Republic, there is one known as **Mt. Radhošť**. For centuries, it was a mountain associated with the worship of a false god. This false god's name was **Radegast**. This god was just one of many false gods worshiped by the Slavs. But one day, the statue of Radegast sitting upon the mountain was destroyed. Missionary brothers Cyril and Methodius visited the mountain. They had the idol torn down. Today, there is a church on the top of Mt. Radhošť. Next to the church is a statue of the two brothers. The statue commemorates their work among the Slavs. That church at the top of Mt. Radhošť is just one picture of how the Christian faith influenced the Slavs. The Lord used these two men to do amazing work among these people.

In this chapter, our attention is on Eastern Europe. There we find countries such as Russia, Ukraine, Bulgaria, and the Czech Republic. Where did these people groups come from? How did their languages form? And how did the Christian faith take root in these regions? Answers to those questions are found in the story of Cyril and Methodius.

Anskar was among the first Christians to reach the Scandinavian lands. For this reason, he is often called the "Apostle to Denmark." The Slavs received the Christian faith through **Cyril** and **Methodius**. They are sometimes called "the apostles to the Slavs." The word "apostle" is sometimes used to refer to the first missionary to a people group. This does not

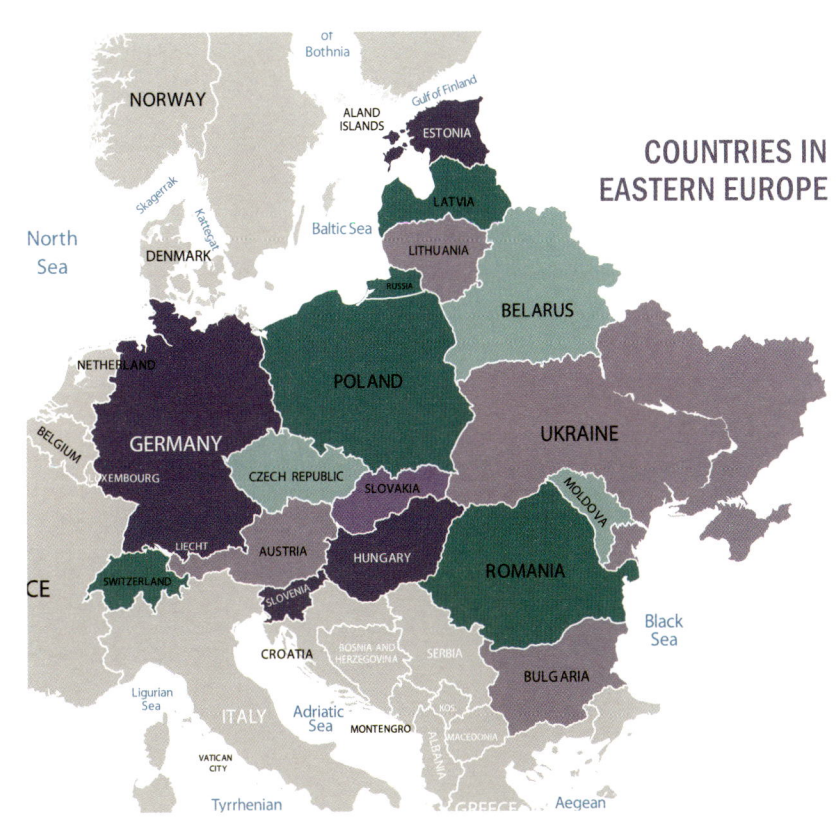

**COUNTRIES IN EASTERN EUROPE**

149

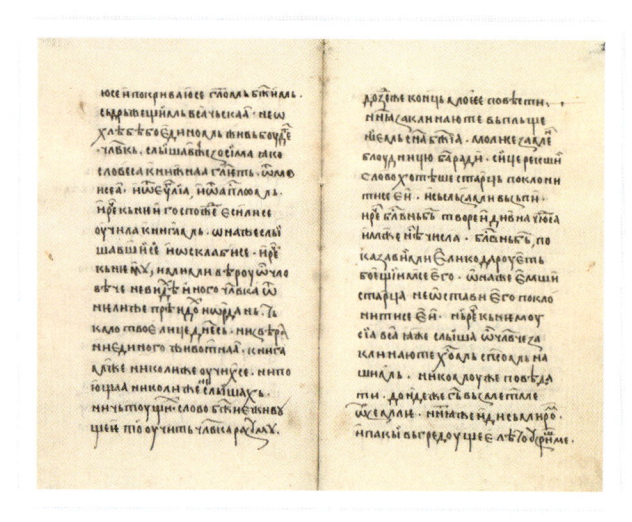

**A TEXT WRITTEN IN CYRILLIC SCRIPT, 13TH CENTURY**

mean these men were apostles in the same sense as Peter, John, or Paul.

Cyril and Methodius are among the most influential men in Eastern European history. They contributed much to the Slavic languages. They worked hard to create an alphabet and standardize the language of the Slavs. Their efforts formed the foundation of numerous languages still spoken today.

The "Slavs" arose in Eastern Europe. From this one people group, numerous different people groups have emerged. Many of the modern nations in Eastern Europe are Slavic in origin. The languages of Russian, Belarussian, Ukrainian, Czech, Bulgarian, and Slovak all trace their origins to the Slavs. Speakers of the various Slavic languages number around 315 million. Many of these languages use a particular script for their alphabets. These letters are called **Cyrillic script**. The script is named in honor of Cyril.

Cyril and Methodius did much to minister to the Slavic peoples. But they were not Slavs themselves. Instead, the two brothers came from Greece. They grew up on the shores of the Aegean Sea. Their hometown was the ancient city of **Thessalonica**.

## CYRIL AND METHODIUS IN THESSALONICA

Cyril and Methodius were two of seven children. Their father was a man named Leo. He held the title **drungarius**. This means Leo was a military official responsible for commanding around one thousand men. Of the two brothers, Methodius was the elder. He was born in AD 815. Cyril was born eleven years later, perhaps in the year AD 826. The brothers grew up in a noble family that had influence in Thessalonica. Both Cyril and Methodius received an extensive education. Their father's wealth provided all they needed for such an education. This training in reading, writing, and languages was important. It equipped them with important tools for their future missionary work.

The native region of the Slavs is north of Greece. But many Slavs lived near or in Thessalonica. Because of this, Cyril and Methodius

**LOCATION OF THESSALONICA**

CHURCH IN THESSALONICA, GREECE

grew up around Slavic people and their language. Inevitably, the Slavs began to trade with the people of Thessalonica. These two people groups wanted to do business together, so they learned each other's language. Some of the Slavs learned Greek. And some of the Greeks learned the Slavonic language. Before their missionary work, both Cyril and Methodius knew some Slavonic.

Because the brothers grew up in a wealthy and influential family, they had many opportunities for social advancement. Methodius was appointed by the emperor to govern a Slavonic-speaking province. This was an important opportunity for him. As a governor, Methodius learned more about the Slav's language and customs. Meanwhile, Cyril was a lover of books, and he advanced in learning. With Methodius' experience as a governor and Cyril's studies, the two brothers were being shaped for their mission.

In time, both Cyril and Methodius joined a monastery. Atop Mount Olympus was the monastery of St. Basil. Here, both brothers dedicated their lives to pursuing God. They spent their days in prayer, study, contemplation, and labor. At this time in church history, there were many monasteries. In many cases, it was monasteries that sent out missionaries. Christians at this time saw the monastic life as an important way to pursue holiness. However, the monastic movement tended to create a division of "sacred" and "secular" that was not biblical. This means that being a "monk" was seen as a life that was holier than an ordinary life of being a blacksmith or a shoemaker. But the Bible teaches that Christians can dedicate their life to God in all different kinds of callings. Nevertheless, the monasteries included many men and women who did faithfully serve the Lord. For Cyril and Methodius, it was another training ground for their mission to the Slavs.

MOUNT OLYMPUS, GREECE

ICONOGRAPHY OF RATISLAV

## KING RATISLAV OF MORAVIA

The loftiness of man shall be bowed down,
And the haughtiness of men shall be brought low;
The LORD alone will be exalted in that day,
But the idols He shall utterly abolish. (Isa. 2:17-19)

The homeland of the Slavic people contains some of the best farmland in Europe. Some of Europe's best agriculture is found in Slavic nations such as Ukraine. Numerous water sources such as lakes, rivers, and marshes provide abundant water. Many flat plains and a varied climate make agriculture fruitful. Farming was the primary occupation of the Slavs.

The Slavs experienced blessings from this fertile land. But they did not know the Savior Jesus. The Slavs worshiped many false gods. Among their gods was a supreme deity whom they thought was the creator, named Praboh. However, they believed in many other gods. They linked each of the elements of nature to various gods. As Romans 1 says, they worshiped the creation rather than the Creator (Rom. 1:25).

Many of the Slavs lived in a region known as Moravia. Emperor Charlemagne, king of the Franks, died in AD 814. By that time, Charlemagne's empire stretched across much of Europe. Charlemagne's son, Louis the Pious, divided the kingdom into four portions. Each of Louis' sons received a portion as their dominion. One of the sons, Louis the German, gained control of much of modern-day Germany. Louis the German then invaded Moravia and conquered it. After conquering Moravia, Louis appointed a Moravian duke named **Ratislav** to act as king.

By the workings of divine providence, this king became a Christian. Ratislav desired his people to be discipled in the Christian faith. King Ratislav sent an appeal to the emperor in Constantinople. He asked the emperor to send Christian teachers to Moravia. Here is a portion of what Ratislav sent to the emperor:

> By the grace of God, we are well. Many teachers have come to us, Christian from the Romans, the Greeks and the Germans, instructing us differently. But we Slavs are a simple people and do not possess one who can teach us and explain the meaning of Christianity. Therefore, O Ruler, send us such a man who will instill in us the entire true faith.

The emperor granted Ratislav's request. He sent Cyril and Methodius to the Slavs.

## THE MISSION TO THE SLAVS

*But you shall receive power when the Holy Spirit has come upon you; and you shall be witnesses to Me in Jerusalem, and in all Judea and Samaria, and to the end of the earth. (Acts 1:8)*

The brothers were well equipped for this mission. Having grown up in Thessalonica, they were familiar with the Slavonic language. Methodius' experience as a governor of a Slavic province was also helpful. Cyril's love for reading, writing, and language was now put to good use.

At this time, the Slavs had a spoken language. But there was no written form. No one in the kingdom knew how to read or write their own language. Cyril knew this problem needed to be remedied. If the Slavs wanted to know the one true God, they would need to read the Bible for themselves. Cyril worked to create an alphabet that would suit the Slavic language well. He began with the letters of the Greek alphabet. He kept some letters and dis-

**THE GOSPEL OF MARK USING THE GLAGOLITIC ALPHABET**

carded others. He also devised new letters to represent certain common sounds in Slavic. By 862, he had produced what is known today as the **Glagolitic alphabet**. This alphabet is very similar to the **Cyrillic alphabet** produced after Cyril's life. Even though Cyril did not produce the Cyrillic alphabet, it was named in his honor at a later time. The later Cyrillic script was based closely upon his Glagolitic alphabet.

After Cyril produced his alphabet, he and Methodius left Thessalonica. They were bound for Moravia to meet King Ratislav. They bore gifts from the emperor. They also carried a letter from the emperor and sealed with his seal. The letter read as follows:

> God, who will have all men come to the knowledge of the truth, has raised you to high rank, seeing your faith and works. This He did in our time and has revealed letters for your language, which from the beginning have not been, in order that you might be added to the great multitude who glorify God in their own tongue.... Endeavor to understand his [Cyril] message and seek God with all your heart. Do not reject salvation but encourage all that they may not delay in following the path of truth; so that you, also, by your labors, leading them to the knowledge of God, might receive your reward in this life and in all eternity for all the souls believing in Christ, our God.

In 863, Cyril and Methodius arrived in the capital. The name of the city was **Velehrad**. This city is located in the modern-day **Czech Republic**. Ratislav welcomed the brothers to the kingdom. Cyril and Methodius got to work right away. They began translating the church liturgy, the New Testament, and the Psalms into Slavonic. Cyril also taught a number of the Slavs the written alphabet he devised. Now, the Slavs could begin teaching others how to read. For the first time, they could communicate in writing. How exciting it must have been for them to read the Word of God using words they knew, in their own language!

However, no missionary can expect to

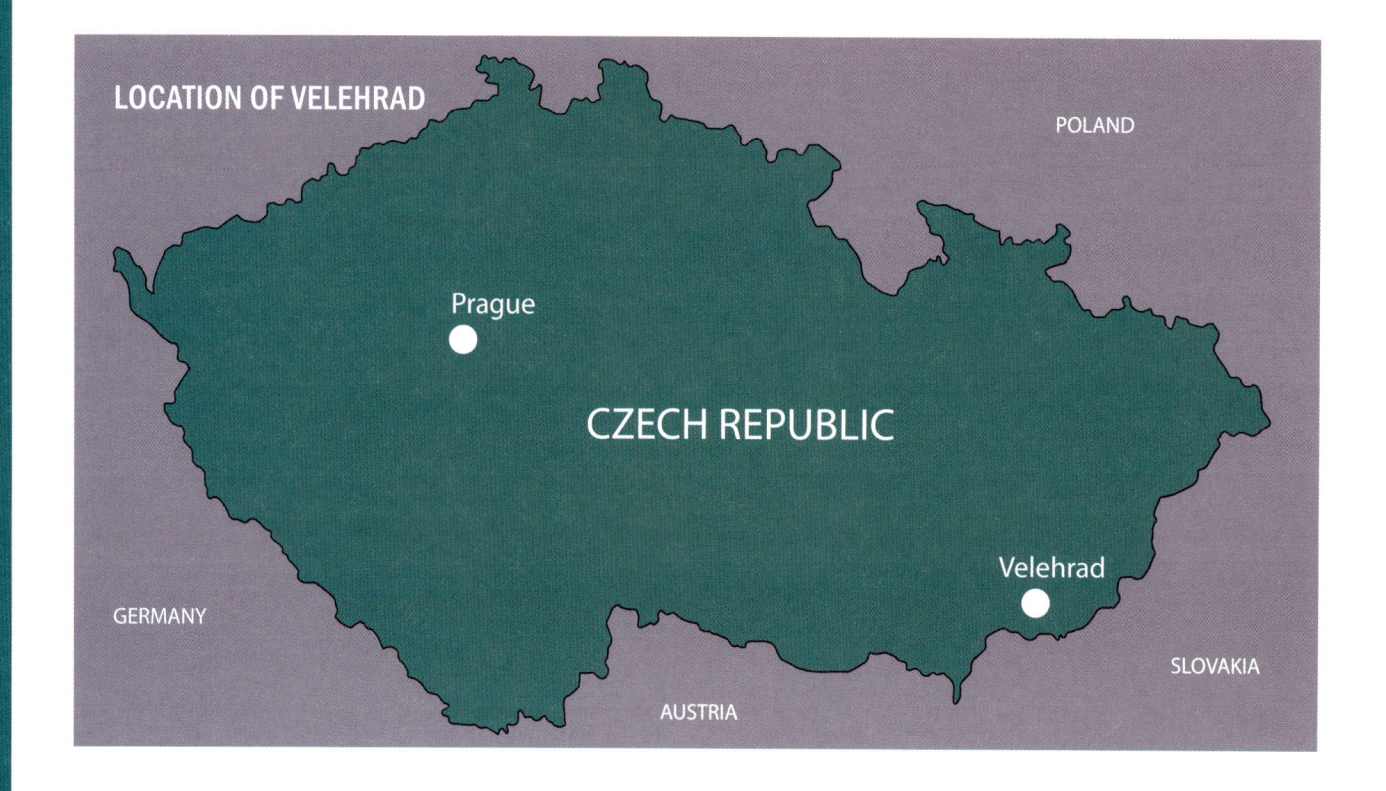

**LOCATION OF VELEHRAD**

CZECH REPUBLIC

Prague

Velehrad

POLAND

GERMANY

AUSTRIA

SLOVAKIA

MOUNTAINS OF THE CZECH REPUBLIC

advance Christ's gospel without opposition. Cyril and Methodius soon encountered difficulty. German bishops who resided in nearby Moravia objected to their translation efforts. Some of these bishops believed the Bible and church liturgy could only be read, sung, and prayed in three languages. Those three languages were Hebrew, Greek, and Latin. These languages happened to be the three languages Pontius Pilate used to inscribe "King of the Jews" on the inscription of Jesus' cross (Luke 23:38). Some believed these were the three sacred languages of worship. As this view became popular, it was known as **tri-linguism** (three-languages). Such a perspective obviously would hamper missionary efforts. How could Cyril and Methodius hope to teach the Slavs about Jesus if they were limited to three languages, none of which the Slavs understood?

The objecting German bishops wrote to the pope. The bishops asked the pope to investigate the matter. Forty months passed after Cyril and Methodius began their work among the Slavs. They were then summoned to Rome to speak with Pope Nicholas I (Pope from 858-867). While the brothers were on their way, Pope Nicolas died. He was succeeded by Pope Hadrian II (Pope from 867-872). After they arrived in Rome, Cyril and Methodius met with Pope Hadrian and a council of other bishops. They vigorously defended their translation work.

The pope agreed with the brothers. Hadrian argued that the account of Pentecost in Acts 2 was justification enough to translate the Bible into other languages. Had not God enabled the people groups on Pentecost to hear the good news in their own languages? Pope Hadrian gave his blessing to their efforts. Hadrian wanted the faith to be one, but he believed it

KIEV, UKRAINE

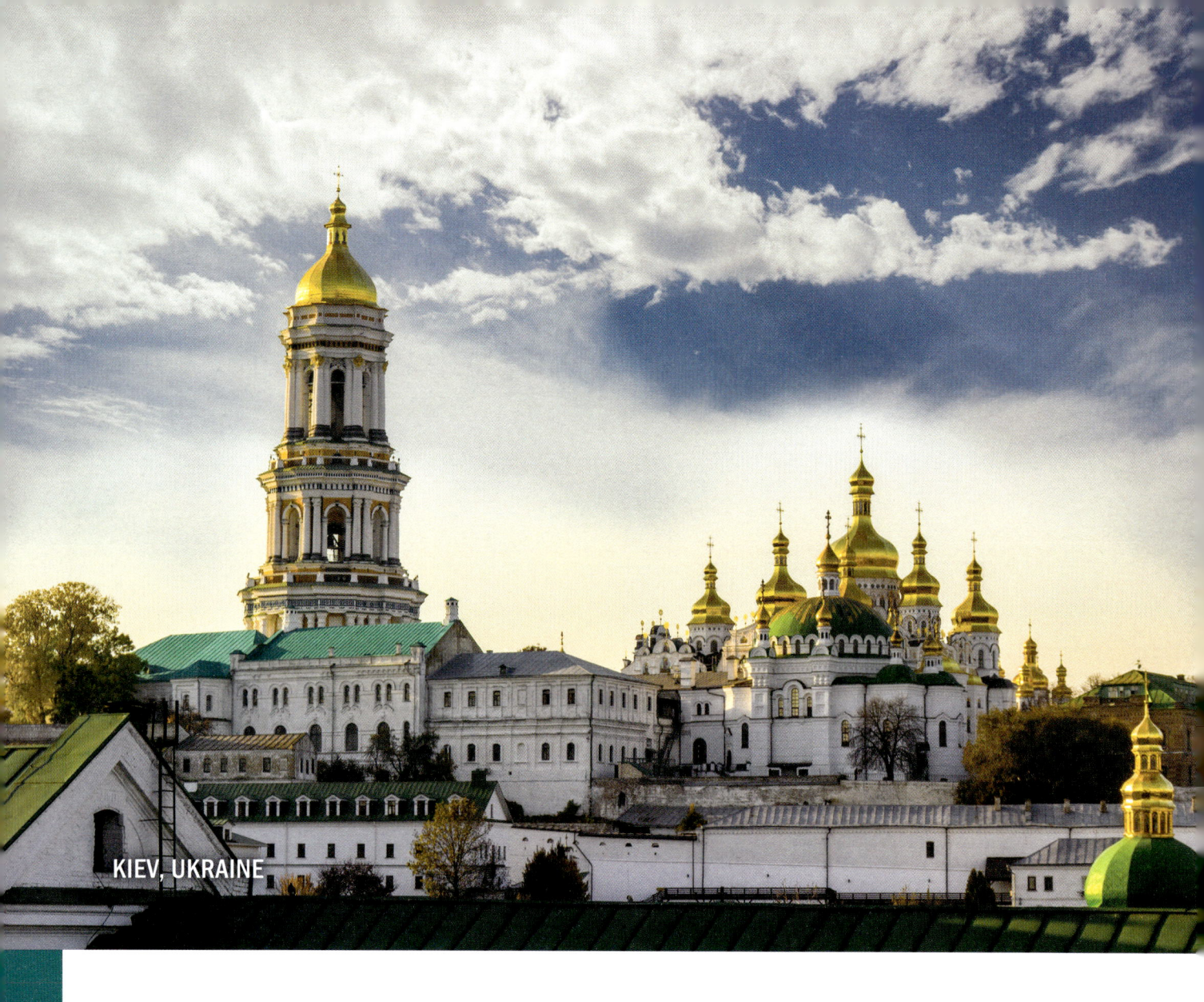

was right that all people groups should worship in their own language. Cyril and Methodius could now return to Moravia and continue their work among the Slavs.

But the brothers did not return together. Instead, Cyril became ill and languished for fifty days in Rome. After over a month of illness, Cyril died. He died in AD 869 at forty-two years of age. Before he passed, Cyril prayed to God for the advance of the gospel among the Slavs. Here is a portion of what was recorded of his prayer:

> O Lord, my God, Who created all the choirs of angels and spiritual beings, set forth the heavens and made the earth and brought forth all living things from non-being into being, and Who always hears those who do Your will, who fear You and obey Your commandments, hear my prayers and guard my flock over which You have placed me, an incapable and unworthy servant. Disperse the ungodly and pagan evildoers who blaspheme You. Destroy the three-language error, increase Your church by multitudes, preserve all in one spirit, make all peoples acknowledge the true faith, implant in their hearts Your Word. For this is Your gift, that at the preaching of the gospel of Your Christ, they accept us, unworthy men, exhorting them to the performance of good works which are pleasing to You.

Methodius grieved the loss of his brother. But the work among the Slavs had to continue. Methodius made the long journey back to Moravia. He continued the missionary work among the Slavs. Translation work continued in the years that followed. Methodius traveled throughout the region but used Velehrad as his home base for the mission.

In 874, the Czech people were also reached for the first time. The Czech prince **Borivoj** was baptized by Methodius. His baptism marked the beginning of gospel work among the Czech. Tradition also records that Methodius' disciples took the faith to the Polish people as well. Other documents from the period indicate that Methodius may have ordained ministers in **Kiev**. This is important because it was from the region of Kiev that the Russian people originated. It is likely that the Russians first received their alphabet from Cyril and Methodius.

Opportunities abounded throughout the surrounding regions. But conflict and opposition continued. The German bishops in the West were not pleased with Methodius' work. Sadly, it seemed that these men were more interested in personal power and political position rather than the salvation of the Slavs. Likewise, the commitment of some to the "tri-lingual" heresy was a major stumbling block to mission work. False accusations and rumors were spread among the bishops. Eventually, Methodius was summoned to appear before the German king in Bavaria. The year was 871. At the meeting, the bishops **deposed** Methodius and imprisoned him. Methodius remained in prison for two and a half years.

When Pope John VIII (Pope from 872-882) heard what had happened to Methodius, he threatened the Western bishops who were involved in deposing Methodius. The pope warned that he would excommunicate the bishops. This threat had its intended effect. Methodius was released in 873. He returned and continued the work of ordaining more men to serve as pastors. He also continued preaching against pagan practices. Not only did Methodius give attention to Bible translation. He also worked to produce legal codes, based upon biblical principles, to be enacted in Moravia.

Methodius continued his work until 885. By the end of his life, he completed the translation of the entire Bible into Slavonic. He died on April 6, 885. In total, he had dedicated twenty-two years of his life to the mission to the Slavs.

## LEGACY OF CYRIL AND METHODIUS

*The memory of the righteous is blessed, But the name of the wicked will rot. (Prov. 10:7)*

After Cyril and Methodius completed their earthly work, the mission to the Slavs continued. Numerous other faithful disciples, many whose names we will never know, continued to spread the faith. The Slavonic translation of the Bible was instrumental in the formation of the Slav's language and literature. The first words the Slavs read in their own language were drawn from the Gospels, the Psalms, and the letters of Paul. That meant their language was shaped by biblical words and concepts.

In some cases, Cyril and Methodius found that the Slavonic language lacked words necessary to translate biblical concepts. To remedy this, the brothers pulled from the Greek language or created new words in Slavonic in order to accurately communicate the biblical message. This also enriched the Slavonic lan-

**Depose** ▪ To depose means to remove someone from office.

SCULPTURE OF CYRIL AND METHODIUS

## Basic Facts about the Czech Republic

| Total population: | 10 million |
| --- | --- |
| Total area: | 30,452 square miles |
| Capital: | Prague |
| Official language: | Czech |
| Primary religions: | Atheist, Agnostic, Roman Catholic |

guage with new words and concepts.

As the Christian faith took root among the Slavs, pagan worship of false gods waned. Today, the Christian influence can still be felt throughout Eastern Europe. With the rise of communism in Eastern Europe, a violent march toward atheism began. But communism failed and Jesus Christ still reigns. The Christian faith has had a culture-shaping influence in Eastern Europe for centuries. But today, far fewer people follow Jesus in these lands. It is important that Christians all over the world pray for the advance of Christ's gospel in Eastern Europe. We know that one day every knee will bow to Jesus, and every tongue will confess that He is Lord.

Returning to Mt. Radhošť, there is a story that reminds us that Jesus still reigns. In 1931, an attempt was made to put a statue of the Slavic god Radegast back on the mountain. As the truck wended its way up the mountain, it got stuck in a steep turn. A heavy rainstorm poured down, and lightning struck and killed one of the men. To this day, Radegast's statue has not returned to Mt. Radhošť. ∎

## PRAYER POINTS: CZECH REPUBLIC

- **Ask God to send light into a dark land:** Among the nations of Europe, the Czech Republic is one of the most atheistic. Over 70% of the population claim to be "non-religious." That means the vast majority of people in the Czech Republic "suppress the truth" about God's existence (Rom. 1:18). This country is deeply in need of God's truth, the Bible, to bring light to a dark land. Pray that God would show the people of the Czech Republic that life is empty and meaningless without the one true God.

- **Pray that God would strengthen and grow the church:** Most of the churches in the Czech Republic are part of the Roman Catholic Church. There are not very many Bible-preaching and Bible-believing churches in this country. Let us pray that God would strengthen the small church that does exist. And let us ask God to grow the church in numbers and influence.

- **Thank God for additional Bible translation and literature distribution:** *Operation World* reports that a new translation of the Bible in the Czech language was published in 2009. It quickly became a best-seller. Let us thank God for providing His Word in the Czech Republic and for the increased distribution of Bibles and Christian literature in this country.

FARMLAND IN SOMERSET, ENGLAND

# ALFRED THE GREAT: CHRISTIAN KING OF WESSEX

The God of Israel said,
The Rock of Israel spoke to me:
"He who rules over men must be just,
Ruling in the fear of God." (2 Sam. 23:3)

In this chapter, we return to the island of Great Britain. Around the same time Methodius and Cyril were reaching the Slavs in Eastern Europe, momentous events were unfolding on the island of Great Britain. A series of invasions by **Norsemen** impacted the churches of the British Isles. Many separate kingdoms existed in Britain at this time. Many of these kingdoms fell to the Vikings. But one kingdom, the kingdom of **Wessex**, stopped the Vikings in their advance. It was **King Alfred** (c. 848-899) who courageously fought back.

Under the reign of Alfred, the kingdom of Wessex repelled Viking invaders. Thereafter, Alfred began unifying the kingdoms of Great Britain under his rule. He worked to further establish the Christian foundations of law in Great Britain. Alfred was a king who acknowledged the lordship of King Jesus. His example of ruling in the fear of God is a model for Christian leaders in the present day.

To understand how Alfred came to have such influence, let's learn about the Viking invasions. In this tumultuous time, the Lord raised up Alfred to defend the kingdom.

## THE VIKING INVASIONS

The historical document *The Anglo-Saxon Chronicle* records the first invasion of the Vikings into Great Britain. This invasion took place around AD 789. The Vikings were a people group who came from the region of modern-day Denmark. They repeatedly invaded Britain to kill, destroy, and rob English towns along the coastline. Between 793 and 795, the monasteries of **Lindisfarne, Iona,** and **Jarrow** were plundered by these ruthless invaders. For God's people in Great Britain, these were crushing trials.

Upon hearing of the destruction of Lindisfarne, **Alcuin of York** wrote to his brethren. As we learned in a previous chapter, Alcuin lived in modern-day France. But he grew up in Northumbria, part of Great Britain. The destruction of Lindisfarne, then, was very personal for him. He urged his fellow Christians to humble themselves before God. He believed these trib-

**ILLUSTRATION OF KING ALFRED**

ulations were a way that God was calling the churches to repentance. This is what he wrote:

> For nearly 350 years, we and our fathers have dwelt in this most beautiful land, and never before has such a terror appeared in Britain, such as the one that we are suffering from this pagan nation.... Carefully consider, brothers, and diligently note, lest this extraordinary and unheard of evil might be somehow merited by the habit of some unspoken wickedness.

Alcuin urged his fellow Christians to examine their actions. Was God disciplining His church because they had strayed from His Word? As the Vikings plundered and killed, the Christians of Great Britain pleaded for God's mercy.

The raids upon villages and monasteries increased year by year. Reports went out all over Great Britain: The Vikings were on the move. There was a common pattern to the attacks. The Vikings (also known as Norsemen) landed. Then they began burning, killing, and stealing. After securing their booty, they returned to their ships and sailed back to their homeland. After a short time, the ruthless marauders returned to Britain for another attack.

In 870, the southern kingdom of Wessex was threatened by Danish Vikings. King Alfred, ruler of Wessex, endured numerous assaults. He was forced to make concessions to the plunderers in hopes of preserving as much of his kingdom as possible. Over time, he lost more territory to the Vikings. At his lowest point, Alfred's army was reduced to a single person—himself. The Viking leader Guthrum took complete control of Wessex.

This did not stop King Alfred. He quietly assembled an army of men loyal to Wessex. Together, they prepared to make one last stand against the tyrant invader. Alfred rebuilt his fighting force starting with a few faithful men. Over time, his army increased in numbers.

In 878, Alfred met Guthrum and his army in battle. This confrontation is known as the **Battle of Edington**. By God's providence, Alfred and his loyal men were victorious. It was a dramatic reversal. Guthrum now had to submit to Alfred.

When the Vikings conquered a kingdom, they frequently killed off any surviving enemy leaders. Alfred did not do this. Instead, he treated his enemies with kindness. Alfred agreed to let Guthrum live. But there were conditions to this. The first condition Alfred imposed on Guthrum was Christian baptism. It wasn't uncommon for Christian rulers in Europe to require baptism of their defeated foes as a condition of peace. This was not biblical.

Alfred also agreed to allow Guthrum to rule over a large part of eastern and northern England. This land was referred to as **Danelaw**. It was called Danelaw because it was a portion of land that was under the law of the Danes.

ALFRED FIGHTS THE VIKING INVADERS

## REBUILDING WESSEX

*This Book of the Law shall not depart from your mouth, but you shall meditate in it day and night, that you may observe to do according to all that is written in it. For then you will make your way prosperous, and then you will have good success. (Josh. 1:8)*

**GUTHRUM BAPTIZED**

Wessex was now secure. Alfred was once again king over the land. But what if the Vikings attacked again? Alfred realized he needed to set up defenses. If Wessex was to repel a future attack, it would need to be ready. Alfred began to strengthen Wessex's defenses. First, he fortified many towns with burhs. These were defensive walls built around the towns. Also, he organized an army for Wessex. The men traveled from town to town, keeping watch against invaders. These defensive measures fortified Wessex and made it more secure.

Alfred was a godly man who loved the Lord. He also wanted the subjects in his kingdom to know the Lord. He believed Christian education was a vital tool to increase his kingdom's growth in godliness. He introduced classic Christian literature into the kingdom. He translated several books into Anglo-Saxon. These translated works included Gregory's *Pastoral Care*, Boethius' *Consolation of Philosophy*, and some of the writings of Augustine of Hippo. With the help of some church leaders, Alfred authored several books of his own. He also likely produced one of the most important documents from this time period. This document is called *The Anglo-Saxon Chronicle* (a history of Anglo-Saxon England). It is a short document, but the *Chronicle* is an important document because it is one of the few records

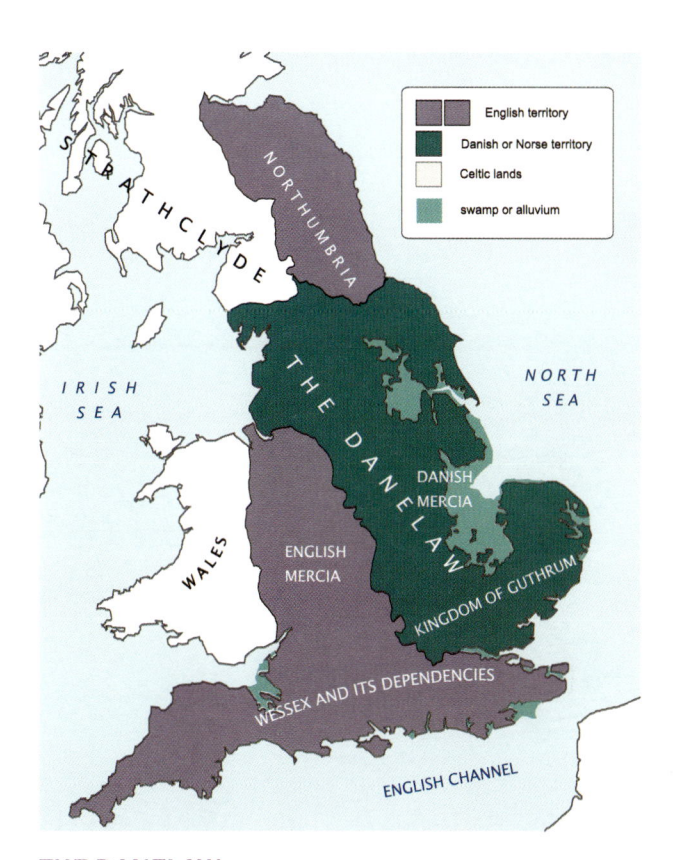

**THE DANELAW**

**ILLUSTRATION OF THE "ALFRED JEWEL," AN ARTIFACT FROM KING ALFRED'S REIGN**

we have from this time period.

At this time, only trained monks could read Latin. Most of the books available in Great Britain, including the Bible, were written in Latin. Alfred was eager to get the Bible and other books translated into the common tongue. He knew that his people would only grow in godliness if they knew the Lord and His Word. The Bible was an essential tool in discipling the nation. Alfred established schools throughout the Wessex countryside. In these schools, children were taught how to read and write in Anglo-Saxon. The local pastors (or bishops) were encouraged to find children who could take time out from their farming to learn how to read. Then Alfred's translations of Christian books were distributed throughout the kingdom for reading material.

Throughout the history of the church, the Book of Psalms has been an essential part of discipleship in the faith. This was the songbook used by Jesus and the apostles. Ever since the early church, the psalms have shaped the faith of Christ's disciples. King Alfred's last translation project was portions of Psalms. He rendered the psalms from Latin into Anglo-Saxon. King David wrote many of the psalms.

That is why so many of the psalms are written in the context of battle. King Alfred was a warrior king just like David. Alfred related to the spirit and mood of the psalms. He knew what it was like to be pursued by a bloodthirsty, dangerous enemy. He faced threats of death many times in his life. And, like King David, Alfred experienced God's saving deliverance many times.

In his translation of Psalm 2, Alfred offered this brief explanation for the meaning of the psalm: "David in this psalm lamented and complained to the Lord about his enemies, both native and foreign, and about all his troubles. And everyone who sings this psalm does likewise with respect to his own enemies. So too did

**ILLUSTRATION OF KING ALFRED AT WORK IN HIS STUDY**

RUINS OF MEDIEVAL CASTLE IN DORSET, ENGLAND

Christ with respect to the Jews."

Here is a portion of Alfred's translation of Psalm 2 rendered into modern English:

> Why do all nations rage, and why do they contemplate useless undertakings?
>
> And why do the kings of the earth rise up, and noblemen come together against God, and against him whom He chose as lord and anointed? . . .
>
> Hear now, you kings, and learn, you judges who judge over the earth:
>
> Serve the Lord and fear Him; rejoice in God, yet with awe.
>
> Embrace learning, lest you incur God's anger and lest you stray from the right path.

Alfred died before he finished translating all the Psalms. He completed the first fifty psalms before his death. Others would complete his translation work. Alfred's effort to translate the Word of God into the common language was a great blessing. His work laid a foundation for future translations by John Wycliffe and eventually William Tyndale.

King Alfred also reshaped the law codes of Wessex. He wrote laws for his kingdom that were based on biblical law as found in the Old and New Testaments. This was evident by how the law code began. It began with a translation of the Ten Commandments. The Ten Commandments are then followed by a large collection of quotations from the various laws found in Exodus 21-23. In addition to the quotations from Exodus, Alfred included sections of Jesus' Sermon on the Mount from Matthew 5-7. After Jesus' words, there are 120 laws listed for the kingdom of Wessex. With this law code, King Alfred formed biblical foundations for justice in the Western world.

Alfred was well known by his people for his wisdom, generosity, and mercy. Like King Solomon, he gave wise judgment in legal disputes when the elders of a community disagreed on some matter. He devoted much of his riches to the work of the church. At this time, it was the church which provided assistance to the poor in the land. Few kings in history retained the title "Great," but King Alfred the Great earned this title because of his courageous leadership and his wise and just government over the kingdom of Wessex. ∎

---

**When a land transgresses, it has many rulers, but with a man of understanding and knowledge,
its stability will long continue. (Prov. 28:2 ESV)**

---

# PRAYER POINTS: UNITED KINGDOM

---

**Therefore I exhort first of all that supplications, prayers, intercessions, and giving of thanks be made for all men, for kings and all who are in authority, that we may lead a quiet and peaceable life in all godliness and reverence. For this is good and acceptable in the sight of God our Savior, who desires all men to be saved and to come to the knowledge of the truth. (1 Tim. 2:1-4)**

---

In this Prayer Points, we will pray for those in civil government in the United Kingdom.

- **Pray for the Monarch of the United Kingdom:** At the time of this book's writing, the reigning monarch in the United Kingdom is Queen Elizabeth II. While the monarch of the United Kingdom has far less power than the kings and queens of the Middle Ages, the monarch is still considered the head of state in the United Kingdom. Pray for the reigning monarch of the United Kingdom: that the monarch would believe in the Lord Jesus Christ and submit to Christ's kingship. Pray that the monarch would be an example of godliness and righteousness to the citizens of the United Kingdom. Ask God to surround the monarch with godly advisers.

- **Pray for the Parliament of the United Kingdom:** The Parliament of the United Kingdom consists of two houses: the House of Lords and the House of Commons. Those members of Parliament (MPs) in the House of Commons are elected by the people of various districts of the United Kingdom. Ask God to raise up more righteous rulers in the United Kingdom. Ask the Lord to put Christians in places of government so that they can seek to apply God's standards of righteousness in the UK. Beseech the Lord to stop those in Parliament who would seek to legislate wicked laws.

## 16. ALFRED THE GREAT: CHRISTIAN KING OF WESSEX

**STATUE OF KING ALFRED THE GREAT**

### Basic Facts about England

*The United Kingdom consists of the nations of England, Wales, Scotland, and Northern Ireland. The facts below pertain to England, one of the countries within the UK.*

| Total population: | 56 million |
|---|---|
| Total area: | 50,000 square miles |
| Capital: | London |
| Official language: | English |
| Primary religions: | Protestant Christian, Atheist, Agnostic |

LAKE DISTRICT, ENGLAND

# ATHELSTAN: FIRST KING OF ENGLAND

*The fear of the LORD is to hate evil;
Pride and arrogance and the evil way
And the perverse mouth I hate.
Counsel is mine, and sound wisdom;
I am understanding, I have strength.
By me kings reign,
And rulers decree justice. (Prov. 8:13-15)*

In 937, somewhere in the north of England, vast armies gathered for battle. On one side was King Athelstan and his army. He was king of the kingdom of Wessex. (The kingdom of Wessex is located in the southwestern portion of modern-day England.) Athelstan inherited the kingdom from his father **Edward the Elder**. In turn, Edward received the kingdom from Alfred the Great. **Athelstan** was Alfred's grandson.

Opposing King Athelstan was a united alliance of kingdoms. Those kingdoms included the king of **Dublin**, the king of **Scotland**, and the king of **Strathclyde**. Together, these kingdoms represented portions of Great Britain and Ireland not yet under the control of Athelstan.

The name of this battle is known as the **Battle of Brunanburh**. We don't know where the battle took place. But we do know the results. The kings of Dublin, Scotland, and Strathclyde were thoroughly defeated by King Athelstan. Historical accounts record the devastating defeat that day. One ancient chronicle says it was the deadliest battle ever fought in Great Britain. The king of Scotland left his son, Prince Alba, dead on the battlefield.

There was an important difference between Athelstan's forces and his enemies. Athelstan was a Christian king leading a Christian kingdom. The other kings did not bow the knee to King Jesus. In fact, they had used sorcery in preparation for the battle. But it had not won them the battle. In God's providence, it was King Athelstan who was victorious. Athelstan's kingdom grew, and the influence of the Christian faith would continue to spread far and wide in Great Britain.

After the Battle of Brunanburh, Athelstan gained the title *Rex Anglorum*. This is translated "King of the English." Athelstan is

**KING ATHELSTAN**

important in our study of Europe for two reasons. First, because it was under his reign that England as a united nation had its beginning. Secondly, much like his grandfather Alfred, Athelstan was a godly king who submitted to the reign of King Jesus.

## ATHELSTAN BECOMES KING

> Mercy and truth preserve the king,
> And by lovingkindness he upholds his throne.
> (Prov. 20:28)

Athelstan was uniquely blessed with consistent Christian discipleship in his early years. In his case, it was his aunt who contributed the most to his Christian upbringing. King Alfred's daughter **Aethelflaed** was called the Lady of Mercia. She held this title because she had married the King of Mercia. (Mercia was located northeast of the kingdom of Wessex.) Her husband Aethelred died in 911, leaving her as ruler over the Mercian kingdom. King Edward sent the young Athelstan to be educated by Aunt Aethelflaed. She was a woman of deep Christian piety. Aethelflaed passed on the Christian heritage from King Alfred down to young Athelstan.

In 917, Aethelflaed died. Then, in 924, Athelstan inherited the throne of Wessex from his father Edward. Athelstan was about thirty years old when he became king. Now, with both Edward and Aethelflaed gone, Athelstan united the kingdoms of Wessex and Mercia.

Athelstan was known for both his powerful leadership and his love for God. He demonstrated Christian virtue in his actions. His father King Edward had been unfaithful in marriage. He divorced several wives and remarried numerous times. Though Athelstan never married, he was faithful to keep God's commandments and lived a pure life.

## ATHELSTAN'S CHRISTIAN KINGDOM

> You shall appoint judges and officers in all your gates, which the LORD your God gives you, according to your tribes, and they shall judge the people with just judgment. You shall not pervert justice; you shall not show partiality, nor take a bribe, for a bribe blinds the eyes of the wise and twists the words of the righteous. (Deut. 16:18-19)

With the kingdoms of Wessex and Mercia united, Athelstan took action to drive out the remaining Vikings from Northumbria. In 927, he held a meeting on the banks of the River

**STATUE OF AETHELFLAED WITH YOUNG ATHELSTAN**

Eamont. There he invited tribal leaders from the Welsh-speaking Cumbrians, the English-speaking Northumbrians, and Norse-speaking Scandinavians. All participants of the meeting were required to take an oath "to renounce all idolatry." Here Athelstan was presented for the first time as *rex totius Britanniae*. This title means "the king of the whole of Britain."

During Athelstan's reign, the ancient habits of witchcraft, Odin-worship, superstition, sun worship, and pagan rituals still existed in some parts of the kingdom. Occasionally, heathen ceremonies took place under cover of night. Athelstan set about to end every remnant of pagan religion. As a result, the Christian faith flourished more than ever across England, Wales, Scotland, and Ireland for the next thousand years. Legislating for all the country of England, Athelstan ordered that "with regard to witchcraft and sorcery, and deadly spells, that if it causes death, and the accused is unable to deny it, then his life shall be forfeit." This meant that those who engaged in witchcraft and sorcery could be put to death if they caused death through their demonic practices.

Athelstan's law code further stated, "There shall be no marketing on Sundays. The offender who violates this law will pay the value of the goods, and pay thirty shillings." This meant that Athelstan's law code respected Sunday as a day of rest and worship. It was unlawful to buy and sell on the Lord's Day.

In matters of justice, Athelstan was also known for his moderate treatment of children

**SILVER PENNY FROM THE REIGN OF ATHELSTAN**

in matters like theft and robbery. In those days, young people were sometimes put to death for minor offenses. The administration of justice could be exceedingly harsh. Athelstan's law code was more reflective of what the Bible teaches. Athelstan stated, "The King thinks it cruel to have such young people put to death, and for such minor offenses, even though this is a common practice. Therefore, it is the stated opinion both of the King and of those with whom he has discussed the matter that no one should be put to death who is under fifteen years of age."

Athelstan also cared for the physical well-being of his subjects. On Christmas Day 932, the great king issued a charter requiring all who worked his estates to be sure that no person should ever starve to death. "My wish it is that you should always provide the destitute with food."

Athelstan's reign is one amazing instance of the powerful influence which Christ had upon one nation. The influence of Christianity in Great Britain continued for some thousand years. It is only in recent centuries that this Christian foundation has been attacked.

During the reign of King Athelstan of England, slavery was still imposed on those who had committed crimes. However, Athelstan moved in the direction of more freedom. He recommended that the nobles "every year set at liberty someone that has for his crimes been condemned to slavery." This pardon for crimes was to take place according to the local pastor-bishop's "testimony" and approval.

This shows Athelstan's respect for the role of Christ's church in society.

In time, more efforts would be made to combat slavery. As Christian influence was furthered in the West, the bishops of Worcester and Canterbury, **Wulfstan** (1008-1094) and **Lanfranc** (1010-1089), joined forces to shut down the slave trade in Bristol. **William the Conqueror** finally banned the English slave trade after the Norman invasion of 1066. However, slavery would re-appear in English society in later centuries.

Athelstan's reign is one good example, among many, of European kings and queens who bowed the knee to King Jesus. Athelstan and other monarchs like him confessed that Jesus Christ is Lord. They acknowledged Jesus' saving power. They worshiped Jesus. And they sought to bring the laws of their kingdom into conformity with the Bible. ∎

# PRAYER POINTS: CIVIL RULERS IN EUROPE

Now therefore, be wise, O kings;
Be instructed, you judges of the earth.
Serve the LORD with fear,
And rejoice with trembling.
Kiss the Son, lest He be angry,
And you perish in the way,
When His wrath is kindled but a little.
Blessed are all those who put their trust in Him. (Ps. 2:10-12)

In this Prayer Points, we will pray for civil rulers in Europe.

- **Pray that Kings, Prime Ministers, Governors, and other major leaders in Europe would submit to Jesus Christ as King of kings and Lord of lords:** Let us ask God to bring His salvation to those rulers in Europe who do not acknowledge Jesus Christ as Savior and Lord.

- **Ask God to raise up righteous leaders who fear God:** The fear of the Lord is the beginning of wisdom. Pray that many government leaders in Europe would stand for righteousness, and seek to punish evildoers, as the Bible requires (Rom. 13).

- **Pray that God would remove unrighteous leaders and demolish unjust laws:** Let us also ask the Lord to remove wicked rulers from their place of authority. Pray that God would bring about a repeal of unjust laws.

# 17. ATHELSTAN: FIRST KING OF ENGLAND

CASTLE ON LINDISFARNE

## Basic Facts about England

The United Kingdom consists of the nations of England, Wales, Scotland, and Northern Ireland. The facts below pertain to England, one of the countries within the UK.

| | |
|---|---|
| Total population: | 56 million |
| Total area: | 50,000 square miles |
| Capital: | London |
| Official language: | English |
| Primary religions: | Protestant Christian, Atheist, Agnostic |

COLOGNE CATHEDRAL, COLOGNE, GERMANY

# UNIT 3
## AD 1000-1500

Return, we beseech You, O God of hosts;
Look down from heaven and see,
And visit this vine
And the vineyard which Your right hand has planted,
And the branch that You made strong for Yourself. (Ps. 80:14-15)

Many dark clouds hung over Europe from AD 1000-1500. Tyranny, war, corruption, and disease all made their mark upon this period. Yet, even among much shadow and gloom, the purposes of God were being fulfilled. The light of Christ could not be extinguished.

A major power shift occurred in Great Britain in AD 1066. England was invaded by the Normans. Crossing the English channel from Normandy, the Normans quickly subdued England. **William the Conqueror** began his conquest of England on the southern coast of Great Britain. The decisive confrontation took place at the **Battle of Hastings**. From AD 1066 to 1154, the House of Normandy ruled over England. The Norman Conquest did have an effect upon the English church. The English church was brought more closely under the Roman church's control. The Pope had a greater say in English church life. In fact, William invaded England with Pope Alexander II's approval. Before the Normans conquered England, most English priests were lawfully married. After the Normans took control, priests in England were no longer allowed to marry.

During this period, a series of conflicts occurred between the Christian West and the Muslim world. These wars are known as the **Crusades**. It began in 1095. At the Council of Clermont, Pope Urban II called for the church to support a war against the Turks and other Muslims in the East. The crowd present cried out, *"Deus vult! Deus vult!"* (God wills it! God wills it!).

A series of crusades took place over the next 200 years. The **First Crusade** was the most successful. The crusaders recaptured Jerusalem and a large part of the Holy Land (by AD 1099). Another five crusades followed the first. These wars had varying levels of success. Some ended in terrible defeat for the European armies. At points, Europe did face real threats of Muslim invasion. But sadly, it seems that almost no one thought of taking the gospel to the Muslims. Instead of the sword of God's Word, many in Europe took the physical sword against the Muslims. It wasn't until missionary **Raymond Lull**, that any real effort was made to convert the Muslims to Christ.

Raymond Lull wrote, "I see many knights going to the Holy Land beyond the seas and thinking that they can acquire it by force of arms. But in the end all are destroyed before they attain that which they think to have. It seems to me that the conquest of the Holy Land ought not to be attempted except in the way in which the Apostles acquired it, namely by love and prayers, and the pouring out of tears and blood." In AD 1315, Raymond Lull poured out his blood on Muslim soil as a martyr. He gave his life for Jesus Christ. He was earnest to see the Muslims come to faith in the Savior.

Corruption in the church's doctrine and practice reached new levels during this period. The **Fourth Lateran Council** (AD 1215) was especially damaging. The council argued that it was the church's responsibility not only to punish heretics, but in some cases, to execute them. The council strengthened the work of the **Inquisition**, which sought to punish doctrinal disagreement, in some cases with the sword. This teaching was in error. The church may use the "power of the keys" to excommunicate unbelievers and evildoers from the church. But it is not the responsibility of the state to banish or execute for unbelief or doctrinal error.

Not all that happened during this period was negative. A major victory for freedom in the West was achieved in AD 1215. The **Magna Carta** (the "Great Charter") was signed by King John in England. After numerous tyrannical abuses of power, the barons in England opposed King John. The document detailed the rights of English citizens under the King. Since the document limited church and state power, it was opposed by Pope Innocent III and other kings in England. Nevertheless, the Magna Carta laid essential foundations for freedom in Europe.

The deadliest plague in human history swept over Europe in the mid-1300s. The **Black Death** killed somewhere between one third or even up to one half of Europe's population. During the Black Death, a light began to shine in the darkness with the work of English scholar, **John Wycliffe**. Wycliffe believed that the plague was the judgment of God on a faithless people and a corrupt church. With Wycliffe, others like John Huss, would seek reformation in the church. Reform-minded men such as these would prepare the church for the soon-to-dawn Protestant Reformation of the 1500s.

At the end of the 15th century, **Christopher Columbus** made a discovery that changed the course of world history. In AD 1492, Columbus' voyage to the east Indies resulted in the European discovery of the American continents. The way was opened for the European colonization of the Americas.

# Timeline of Key Events

| | |
|---|---|
| AD 1066 | William the Conqueror invades Great Britain |
| AD 1096 | Beginning of the First Crusade |
| AD 1170 | Peter Waldo begins the Waldensian movement |
| AD 1198-1216 | Pope Innocent III declares himself vicar of Christ on earth |
| AD 1209-1229 | Crusade against the Albigense or Cathars |
| AD 1215 | King Johns signs the Magna Carta |
| AD 1215 | Fourth Lateran Council |
| AD 1271 | Marco Polo begins his voyage to the East |
| AD 1330 | John Wycliffe born |
| AD 1347 | Beginning of the Black Death in Europe |
| AD 1378 | The Great Western Schism (papacy divided) |
| AD 1395 | Wycliffe/Purvey English Bible completed |
| AD 1414-1418 | Council of Constance |
| AD 1415 | John Huss executed at the Council of Constance |
| AD 1453 | Constantinople falls to the Turks |
| AD 1492 | Christopher Columbus discovers the American continents |
| AD 1498 | Girolamo Savonarola executed in Florence |

CARCASSONNE, FRANCE

# THE CRUSADE AGAINST THE CATHARS

Since the time of our Lord's ascension, the church of Jesus Christ has advanced throughout the world. The advance of the church is not without conflict. There are enemies outside the church. And there are sins, heresies, and divisions that afflict the church from within. The church on earth is fighting in a spiritual battle. Because of this, there is no Christian church on earth that is perfect. No church is wholly without sin or error. None of Christ's people will be perfect before the day of His return.

In certain periods of church history, the truth of the gospel has blazed forth with remarkable clarity. These are times of reformation and revival. At other times, the light of the gospel has been significantly dimmed. The dimming occurs when God's Word is not faithfully proclaimed. It also occurs because of heresy and division in the church. Sometimes it might look like the church is in retreat. At other times, the church appears to advance. Whatever the appearance may be, our Lord Jesus promised that the gates of hell will collapse as the church marches on (Matt. 16:18).

Numerous missionaries worked very hard to bring the gospel into Britain and the rest of Europe from AD 400 to 1000. King Jesus did amazing things. The Christian faith brought remarkable shifts in culture to every man, woman, boy, and girl living in Europe. Of course, these years of missionary advance were not without sin, heresy, and conflict. But much good was done during this time. In the 10th century, things began to change. For the next six hundred years, the church in Europe would experience a decline like nothing else in history to that point.

## TYRANNY AND CORRUPTION IN THE CHURCH

> For the time will come when they will not endure sound doctrine, but according to their own desires, because they have itching ears, they will heap up for themselves teachers; and they will turn their ears away from the truth, and be turned aside to fables. (2 Tim. 4:3-4)

Between AD 955 and 1517, the European church became filled with error and corruption. As the power of the papacy continued its rise, corruption came with it. Pastors or bishops were no longer chosen because they were godly. Instead, they were chosen because they were rich. Church offices were often sold to the highest bidder. This practice was known as "**simony**." The popes of the Roman Church would go so far as to kill people they didn't like. The popes began to assume political power over kings and national governments. **Pope Innocent III** (Pope from AD 1198-1216) was probably the most powerful pope ever. He assumed the title "**vicar of Christ**" (the earthly representative of Christ). He even claimed that he was the visible manifestation of Christ on earth, exercising Christ's authority over the whole world. He claimed: "The Lord Jesus Christ has established one sovereign [the pope] over all as His universal vicar, whom all things in heaven and hell should obey, even as they bow the knee to Christ." This man truly believed he was the ruler of the world as the representative of Christ.

The Bible didn't create this powerful structure in the church. In fact, Peter called himself an "elder" just like the other elders and pastors in the church. It is true that Peter, as an apostle, held unique authority. But when he wrote to the churches in Cappadocia, he appealed to the elders as "a fellow elder."

> The elders who are among you I exhort, I who am a fellow elder and a witness of the sufferings of Christ, and also a partaker of the glory that will be revealed. (1 Pet. 5:1)

Peter does not present himself as a pope over the whole church. He taught that both elder and apostles were under the chief Shepherd, our Lord Jesus Christ.

Putting too much power in the hands of one man is a recipe for disaster. **Lord Acton** famously stated that "absolute power corrupts absolutely [or completely]." The truth of Lord Acton's proverb was vindicated time and time again during this period of the church. In time, this power-hungry church began to persecute people who did not conform at every point to the thinking of the Roman Church. This absolute power wielded by church leaders turned dangerous, and many people were killed as a consequence.

## THE CATHAR HERESY

> For many deceivers have gone out into the world who do not confess Jesus Christ as coming in the flesh. This is a deceiver and an antichrist. Look to yourselves, that we do not lose those things we worked for, but that we may receive a full reward. (2 John 7-8)

Members of the church witnessed the tyranny and corruption of the church. As a result, many were attracted to promises of change and renewal. But not every renewal movement was healthy. Insofar as Holy Scripture was the guide, movements of change in the church were healthier. The **Waldensian movement**, which you will learn about in the next chapter, had many healthy elements. But the **Cathar movement**, studied in this chapter, was truly a heresy. The Cathars radically departed from the Christian faith. For this reason, this movement did not bring health to the church.

In the late 1100s, a new movement originated in southern France. The people involved in it were called the **Albigenses** because many of them came from the town of Albi, France. They were also called the **Cathars** (a Greek word meaning "pure ones"). Though the Cathars pursued purity, their doctrine and practice were not biblically pure. Sadly, these people radically departed from the Christian faith.

The Cathars held to an unbiblical view of God. They claimed that the physical world was not created by a good god. Instead, they taught that the world was created by an evil force. Because of this, they viewed physical things (like the human body, trees, or animals) as corrupt. The Cathars weren't very concerned about being saved from sin and death. Instead, they wanted to be saved from a physical existence. This is quite different than the teaching of the Bible. In biblical teaching, Jesus destroys all death (spiritual and physical) through His death and resurrection. And, according to 1 Corinthians 15, we look forward to the resurrection of our physical bodies.

The Cathars did not see it this way. They taught that the soul had been kidnapped by Satan. The physical body was just Satan's prison house. They also taught that Christ did not have a physical body and that He never died on the cross. This rejection of the biblical doctrine of Christ comes under the direct condemnation of Scripture. For example, in 1 John, we read:

> By this you know the Spirit of God: Every spirit that confesses that Jesus Christ has come in the flesh is of God, and every spirit that does not confess that Jesus Christ has come in the flesh is not of God. And this is the spirit of the Antichrist, which you have heard was coming, and is now already in the world. (1 John 4:2-3)

Because they viewed the physical world as evil, the Cathars would frequently fast. They would avoid certain foods like eggs, milk, and cheese. They believed these foods were particularly tainted with corruption. However, because the Cathars were still in physical bodies, they had to eat something. In between frequent fasts, they would eat foods like wine and fish. Paul warned about such false and dangerous doctrines in 1 Timothy 4:

> Now the Spirit expressly says that in latter times some will depart from the faith, giving heed to deceiving spirits and doctrines of demons, speaking lies in hypocrisy, having their own conscience seared with a hot iron, forbidding to marry, and commanding to abstain from foods which God created to be received with thanksgiving by those who believe and know the truth. (1 Tim. 4:1-3)

The Cathars also rejected the sacraments of the church. They isolated themselves from the church and avoided all public worship. The people within this heretical movement believed that they alone were the true disciples of Christ. They thought no one could be saved unless they believed everything the Cathars did.

ALBI, FRANCE

# TAKING EUROPE FOR JESUS

**POPE INNOCENT III**

The Cathar movement grew rapidly. It soon had a strong grip on southern France. At first, church leaders tried to persuade the Cathars to return to the church. But these efforts did not make much progress. When missionary efforts to the Cathars failed, the Roman Church turned to the use of the sword to stop this false teaching. Pope Innocent III initiated a crusade against the Cathars. He gave these people only two options: (1) reject Cathar teachings or (2) die. By turning to the power of the sword, the church gave up God's appointed means of combating false teaching: the preaching of the Word of God. We shouldn't use the sword to force people to stop believing wrong teaching. The Apostle Paul tells Timothy to continue to patiently correct false doctrine and preach the truth. We should do the same. Then we should wait for God to grant repentance.

---

And a servant of the Lord must not quarrel but be gentle to all, able to teach, patient, in humility correcting those who are in opposition, if God perhaps will grant them repentance, so that they may know the truth, and that they may

**VINEYARDS IN SOUTHERN FRANCE**

come to their senses and escape the snare of the devil, having been taken captive by him to do his will. (2 Tim. 2:24-26)

Pope Innocent III promised eternal rewards to those who would join the crusade against the Cathar heretics. Innocent's offer was an attractive one. Thousands participated in the bloodshed. Over a period of twenty years (AD 1209-1229), the Cathars were systematically wiped out. This crusade was one of the most atrocious acts in European history. The Crusaders attacked the cities in southern France, killing men, women, and children. They even killed some of those who were faithful to the Christian church simply because they lived in the same city as that inhabited by the Cathars. Before the crusade, this region known as **Languedoc** was a prosperous and beautiful land. After two decades of bloodshed, Languedoc lay in ruins. Pope Innocent III's goal was largely achieved—the

**THE SIEGE OF TOULOUSE IN 1218**

**LOCATION OF LANGUEDOC PROVINCE WITHIN FRANCE**

heresy was almost completely eliminated from southern France.

The crusade against the Cathars would be a major driving factor in what became known as the **Inquisition**. This was the horrible Medieval court which pursued those who didn't agree with the Roman Catholic Church, sometimes resorting to torture and execution. A major doctrinal error that drove this crusade was the unbiblical idea that the church held the power of the sword. God didn't give His church the power of the sword. The church of Jesus Christ is entrusted with the keys of Christ's kingdom. These keys are exercised through the proclamation of the gospel and church discipline (Matt. 16:18-19; 18:15-20). The church can excommunicate heretics or unrepentant sinners (1 Cor. 5:1-13). But the church is not given the duty to execute heretics.

In Matthew 13, the Lord Jesus taught a

**184** TAKING EUROPE FOR JESUS

ILLUSTRATION OF THE ALBIGENSIAN CRUSADE

> No, lest while you gather up the tares you also uproot the wheat with them. Let both grow together until the harvest, and at the time of harvest I will say to the reapers, "First gather together the tares and bind them in bundles to burn them, but gather the wheat into my barn." (Matt. 13:29-30)

parable often called the Parable of the Wheat and Tares. In this parable, the Lord likens the kingdom of heaven to a field. In that field there are both wheat and tares. Good seed is sowed in the field. But the enemy (Satan, the evil one) comes and spreads tares in the field. When the servants ask the master, "Do you want us then to go and gather up the tares?" the master responds:

The final sorting out of wheat and tares in the kingdom of God will happen at the final judgment. This isn't our job to do. When the Lord Jesus returns, all heretics and evildoers will be judged. And the wheat (God's true people) will be gathered into the barn. These matters aren't in the hands of the church. They are in the hands of the chief Shepherd, Jesus Christ. ∎

## Basic Facts about France

| Total population: | 67 million |
|---|---|
| Total area: | 247,000 square miles |
| Capital: | Paris |
| Official language: | French |
| Primary religions: | Roman Catholic, Atheist, Islam |

# PRAYER POINTS: FRANCE

- **Pray for dead hearts to be awakened to the things of God:** Since the radically secular French Revolution of 1789, France has been one of the most secular nations in Europe. Yet, like most nations in Europe, it has a Christian heritage that goes back almost to the beginning of Christianity. It is estimated that only six percent of the population in France attend church on a weekly basis. Most French people are "without God and without hope in the world" (Eph. 2:12). Ask the Lord to awaken dead hearts to the things of God. Pray that God would send forth faithful Christians who would share God's Word with the unbelievers of France.

- **Pray in light of changing demographics:** The population of France is changing. Many immigrants, especially from Muslim backgrounds, are now living in France in greater numbers than ever before. The birth rate among French families is falling. This likely means that in the future, more people in France will be born with a heritage from a nation elsewhere in the world, especially from Muslim nations. Pray that God would use this change in France as an opportunity for the gospel to penetrate both into the French people as well as the foreign immigrants now in France.

- **Pray against the forces of darkness in France:** *Operation World* reports that there are ten times more people earning a living by occult practices (witchcraft and sorcery) than there are evangelical pastors in France. This means that for every ten people actively practicing occultic rituals, there is just one Bible-believing pastor. Pray against the demonic forces that are bringing destruction to the people of France. Pray that God would raise up more faithful missionaries and pastors in France.

PIEDMONT REGION, ITALY

# THE WALDENSIAN MOVEMENT

Blessed is the man
Who walks not in the counsel of the ungodly,
Nor stands in the path of sinners,
Nor sits in the seat of the scornful;
But his delight is in the law of the LORD,
And in His law he meditates day and night.
He shall be like a tree
Planted by the rivers of water,
That brings forth its fruit in its season,
Whose leaf also shall not wither;
And whatever he does shall prosper. (Ps. 1:1-3)

In the last chapter, we learned about the Cathars. They were known for their radical denial of the most foundational truths of Christianity. Because of their heresies, the Cathars were heavily persecuted by the authorities in the Roman Catholic Church. The Cathars were not the only major "dissent" movement around this time. In AD 1170, another movement took root in the region of modern-day France. This is known as the **Waldensian** movement. The Waldensians were much more biblical than the Cathars in their beliefs and practices. Their effort to reestablish a faithful church is a noteworthy story in Europe's Christian history.

## PETER WALDO

The Waldensian movement began in the city of Lyons (pronounced "Lee-awn"). We learned about Lyons in a previous chapter. This was the city where Irenaeus was once a pastor. In 1170, a wealthy merchant named Pierre Valdes lived in Lyons. Pierre's name is often written in English as **Peter Waldo**. Little is known about this man. But there is a traditional story concerning Peter Waldo's spiritual awakening. This is how the story is recorded in history.

One day, one of the leading men of Lyons died unexpectedly. This sudden passing awakened Waldo. It reminded him that life is short and that he could die at any time. He consulted a priest. "What should I do to follow Christ?" he asked. The priest read to Waldo the account of the rich young ruler in the Bible. In that story, the Lord Jesus told the rich young ruler to sell all that he had and to follow Him.

Jesus said to him, "If you want to be perfect, go, sell what you have and give to the poor, and you will have treasure in heaven; and come, follow Me." (Matt. 19:21)

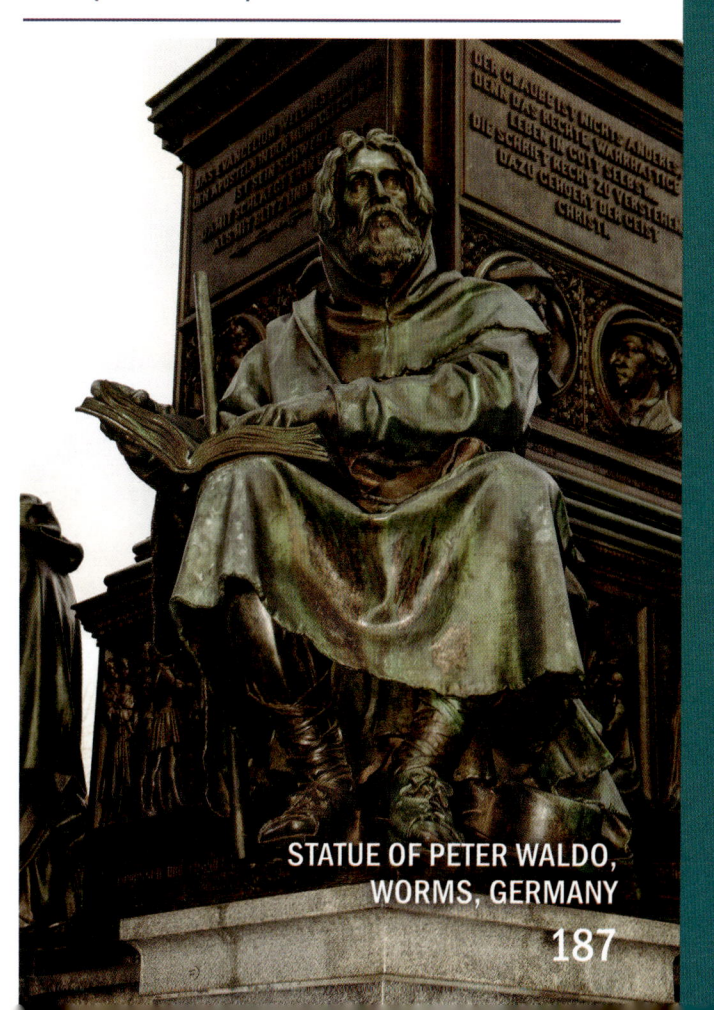

STATUE OF PETER WALDO, WORMS, GERMANY

Waldo followed the priest's counsel. He distributed his goods to the poor. He began to read the Bible. He commissioned a few men to translate parts of the Gospels into the common tongue spoken in Lyons. He was burdened to share the word of Christ with others. Waldo began preaching in the streets of Lyons. Soon, others joined him in a life of poverty and preaching. The movement grew rapidly.

From the beginning, the Waldensian movement had three common characteristics: poverty, preaching, and obedience to the word of Christ. Those following Waldo became known as "**the poor of Lyons**." The Waldensians retained this title for centuries. Others called them "Waldensians." However, it took a few hundred years before the Waldensians used this name themselves. They did not wish to be called by the name of one man.

The Waldensians were considered strange and dangerous by many. Authorities in Lyons and in the surrounding region began to oppose them. During that time, men who were part of the priesthood were the only ones who were allowed to preach. It was not lawful for anyone else to proclaim the Bible in a public place. Additionally, the church considered it inappropriate for laypeople to read and interpret the Bible for themselves. The Waldensians did not submit to these rules. Both men and women of the Waldensians proclaimed the Bible in the streets. They also translated and shared portions of the Bible with the common people.

Eventually, local authorities commanded Peter Waldo to stop preaching. But he refused to submit. He, with his other followers, believed it to be their obligation to keep on preaching. Because he refused to submit, Peter Waldo was excommunicated from the church in 1182. Then, at the **Council of Verona** in 1184, all Waldensians were declared to be heretics. In the church's eyes, the Waldensians were just as bad as the Cathars. After the declaration of 1184, things became more difficult and more dangerous for the Waldensians.

## WALDENSIAN BELIEFS AND PRACTICES

What did the Waldensians believe? Were they true Christians? Or did they reject the true faith like the Cathars?

The Waldensians loved to read and memorize the Bible. Peter Waldo and his followers believed the Bible was the final and only infallible authority. Because of this, their beliefs and practices were often faithful to Scripture. But they did have some wrong beliefs too. They tended to emphasize the New Testament more than the Old Testament. Also, the Waldensians did not always have access to the entirety of

A PICTURE OF WALDENSIANS PORTRAYED AS WITCHES. THE WALDENSIANS WERE ACCUSED OF MANY UNTRUE CHARGES.

**WALDENSIAN CHURCH IN ROME, THE ITALIAN "CHIESA VALDESE" WHICH MEANS "WALDENSIAN CHURCH" IN ENGLISH**

the Bible in their native language. Because of this, they sometimes were wrong about certain doctrines. The **Protestant Reformation** (in the 1500s) brought further progress in understanding the Bible.

The Waldensians did see that many Roman Catholic beliefs were in error. They rejected some Roman Catholic teaching, including the authority of the pope, purgatory, prayers for the dead, and indulgences.

The Waldensians also held other unique views. They refused to take oaths of any kind. They believed that Jesus forbids Christians to take oaths when He said:

> Again you have heard that it was said to those of old, "You shall not swear falsely, but shall perform your oaths to the Lord." But I say to you, do not swear at all. (Matt. 5:33-34)

The Waldensians also opposed the death penalty. They misunderstood the Bible and thought God didn't want rulers to execute anyone. But in this case, they never had the ability to implement their perspective. Waldensians were never in civil power. They were frequently at the other end of the sword at different times in history.

Some of the things the Waldensians believed were not correct. Not all of their practices and doctrines had firm Biblical rooting. However, their respect for Scripture was noteworthy and commendable in its time. In many ways, the Waldensian movement was a preview of the Protestant Reformation.

## PERSECUTION AND DISPERSION

Waldensian teaching spread far and wide from Lyons. It spread to Languedoc, Spain, Austria, and Germany. After the Cathars, the Waldensian movement was the second-largest movement to separate from the Roman Church. Because they loved God's Word, the Waldensians shared it with others. Some Waldensians infiltrated the universities of Europe and converted people to the Faith. Other Waldensians traveled as poor merchants and built relationships with others through buying and selling.

The Roman Church did not see much difference between the Waldensians and the Cathars. They saw them as equally dangerous. Both Cathars and Waldensians were a threat to the pope's authority. The Cathars were mostly wiped out by violent attack. By God's sovereign protection, the Waldensians still exist to this day.

After most of the Cathars were wiped out, church leaders turned their attention to the Waldensians. They were now the primary target. As persecution increased, the Waldensian movement also changed.

The poor of Lyons remained committed to evangelism. But when evangelism meant death, what was a father to do? What about his family? Many Waldensians were faced with this question: should I convert others, or should I pass on my faith within my family in order to survive? These were challenging questions.

The Waldensian movement became more secretive in many parts of Europe. The movement continued to spread quietly, but there was not as much street preaching as at the beginning. Waldensian evangelism began to happen in private conversations rather than in public places.

Another difficulty faced by the Waldensians occurred when they were discovered and put on trial. Those on trial were called to take an oath and answer whether they were Waldensians or not. Because of their unique belief about oaths, the Waldensian on trial would not take an oath. This immediately revealed their convictions. Likewise, their refusal to pray to the saints or participate in certain religious holidays made it difficult to hide their convictions.

If the Waldensians were to survive, they needed a place of refuge. Many of them hid in the rocky crags of the Alps in northern Italy. The region of northern Italy known as **Piedmont** became the center of the Waldensian community. To this day, there are many Waldensians still living in the Piedmont region.

For over three hundred years, the Waldensians faced persecutions from the Roman Church and other state authorities. Sometimes they were ignored, and they would increase for a generation or so. But eventually, they were to face another assault. During the crusade against the Cathars, a number of Waldensians were caught up in the bloodbath and were executed. In 1487, another pope named **Innocent VIII** (Pope from 1484-1492) planned to wipe out the poor of Lyons. Inspired by his predecessor **Innocent III** (Pope from 1198-1216), he called for another attack on the Waldensians living in Piedmont. Again, a great many

**REGION OF PIEDMONT, ITALY**

were killed. Waldensians were scattered as far as the Netherlands, Germany, Poland, Bohemia (modern-day Czech Republic), and England. Eventually, reformation would occur in these same areas in the 1500s.

## WALDENSIANS JOIN THE REFORMATION

Oh, bless our God, you peoples!
And make the voice of His praise to be heard,
Who keeps our soul among the living,
And does not allow our feet to be moved.
(Ps. 66:8-9)

The Protestant Reformation came first to Germany. It then spread to Switzerland, France, and England. Many of the Waldensians joined the Protestant churches in France and Germany. Joining the Reformation meant the Waldensians left behind certain beliefs. The Protestant Reformers taught that Jesus Christ instituted only two sacraments. Those two sacraments or ordinances are baptism and the Lord's Supper. The Roman Catholic Church believed there were seven sacraments. The Waldensians previously agreed with the Roman Catholic Church. But when the Reformation began, they adopted this Protestant view of two sacraments.

Also, the Reformation teaching of justification by faith alone was new to the Waldensians. It took some time for them to understand and embrace biblical teaching on justification. The Reformers made it their aim to reform biblical doctrine and practice using the entire Bible. But for centuries, the Waldensians had primarily drawn from the New Testament. And certain parts of the New Testament were neglected by them. This began to change as they learned from **Martin Luther**, **John Calvin**, **Martin Bucer**, and others.

The Waldensians also joined the Reformers in producing a French Bible. This Bible trans-

**JOHN CALVIN (1509-1564)**

lation became a vital tool in spreading the faith. For the first time, the Waldensians also produced a confession of faith. Eventually, most of the Waldensians were integrated into the Reformed churches of Switzerland, France, and Germany.

This rising Reformation, joined with the Waldensian movement, provoked a violent reaction from **King Francis I** of France. In January 1545, the king assembled an army to attack the Waldensian believers living in Provence, France. The massacre resulted in hundreds of deaths. Twenty to thirty villages were completely destroyed.

The worst was yet to come, however. The Duke of Savoy led an army against Piedmont in 1655. He gave the Waldensians twenty days to attend Catholic mass or leave all their possessions behind and flee Piedmont. The Walden-

O'er all th' Italian fields where still doth sway
The triple tyrant; that from these may grow
A hundredfold, who having learnt thy way
Early may fly the Babylonian woe.

Despite many persecutions, the Waldensians continued steadfastly in the faith. While European Christianity was breaking down and darkness prevailed, this small group of Christians kept the light burning for three hundred years. This was how the Lord preserved the faith in Europe between 1175 and 1517. ■

---

**Then they will deliver you up to tribulation and kill you, and you will be hated by all nations for My name's sake. And then many will be offended, will betray one another, and will hate one another. . . . But he who endures to the end shall be saved. (Matt. 24:9-13)**

---

**KING FRANCIS I (REIGNED FROM 1515-1547)**

sians refused to convert to the Roman Church, so the duke and his army proceeded to slaughter 2,000 men, women, and children. News of these horrible killings spread throughout Europe. People responded with outrage and grief. The English poet, **John Milton** (1608-1674), wrote a poem about this event. In the poem, Milton prayed for God's vengeance.

> Avenge, O Lord, thy slaughtered saints, whose bones
> Lie scattered on the Alpine mountains cold,
> Even them who kept thy truth so pure of old,
> When all our fathers worshiped stocks and stones;
> Forget not: in thy book record their groans
> Who were thy sheep and in their ancient fold
> Slain by the bloody Piedmontese that rolled
> Mother with infant down the rocks. Their moans
> The vales redoubled to the hills, and they
> To Heaven. Their martyred blood and ashes sow

**JOHN MILTON (1608-1674)**

# PRAYER POINTS: ITALY

- **Thank God for the Christian heritage of Italy:** Godly pastors and faithful churches were planted here in the first centuries of the church. Thank the Lord for what He has done in the past in Italy. It was to Rome, Italy that Paul wrote his inspired letter (Romans) that continues to change the world. From Italy, the message of the gospel went forth into other parts of Europe.

- **Pray for Biblical reformation in Italy:** The seat of the Roman Catholic Church is in Rome, the capital city of Italy. For this reason, Italy has long been dominated by the Roman Catholic Church. Today, about 85% of Italians profess some kind of connection to the Roman Church. In contrast, only about half of 1 percent of the Italian population describes itself as Protestant. Italy never experienced the fruits of the Protestant Reformation like other parts of Europe. But if God so wills, that Reformation could come to Italy in our generation. Let us pray that the church would be reformed in Italy.

- **Pray for the light of the Gospel to overcome secularism:** Like many nations in modern Europe, Italy is becoming more secular. This means that increasingly, many citizens of Italy do not believe in any religion. They may be atheists (those who do not believe in the existence of any God) or agnostics (those who don't know or care about God's existence). A godless view of the world is one of the strategies Satan uses to send people to hell. A secular worldview among many in Europe makes them indifferent to the things of God. Pray that Christ would once again send His light into Europe and awaken dead hearts.

## Basic Facts about Italy

*The Waldensians were first based in the region of modern-day France. However, in later centuries, the movement was largely centered in Piedmont. This is a mountainous region in northwestern Italy.*

| | |
|---|---|
| Total population: | 60 million |
| Total area: | 116,000 square miles |
| Capital: | Rome |
| Official language: | Italian |
| Primary religions: | Roman Catholic |

ST. PANCRAS CHURCH, KINGSTON NEAR LEWES, EAST SUSSEX, ENGLAND

# THE BLACK DEATH

> For the time has come for judgment to begin at the house of God; and if it begins with us first, what will be the end of those who do not obey the gospel of God? (1 Pet. 4:17)

The history of God's world is filled with God's acts of judgment and salvation. The Lord's reign over all things should cause us both to rejoice (Ps. 97:1) and also to tremble (Ps. 99:1). As we behold the judgments of God in the earth, we should respond in reverent fear. Also, when we see suffering and death in this world, it reminds us of the terrible consequences of sin. This should make us pray, "Come, Lord Jesus." We long for the day when every tear will be wiped from our eyes and death will be no more (Rev. 21:3-4). Thanks be to God that in Jesus Christ, death is defeated. All those who have put their trust in Jesus join in that victory. Death has no sting for the Christian. The Word of God declares, "to be absent from the body [is] to be present with the Lord" (2 Cor. 5:8).

It is important to remember these biblical truths as we learn something about one of the most devastating events in European history. The mid-1300s was unlike any other time in Europe's history. A terrible, deadly plague swept through the entirety of Europe. The plague was known as the **Black Death**. This was among the deadliest epidemics in world history. It is estimated that around one third or even up to one half of Europe's population died from this scourge.

Before we turn to the specific events of the plague, we need to understand other important events in European history.

KUBLAI KHAN (1215-1294)

GENGHIS KHAN (1158-1227)

195

## THE EXPLORATIONS OF MARCO POLO

In the late Middle Ages (1250-1500), exploration and trade to other parts of the world increased. One important explorer was **Marco Polo** (c. 1254-1324) of Venice, Italy. Polo was only a teenager when he left for China with his father and uncle who had traded with the East for many years. Their travels throughout China lasted for seventeen years. Many of those years were spent in the service of the Great **Kublai Khan** (1215-1294). Kublai Khan was the Mongol emperor and grandson of the Mongol conqueror **Genghis Khan** (1158-1227).

When the Polos returned to Europe, they had been gone for so long that at first hardly anyone recognized them. When the explorers were invited to a banquet held in their honor, they shocked their hosts with a dramatic display. They held knives to their chests and slashed open their cloaks. Around their necks hung a wealth of diamonds and other jewels. The Polos had brought back numerous foreign treasures. The guests were dazzled by the display.

Their fame was instantly established. In addition to great wealth, Marco Polo brought back something far more valuable: a tale of his adventures in a faraway and mysterious land. His exploits were published as *The Book of Sir Marco Polo Concerning the Kingdoms and Marvels of the East*, or simply *The Travels of Marco Polo*. Soon all of Europe was burning with curiosity about the world beyond its small, familiar communities. Trade routes to the East opened Europe's eyes to the great wealth of China and other Asian countries including Japan, Siam (Thailand), Tibet, India, Burma, and Ceylon (Sri Lanka). As Europeans clamored for luxury goods from the East, traders and seamen dreamed of wealth beyond the waves.

## THE PLAGUE STRIKES EUROPE

> When He opened the fourth seal, I heard the voice of the fourth living creature saying, "Come and see." So I looked, and behold, a pale horse. And the name of him who sat on it was Death, and Hades followed with him. And power was given to them over a fourth of the earth, to kill with sword, with hunger, with death, and by the beasts of the earth. (Rev. 6:7-8)

In God's providence, traders imported more than just treasures from the East. They unknowingly carried to European ports rats infested with plague-ridden fleas. The Black Death began its march of destruction through Europe in 1347. The plague killed tens of millions of people. Historians are divided on what percentage of Europe's population died during the epidemic. Estimates vary from between one third and one half of the entire European population. There is no way to know the

MARCO POLO (C. 1254-1324)

**SPREAD OF THE BLACK DEATH**

exact number. But firsthand accounts from this period certainly reinforce a very high percentage. No war has ever claimed so many lives as the Black Death.

The plague may have spread as the Mongols expanded their trade routes across Asia to the city of Constantinople. In addition, European traders brought disease into the docks of Genoa, Naples, Venice in Italy, Marseilles in France, and other Mediterranean port cities. Merchants from these cities unknowingly took the plague home with them and infected their families. For people in northern Europe such as England, the plague remained far away for a time. News reports came from southern Europe about the terrible plague, but people hoped it would not reach the shores of Great Britain. Eventually, however, it did. There was almost no part of Europe that was untouched by the deadly pestilence.

The **Bubonic Plague**, also known as the Black Death, gets its name from the swelling of the lymph nodes or buboes. It was called the "black death" because of the black blotches which appeared on the skin. The disease was initially transmitted to humans by fleas from infected rats, not from human contact. The Black Plague later affected the lungs and changed to "pneumonic plague," spreading rapidly from person to person without the need of fleas as carriers. The death rate was so high that at times there weren't enough people left alive to bury all the dead. Half the population died in Avignon, France, where the pope lived. The pope consecrated the Rhine River to permit corpses to be thrown into it for a mass burial.

The bustling cities of Europe provided a perfect environment for the rapid spread of the plague. The epidemic was especially severe because of the people's low resistance to disease in general. Malnutrition made them particularly vulnerable to new illnesses. Poor sanitation made matters worse. The results of the plague were evident everywhere. As a

**JOHN WYCLIFFE (1330-1384)**

response, many fled the cities to find refuge in smaller villages where they hoped to avoid infection. Even still, most villages at some point or another experienced an outbreak. Crops were left to rot in the fields, and farm animals were left to die. One pastor in the English countryside wrote an eyewitness account of how the plague affected the more sparsely populated parts of England. Henry Knighton of Leicester wrote: "In this same year, a great number of sheep died throughout the whole country, so much so that in one field alone more than five thousand sheep were slain. Their bodies were so corrupted by the plague that neither beast nor bird would touch them." Fields remained unplowed and unplanted. A dramatic decrease of food production drove prices for basic necessities sky high.

It is not surprising that religious leaders believed this was the end of the world. By 1348, the plague had crossed the English Channel into England. In less than a year, half the population of London (some 100,000 persons) had been wiped out. Two thirds of the students at Oxford University died. One gravestone tells the tale:

> Was it not sad and painful to relate
> I died with thirteen of my house on the same date?

In that same year, an English ship carried the pestilence to Iceland where half the population perished. The following year, plague broke out in Norway and destroyed two thirds of its population. Sweden also was affected. By the end of 1350, one third of Europe's entire population had died.

As the plague ravaged Europe, church leaders called God's people to repent for their sins and turn back to God in faith. For example, Archbishop Zouche of York wrote to the people of his city in July 1348, urging them to call upon God. The plague was threatening England. The archbishop wrote:

> Almighty God sometimes allows those whom He loves to be chastened. This is so that their strength can be made complete by the outpouring of spiritual grace in their time of infirmity. Everyone knows, since the news is now widely spread, what great pestilence, mortality and infection of the air there are in various parts of the world. At this moment, the pestilence threatens the land of England. This surely must be caused by the sins of men who, made complacent by their prosperity, forget the bounty of the Most High Giver.

In 1350, King Magnus II of Sweden gave a similar statement. He made a proclamation to his people, saying:

> God for the sins of men has struck the world with this great punishment of sudden death. By it most of the people in the land to the west of our country are dead. It is now ravaging Norway and Holland and is

approaching our kingdom of Sweden.

The king urged the Swedes to fast and pray, begging God to be merciful to their kingdom.

One chronicler in one of the English monasteries described his experience this way:

> This plague slew Jew, Christian, and Muslim alike. It filled the whole world with terror. So great an epidemic has never been seen nor heard of before this time, for it is believed that even the waters of the flood which happened in the days of Noah did not carry off so vast a multitude.

The Black Death did not kill nearly the percentage of people that Noah's flood did (100% except for Noah and his family). However, this contemporary account does give us a sense for how dire the times were.

After 1350, the plague in Europe began to abate. Nevertheless, outbreaks of the bubonic plague would continue to appear occasionally in the centuries that followed. The disease still exists in some parts of the world today.

In the midst of the Black Death, a light began to shine in the darkness with the work of a brilliant English scholar, John Wycliffe (1330-1384). Wycliffe believed that the plague was the judgment of God on a faithless people and a corrupt church. He charged his audience to turn back to the Bible and to God in repentance. To Wycliffe's story, we turn next. ∎

## PRAYER POINTS

In this Prayer Points, we will pray in light of the resurrection hope we have in Jesus Christ. First Corinthians 15 teaches:

> So when this corruptible has put on incorruption, and this mortal has put on immortality, then shall be brought to pass the saying that is written: "Death is swallowed up in victory." "O Death, where is your sting? O Hades, where is your victory?" The sting of death is sin, and the strength of sin is the law. But thanks be to God, who gives us the victory through our Lord Jesus Christ. (1 Cor. 15:54-57)

- **Let us praise our Lord Jesus for overcoming sin and death:** No matter what suffering we may encounter in this life, we can praise Jesus Christ for overcoming sin and death for us! And we can look forward to the day of resurrection with confidence. Give thanks to our Lord Jesus Christ for accomplishing so great a salvation for us.

- **Let us pray that we would fear God:** The fear of the Lord is the beginning of wisdom (Prov. 1:7). Let us remember that our God is a Holy God whose name is to be hallowed. When we see the judgments of God, let us fear Him. Let us acknowledge Him. Let us praise Him.

- **Give thanks for deliverance from the fear of death:** Hebrews 2:15 says that Jesus came to set us free from the fear of death. We should not fear death because Jesus has overcome death. We know that one day our bodies will be raised to new life, and we will live forever with Christ. Let us thank Jesus for this deliverance and ask for faith to believe the promises of the Bible.

OXFORD, ENGLAND

# JOHN WYCLIFFE AND THE LOLLARDS

> And so we have the prophetic word confirmed, which you do well to heed as a light that shines in a dark place, until the day dawns and the morning star rises in your hearts; knowing this first, that no prophecy of Scripture is of any private interpretation, for prophecy never came by the will of man, but holy men of God spoke as they were moved by the Holy Spirit. (2 Pet. 1:19-21)

In some of the northernmost regions of the world, the light of the sun will not appear for up to thirty days. When the sun does not shine at all, temperatures drop to extreme levels of cold. Plants cannot grow. Without the light of the sun, there is no life.

In a similar way, when the light of God's Word does not shine, the church suffers. From a spiritual standpoint, the late Middle Ages (1300s to 1500s) are much like those thirty long days of night. For too long, the clarifying, penetrating, life-giving power of God's Word was hidden. For too long, God's people did not hear the Bible preached faithfully. For too long, priests and popes lived for themselves rather than to feed God's flock.

In the mid-1300s, a sliver of light dawned in England. In the university town of Oxford, a man named **John Wycliffe** (1330-1384) called God's people to read the Bible, preach the Bible, practice the Bible, and love the Bible. Wycliffe believed the church had gone astray on many matters of faith and practice. In order to equip the church to know the Bible, he labored to translate the Scriptures into English. Through writing, preaching, and translating, Wycliffe became known as **"the morning star of the Reformation."** He is known by this title because he prepared the way for the Protestant Reformation of the 1500s.

## WYCLIFFE BECOMES CONTROVERSIAL

At age fifteen, Wycliffe attended Oxford to study. This was around the year 1345. He spent many years at Oxford. However, his studies were interrupted by the repeated waves of the Black Death. From 1349 to 1353, Oxford lost many of its residents to the dreaded plague. After graduating as a theology student, Wycliffe remained at Oxford. He spent his time teaching, writing, and preaching. He was also ordained a priest.

As Wycliffe taught and preached, his views became increasingly different from the church of that age. Some considered what he was teaching to be heresy. Wycliffe was repeat-

**JOHN WYCLIFFE (1330-1384)**

edly summoned by civil and church authorities to answer for his doctrine. In February 1377, **Bishop Courtney** summoned Wycliffe to London. Courtney demanded Wycliffe to give an answer for his views. But Wycliffe had many who supported him. Among those supporters was **John of Gaunt**. This man was the son of King Edward III. John of Gaunt protected Wycliffe from any harm.

Only months later, in May 1377, **Pope Gregory XI** (Pope from 1370-1378) commanded Wycliffe to appear in Rome. Wycliffe was charged with teaching false doctrine. But Wycliffe did not believe he had to obey the pope's demands. He refused to go. Even though he refused, the English authorities did not do anything about this. God protected Wycliffe.

A third attempt was made to stop Wycliffe. In January 1378, the archbishop of Canterbury sought to hold a trial to condemn Wycliffe. But a large mob supporting Wycliffe put a stop to the meeting. Wycliffe frequently condemned immoral leaders. This gained him popular support from English citizens. He became a national hero of sorts.

**Heresy** • A belief or practice contrary to sound biblical doctrine. The Bible warns about destructive heresies in 2 Peter 2:1.

BALLIOL COLLEGE, OXFORD

## 21. JOHN WYCLIFFE AND THE LOLLARDS

## WYCLIFFE'S TEACHINGS

What was it that made John Wycliffe so controversial? Why did popes and other church leaders condemn him? The answer can be found by examining Wycliffe's teachings. Wycliffe's sermons and writings taught the truth of the Scriptures even when this truth contradicted what the church of his day was teaching. Much of what he taught would make its appearance again during the Protestant Reformation. That is why Wycliffe earned the title "the morning star."

In 1378, a significant event in church history occurred. Today it is called the **Great Schism** or the **Western Schism**. The word "schism" means a "division." In that momentous year, Pope Gregory XI died. To replace Gregory, two different popes were elected. Urban VI was one of them. He resided in Rome. The second man who claimed to be pope was Clement VII. He resided in Avignon, France. Thus, for a time, there were two men claiming the single office of pope. Kings and nations took sides and chose whomever they believed to be the true pope. Some followed Urban VI. Others followed Clement VII.

Such division and confusion gave Wycliffe a unique opportunity. Soon after Gregory died, Wycliffe wrote a book called *The Truth of Holy Scripture*. In this book, he argued that the Bible was the only infallible source of truth for Christian faith and practice. Since the Bible is God's Word, it should judge the teachings of popes and councils. Popes shouldn't decide what is right; the Bible should decide this. In the Medieval church, this order was often reversed. Often it was popes and councils who judged Scripture. Wycliffe was correct in asserting the final authority of the Bible. This is what the Bible itself teaches.

As Isaiah prophesied to God's people long ago, it is God's "law and testimony" that must guide us.

---

**And when they say to you, "Seek those who are mediums and wizards, who whisper and mutter," should not a people seek their God? Should they seek the dead on behalf of the living? To the law and to the testimony! If they do not speak according to this word, it is because there is no light in them. (Isa. 8:19-20)**

---

Since Wycliffe so revered God's Word, it is natural that he wanted to translate the Bible into English. At the time, portions of the Bible were available in English, but no complete translation existed. To remedy this, Wycliffe began translating the Latin version of the Bible into English. (This Latin Bible is known as the **Latin Vulgate**.) Wycliffe did not finish translating the entire Bible. But his followers, often called **Lollards**, continued the translation work.

**ILLUSTRATION OF WYCLIFFE SENDING OUT THE LOLLARDS**

The most important of these translations was completed by Wycliffe's secretary in 1395. The secretary's name was John Purvey. Here are a few verses from Wycliffe's Bible. On the left is the 1395 English translation. On the right is a modern English translation of the same verses.

### MATTHEW 5:3-6

| Wycliffe Bible (1395) | New King James Version (1982) |
|---|---|
| *Blessed ben pore men in spirit, for the kyngdom of hevenes is herne.* | *Blessed are the poor in spirit, For theirs is the kingdom of heaven.* |
| *Blessid ben thei that mornen, for thei schulen be coumfortid.* | *Blessed are those who mourn, For they shall be comforted.* |
| *Blessid ben mylde men, for thei schulen welde the erthe.* | *Blessed are the meek, For they shall inherit the earth.* |
| *Blessid ben thei that hungren and thristen riytwisnesse, for thei schulen be fulfillid.* | *Blessed are those who hunger and thirst for righteousness, For they shall be filled.* |

Can you spot the similarities in these translations? What words are the same? What words are different? As you can see, English has changed since 1395. However, the foundational translation work of Wycliffe was a steppingstone for future translations. During the Reformation period, English Bible translation would be furthered by **William Tyndale** (1494-1536).

By making the Bible more available to English citizens, Wycliffe's translation enabled ordinary Christians to examine the church's teachings and practices. Were those teachings and practices consistent with God's Word? Or was the church in error? As God's Word began to be read by more people, many concluded with Wycliffe that the church was in grave error.

Wycliffe wrote a second book in 1378. The title of the second book was *On the Church*. In this work, Wycliffe struck another blow against common church teaching. He argued that the true church was not just those who were joined outwardly to the church through baptism or through church offices. Instead, Wycliffe taught, the church was God's elect. "Elect" refers to God's chosen people, predestined by God to be saved. Therefore, in Wycliffe's defi-

**BEGINNING OF THE GOSPEL OF JOHN FROM A WYCLIFFE POCKET TRANSLATION**

nition, the church was made up of those who were saved by God. This meant that some within the visible organized church may not be elect.

The next year, Wycliffe argued that the institution of the papacy was not ordained by God. If the pope was faithful to follow the example of the apostles, he was a good leader. But if he did not, then he should be considered an antichrist. Wycliffe's critique of the papacy was a bold act. To question the authority of the pope was considered heresy.

MODERN-DAY LUTTERWORTH, ENGLAND

Next, Wycliffe challenged the doctrine of **transubstantiation**. Transubstantiation is the doctrinal belief that the physical elements of bread and wine in the Lord's Supper are turned into the actual physical body and blood of Jesus Christ. According to the Roman Catholic Church, this happens when the priest consecrates the elements of bread and wine. To "consecrate" the elements means to set them apart from ordinary use. The Roman Church also teaches that even though the bread and wine have changed into the body and blood of Christ, they still appear to our senses as ordinary bread and wine. Wycliffe argued that this doctrine was contrary to the Bible and conflicted with ordinary human senses. The bread still tasted like bread and appeared to be bread. Likewise, the wine still tasted like wine and smelled like wine.

Wycliffe also argued that transubstantiation encouraged idolatry among members of the church. If the bread and wine was truly Christ's physical body and blood, then to worship the elements was the same as worshiping Jesus Christ. Such idolatry was common. When people saw the consecrated bread and wine, they would say they were "seeing their Maker." Many priests used blasphemous language to describe the act of consecrating or "setting apart" the bread and wine. Some even would describe this act as "making God." One Irish priest from the 1480s boasted of his ability to make Christ present, and then to make Christ disappear. Such idolatry and blasphemy turned God's worship into a sort of magic show.

Wycliffe was right to attack this false doctrine. But it cost him his teaching position at

Oxford. Much of the English nobility did not support his teachings about the Lord's Supper. As a result, Wycliffe retired to the countryside. For the last years of his life, he served as a priest at the parish church in Lutterworth. He continued his ministry in seclusion until 1384. That year, he died. He lived until about fifty-four years of age. Though Wycliffe was gone, he left behind many followers.

## WYCLIFFE'S LOVE FOR GOD'S WORD

Your word is a lamp to my feet
And a light to my path.
I have sworn and confirmed
That I will keep Your righteous judgments.
(Ps. 119:105-106)

From Wycliffe's writings, we learn how important the Bible was to John Wycliffe. He was a man who loved God's Word, diligently studied it, and wanted to see it applied. His trust in and use of the Bible is a model for Christians today. We need the light of God's Word to guide our path in this dark world.

What did John Wycliffe say about the Bible? Here are a few important quotes from his writings.

Wycliffe believed that because God **inspired** the Bible, the Bible is without error. He wrote, "The Holy Scripture is the faultless, most true, most perfect, and most holy law of God which it is the duty of all men to learn, to know, to defend, and to observe."

Wycliffe also taught that the Bible is **sufficient**. This means that God gave us in His Word exactly what we need for faith and life. Wycliffe explained, "Everything necessary is found in Scripture, and what is not there is unnecessary."

Because the Bible is God's Word, it is therefore the **supreme authority**. There is no higher authority than the one true and living God. Wycliffe taught that the Bible is "alone the supreme law that is to rule church, state, and Christian life, without traditions and statutes."

## THE LOLLARDS

Whatever I tell you in the dark, speak in the light; and what you hear in the ear, preach on the housetops. And do not fear those who kill the body but cannot kill the soul. But rather fear Him who is able to destroy both soul and body in hell. (Matt. 10:27-28)

After Wycliffe went to be with the Lord, his followers were scattered throughout England. They took with them portions of Scripture in English, and they sometimes had short tracts written by Wycliffe. Over time, they became known as **Lollards**. The exact meaning of this word is debated, but most believe it means something like "mumbler" or someone who "lolled." The name was not meant as a compliment. Many would have rejected the open-air preaching of the Lollards as just a bunch of "mumbling."

For decades after Wycliffe's death, the Lollards kept on with their "mumbling." Wycliffe's teaching and his translations of the Bible touched every part of England to some degree or another. Lollards preached in the open and gained many followers. Sometimes local church leaders would have Lollards arrested and punished. But for many years, the Lollards got away with much of their activity. By the early 1400s, more opposition against the Lollards arose. Open-air preaching was more often suppressed. Some Lollards were executed. One particular English nobleman named **Sir John Oldcastle** (1378-1417) was a leader among

## Basic Facts about England

*The United Kingdom consists of the nations of England, Wales, Scotland, and Northern Ireland. The facts below pertain to England, one of the countries within the UK.*

| | |
|---|---|
| **Total population:** | 56 million |
| **Total area:** | 50,000 square miles |
| **Capital:** | London |
| **Official language:** | English |
| **Primary religions:** | Protestant Christian, Atheist, Agnostic |

the Lollards. When Sir Oldcastle staged a rebellion against the king in 1414, he gave the Lollards a bad reputation. Oldcastle was executed in 1417. After that time, the Lollard movement largely went underground.

From 1417 until the time of the Reformation, "Lollardy" continued as a quiet but always present movement in England. Most Lollards passed on their teaching in private house meetings. Lollard teaching was also passed on from generation to generation by parents who taught their children. They were a people dedicated to knowing and applying the Bible. When the Reformation took England by storm, some of the Lollards joined the reformation efforts.

As we will see in the next chapter, Wycliffe's ideas did not stay limited to England. Soon, mainland Europe would also see its own reforming movement. It would take place especially in the land of Bohemia. ■

THE EXECUTION OF JOHN OLDCASTLE

# PRAYER POINTS: ENGLAND

In this Prayer Points, we will pray for the ministry of Bible distribution, preaching, and teaching in England. Wycliffe and the Lollards believed in the power of God's Word. Let us follow them in that belief. Let us pray that God's Word would accomplish great things in England.

For as the rain comes down, and the snow from heaven,
And do not return there,
But water the earth,
And make it bring forth and bud,
That it may give seed to the sower
And bread to the eater,
So shall My word be that goes forth from My mouth;
It shall not return to Me void,
But it shall accomplish what I please,
And it shall prosper in the thing for which I sent it. (Isa. 55:10-11)

- **Give thanks to God for a rich heritage of English Bible translation:** Among the many languages of the world, English speakers are blessed with an abundance of Bible translations. Give thanks to God for Bible translators like John Wycliffe, William Tyndale, Miles Coverdale, the King James Bible translators, and others. Let us be thankful to God that we have such an abundance of access to God's Word in the English language.

- **Pray for Bible distribution in England:** Even though the Bible is so accessible in England, most of the people in England have no interest in God's Word. Pray that as the Bible is distributed, read, and studied, it would bring forth life in the people of England. Ask God to put Bibles into the hands of many unbelievers in England.

- **Pray for faithful Bible preaching:** Ask God to raise up faithful men who are gifted and called to preach the Bible. Pray that God would give such men faith and boldness. Pray that He would make these men fearless so that the whole counsel of God contained in the Bible would be preached faithfully, without fear or apology.

SUNRISE IN ENGLISH COUNTRYSIDE

CHARLES BRIDGE, PRAGUE, CZECH REPUBLIC

# JOHN HUSS: THE PREACHER OF PRAGUE

**And so we have the prophetic word confirmed, which you do well to heed as a light that shines in a dark place, until the day dawns and the morning star rises in your hearts. (2 Pet. 1:19)**

On June 10, 1415 the Czech preacher **John Huss** wrote a letter to his own people. On this date, Huss was in prison awaiting trial. For months, he had been dwelling in the city of **Constance**. A church council was being held in this city, and Huss' teaching was one of the topics under discussion. Huss had been charged with numerous heresies, and he knew his life was in danger.

Writing on June 10, Huss exhorted his people:

> Faithful and beloved of God, lords and ladies, rich and poor! I entreat you and exhort you to love God, to spread abroad His word, and to hear and observe it more willingly. I entreat you to hold fast the truth of God, which I have written and preached to you from the Holy Scriptures and the utterances of His saints. I entreat you also, if any have heard in my preaching or private conversation that which is opposed to God's truth, or if I have ever written anything of that kind—I trust God that it is not so—not to hold to it. I entreat you, if any have noticed frivolity in my words or actions, not to imitate it, but to pray God that it may please Him to pardon me.... I write this letter to you in prison, bound with chains and expecting on the morrow the sentence of death, yet fully trusting in God that I shall not swerve from His truth nor swear denial of the errors whereof I have been charged by false witnesses. What grace God hath shown me, and how He helps me in the midst of strange temptations, you will know when by His mercy we meet in joy in His presence.

Huss' final letters from prison tell us much about this man's faith. Huss was a man committed to the truth of God's Word. He was a man of principle. He was a man of courage. And he was a humble man.

About one month later, on July 6, 1415, John Huss was condemned to death by the **Council of Constance**. He was burned at the stake for his refusal to renounce his belief in

**JOHN HUSS (1372-1415)**

the truth of the Word of God.

By his death, Huss left behind an impactful testimony that has created ripple effects in the history of Christ's church ever since.

In order to understand why it was that Huss gave up his life on July 6, 1415, we must review the rest of his story. We must journey from Constance back to the Bohemian capital of **Prague** (today the capital of the Czech Republic). There in Prague, at the university and in the **Bethlehem Chapel**, Huss became a leader among his people.

## THE MINISTRY OF HUSS IN PRAGUE

"Is not My word like a fire?" says the LORD, "And like a hammer that breaks the rock in pieces?" (Jer. 23:29)

It was through a royal marriage that a unique tie between England and Bohemia was formed.

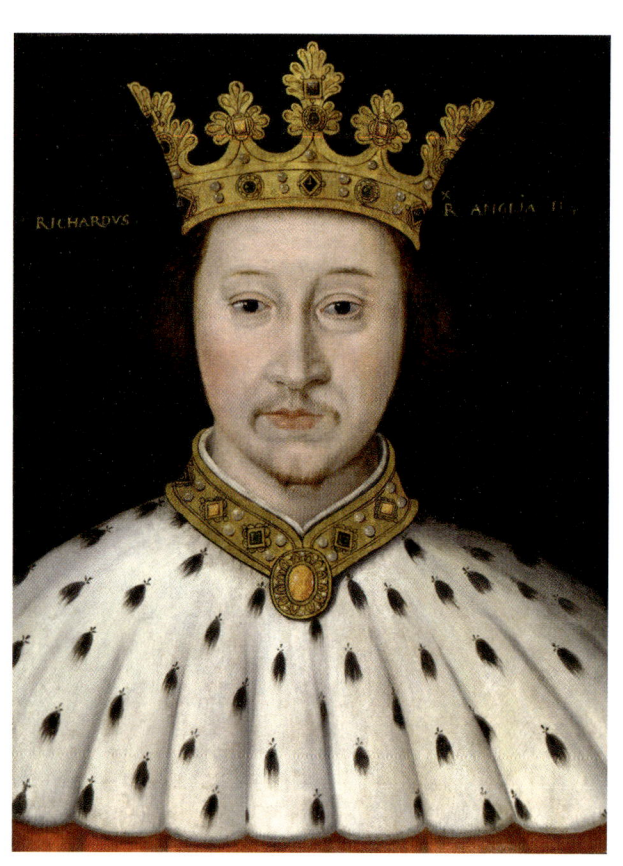

**KING RICHARD II (REIGNED 1377-1399)**

**King Richard II** of England married **Anne of Luxembourg**. Anne happened to be the sister of the king of Bohemia. (Today, the region of Bohemia is known as the Czech Republic.) After this marriage, students from Bohemia made the journey to England to study in the universities of England. This took place in the mid-1300s. At this time, **John Wycliffe** was a professor in the University of Oxford. As we learned in the previous chapter, Wycliffe was a controversial figure in his time. Many of his teachings were similar to the teachings of the Protestant Reformers of the 1500s.

As Bohemian students returned to their native land, many brought Wycliffe's teachings with them. Soon, Wycliffe's controversial writings were in Bohemia as well. In the early 1400s, John Huss began to read Wycliffe's writings and was influenced by them. Starting in 1402, Huss was appointed as preacher in the Bethlehem Chapel in Prague.

The Bethlehem Chapel was established in 1391 by two men who were passionate for preaching God's Word in the Czech language. It was called Bethlehem Chapel because it was to be a place where the Bohemians were fed with the bread of God's Word. "Bethlehem" in Hebrew means "house of bread."

For over a decade, Huss preached God's Word in the Bethlehem Chapel. The effect of his teaching and preaching was monumental. Huss became a beloved leader among the people of Prague.

As Huss studied the Bible and read the writings of Wycliffe, his views began to change. Wycliffe's commitment to the supreme authority of the Bible deeply influenced Huss. In time, Huss developed the same commitment. He became a man who submitted his life to the authority of God's Book.

The time for reform in the church was ripe. The unity of the church in Europe was being

**RECONSTRUCTED BETHLEHEM CHAPEL IN PRAGUE**

**INTERIOR OF THE BETHLEHEM CHAPEL**

torn asunder. A schism in 1378 led to a strange situation. There were now two popes, each claiming to be the true leader of the universal church. In 1409, the situation became even more perplexing. **The Council of Pisa** elected a third pope. For a time, then, three rival popes all claimed to be the head of the Roman Catholic Church. This conflict and division made it clear that the church was in need of reform. Besides this division, the church was also filled with moral corruption. Ungodly priests, bishops, and popes brought reproach upon the name of Christ because of their wicked lives.

Huss' zeal for reform resonated with the Bohemian people. Huss' bold preaching and godly character won the hearts of the Bohemians. Even **King Wenceslas** (reigned 1378-1419) supported Huss' leadership in Prague. Huss became a national leader of sorts.

THE STATUE OF SAINTS NORBERT OF XANTEN, WENCESLAS AND SIGISMUND ON CHARLES BRIDGE IN PRAGUE

## CONTROVERSY, DISCIPLINE, AND BANISHMENT

Blessed are you when they revile and persecute you, and say all kinds of evil against you falsely for My sake. Rejoice and be exceedingly glad, for great is your reward in heaven, for so they persecuted the prophets who were before you. (Matt. 5:11-12)

Because of Huss' unique preaching, his name became controversial in the wider church. His views eventually gained the attention of one of the rival popes. It was in 1411. That year, Huss preached against the common practice of indulgences. An indulgence was something a person could purchase from the pope. The pope declared that an **indulgence** would lessen the time someone would have to spend in **purgatory**. (The Roman Catholic Church taught that purgatory was where many Christians went when they died. Purgatory was a place of cleansing or "purgation.") If someone wanted to avoid going to purgatory, they could pay money to the church to receive an indulgence. The popes used this money to fund various projects. Later, in the 1500s, indulgences would be a major concern for Reformer Martin Luther.

Pope John XXIII (Pope from 1410-1415) was a rival pope to Pope Gregory XII (Poope from 1406-1415). Pope John XXIII was planning a war against Gregory. In order to fund this effort, Pope John XXIII used the sale of indulgences. They also brought peace of mind to the people buying them. People believed that their time in purgatory would be lessened by this purchase. It seemed to be a good investment.

**LOCATION OF PRAGUE IN THE CZECH REPUBLIC**

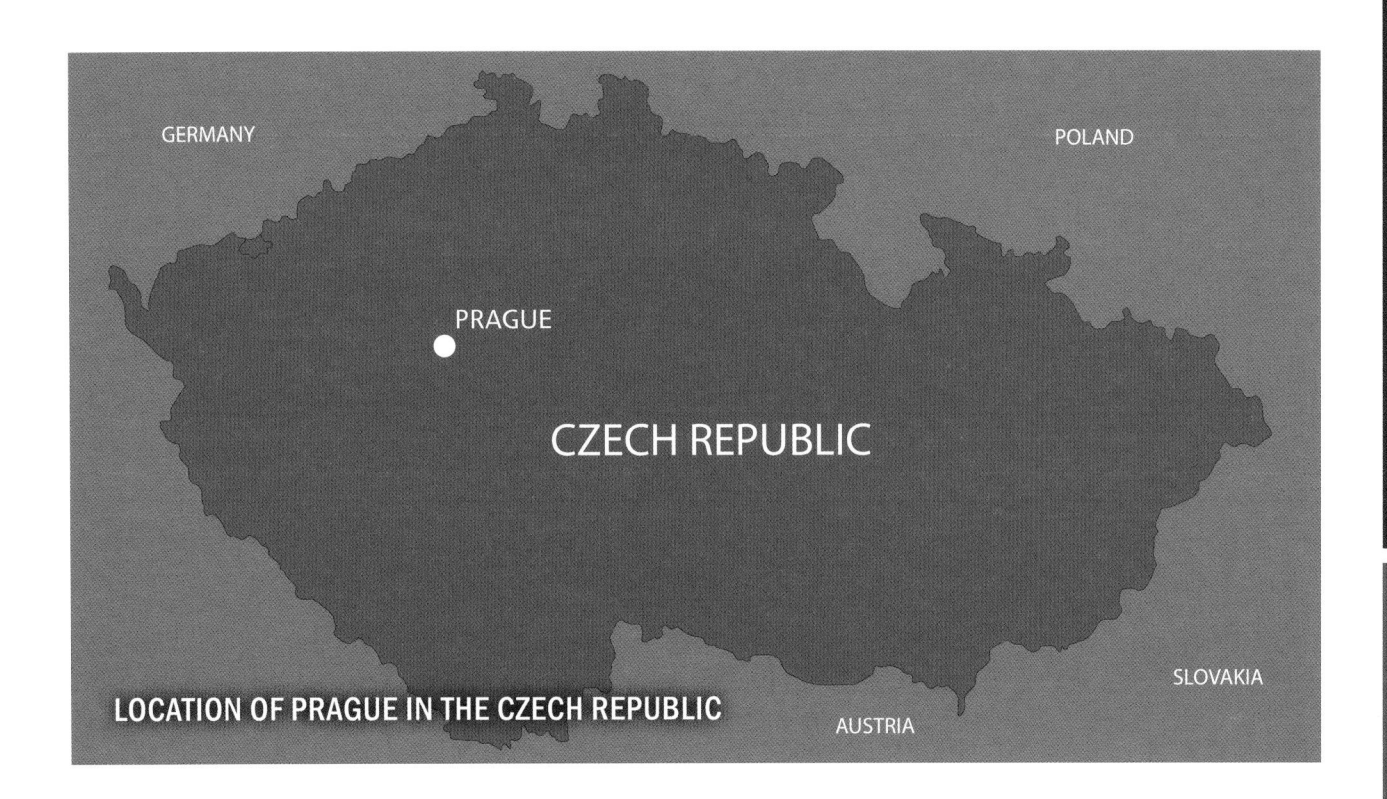

Huss knew the pope was wrong to sell indulgences. He preached vigorously against this. He argued that God freely forgives sinners who repent.

As would be expected, Pope John XXIII was not happy with Huss' perspective. The pope's fundraising efforts were in jeopardy. John moved swiftly to **excommunicate** John Huss. By excommunicating Huss, the pope declared that Huss was outside of the church. The pope also placed the city of Prague under an **interdict**. This meant that all of Prague was excommunicated as well.

King Wenceslas asked Huss to leave Prague in order to free the city from the interdict. Huss submitted to the king's request and began an exile that lasted from 1412 to 1414. In October 1412, Huss left the city and lodged in villages or towns in the countryside. While in exile, he continued to communicate with friends in Prague. One man named Christian was the rector of the University of Prague. Huss wrote to his friend Christian, saying, "I want to live godly, and it behooves me to suffer in the name of Christ and thus to imitate Christ in his trials."

While in exile, John Huss did not stop preaching. Without his beloved Bethlehem Chapel, he had to preach in the open air. Exile was difficult, but Huss embraced this new opportunity. He preached in castles, open fields, town squares, and along highways. Wherever he preached, large crowds assembled to hear him.

## THE COUNCIL OF CONSTANCE

From 1414 to 1418, a church council of great historical significance was held in Constance. It is known as the **Council of Constance**. One purpose of this council was to heal the division among the popes. The reform of the church in terms of morals and practice was another goal. It was to this council that Huss was summoned in 1414. Huss was called to answer for his teachings. He knew that traveling to Constance could result in his death. But he was promised a safe conduct. This meant that no one would harm him at the council. The brother of King Wenceslas, Emperor **Sigismund** (reigned from 1410-1437), promised Huss safe conduct. Before departing Bohemia, Huss prepared his will in case he didn't return.

Upon arriving in Constance, the emperor's promise was shown to be empty. Huss was quickly imprisoned. For over half a year, Huss suffered in various prisons in Constance, awaiting trial. While in prison, he suffered numerous physical maladies and almost died several times due to illness. However, he did what he could to continue his ministry through letter writing.

While in prison, Huss' disciples in Prague began a practice that was considered heretical at the time. This was the practice of allowing the congregation to partake of both elements in communion. For some time, it was the practice of the Medieval church to only give the bread of the Lord's Supper to the congregation. Only the ordained priest would partake of the wine. To modern-day Christians, this practice of the Medieval church seems bizarre and obviously unbiblical. One reason for this practice was a belief in the doctrine of **transubstantiation**. There was a concern that if someone dropped the cup of Christ's blood, they would desecrate Christ's blood. Another possible reason was to reinforce a strong distinction between the ordained priests and the people.

These reasons given for the practice are not consistent with the teaching of the Bible. In 1 Corinthians, Paul taught that at the Lord's Supper all believers should partake of both the bread and the wine.

---

**Therefore whoever eats this bread or drinks this cup of the Lord in an unworthy manner will be guilty of the body and blood of the Lord. But let a man examine himself, and so let him eat of the bread and drink of the cup. (1 Cor. 11:27-28)**

---

This withholding of the cup from God's people shows just how far the church had departed from the plain teaching of God's Word. Huss was in support of his fellow disciples in Prague. He encouraged them to give both the bread and the wine to all of God's people. For his support of this doctrine, he would be charged with heresy.

In June and July 1415, Huss was brought before church and civil authorities repeatedly. He was bullied to renounce his teachings. He was also falsely accused. Just what was it that Huss was accused of?

On some matters, Huss was indeed "guilty" of teaching certain doctrines that were considered heresy. Huss taught that immoral and wicked clergy should not be followed if they lead God's people astray. In this way, Huss challenged the authority of the church. He even argued that the pope could be disobeyed if the pope was not following God's Word. The authorities at the council believed it was heresy to submit the authority of the church to the rule of God's Word. For Huss to elevate the Scriptures to the role of supreme authority was a central issue.

Huss was also accused of being a "Wycliffite." This meant that he was accused of fol-

> **Transubstantiation** ▪ Transubstantiation is the doctrinal belief that the physical elements of bread and wine in the Lord's Supper are turned into the actual physical body and blood of Jesus Christ. According to the Roman Catholic Church, this happens when the priest consecrates the elements of bread and wine. The Roman Church also teaches that even though the bread and wine have changed into the body and blood of Christ, they still appear to our senses as ordinary bread and wine.

JOHN HUSS AT THE COUNCIL OF CONSTANCE

lowing the teachings of John Wycliffe, who was seen as a heretic. It is true that Huss agreed with much of Wycliffe's writings. However, Huss did not agree with everything Wycliffe said. Sadly, clarity and truth did not seem to be a high priority for the leaders of the council.

To make Huss look really bad, false witnesses were brought in. Some accused Huss of teaching that there were more than three persons in the Godhead. Huss was accused of adding to the Trinity a fourth person. And, the false witnesses claimed, that fourth person was Huss himself! To this charge, Huss protested vigorously. He argued he had never taught such a blasphemous doctrine. He explained he had always taught that there is one God eternally existing in three persons.

A verdict was soon reached. Huss was declared guilty of heretical teaching. He was also declared guilty of refusing to submit to the church's authority. The sentence was death.

When the verdict was read, Huss fell to his knees and prayed to God. He prayed that Christ, out of His great mercy, would pardon his enemies. As Huss prayed, the council sneered at him.

The bishops surrounded Huss and stripped him of his priestly robes. They also took a chalice they had put in his hands and said, "O cursed Judas, who has spurned the counsels of peace and have taken counsel with the Jews, we take from you this cup of redemption." Symbolically, they were saying that Christ's blood would not save Huss.

Huss was not silent. He replied, "My trust is in the Lord God Almighty, for whose name I patiently suffer this blasphemy, for He will not take away from me the cup of His redemption. And I firmly hope that today I shall drink it in His kingdom."

Then, a paper cap of eighteen inches height was placed upon Huss' head. The cap had

**EXECUTION OF JOHN HUSS**

three demons pictured on it. Each of the three demons were tugging at a man's soul. The word "heresiarch" was also written on the cap. This word means "founder of a heresy." The bishops then proclaimed, "We commit your soul to the devil."

Huss raised his hands to heaven and said, "And I commit it to my most gracious Lord, Jesus Christ. The crown my Savior wore on His most sacred head was heavy and irksome. The one I wear is easy and light. He wore a crown of thorns even to the most awful death. And I will wear this much lighter one humbly for the sake of His name and the truth."

Huss was led to the stake where he would be burned. Kneeling before his execution, he prayed, "Lord Jesus Christ, I wish to bear most patiently and humbly for Your Gospel's sake and the preaching of Your Word, this dire, ignominious, and cruel death."

Huss was bound to the stake with chains as the wood was placed underneath him. Looking at the executioners, Huss spoke, "The Lord Jesus Christ, my Redeemer, was bound with a harder chain, and I, a miserable sinner, am not afraid to bear this one, bound as I am for His name's sake." Having said these words, Huss died in the flames as he commended his soul to God.

## THE MORAVIANS

John Huss' earthly life ended at the Council of Constance in 1415. But his legacy lived on. He left behind him committed disciples in Bohemia. In the centuries that followed, the **Hussites**, as they were known, lived on. Sometimes called the **Bohemian Brethren** or the **Moravian Brethren**, Huss' leadership continued as the foundation of this reforming movement. The Moravians were fiercely persecuted by the Roman Catholic Church. But as a group, they continued into the time of the Protestant Reformation. At that time, they supported the efforts of the Reformers.

## Basic Facts about the Czech Republic

| | |
|---|---|
| **Total population:** | 10 million |
| **Total area:** | 30,452 square miles |
| **Capital:** | Prague |
| **Official language:** | Czech |
| **Primary religions:** | Atheist, Agnostic, Roman Catholic |

In 1722, two Moravian families settled near Dresden, Germany. They formed a community known as **Herrnhut**. They settled on land owned by a local nobleman named Count Zinzendorf. In time, this community would become one of the most productive missionary-sending centers in church history. From this community and others like it, the Moravian Brethren would go to Greenland, Canada, the Caribbean, Australia, South Africa, and many other places in the world. In a later chapter, you will learn more about this important event in European church history. ∎

# PRAYER POINTS: CZECH REPUBLIC

- **Ask God to send light into a dark land:** Among the nations of Europe, the Czech Republic is among the most atheistic. Over 70% of the population claim to be "non-religious." That means the vast majority of people in the Czech Republic "suppress the truth" about God's existence (Rom. 1:18). This country is deeply in need of God's truth, the Bible, to bring light to a dark land. Pray that God would show the people of the Czech Republic that life is empty and meaningless without the one true God.

- **Pray that God would strengthen and grow the church:** Most of the churches in the Czech Republic are part of the Roman Catholic Church. There are not many Bible-preaching and Bible-believing churches in this country. Let us pray that God would strengthen the small church that does exist. And let us ask God to grow the church in numbers and influence.

- **Thank God for additional Bible translation and literature distribution:** *Operation World* reports that a new translation of the Bible in the Czech language was published in 2009. It became a quick best-seller. Let us thank God for providing His Word to the Czech Republic and for the increased distribution of Bibles and Christian literature in that country.

CHURCH IN HERRNHUT, GERMANY

FLORENCE, ITALY

# GIROLAMO SAVONAROLA: REFORMER OF FLORENCE

---

Wash yourselves, make yourselves clean;
Put away the evil of your doings from before My eyes.
Cease to do evil,
Learn to do good;
Seek justice,
Rebuke the oppressor;
Defend the fatherless,
Plead for the widow. (Isa. 1:16-17)

---

On the morning of September 21, 1494, the people of Florence were anxious and worried. During the past few weeks, word had arrived that an invading army was approaching. Soon, soldiers would be at the gates of the city. The French army of Charles VIII was marching on Florence. What would this mean for the city? Economic ruin? Destruction of the city? Violence and death? And who would stop Charles VIII? Could he be stopped?

Thousands of Florentines gathered under the dome of San Marco Cathedral. Apprehension and fear filled the air. Many hoped to hear a word of comfort and encouragement. Fearful times called for a word from the Lord.

A Dominican friar in black garb ascended the pulpit. Then he read the words of his passage from the Bible.

---

And behold, I Myself am bringing floodwaters on the earth, to destroy from under heaven all flesh in which is the breath of life; everything that is on the earth shall die. (Gen. 6:17)

---

These were hardly the words the agitated Florentines wanted to hear. This was no word of comfort.

The friar's name was **Girolamo Savonarola**. He warned the Florentines that the French army would descend upon the Italian countryside like a flood. For many years, Savonarola warned Florence of the judgment to come. King Charles of France was a sword in the Lord's hand to chastise Florence for her sins.

Known for its art, literature, and architecture, the city of Florence was also known for its many sins. Florence's sin list was long: pride, self-indulgence, theft, drunkenness, prostitution, homosexuality, **usury**, and corruption in high places. And the list went on. Though it was a place of high culture, it was also a city degraded by sin and misery.

Throughout the 1490s, Savonarola came

**GIROLAMO SAVONAROLA (1452-1498)**

223

> **Usury** ▪ The practice of lending money at unreasonably high interest rates. This practice was condemned because it took advantage of vulnerable poor and further enlarged the wealth of lenders, who often cared nothing for the poor.

to wield enormous influence in Florence. At times, over 10,000 people would gather to listen to his preaching. Word of his preaching spread throughout Italy. The Lord elevated him to a place of authority at a critical time in Florence's history. Dying in 1498, Savonarola lived within twenty years of the birth of the Protestant Reformation. He would not live to see the Reformation's effects, but in his own way, he was an early Reformer. He was a kind of "John the Baptist" for Florence. He called the Florentines to repentance, warning the city of God's coming judgment. As Jonah warned Nineveh, so Savonarola warned Florence that destruction would come. That is, destruction would come unless the people humbled themselves before Almighty God.

How then did a monk come to have such influence in Florence? To answer that question, we begin with Girolamo's childhood.

## GIROLAMO GROWS UP

*And in Your book they all were written,
The days fashioned for me,
When as yet there were none of them.
(Ps. 139:16)*

Savonarola was born in 1452 in the city of Ferrara. That same year, artist and **polymath Leonardo da Vinci** (1452-1519) was also born. We remember da Vinci for his many works of art and inventions. Savonarola lived during the years of the growing Italian Renaissance. The Renaissance is considered by many historians

**LOCATION OF FLORENCE**

**LEONARDO DA VINCI (1452-1519)**

as a "rebirth" or "revival" of literature, art, and architecture. Italians rediscovered the writings of the classical world. These writings were primarily Greek and Roman literature. For many, this rediscovery of the classics became a reason to grow in pride.

> **Polymath** ▪ A polymath is someone with a wide range of learning and knowledge in many subjects. Many people consider Leonardo da Vinci a polymath because he was learned in multiple subjects including biology, physics, art, engineering, astronomy, and more.

As Christians, we should always remember that in seeking knowledge, we must always begin with the fear of the Lord (Prov. 1:7).

But there was one good thing that happened during the Renaissance period. More men and women began studying the Bible. The movable-type printing press developed by **Johann Gutenberg** (1400-1468) made printed texts more widely available. Soon, new editions and translations of the Bible became available to more and more people.

As a young man, Girolamo was influenced by his grandfather Michele. Michele was a medical doctor. Girolamo's father was also a doctor. Like all young boys in Italy, Girolamo was surrounded by the institutions of the Roman Catholic Church. Churches and priests were everywhere. But this did not mean people knew God's Word. There was little to no preaching of the Bible in the churches. The pure gospel of Jesus Christ was shrouded in centuries of ritual and tradition. However, Girolamo was blessed with a grandfather who read the Bible. Michele

**CATHEDRAL IN FERRARA, ITALY**

shared God's Word with Girolamo. Girolamo began to read the Bible on his own.

As Girolamo grew older, it became time to choose a trade or profession. His father and grandfather were both medical doctors. Naturally, Girolamo's father wanted him to also become a physician. It was the family business. Girolamo would carry on the torch. Therefore, Girolamo's father Niccolo sent him to the University of Bologna. A university education would prepare Girolamo for medical studies. But what awaited him at the university was only disappointment. Girolamo was appalled by the immoral lifestyle of his classmates. He despised university life. He wrote later:

> To be considered a man here, you must defile your mouth with the most filthy, brutal, and tremendous blasphemies. . . . if you live chastely and modestly, you are considered a fool. If you are pious, you are considered a hypocrite. If you believe in God, you are considered an imbecile.

Girolamo's classmates ran after youthful lusts. But Girolamo ran in the other direction. He wanted to seek God. His peers had no interest in the Lord. Girolamo spent his time in prayer and study rather than joining in recreation. He feared God and was burdened by his sins. But what could he do with his guilt? This question haunted him.

## GIROLAMO DEDICATES HIS LIFE TO GOD

**When You said, "Seek My face," My heart said to You, "Your face, LORD, I will seek." (Ps. 27:8)**

Girolamo's parents urged him to continue his medical studies. They wanted him to become a doctor. But one day, Girolamo decided on a different path. In order to serve God, he decided to become a monk. Girolamo's parents were disappointed. They wanted financial stability for the family. If Girolamo became a doctor, the family would benefit. But God had other plans.

Girolamo explained his decision in a letter to his father. He wrote:

> My honored father, I do not doubt that my departure has been painful to you. . . . Yet I would that by this letter my mind and intention may be fully revealed to you, that thus you may be of a better courage and may understand that I was led unto the purpose in question by no means in that light and childish spirit as I hear is believed by many persons. . . . The chief reason which led me to the religious life and to a monastery [is] the boundless misery of this world and the extreme unrighteousness of most men. . . . You must not weep. Nay, you must render unceasing thanks to the Lord Jesus.

Girolamo desired to escape the defilements of this world. He knew the misery sin produced. He saw it in others. He also saw it in his own heart. Yet, because of unbiblical teaching, it was hard for him to be at peace. He did not rightly understand what Jesus' death and resurrection accomplishes for sinners.

In order to achieve God's favor, Savonarola would pray for hours on end. He would fast for days. He would punish himself with self-inflicted wounds. He took the dirtiest job at the monastery and gladly cleaned the latrines. He thought this would help him pay for his sins. Of course, nothing we do can bring peace between us and God. It is by faith alone that we are justified in God's sight. It is by the Holy Spirit's work in us that we grow more holy. But these truths were not taught in Savonarola's time.

## PREACHER OF RIGHTEOUSNESS

"Now, therefore," says the LORD,
"Turn to Me with all your heart,
With fasting, with weeping, and with mourning."
So rend your heart, and not your garments;
Return to the LORD your God,
For He is gracious and merciful,
Slow to anger, and of great kindness;
And He relents from doing harm.
(Joel 2:12-13)

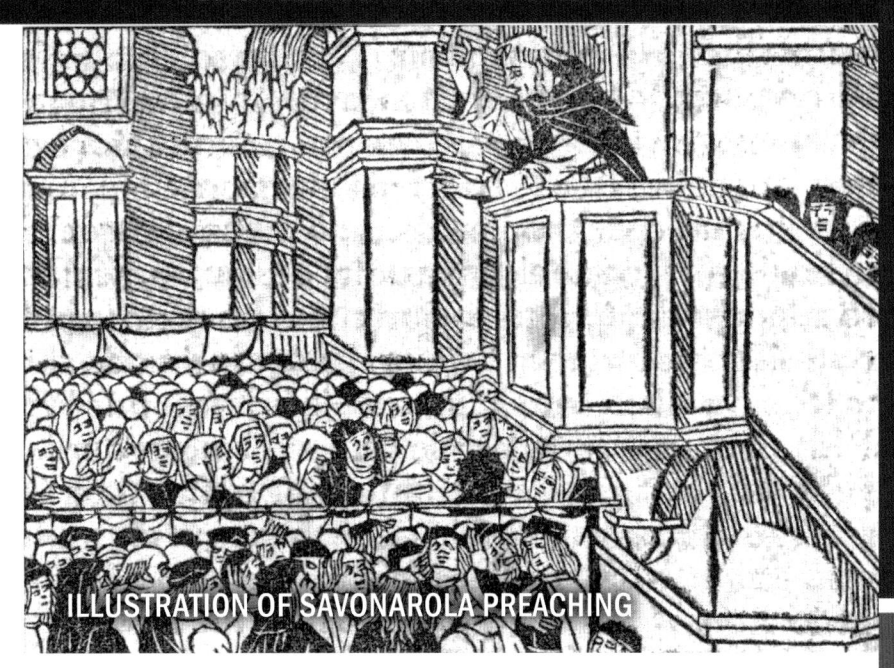

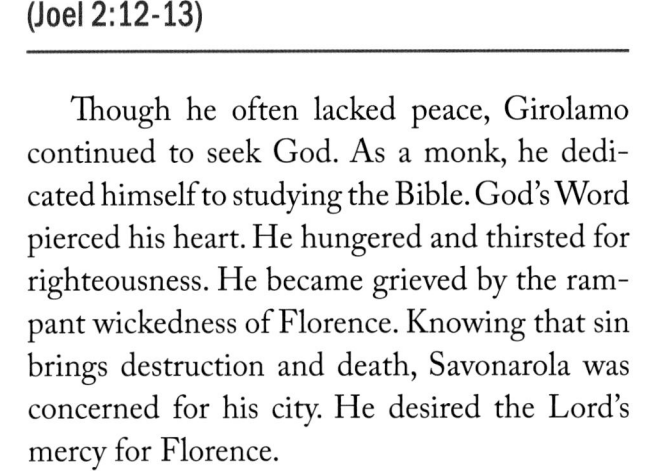

*ILLUSTRATION OF SAVONAROLA PREACHING*

Though he often lacked peace, Girolamo continued to seek God. As a monk, he dedicated himself to studying the Bible. God's Word pierced his heart. He hungered and thirsted for righteousness. He became grieved by the rampant wickedness of Florence. Knowing that sin brings destruction and death, Savonarola was concerned for his city. He desired the Lord's mercy for Florence.

The prior, the head of the Dominican monastery, decided to give Girolamo a chance to preach. Girolamo's first assignment was to preach in a small church near the monastery. His first sermon was not well received. Girolamo stumbled through his notes and didn't speak very clearly. But in time, he learned how to communicate the Bible with more clarity and power. In time, he became a gifted preacher. What made him unique in the 1400s was this: Savonarola preached from the Bible. Most preachers in his day quoted from the Bible sparingly. They certainly did not preach through books of the Bible. But Savonarola did. This is one way that he was a forerunner of the Protestant Reformation.

In 1491, Savonarola became the pastor of San Marco Cathedral in Florence. His preaching was fiery. He drew from biblical passages and made direct application to the people of Florence. Preaching to the conscience won him supporters. But it also turned other people into enemies. Girolamo did not shirk from preaching against the fashionable sins in Florence. He preached against the vanity of fashion and outward beauty. He denounced the wealthy who took advantage of poor Florentines. He called tyrannical rulers to repentance. He also condemned much of the art and literature of Florence as sinful. This attack upon the art and literature of the Renaissance offended many. He once preached:

> The literature and art are pagan. The humanists merely pretend to be Christians. Those ancient authors ... are strangers to Christ and the Christian virtues, and their art is an idolatry of heathen gods, or a shameless display of naked women and men.

In these words, Savonarola argued that the literature so popular in Florence was pagan. It was not Christian. He believed the Roman and Greek classics corrupted the morals of the people. He also censured the Roman and Greek art, which was often immodest. It wasn't just the "worldly people" of Florence who received rebuke. Savonarola reprimanded the clergy as well. No one in Florence was immune from the correction of God's Word. That included Girolamo Savonarola himself.

At this time, Florence was governed by a city council of elected officials. But in reality, one powerful family ruled Florence. For generations, the wealthy and influential Medici family tyrannized Florence for their own benefit. When Savonarola became preacher at San Marco, a man named **Lorenzo de Medici** (1449-1492) was in power. It was easy for Savonarola to get away with preaching against some people in Florence, but it wasn't wise for him to be so direct with Lorenzo de Medici. After all, Lorenzo was a powerful man. But Savonarola wasn't afraid. Such concerns did not stop him. He risked Lorenzo's wrath. He was a bold man. He was no "respecter of persons." For him, faithfulness to the Lord's Word was of the highest importance. Eventually, that boldness would get Savonarola killed.

One day, Savonarola was granted an audience with Lorenzo. The powerful Medici ruler thought to himself, "Surely, the preacher will be careful with his words. He is in my home." Savonarola did not mince words. He drew a comparison between Lorenzo and the Pharisees of Jesus' day. Our Lord did not hold back in rebuking those leaders of old. Savonarola did the same. He exhorted Lorenzo to repent and fulfill his God-given duty.

> I shall say, therefore, that all the evil of a city depends on its head, whose responsibility is great even for small sins. For if he followed the right path, the whole city would become holy... It is your duty, therefore, to root out dissension, to do justice, and to demand honesty of everyone.

History does not record how Lorenzo received Savonarola's exhortations. But we do know that not long after Savonarola's visit, Lorenzo de Medici fell ill and was near death. Lorenzo summoned Savonarola to visit him one last time. Lorenzo wanted absolution for his sins. He desired assurance that upon death, he would enter into eternal life. (It is important to note that the Bible does not require a priest to grant forgiveness of sins. The Bible teaches that if we confess our sins to God, we can be assured we are forgiven.)

Lorenzo hoped for an easily granted assurance from the friar. But Savonarola pressed Lorenzo for real repentance. Lorenzo confessed his sins to the friar. But Savonarola wanted to know what Lorenzo would do about it before he died. The preacher explained that Lorenzo must do three things. First, he told Lorenzo to "have a strong faith in God's mercy." Second, Lorenzo must restore any wealth that was unjustly taken from others. And thirdly, Savonarola explained, "you must instruct your sons to

**LORENZO DE MEDICI (1449-1492)**

give Florence back her liberties."

It was easy enough to confess a few sins. Savonarola's point in pressing these exhortations was to test whether Lorenzo was truly repentant. Did Lorenzo really believe in Christ? Was there any works to show that Lorenzo's faith was real (Jas. 2:14-26)? But Lorenzo was unwilling to follow through with action before his death. Savonarola left without giving Lorenzo any assurance of God's mercy.

A few hours later, Lorenzo de Medici was dead. The year was 1492. It was the same year Christopher Columbus discovered the Americas.

## FLORENCE INVADED

In 1494, **Charles VIII** (1470-1498), king of France, invaded the Italian Peninsula. The French army was an enormous fighting force. Forty thousand men with an array of horses and cannons lumbered south. The Italian armies were no match for the French army. City after city fell without much of a fight. Lorenzo's son Piero de Medici knew that Charles VIII could not be stopped. The Medici family fled Florence before the French army arrived. The Medici family were rulers in Florence, but the people of Florence would not miss Piero. They were glad to be rid of the tyrannical Medici family.

On November 17, 1494 Charles VIII reached the gates of Florence. He marched right into the city with no opposition. Charles then took up residence in the Medici mansion. Savonarola's influence was well known in the city. For this reason, Charles invited the preacher of San Marco to visit him. Savonarola welcomed Charles VIII to Florence. He then delivered an exhortation to the French king. Again, Girolamo did not fear man. As he had done with Lorenzo, Savonarola instructed Charles to act justly.

Therefore, most Christian king, listen carefully to my words and bind them to your heart. Be merciful, especially with Florence, where God has many servants, despite its sins. Guard and defend the innocents ... God elected you in the interest of the church. You must obey the Lord.

Charles VIII heeded Savonarola's words. He left Florence unharmed and moved on. On November 28, the city was free. With the Medici family gone, the people of Florence had a unique opportunity. Now it was time to reorganize the government of Florence into a true republic. Savonarola led the way in encouraging moral and political change. A council was established with a balance of powers. The Florentines wanted nothing to do with the tyranny of the Medici family. It was a new day for Florence. Savonarola urged the council to pursue moral reform as well. Certain behaviors such as gambling, profanity, and unclean songs were forbidden.

Freedoms were restored. Morality was

**CHARLES VIII (1470-1498)**

improving. Florence was heading in a good direction. But would the changes last? Girolamo Savonarola soon learned that moral change was not enough. Without the gospel of Jesus Christ changing a people, true transformation does not last. Without new life in Christ, people will go right back to their sins.

## OPPOSITION MOUNTS

And this is the condemnation, that the light has come into the world, and men loved darkness rather than light, because their deeds were evil. For everyone practicing evil hates the light and does not come to the light, lest his deeds should be exposed. (John 3:19-20)

Savonarola's bold preaching made him famous throughout Italy. But for some in the church, Savonarola was infamous. Girolamo's forceful denunciations of the sins of the clergy were offensive to many. This was especially the case for those clergy committing the very sins Savonarola censured. News of Savonarola's preaching reached **Pope Alexander VI** (pope from 1492-1503). The pope wanted to speak with the outspoken monk of Florence, so the pope summoned Savonarola to Rome.

The pope was shocked when Savonarola refused to come. The friar of Florence explained in his reply letter that he was busy with important reform work in Florence. His delay to the pope's summons would not be permanent. Savonarola wrote, "I trust therefore that your holiness will kindly admit this delay in order that we may bring to perfection this reform begun by the will of the Lord."

The pope was furious. Savonarola had acted

BRIDGES IN FLORENCE

boldly before, but to defy the pope could be deadly. The pope sent another letter ordering Savonarola to end his preaching. Additionally, the pope indicated that the friar would be reassigned to another location. The people of Florence wrote back to the pope, urging him to relent. Reluctantly the pope agreed. But a bishop was sent to monitor Savonarola's preaching. This enabled the pope to scrutinize Savonarola's ministry. The preacher of San Marco continued his preaching. Moral reform continued in Florence. But the pope's temporary grant to Savonarola did not last.

## EXCOMMUNICATED AND EXECUTED

Savonarola was a preacher first and foremost. He did not intend at first to be entangled in the civil government of Florence. But as his influence grew, he became a prominent leader in Florence. As Savonarola's preaching became increasingly earnest, the pope's patience diminished. Eventually, Savonarola condemned the pope in his preaching. He denounced Pope Alexander as a servant of Satan. He warned Florence about the corrupt innerworkings of the papal court. In the pope's judgment, Savonarola had gone too far. On May 12, 1497 Pope Alexander VI excommunicated Savonarola. By the pope's edict, Savonarola was no longer a member of the church. The pope also threat-

> **Interdict** ▪ An interdict was a pronouncement made by the Roman Catholic Church that meant an entire city or region was excommunicated from the church.

ened Florence with an **interdict**.

Now, support for Savonarola in Florence waned. In response to the papal decree, the city authorities arrested Savonarola. He was then tortured. The authorities pressed Savonarola to repent of his teachings. He was then left in prison to await execution. Girolamo had dedicated himself to the moral and political reform of Florence. But now, the world was turned against him. Change had not lasted. Savonarola stood rejected. Now, facing the end of his earthly life, in the time of his greatest need, Savonarola looked to the Lord for help. He found hope in the Word of God.

> Sinner that I am, where shall I turn now? To the Lord whose mercy is infinite. No one can glory in himself; all the saints say, not of us but of the Lord is glory. They were not saved by their merit, nor by their work, but by the goodness and grace of God, that nobody may glory in himself.

In these words, we learn that Savonarola understood the grace of God. His own pursuit of righteousness would not save him. Savonarola's understanding of God's grace was not always clear in his preaching. But by the end of his life, the Lord had given him a deeper understanding of His mercy. Savonarola knew: it was Jesus Christ alone who would save him.

On May 23, 1498 Savonarola was hanged and then burned at the stake in the plaza of Florence. He was excommunicated by the church. He was executed by the people of Florence. Savonarola's life appeared to be a failure. But it was not. He was a voice in the wilderness decrying corruption and unrighteousness. He boldly preached against sin. He even stood up to the pope. In these ways, he was like the Protestant Reformers who came after him. Savonarola's unique contributions to his time include preaching from the Bible, urgent calls of repentance and moral reform, and challenging tyrants.

Men such as Martin Luther, William Farel, Martin Bucer, and John Calvin would lead the way to a rediscovery of the biblical gospel. As the Reformation began, the light of Holy Scripture burst into the darkness of medieval Europe. That piercing light would expose the wickedness and corruption of European society. But exposing sin was not enough to bring change. Others like Savonarola had exposed sin and corruption. Moral reforms such as what Savonarola preached did not go far enough. Moral reform doesn't change the heart. Only the gospel of Jesus Christ can do that.

We must thank God for glimmering lights in dark places. Such was Girolamo Savonarola in Florence. ■

---

And so we have the prophetic word confirmed, which you do well to heed as a light that shines in a dark place, until the day dawns and the morning star rises in your hearts. (2 Pet. 1:19)

---

## PRAYER POINTS: ITALY

- **Thank God for the Christian heritage of Italy:** Godly pastors and faithful churches were planted here in the first centuries of the church. Thank the Lord for what He did in the past in Italy. It was to Rome that Paul wrote his inspired letter (Romans) that continues to change the world. From Italy, the message of the gospel went forth into other parts of Europe.

- **Pray for Biblical reformation in Italy:** The seat of the Roman Catholic Church is in Rome, the capital city of Italy. For this reason, Italy has long been dominated by the Roman Catholic Church. Today, about 85% of Italians profess some kind of connection to the Roman Church. In contrast, only about half of 1 percent of the Italian population describes itself as Protestant. Italy never experienced the fruits of the Protestant Reformation like other parts of Europe. But if God so wills, that Reformation could come to Italy in our generation. Let us pray that the church would be reformed in Italy.

- **Pray for the light of the gospel to overcome secularism:** Like many nations in modern Europe, Italy is becoming more secular. This means that increasingly, many citizens of Italy do not believe in God. They may be atheists (those who do not believe in the existence of any God) or agnostics (those who don't know or care about God's existence). A godless view of the world is one of the strategies Satan uses to send people to hell. A secular worldview among many in Europe makes them indifferent to the things of God. Pray that Christ would send His light into Europe once again and awaken dead hearts.

## Basic Facts about Italy (Italian Republic)

| | |
|---|---|
| Total population: | 60 million |
| Total area: | 116,000 square miles |
| Capital: | Rome |
| Official language: | Italian |
| Primary religions: | Roman Catholic |

SAVONAROLA EXECUTED

ST. GILES CATHEDRAL, EDINBURGH, SCOTLAND

# UNIT 4
## AD 1500-2000

Let Your hand be upon the man of Your right hand,
Upon the son of man whom You made strong for Yourself.
Then we will not turn back from You;
Revive us, and we will call upon Your name.
Restore us, O LORD God of hosts;
Cause Your face to shine,
And we shall be saved! (Ps. 80:17-19)

By the 1500s, the church in Europe languished. Scandal, false teaching, and corruption marked much of the church's leadership. The average Christian in Europe was ignorant of the Bible. Under such conditions, the church could not fulfill Christ's Commission to disciple the nations. Even still, the Lord Jesus was shepherding His church.

In AD 1517, the prayers of reform-minded men such as John Wycliffe and John Huss were answered. The **Protestant Reformation** began. Faithful and courageous men led the way in translating and teaching the Word of God. Men such as Martin Luther, William Tyndale, John Knox, John Calvin, Martin Bucer, and others dedicated their lives to the cause of reformation. This was a mighty work of God much needed in Christ's church.

One of the greatest benefits of the Reformation was the translation and distribute of the Bible into the common tongues of Europe. Martin Luther produced a complete Bible translation for the German people. Across the English Channel, in Britain, William Tyndale's translation of the New Testament ignited the fires of reform throughout England. The Word of God was like a hammer that broke the rock in pieces (Jer. 23:29). The Bible broke through the rock of human traditions. It decimated false teaching. It shattered hard hearts. Through the preaching and teaching of God's Word, Europe was dramatically transformed. The effects of the Protestant Reformation can still be seen today.

The work of reformation in the church continued over the centuries that followed. In the 1600s, the **Puritans** labored for the purity of Christ's church in England. Likewise, the **Scottish Covenanters** of the 1600s were committed to the lordship of Jesus Christ over His church. Efforts to be faithful to the gospel and to Christ always come with opposition. So it was with the Puritans and Covenanters. In some cases, Puritans lost their ministry. For many of the Covenanters, the cost of faithfulness required them to give up their lives.

The 1700s and 1800s were marked by significant advances in the cause of missions. The **Moravian** mission movement of the 1700s played a significant role in advancing the name of Jesus Christ in all different parts of the world. Many, inspired by the Moravians dauntless courage and love, would follow in their footsteps.

The 1800s are sometimes called "the greatest century of missions." Missionaries from all over

Europe and America made their way into regions of the world that had not seen a Christian missionary for centuries. In some cases, the remotest regions of earth had never seen a missionary. Such was the case with the remote islands of the **New Hebrides**. It was not until the mid-1800s that a Christian missionary set foot on the islands of the cannibals. Thanks be to God He poured out a zeal to take the gospel to the uttermost parts of the earth. Whether it was the frigid temperatures of the far north, or the oppressive and humid heat of the African interior, missionaries from Europe and America journeyed to all different parts of the world.

A wave of ungodly ideas swept through Europe in the 17th and 18th centuries. This period is sometimes called the **Enlightenment** or the **Age of Reason**. This movement elevated human reason, or for others, sense experience to be the ultimate authority in truth. Those who adopted such worldviews rejected God's Word as a source of knowledge and truth. Professing to be wise, they became fools, as Paul says (Rom. 1:22). The effect of these intellectual movements in Europe would bring about catastrophic consequences in the 1800s and 1900s. Those who reject God are given over to all different kinds of wickedness. The violent **French Revolution** was one example of the consequences of bad ideas.

Still, many philosophers and writers in Europe were optimistic about human progress. Perhaps the evils of society could be done away with through education? Perhaps technology would help? Or perhaps governments could bring about a more equal and fair society? Those who had such dreams were rudely awakened in the 1900s. Two world wars brought about devastation all over Europe. **World War I** (1914-1918) and **World War II** (1939-1945) brought war, famine, poverty, and sorrow to the nations of Europe. These two conflicts were evidence of the terrible evil still in the human heart.

During the 1900s, the nations of eastern Europe became subject to the tyranny of **Communism**. Soviet leaders such as **Vladimir Lenin** and **Joseph Stalin** imposed atheism upon the peoples of eastern Europe. (An atheist is one who does not believe in God.) Russia, Ukraine, Romania, Poland, and other nations were ruled by wicked and oppressive rulers. The churches of these lands were suppressed. But eventually, communism in Europe failed. In 1991, the Soviet Union was dissolved. The door for Christian missions in eastern Europe was opened once again.

For thousands of years, Europe was the center of Christianity in the world. But in time, the center shifted to North America. And now, the largest Christian populations are found in Africa and Asia. Today, the peoples of Europe are increasingly forgetting about their Christian heritage. But as Christians, it is for us never to forget what God has done in Europe. Let us praise the Lord Jesus Christ for His redeeming work in Europe!

## Timeline of Key Events

| | |
|---|---|
| AD 1517 | The Protestant Reformation begins in Wittenberg, Germany |
| AD 1519 | Ferdinand Magellan sails around the world |
| AD 1536 | John Calvin publishes his first edition of the *Institutes of the Christian Religion* |
| AD 1554 | Lady Jane Grey executed by Queen Mary |
| AD 1572 | St. Bartholomew's Day Massacre |
| AD 1588 | England defeats the Spanish Armada |
| AD 1598 | Edict of Nantes granting limited toleration to the Huguenots |
| AD 1620 | The Separatist Pilgrims leave Europe for North America |
| AD 1700 | Count Nicolaus Ludwig von Zinzendorf born |
| AD 1700 | Period of the "Enlightenment" begins paving the way for secularization in Europe |
| AD 1732 | First Moravian missionaries set out for St. Thomas |
| AD 1739 | George Whitefield preaches in the open-air for the first during the Great Awakening |
| AD 1773 | John Newton writes *Amazing Grace* |
| AD 1789 | Beginning of the French Revolution |
| AD 1807 | Britain abolishes the slave trade |
| AD 1818 | Karl Marx, creator of Communism, born |
| AD 1854 | Charles Spurgeon becomes pastor of New Park Street Church (later Metropolitan Tabernacle) |
| AD 1914-1918 | World War I |
| AD 1917 | Communist Revolution in Russia |
| AD 1938 | Dr. D. Martyn Lloyd-Jones becomes pastor of Westminster Chapel |
| AD 1939-1945 | World War II |
| AD 1991 | Fall of the Soviet Union (USSR) |

SEMUR EN AUXOIS, BURGUNDY, FRANCE

# THE REFORMATION IN FRANCE

> You are the light of the world. A city that is set on a hill cannot be hidden. Nor do they light a lamp and put it under a basket, but on a lampstand, and it gives light to all who are in the house. Let your light so shine before men, that they may see your good works and glorify your Father in heaven. (Matt. 5:14-16)

In previous chapters, we learned how God raised up faithful men like Wycliffe and Huss. But by the beginning of the 1500s, Wycliffe and Huss were gone. Yet, in God's providence, these early lights were not entirely extinguished. Huss' followers, later known as the Moravian Brethren, continued preaching and discipling. The Lollards (followers of Wycliffe) continued to travel throughout their country, teaching the Bible to the common folk in England. A desire to return to the authority of God's Word and its proclamation burned in the hearts of many. Heaps of tradition and ritual had buried the powerful and glorious gospel of Jesus Christ. The church needed reformation and spiritual revival.

A pivotal moment in the history of Christ's church was about to take place. In the early 1500s, God raised up men in Germany and Switzerland to reform the church.

A monk in Wittenberg named **Martin Luther** (1483-1546) nailed a document listing **95 Theses** to a church door on October 31, 1517. Luther was concerned about the abuse of authority by church leaders. He was also grieved by the corruption of the church in doctrine and practice. Luther was passionate for reformation. His work in preaching, teaching,

**MARTIN LUTHER (1483-1546)**

**WILLIAM TYNDALE (1494-1536)**

239

and Bible translation changed the world.

Luther's writings served as a wake-up call for men like **William Tyndale** (1494-1536) in England, **John Calvin** (1509-1564) in France, and **John Knox** (1514-1572) in Scotland. It wasn't long before the doctrines of Biblical authority and justification by faith alone had spread throughout Europe. Practically every country in Europe was affected in some way or another. The world would never be the same.

We call this time in church history the **Protestant Reformation**. It is called "Protestant" because those seeking reformation were protesting the unbiblical doctrines and practices common at the time. It is called the "Reformation" because the goal was to reshape the teaching and practice of the church according to what the Bible teaches.

During this time, German Protestants were somewhat protected from persecution by their princes. Many of the German princes joined the Reformation. English Protestants were also somewhat protected from persecution. **King Henry VIII** (1491-1547) severed the English Church from the authority of the pope and the Roman Catholic Church. He proclaimed himself "head of the church." King Henry did this because the pope would not allow him to end his first marriage. Henry's reasons for making the English Church independent were not godly reasons. But the Lord used even this sinful king to open the door to reformation in England. For a time, many German Protestants and English Protestants were protected from persecution.

However, the situation for Protestants in France was quite different. During the Protestant Reformation, it was particularly French Protestants who suffered persecution for their convictions.

## THE FRENCH HUGUENOTS

As we learned in previous chapters, much persecution occurred in France. Heretical groups like the Cathars were violently attacked. Others more faithful to the Bible, like the Waldensians, also suffered. This pattern of violence in France would continue during the Protestant Reformation. The French Protestants, known as the **French Huguenots**, were brutally persecuted for many years. At times, the Huguenots were forced to flee the country for safety.

Despite frequent attacks, the French Protestant Church grew rapidly through the 1540s and the 1550s. French believers were assisted by the reformation efforts in **Geneva**. (Geneva was a city located just across the French

**KING HENRY VIII (1491-1547)**

> **French Huguenots, French Reformed Church, French Protestants** ▪ These three terms are used interchangeably in this chapter. The French Huguenots were also known as the French Reformed. They were called "reformed" because they were connected with the reforming church work taking place in both Geneva and in Switzerland.

border.) Christians from all over Europe traveled to Geneva to be discipled. Here **William Farel** (1489-1565), **Pierre Viret** (1511-1571), and John Calvin labored to root and ground God's people in the Bible.

Under the leadership of Reformer John Calvin, a training academy was established in Geneva. This academy would prepare thousands of young men for ministry as pastors and evangelists. Men from France traveled to Geneva to study. After months or years of study, they returned to their native land to proclaim the gospel of God's grace. Reformation ideals spread like wildfire throughout France. Roman church leaders in France began complaining that "all these Protestant pastors were spreading dangerous ideas throughout France." Roman church leaders wanted to stop the Protestants. Some of them realized that violent force would be necessary.

French Protestants began to experience slander and violence. As a result, they met in secret when they came together to worship God. Sometimes they gathered in private houses for worship. Sometimes they gathered in the forest. These faithful men and women were committed to hold fast to the true gospel. Even if it meant giving up their lives, the Huguenots held fast to what they had discov-

LAKE GENEVA, SWITZERLAND

ered in the pages of Scripture. And for some, it would cost them their lives.

When believers of the French Reformed Church met for worship, their services included expository preaching of the Bible, the singing of the Psalms, and the celebration of the Lord's Supper. Even though they were persecuted, the French Protestants maintained an evangelistic spirit. They wanted others to know the precious truths found in the Bible. Many of the pastors would preach openly in town squares. As they cried out in the town square, they preached Christ crucified. They called men and women, boys and girls, to believe in Jesus Christ and repent of their sins.

> I charge you therefore before God and the Lord Jesus Christ, who will judge the living and the dead at His appearing and His kingdom: Preach the word! Be ready in season and out of season. Convince, rebuke, exhort, with all longsuffering and teaching. (2 Tim. 4:1-2)

## THE GROWTH OF THE FRENCH REFORMED CHURCH

> Let the word of Christ dwell in you richly in all wisdom, teaching and admonishing one another in psalms and hymns and spiritual songs, singing with grace in your hearts to the Lord. (Col. 3:16)

The French Huguenots experienced a brief period of peace in the 1550s. This happened because several French nobles embraced the Biblical gospel in the 1550s. Two of the most influential of these nobles were **Louis of Conde** (1530-1569) and Admiral **Gaspard de Coligny** (1519-1572). These Christian noblemen worked hard to protect their fellow believers from persecution. For a while, the Huguenots were able to meet for worship more openly. No longer did they have to meet covertly in homes and forests.

By 1559, the French Reformed Church was quite large. An assembly was called to organize a common church government. They adopted a **Presbyterian** form of church government.

The pastors and elders of the French Huguenots convened frequently as a presbytery. The 1559 assembly adopted a confession of

**GASPARD DE COLIGNY**

## 24. THE REFORMATION IN FRANCE

> **Presbyterian church government**
> The form of church government called "Presbyterian" comes from the Greek word for *elder* used in the New Testament (*presbuteros*). Churches with a Presbyterian form of church government are ruled by appointed elders. In most cases, Presbyterian churches are connected with other Presbyterian churches. A local presbytery consists of the pastors and elders from each of the local churches. Together, the pastors and elders of that region will meet together and discuss matters and make decisions.

faith known as the **French Confession**. This confession is also called the **Gallican Confession**. Most of the document was written by the Genevan Reformer John Calvin. Here is one portion of the Gallican Confession translated into English:

> We believe that by the perfect sacrifice that the Lord Jesus offered on the cross, we are reconciled to God, and justified before him. For we cannot be acceptable to him, nor become partakers of the grace of adoption, except as he pardons all our sins, and blots them out. Thus we declare that through Jesus Christ we are cleansed and made perfect. By his death we are fully justified, and through him only can we be delivered from our iniquities and transgressions. (Gallican Confession, Article 17)

The words quoted above summarize the biblical doctrine of justification. Thanks be to

LA ROCHELLE, FRANCE

## Basic Facts about France (French Republic)

| Total population: | 67 million |
|---|---|
| Total area: | 247,000 square miles |
| Capital: | Paris |
| Official language: | French |
| Primary religions: | Roman Catholic, Atheist, Islam |

God for the clarity of truth expressed in these words! We are cleansed and made perfect through Jesus Christ alone! The French Confession contains many precious truths such as this one.

By 1561, there were over 2,000 Reformed churches in France. This was Admiral Coligny's estimate. The church of Jesus Christ was steadily growing. Many Roman Catholic priests converted to the faith. Some of the Roman church buildings were used for Protestant worship. A church in Rouen, France was estimated to have over 10,000 members. With these growing numbers, it became more difficult for the French authorities to persecute the Huguenots.

Then, in 1559, King Henry II died. The throne passed to his sixteen-year-old son Francis II. However, Francis II died the next year. Then the throne passed to Francis' brother Charles IX. He was also quite young (being only ten years old). Because Charles was still a young boy, his mother Catherine de Medici (1519-1589) ruled on his behalf. As a committed Italian Catholic, **Catherine de Medici** was fiercely opposed to the Protestants. However, many of the French nobles were now Huguenots. Catherine realized that she must tolerate the Protestants to avoid civil war. In 1562, she issued a royal edict granting a degree of toleration to the French Huguenots. The edict allowed the Huguenots to worship in private outside the city walls, but not in towns. It also allowed the Huguenots to hold synods (church assemblies or presbytery meetings).

The edict brought some peace to France. But it was short-lived. French persecutions resumed in the following years. In a later

**CATHERINE DE MEDICI (1519-1589)**

# PRAYER POINTS: FRANCE

In this Prayer Points, we will pray for Protestant, gospel-preaching, Bible-believing churches in France.

- **Pray for the increase of faithful, Christ-following, Bible-believing churches:** According to *Operation World*, only around 1% of the French population claims to be Protestant Christian. Though France once had a large, strong Protestant church, it has diminished in size due to persecution and secularization. Let us ask God to establish more faithful churches in France where Christ is preached and where God is worshiped in spirit and truth.

- **Pray for God's strength for faithful disciples in France:** Though the population of gospel-believing Christians in France is small, there are still some true disciples of Jesus Christ in France. Let us ask God to strengthen them so that they would not give up. Ask the Lord to equip them with faith, boldness, power, love, and a sound mind in order to keep the faith in a difficult country.

chapter, you will learn about how the Huguenots suffered and survived. Though oppressed and mistreated, the French Reformed Church still persevered and continued to grow. Theodore Beza, a friend and disciple of John Calvin, once said, "The church is an anvil that has worn out many hammers." The hammers of state-government persecution did break eventually, and sure enough, the anvil of the true church prevailed. ∎

THUN CITY, SWITZERLAND

# PIERRE VIRET: EVANGELIST TO FRANCE

*You therefore, my son, be strong in the grace that is in Christ Jesus. And the things that you have heard from me among many witnesses, commit these to faithful men who will be able to teach others also. You therefore must endure hardship as a good soldier of Jesus Christ. (2 Tim. 2:1-3)*

As we learned in the previous chapter, the city of Geneva was an important center of reformation. It became one of the most prolific missionary-sending bases in all of Europe. The Academy of Geneva commissioned thousands of evangelist missionaries. Those faithful men took the gospel all over Europe. Some would even travel as far as South America. Geneva's discipleship ministry was largely directed by the careful, mature guidance of John Calvin (1509-1564). But there were other brothers who served alongside Calvin. These included such men as **William Farel** (1489-1565), **Theodore Beza** (1519-1605), and **Pierre Viret** (1511-1571).

Though largely forgotten by history, Pierre Viret (pronounced "vee-ray") was a pivotal leader of the Protestant Reformation. Viret was born in 1511 in the village of **Orbe** (located in modern-day Switzerland). He was first exposed to the teachings of the Reformation by his schoolteacher. At sixteen years of age, the young man traveled to Paris for college. There he quickly grew in his knowledge of the Scriptures. After completing his college studies, he returned to his hometown in Switzerland. Orbe was a much safer place for a Protestant than was Paris.

When Pierre Viret was twenty years of age, the reformer William Farel came to Orbe for a visit. Farel visited the village to preach God's Word, and while there, he met Viret. Farel was impressed by Viret's zeal for the gospel and his gifts. Farel encouraged the young man to preach the Word. Viret took this advice and began testing his gift for preaching in Orbe. It was not long before the townsfolk were impressed by Viret's preaching. Viret had a unique ability to win his audience by gentleness and faithfulness to the Word. The young preacher earned the title "the Angel of the Reformation" because of his peaceableness and gentleness. In numerous situations, Viret

**PIERRE VIRET (1511-1571)**

would be called upon to mediate disputes.

"Blessed are the peacemakers,
For they shall be called sons of God." (Matt. 5:9)

But the fruit of the Spirit is love, joy, peace, longsuffering, kindness, goodness, faithfulness, gentleness, self-control. Against such there is no law. (Gal. 5:22-23)

In 1534, Viret traveled to **Geneva** to join Farel. These two reformers longed to see Geneva reformed according to God's Word. Not everyone in Geneva wanted reformation. The remaining Catholics in Geneva hatched a plot to kill both Farel and Viret. A Roman Catholic woman by the name of Antonia Vax was selected to carry out the assassination. This woman deceived the reformers by presenting herself as a Huguenot refugee. She became a cook for the Genevan pastors. One day, she mixed poison in a pot of spinach soup. It was her intention to kill both Farel and Viret with the deadly soup. At supper, Antonia placed the soup bowls before the two reformers.

Farel took a taste of the soup and turned it away. However, Pierre Viret kept eating. As Antonia watched Viret take sips of the soup, her conscience was deeply disturbed. She saw that she was to be responsible for the death of an innocent man. She rushed over to Viret, but it was too late. Antonia later confessed the evil plot. Thankfully, by God's mercy, Viret did not die from the poisoned soup. However, he became quite ill. Though he recovered, Viret had lingering health effects the rest of his life. As God ordained it, the preacher from Orbe would continue to minister in much weakness, as the Apostle Paul did.

ORBE, SWITZERLAND

**JOHN CALVIN (1509-1564)**

> And He said to me, "My grace is sufficient for you, for My strength is made perfect in weakness." Therefore most gladly I will rather boast in my infirmities, that the power of Christ may rest upon me. Therefore I take pleasure in infirmities, in reproaches, in needs, in persecutions, in distresses, for Christ's sake. For when I am weak, then I am strong. (2 Cor. 12:9-10)

After ministering in Geneva for a few years, Viret was called to the neighboring city of Lausanne. There he ministered for another twenty-two years until disagreements with the authorities of Bern forced him out. He returned to Geneva in 1559.

Viret continued working alongside Calvin until 1561. His duties included preaching in the churches of Geneva and training students at the **Academy of Geneva**. Due to his ongoing health problems, he took the counsel of doctors and left the city for southern France. The climate in southern France was easier on his body. Always the minister of the gospel, Viret wasn't there for a vacation. He took up a preaching ministry throughout France. He advanced the French Reformation and built up his Huguenot brothers and sisters in the faith. Invitations for him to preach came from all over France.

The cities of **Montpellier, Nimes,** and **Lyons** were particularly affected by Viret's ministry. His preaching attracted thousands upon thousands. Many turned to the Lord from the false religion of Roman Catholicism. Many eyes were opened to the gospel of God's free grace. During the Christmas of 1561, Viret preached in the city of Nimes. While there, he led a communion service with over 8,000 in attendance. Many Roman Catholic authorities in the city repented of their sins and believed in Jesus Christ.

**JEANNE D'ALBRET (1528-1572)**

Viret's proclamation of the gospel was not well received by many of the French authorities. By royal decree, Viret was banished from France in 1566. After being banished, he sought refuge with **Jeanne d'Albret** (1528-1572), the queen of **Navarre**. The kingdom of Navarre would later become part of France, but at this time Navarre was a separate kingdom. Navarre was located between the border of France and Spain.

For a time, Protestants flourished under the protection of Jeanne d'Albret. Viret was appointed by the queen to be the superintendent of the academy at Orthez. He continued his labors there for the gospel of the Lord Jesus until his death in 1571.

---

Then I heard a voice from heaven saying to me, "Write: 'Blessed are the dead who die in the Lord from now on.' 'Yes,' says the Spirit, 'that they may rest from their labors, and their works follow them.' " (Rev. 14:13)

---

Pierre Viret was used mightily by God during the Reformation. Many were converted to the true gospel. Many saints were equipped for the work of ministry. The church was edified. Viret left over fifty books for the building up of the future church. Many of these books are being translated into English today. In these memorable words, Viret gave testimony to his willingness to die for the gospel:

> It is necessary always to stand upon this, that we must hold the glory of God in greater esteem than our life, and we should always elect a thousand deaths rather than violate a single commandment of God.

Amen. May God grant all of us that faith of Pierre Viret to seek the glory of God above all else in this life. ■

## PRAYER POINTS: SWITZERLAND

- **Praise God for the Reformation heritage of Switzerland:** It was in Switzerland, along with Germany, that the Reformation took root and spread elsewhere. It was God's grace to raise up teachers, translators, evangelists, and missionaries in Switzerland. Give thanks to God for this rich heritage of faith.

- **Ask God to revive this rich heritage:** Like much of Europe, Switzerland is becoming more godless in its culture. Let us pray that many would discover the rich heritage of gospel teaching found in the Swiss Reformation. Let us ask God to raise up faithful new evangelists in Switzerland who would teach the Bible to the Swiss people.

- **Pray that God would strengthen Christian families:** There are faithful Christian families in Switzerland who desire to pass on the faith to their children. Ask God to strengthen and protect these families. Pray that God would sustain the faith into future generations.

25. PIERRE VIRET: EVANGELIST TO FRANCE 251

ORTHEZ, FRANCE

## Basic Facts about Switzerland (Swiss Confederation)

| Total population: | 8.5 million |
| --- | --- |
| Total area: | 16,000 square miles |
| Capital: | Bern |
| Official language: | German, French, Italian |
| Primary religions: | Roman Catholic, Protestant Christian |

GORDES, PROVENCE, FRANCE

# THE SUFFERINGS OF THE HUGUENOTS

---

**Yes, and all who desire to live godly in Christ Jesus will suffer persecution. (2 Tim. 3:12)**

---

As we learned in a previous chapter, the royal edict of 1562 gave limited toleration to the Huguenots in France. Huguenots could worship in the countryside, but they were barred from worshiping in the towns of France. Even this limited toleration was short-lived. Not only did the Roman Catholics and Protestants disagree on matters of doctrine, but there were political divisions as well. The accumulated political and theological disagreements turned into open conflict.

Persecution of the Huguenots began to increase in 1562. It began in the town of **Vassy**. There a horrific attack took place in which sixty-three Huguenots were cruelly massacred. It was Sunday, March 1, 1562. As the duke of Guise was on his way to the Roman mass, he ordered his men to set fire to a Huguenot church. Sixty-three innocent Huguenots were burned to death in the conflagration. Additional massacres followed in other French towns as other Roman Catholics joined in the bloodshed.

Violence continued to increase all over France. Those French nobles who were also Huguenots realized that they must act to protect God's people. As civil rulers, they had an obligation to protect God's people and punish evildoers. One night, **Admiral Coligny** was awakened by his wife. She was weeping. Coligny's wife told him, "Sir, I have on my heart and conscience all our people's blood that has been shed. This blood and your wife cry to God in heaven and in this bed against you, to warn you that you will be guilty of murdering those whom you do not prevent from being murdered."

Gaspard de Coligny's wife was calling her

**ILLUSTRATION OF FRENCH HUGUENOTS**

husband, as a godly civil leader in France, to do something. Her words are similar to the exhortation of Proverbs 24:

Deliver those who are drawn toward death,
And hold back those stumbling to the slaughter.
If you say, "Surely we did not know this,"
Does not He who weighs the hearts consider it?
He who keeps your soul, does He not know it?
And will He not render to each man according to his deeds? (Prov. 24:11-12)

Admiral Coligny and others in the French nobility took action. The Protestant French nobles began to fight back against the tyrannical persecutions of the Huguenots. A series of civil wars rocked France in the following years. These conflicts culminated in a horrific atrocity. This atrocity is known as the **St. Bartholomew's Day Massacre** of 1572. Peace had almost been achieved. But then the devil stirred up the hearts of the French monarchy to do great wickedness.

## THE ST. BARTHOLOMEW'S DAY MASSACRE

Before the massacre, an event took place intended to bring peace between Protestant and Roman Catholic. In August 1572, both Roman Catholic and Huguenot nobles gathered in Paris. They had come together to witness the wedding of a Huguenot prince, Henry of Navarre, to Margaret, a Roman Catholic princess and the sister of Charles IX. Many hoped this marriage would seal something of a political peace between Roman Catholics and Huguenots. In God's providence, it did the opposite. Four days after the wedding, an assassination was orchestrated by Catherine de Medici. Her target: Admiral Gaspard de

VIOLENCE AGAINST THE HUGUENOTS

Coligny. But her assassination failed. Coligny survived the attack. Fearing the Huguenots would take revenge, **Catherine de Medici** and others of the nobility planned a surprise massacre on the whole Huguenot population in France.

On August 24, 1572, on the feast day of St. Bartholomew, armed men swarmed through Paris and other major cities in France. Huguenots everywhere were killed. It was the largest single massacre during the Protestant Reformation. It is estimated that around 20,000 Huguenots died. Among those slain was Admiral Gaspard de Coligny. The massacre has since lived in infamy as the "St. Bartholomew's Day Massacre." It remains one of the most wicked acts committed against Christ's church. The French Reformed Church experienced a serious setback with the loss of so many of their leaders. After the massacre, the French monarchy continued its attempts to purge the Huguenot Christians. These various conflicts are known today as the **French Wars of Religion**.

## THE HUGUENOTS RESIST TYRANNY

How do Christians react to these massacres inspired by evil kings and rulers? Some Huguenot leaders were led to reexamine the role of civil government. The Huguenots found much teaching in the Bible to guide their thinking. Clearly, human authority must be limited and restrained by a higher authority. The highest authority must always be the authority of God's law. One of the most influential Huguenot thinkers was a man named **Philip Duplessis Mornay** (1549-1623). He was a Huguenot soldier and diplomat. He wrote an important book titled *A Defense of Liberty Against Tyrants*. The book was published in 1579.

In his book, Mornay carefully explained what the Bible teaches about this topic. Mornay insisted that a king's authority was not unlimited. A king could not kill his citizens whenever he wanted to. Even the king was subject to the law of God as well as the laws of his own country. If a king disregarded the laws of the land, that king could be opposed by other civil rulers.

For example, the president of the United States is not supreme. The president is under God's authority. The president, like all civil rulers, is required to obey God. Second, the president is also bound to obey the law of the land. In this case, that law is the Constitution of the United States. The president cannot simply kill people with whom he disagrees. Mornay went on to explain that kings or presidents who act as tyrants, ignoring the law of God or the laws of the land, could be lawfully opposed. Mornay even believed that tyrants and wicked rulers could be opposed with military force. However, it was important that those who led the opposition were civil rulers themselves (such as other noblemen). These were called **"lesser magistrates"** because they did not have the same degree of authority as someone like the king, but they were still civil rulers. And it was their job to uphold law in the land.

Mornay's views of government, law, and authority would later have an influence in other major events, including the American War for Independence. In fact, Mornay's book was referenced by some of America's founding fathers.

---

Therefore I exhort first of all that supplications, prayers, intercessions, and giving of thanks be made for all men, for kings and all who are in authority, that we may lead a quiet and peaceable life in all godliness and reverence. For this is good and acceptable in the sight of God our Savior, who desires all men to be saved and to come to the knowledge of the truth. (1 Tim. 2:1-4)

**KING HENRY IV (REIGNED 1589-1610)**

## LATER PERSECUTIONS OF THE HUGUENOTS

I have seen the wicked in great power,
And spreading himself like a native green tree.
Yet he passed away, and behold, he was no more;
Indeed I sought him, but he could not be found.
(Ps. 37:35-36)

The Huguenots sustained wave after wave of war and persecution. By God's mercies, peace was finally restored in 1598. That year, the **Edict of Nantes** was issued by **King Henry IV** (reigned 1589-1610). As a Huguenot himself, King Henry wanted protection for his fellow believers. This edict secured freedom of worship for the Huguenots throughout France. There were a few exceptions such as major cities like Paris. Huguenots were free to raise their children in their own faith. All positions in civil government were also open to Huguenots. The Edict of Nantes was a landmark achievement for religious liberty.

For many decades following the Edict of Nantes, the Huguenots flourished in France. They influenced government, education, and science. They built their own educational institutions throughout France. And the churches continued to grow. However, in the 1630s, troubles for the Huguenots returned. After thirty years of relative peace, conditions worsened as Roman Catholicism increased in France. The Jesuit order of the Roman church initiated more persecutions against the Huguenots. Then, in 1685, the Edict of Nantes was formally revoked by Louis XIV and replaced with a new edict of persecution. This reversal edict was known as the **Edict of Fontainebleau**. Hundreds of thousands of Huguenots fled to other nations. Many of them left for England and the American colonies.

By persecuting the French Huguenots,

HUGUENOTS DEFENDING THEIR HOME AFTER THE EDICT OF NANTES WAS REVOKED

France expelled many of its most godly citizens. The country lost many of its best and brightest. With those righteous men and women who fled went much of the learning, industry, and innovation that always comes with true faith. However, France's loss was the world's gain. It wasn't long before French Huguenots had spread all over the world. Wherever they went, the Huguenots brought with them robust faith, God-centered worship, and faithfulness in their character and work. England, Switzerland, the Netherlands, South Africa, Brazil, and America all received the Huguenots with open arms. God would bless these nations with an outpouring of the biblical faith in the centuries to come. ∎

---

Blessed is the nation whose God is the LORD, The people He has chosen as His own inheritance. (Ps. 33:12)

---

## Basic Facts about France (French Republic)

| Total population: | 67 million |
| --- | --- |
| Total area: | 247,000 square miles |
| Capital: | Paris |
| Official language: | French |
| Primary religions: | Roman Catholic, Atheist, Islam |

# PRAYER POINTS: FRANCE

- **Pray for dead hearts to be awakened to the things of God:** Since the radically secular French Revolution of 1789, France has been one of the most secular nations in Europe. Yet, like most nations in Europe, it has a Christian heritage that goes back almost to the beginning of Christianity. Only about six percent of the population of France attend church on a weekly basis. Most French people are "without God and without hope in the world" (Eph. 2:12). Ask the Lord to awaken dead hearts to the things of God. Pray that God would send forth faithful Christians who would share God's Word with the unbelievers of France.

- **Pray in light of changing demographics:** The population of France is changing. Many immigrants, especially from Muslim backgrounds, are now living in France in greater numbers than ever before. The birth rate among French families is falling. This means that in the future, more people in France will likely be born with a heritage from a nation elsewhere in the world, especially from Muslim nations. Pray that God would use this change in France as an opportunity for the gospel to penetrate both into the French people as well as the foreign immigrants now in France.

- **Pray against the forces of darkness in France:** *Operation World* reports that there are ten times more people earning a living by occult practices (witchcraft and sorcery) than there are evangelical pastors in France. This means that for every ten people actively practicing occultic rituals, there is just one Bible-believing pastor. Pray against the demonic forces that are bringing destruction to the people of France. Pray that God would raise up more faithful missionaries and pastors in France.

HUGUENOT CHURCH IN CHARLESTON, SOUTH CAROLINA

TOWER OF LONDON

# LADY JANE GREY: NINE DAY QUEEN OF ENGLAND

And they overcame [Satan] by the blood of the Lamb and by the word of their testimony, and they did not love their lives to the death. (Rev. 12:11)

Within a jail cell in the **Tower of London**, a young woman sixteen years old awaited execution. From July 1553 to February 1554, Jane had been confined in the same cell. A victim of political forces outside her control, **Lady Jane Grey** (1537-1554) was charged with treason against the reigning monarch. **Queen Mary** (1516-1558), known to history as "Bloody Mary," had ordered Jane's execution.

Lady Jane Grey inherited the throne of England after the death of **King Edward VI** (1537-1553). On July 6, 1553, Edward had died of tuberculosis at fifteen years of age. At this time in England, the future of the Protestant church hung in the balance. Would the churches of England be aligned with Rome and its pope? Or would the churches in England join the Protestant Reformation? Would the Word of God be of supreme authority in England, or would the Roman Church act as the ultimate authority?

Though Edward was young, he died a committed Protestant. Some of his dying prayer is recorded for us.

**LADY JANE GREY (1537-1554)**

**EDWARD VI (1537-1553)**

261

Lord God, deliver me out of this miserable and wretched life.... Lord, I commit my spirit to You. O Lord, you know how happy it were for me to be with You.... O my Lord God! Bless Your people, and save Your inheritance! O Lord God, save Your chosen people of England! O my Lord God, defend this realm from papistry, and maintain Your true religion; that I and Your people may praise Your holy name, for Your Son, Jesus Christ's sake!

## LADY JANE BECOMES QUEEN

Before Edward died, he was advised to sign a document indicating who his successor would be. Some people feared that Mary, Edward's older sister, would take the throne. Mary was committed to returning the English Church to Roman control. She wanted to see England return to Roman Catholicism and abandon the Reformation. Many in England agreed with her. But others, including **Thomas Cranmer** (1489-1556), the archbishop of Canterbury, earnestly desired reformation in England.

In order to prevent Mary's accession to the throne, Edward signed a document indicating that his cousin, Lady Jane Grey, should inherit the throne. Lady Jane was a Protestant, but she stood fourth in line to the throne. Edward's father Henry VIII had complicated matters by disinheriting his daughters Mary and Elizabeth. For this reason, legal questions remained. Who was the rightful heir to the throne? Mary was the oldest child of Henry VIII. It seemed that Mary was obviously the rightful heir to succeed her younger brother Edward. But fearing Catholic influence, many wanted Lady Jane to reign instead.

In his last days, Edward signed a document that specifically stated that Lady Jane Grey should be his heir. Senior lawyers in the kingdom argued that without Parliament approving this, the document would not be legal. But Edward died before Parliament had a chance to consider the decision. When he died, Edward left the kingdom in a precarious position. Two days after his death, the news reached his sisters Mary and Elizabeth. Mary assumed she was the rightful heir. She began her journey from the north to London.

Meanwhile, those in support of Edward's special "devise" of succession informed Lady Jane Grey that

**THOMAS CRANMER (1489-1556)**

she was now to be the queen of England. Young Jane was stunned and frightened by this news. She was reluctant to accept the throne. She did not understand all the legal matters at stake. Nor did she understand the risk that was posed by Mary who was on her way to London. But she humbly accepted what had been presented to her. She prayed to God, "If what has been given to me is lawfully mine, may Your divine Majesty grant me such grace that I may govern to Your glory and service, to the advantage of this realm."

## ARRESTED

For about nine days, Jane served as the queen of England. But as word spread that Mary was on her way to claim the throne, Jane's support quickly evaporated. With Mary came an army that would take the throne by force if necessary. It became evident to Jane's supporters that Mary would succeed in taking the throne from Lady Jane. By the time Mary arrived in London, practically everyone had already abandoned Jane. Those who had arranged for Jane to be made queen were now in danger. They realized they would be executed for treason if Mary found out they had been involved in bringing Jane to the throne.

**MARY I (1516-1558)**

Nine days after accepting the crown, Lady Jane was arrested and imprisoned in the Tower of London. The date was July 19, 1553. Jane was charged with high treason. Along with Jane, her young husband **Guildford Dudley** (1535-1554) was also charged with treason. Archbishop Thomas Cranmer was charged with the same crime.

That September, Parliament declared Mary the rightful successor to Edward. Jane was declared a treasonous usurper. For months, Jane remained in a jail cell in the Tower. It was not clear whether Mary would order Jane's execution. Would Mary have mercy on Jane? After all, Jane was the victim of circumstances outside her control. She had had no intention of committing treason. She believed she had acted lawfully.

While Jane awaited news of her fate, there was unrest throughout England. Queen Mary, though thirty-nine years of age, was not married. If she would have an heir of her own, she would need to be married. She began to make arrangements to marry Prince Philip of Spain. This potential marriage made many in England anxious. Many feared that such a marriage would put England under Spanish control. The English church was also in peril. Would the English church be under the control of the pope? What would come of the Reformation's progress in England?

These were pressing questions in Lady Jane's day. Such questions were especially concerning to fellow Protestants who longed to see the reformation of England continue.

## SENTENCED TO EXECUTION

Queen Mary's plan to marry Prince Philip of Spain was deeply unpopular. Many people

THE WHITE TOWER, WITHIN THE TOWER OF LONDON

in England feared that their country would be ruled by this foreigner. In January 1554, a rebellion was staged against Queen Mary. Jane's father Henry Grey was one of the main conspirators of the rebellion. Jane's two uncles also joined Henry Grey in the rebellion. With Henry Grey, a man named Thomas Wyatt coordinated the rebellion. An army was raised and marched on London. But Mary's supporters quelled the rebellion. This event is known as Wyatt's Rebellion.

The rebellion showed Queen Mary that Jane was still a threat to her reign. If the rebels had succeeded, they might have made Jane queen again. In order to ensure that she would reign unchallenged, Mary decided to have Jane executed. With Jane, her husband Guilford Dudley was also to be put to death.

## LADY JANE STANDS FAST

> For whoever desires to save his life will lose it, but whoever loses his life for My sake will save it. For what profit is it to a man if he gains the whole world, and is himself destroyed or lost? For whoever is ashamed of Me and My words, of him the Son of Man will be ashamed when He comes in His own glory, and in His Father's, and of the holy angels. (Luke 9:24-26)

Lady Jane's execution was to occur in early February 1554. Though Jane was to be put to death, Mary hoped that Jane might turn away from her "heretical" Protestant beliefs. Perhaps Jane could be persuaded to return to the Catholic faith. On February 8, Queen Mary sent her personal chaplain to Lady Jane. The name of her chaplain was **Dr. John Feckenham** (c. 1515-1584). He was a man thoroughly committed to the Roman Church and its false doctrines. Despite his wrong views, Dr. Feckenham came out of concern for Lady Jane's soul.

As Dr. Feckenham talked with Lady Jane, he was amazed by her responses to his questions. Lady Jane was a young woman who knew what she believed. She asked Dr. Feckenham to leave her to pray. She was preparing for her execution the next day.

Dr. Feckenham returned to Queen Mary and reported what had happened. He told the queen that if he could have a few more days to speak with Lady Jane, she would surely embrace the Catholic faith. Queen Mary gave permission to Dr. Feckenham to return to Lady Jane's cell and continue the discussion. Not only that, but Dr. Feckenham was to inform Lady Jane that if she converted, she would be spared execution. Jane would save her life if she would only repent of her Protestant beliefs.

Dr. Feckenham returned to the Tower with the good news. But he was quickly disappointed by Lady Jane's reply. She told Dr. Feckenham:

> Alas sir, it was not my desire to prolong my days. You are much deceived if you think I have any desire for longer life. For I assure you, since the time you went from me, my life has been so tedious to me, that I long for nothing so much as death.

Though Jane had not immediately given in, Dr. Feckenham thought he might still have a chance to convince her, so he challenged her to a public debate in the chapel. A debate on matters of doctrine would be held on February 10 in the chapel of the Tower of London. Perhaps there Dr. Feckenham could show Jane the error of her ways.

Lady Jane agreed to the debate. A portion of the debate was written down by Jane before her death. It is a remarkable testimony. In it, we learn that Lady Jane was a diligent student of the Bible. We learn that she was a woman of remarkable faith. She was a faithful follower of Jesus Christ. Here is a part of what she wrote:[1]

---

[1] The language of the debate between Lady Jane Grey and Dr. Feckenham has been modernized at points for the reader.

Feckenham: What thing is required in a Christian?

Jane: To believe in God the Father, in God the Son, in God the Holy Ghost, three persons and one God.

Feckenham: Is there nothing else required in a Christian, but to believe in God?

Jane: Yes. We must believe in him, we must love him, with all our heart, with all our soul, and all our mind, and our neighbor as ourselves.

Jane explained to Dr. Feckenham that a Christian must believe in God and must love God and love neighbor. So far they were both agreed. But Dr. Feckenham wanted to trap Jane. He wanted to disprove the Reformation doctrine of justification. Lady Jane believed that we are declared righteous in God's sight by faith alone.

Feckenham: Why then does faith not justify or save?

Jane: Yes, verily, faith (as St. Paul says) only justifies.

Feckenham: St. Paul says, if I have all the faith of the world, without love, it is nothing.

Jane: True it is, for how can I love him I trust not, or how can I trust in him whom I love not? Faith and love ever agree together, and yet love is comprehended in faith.

Feckenham: How shall we love our neighbor?

Jane: To love our neighbor is to feed the hungry, clothe the naked, and to give drink to the thirsty, and to do to him as we would do to ourselves.

Feckenham: Why then it is necessary to do good works in order to be saved, and it is not sufficient to believe?

Jane: I deny that. I affirm that faith only saves. For it is necessary for all Christians, to show that they follow their master Christ, to do good works. Yet may we not say, nor in any wise believe, that they profit to salvation. For although we have done all that we can, yet we are unprofitable servants, and the faith we have only in Christ's blood and his merits, saves.

Jane explained that it is by faith alone that we are saved. True Christians will show their faith by good works. True Christians love Jesus Christ. They will obey His commands. But our good works cannot in any way contribute to our salvation.

Then Dr. Feckenham moved to another topic dividing Protestants and Catholics. He debated the sacraments with Lady Jane Grey.

Feckenham: How many Sacraments are there?

Jane: Two: the one the Sacrament of Baptism, and the other the Sacrament of the Lord's Supper.

Feckenham: No, there be seven Sacraments.

Jane: By what Scripture do you find that?

Jane challenged Dr. Feckenham and asked, "What Scripture do you use to prove there are seven sacraments?" Not able to answer, Dr. Feckenham proceeded with more questions for Jane.

Feckenham: Well, we will talk of that hereafter. But what is signified by your two sacraments?

Dr. Feckenham challenged Jane on the meaning of baptism and the Lord's Supper. As with her other replies, Jane responded with biblical truth.

Finally, Dr. Feckenham accused Jane of basing her faith upon the opinions of men.

> Feckenham: You ground your faith upon such authors as say and unsay, both with a breath, and not upon the church, to whom you ought to give credit.

To this, Jane replied that her faith was not based on the opinions of Martin Luther or John Calvin. Instead, her faith was grounded on the sure foundation of the Bible.

> Jane: No, I ground my faith upon God's word, and not upon the church. For if the church be a good church, the faith of the church must be tested by God's word, and not God's word by the church.

Jane believed that the church's teaching must be tested by the only standard without error: the standard of the Bible.

The debate continued for some time, but eventually Dr. Feckenham gave up. Lady Jane had stood firm. She would not reject her biblical beliefs. Dr. Feckenham then said to Jane, "I am sorry for you, for I am sure that we shall never meet again."

To this Jane replied, "It is true that we will never meet again except if God changes your heart. For I am sure, unless you repent and turn to God, you are in an evil condition. I pray that God would, in His mercy, send you His Holy Spirit. He has given you the gift of speech. May He also open the eyes of your heart."

## EXECUTED FOR HIGH TREASON

The next evening, February 11, Lady Jane prepared for her execution. It was scheduled for the morning of February 12. Before Jane went to sleep, she wrote a brief letter for her sister Katherine. Not having any writing paper at hand, Jane wrote the letter in the back of her Greek New Testament.

For years, Jane had dutifully studied the Greek New Testament. From its pages, she had come to a saving understanding of the gospel. Her faith was in Christ. Her hope was in His death and resurrection. Jane hoped that her sister Katherine would also know Jesus to the saving of her soul. Here is a portion of what Jane wrote to her sister:

> I have here sent you, good sister Katherine, a book, which, although it is not outwardly trimmed with gold, yet inwardly it is worth more than precious stones. It is the book, dear sister, of the law of the Lord ... [it] shall lead you to the path of eternal joy. And, if you with a good mind read it, and with an earnest mind do purpose to follow it, it shall bring you to an immortal and everlasting life.

The next morning, Jane's husband Guilford Dudley was marched past her prison cell. He was then executed. Jane was next.

She was taken to Tower Green, within the Tower of London. Before she was to be executed, Lady Jane was given an opportunity to speak. She said:

> I pray you all, good Christian people, to bear me witness that I die a true Christian woman. I do look to be saved by no other means, but only by the mercy of God, in the blood of His only Son Jesus Christ.

Before the execution proceeded, Jane knelt and recited the words of Psalm 51:

---

**Have mercy upon me, O God,
According to Your lovingkindness;
According to the multitude of Your tender mercies,
Blot out my transgressions.
Wash me thoroughly from my iniquity,
And cleanse me from my sin. (Ps. 51:1-2)**

---

Lady Jane continued by reciting all nineteen verses of the psalm. Having recited this

**THE EXECUTION OF LADY JANE GREY**

## Basic Facts about England

*The United Kingdom consists of the nations of England, Wales, Scotland, and Northern Ireland. The facts below pertain to England, one of the countries within the UK.*

| | |
|---|---|
| Total population: | 56 million |
| Total area: | 50,000 square miles |
| Capital: | London |
| Official language: | English |
| Primary religions: | Protestant Christian, Atheist, Agnostic |

last prayer, she said, "Lord, into your hands I commit my spirit!" Having said these words, Lady Jane Grey was executed. She was sixteen years old. To the end of her short life, Lady Jane kept the faith.

## THE YEARS THAT FOLLOWED

As expected, Queen Mary continued to bring the English church under Roman control. Many English Reformers were put to death. Queen Mary soon earned the name Bloody Mary because of the executions she ordered. Many of the men who mentored Lady Jane Grey were executed during her bloody reign. These men include Thomas Cranmer, **Nicholas Ridley** (c. 1500-1555), and **Hugh Latimer** (c. 1487-1555). Much of Mary's persecution against faithful men and women is recorded in **John Foxe's** *Book of Martyrs*.

In October 1555, Nicholas Ridley and Hugh Latimer were burned at the stake together. Queen Mary had sentenced them to death for heresy. Latimer's last words were recorded by John Foxe as follows:

> Be of good comfort, and play the man, Master Ridley; we shall this day light such a candle, by God's grace, in England, as I trust shall never be put out.

Latimer was right. The bloody persecutions of Queen Mary did light a candle in England. The works of darkness were exposed. The truth of God's Word would shine more brightly in the years that followed.

Queen Mary died in 1558. She was forty-two years old. Having died without any children, Mary's sister Queen Elizabeth took the throne. Under Queen Elizabeth's reign, persecutions against Protestants largely ended. The work of reformation in England continued. ∎

---

**In him was life, and the life was the light of men. The light shines in the darkness, and the darkness has not overcome it. (John 1:4-5 ESV)**

---

**BURNING OF RIDLEY AND LATIMER FROM *FOXE'S BOOK OF MARTYRS***

# PRAYER POINTS: UNITED KINGDOM

> Therefore I exhort first of all that supplications, prayers, intercessions, and giving of thanks be made for all men, for kings and all who are in authority, that we may lead a quiet and peaceable life in all godliness and reverence. For this is good and acceptable in the sight of God our Savior, who desires all men to be saved and to come to the knowledge of the truth. (1 Tim. 2:1-4)

In this Prayer Points, we will pray for those in civil government in the United Kingdom.

- **Pray for the Monarch of the United Kingdom:** At the time of this book's writing, the reigning monarch in the United Kingdom is Queen Elizabeth II. While the monarch of the United Kingdom has far less power than the kings and queens in Bloody Mary's day, the monarch is still considered the head of state in the United Kingdom. Pray for the reigning monarch of the United Kingdom: that the monarch would believe in the Lord Jesus Christ and submit to Christ's kingship. Pray that the monarch would be an example of godliness and righteousness to the citizens of the United Kingdom. Ask God to surround the monarch with godly advisers.

- **Pray for the Parliament of the United Kingdom:** The Parliament of the United Kingdom consists of two houses: the House of Lords and the House of Commons. Those members of Parliament (MPs) in the House of Commons are elected by the people of various districts of the United Kingdom. Ask God to raise up more righteous rulers in the United Kingdom. Ask the Lord to put Christians in places of government so that they can seek to apply God's standards of righteousness in the UK. Beseech the Lord to stop those in Parliament who would seek to legislate wicked laws.

HERRNHUT, GERMANY

# COUNT ZINZENDORF AND THE MORAVIAN BRETHREN

So the nations shall fear the name of the LORD,
And all the kings of the earth Your glory.
For the LORD shall build up Zion;
He shall appear in His glory. (Ps. 102:15-16)

The year 1700 is an important year in the history of Christianity in Europe. It was the year a man named Count **Nicolaus Ludwig von Zinzendorf** (1700-1760) was born. He was born into a family of Austrian nobility. Zinzendorf would be used by God in amazing ways to further the cause of Christian missions. His commitment to the cause of Christ, and his investment in a group of Christians known as the Moravian Brethren, led to an ambitious new wave of missionary efforts all over the world.

Days after his birth, Zinzendorf's mother wrote a prayer of dedication for her son. She wrote in the front of the family Bible:

> On May 26, in the year 1700, on Wednesday evening about six o'clock, Almighty God blessed me in Dresden with the gift of my firstborn son, Nicolaus Ludwig. The Father of mercy govern the heart of this child that he may walk blamelessly in the path of virtue. May he allow no evil to have control over him, and may his path be fortified in his Word. Thus that which is good will not fail toward him, neither in this temporal world nor beyond in eternity.

This was a prayer the Lord answered in Count Zinzendorf's life. From his youth to the end of his days, Nikolaus Zinzendorf was a committed follower of Jesus Christ.

## EARLY CHRISTIAN NURTURE

By You I have been upheld from birth;
You are He who took me out of my mother's womb.
My praise shall be continually of You. (Ps. 71:6)

Six weeks after Zinzendorf was born, his father passed into glory. As his father died of tuberculosis, he spoke a blessing over his son Nikolaus. Though Nikolaus' father passed away at such a young age, Nikolaus was abundantly provided for by the Lord. His mother and others in the extended family were committed Christians. They raised Nikolaus in the fear and admonition of the Lord.

**COUNT ZINZENDORF (1700-1760)**

Nikolaus was born into a family of wealth and power. Going back to the 11th century, the Zinzendorf name was associated with nobility in Austria and Germany. At birth, Nikolaus inherited the title of **Count**. A count was a German nobleman. As a count, Nikolaus would live a life of public service and civic duty. This would always be a struggle for him. He wanted to dedicate his life to the work of Christ's church, but there were public demands on him. However, the Lord had a purpose in making Zinzendorf a count. It was because of Count Zinzendorf's wealth and influence that he was able to provide a place for refugees from Moravia. If he hadn't been a count, Zinzendorf could not have done what he did for the cause of Christ's kingdom.

Zinzendorf's earliest years were spent in a family castle in **Gross-Hennersdorf**. In this beautiful country castle, he received his early training in the Christian faith. His Aunt Henrietta in particular was influential in teaching the gospel to young Nikolaus. In later years, the count reflected on the blessings he received as a boy.

> Up to my tenth year there was more care bestowed upon me by way of shielding me from evil influences and fostering in my heart the work of God's grace than would have been possible anywhere except in a well-ordered church of Jesus Christ. I can say with truth that my heart was religiously inclined as far back as I can recollect....

**CHURCH IN GROSS-HENNERSDORF**

**AUGUST HERMANN FRANCKE (1663-1727)**

**PHILIP JAKOB SPENER (1635-1705)**

My very dear Aunt Henrietta endeavored to keep me in this frame of mind by often speaking to me loving and evangelical words.

Zinzendorf grew up hearing the words of the Bible each day. He was also taught Martin Luther's *Small Catechism*. From this early training, Zinzendorf was firmly rooted in the gospel.

In 1710, Zinzendorf was sent to boarding school for further education. He went to a school in Halle. Nine years previously, a man named **August Hermann Francke** (1663-1727) founded a school in his home in **Halle**. It was Francke's desire to train up men for Christian missions. Francke was a committed leader of a movement that came to be known as **Pietism**. Pietist leaders such as Francke were concerned that the faith in Germany lacked spiritual life. The Pietists were concerned that for many professing Christians, their beliefs did not affect their lives. The established state church was Lutheran in its background. It had a rich heritage going back to Martin Luther and the Protestant Reformation. But to Francke and others, much of the church in Germany seemed to lack spiritual life. The Pietists wanted to see a restoration of zeal and love for the Lord. They were not content with a dead faith.

Along with Francke, a man named **Philip Jakob Spener** (1635-1705) was responsible for this effort. Spener is commonly recognized as the founder of Pietism. Movements within Protestantism have generally originated around certain emphases that had been lost somehow by previous generations. The Pietists accepted the doctrines of the Lutheran church. But their desire was to return to certain important practices and emphases in the church. Spener's classic work, *Pia Desideria*, summarized the emphases of the Pietists in six points:

1. To better acquaint believers with Scripture by adding private readings and study groups to preaching
2. To emphasize the gifts of the body and to encourage involvement of all the members in spiritual ministry to one another

3. To emphasize that believers be "doers of the Word" and not hearers only, to apply their faith and knowledge of God
4. To restore humility and love in the Church, avoiding unnecessary controversy
5. To ensure that pastors live pious lives while also assuring that they are well taught in the Word
6. To focus preaching on developing faith in ordinary believers

It was in the context of this movement that Zinzendorf received his schooling. Zinzendorf benefited from Francke's discipleship. But school was not easy. Zinzendorf endured frequent mistreatment by classmates. His fellow schoolboys were hardly the best examples of godly piety. Furthermore, Zinzendorf was sometimes disinterested in his studies. His calling as a count, determined before he was born, was not to his liking. Zinzendorf wanted to be a pastor. But that was not his family's wish. It was unheard of for a count to be a pastor. A count was to be a count. A pastor was to be a pastor. The two callings were not normally combined.

It was during his time at Halle that Zinzendorf continued to grow in his commitment to the Lord. As a young man, he took the lead in gathering other classmates for prayer and sharing the Word with them. By the time he left school, he had formed seven different prayer groups. He also formed Christian clubs of young people who were committed to sharing their faith with others. One of the clubs Zinzendorf formed was called the Order of the Grain of the Mustard Seed. This title came from Jesus' Parable of the Mustard Seed. In that parable, our Lord Jesus teaches that the kingdom of God starts from a small seed. But, as time progresses, the mustard seed grows into a large tree. Zinzendorf's club was committed to spreading Christ's kingdom just like the Lord taught in the mustard seed parable.

At age sixteen, Zinzendorf moved to the **University of Wittenberg**. It was here that

**MARKET SQUARE OF WITTENBERG WITH STATUE OF MARTIN LUTHER**

HERRNHUT, CENTER OF THE MORAVIAN CHURCH

Martin Luther began his reformation efforts in the 1500s. However, Zinzendorf had come to Wittenberg to complete his studies in law. As a count and as a public official-to-be, Zinzendorf was required to be trained in law. He did complete his studies, but he found them difficult because his heart was drawn more to study and meditation in God's Word. He wrote:

> My mind inclined continually toward the cross of Christ. My conversation always turned to that subject; and since the theology of the cross was my favorite theme, and I knew no greater happiness than to become a preacher of the gospel.

For years, Zinzendorf struggled between the desire to be a pastor and his duty as a count. But in time, the Lord's purposes in his life became evident.

## THE COMMUNITY OF HERRNHUT

I, therefore, the prisoner of the Lord, beseech you to walk worthy of the calling with which you were called, with all lowliness and gentleness, with longsuffering, bearing with one another in love, endeavoring to keep the unity of the Spirit in the bond of peace. (Eph. 4:1-3)

At age twenty-one, Zinzendorf came into possession of a large estate. It remained his mother's desire that he would serve faithfully as a count. In order to honor his mother's wishes, Zinzendorf fulfilled that calling. For five years he served in public service at Dresden. He served under the chancellor of the region, who would occasionally assign Zinzendorf various tasks. Even with his public service responsibilities, Zinzendorf had plenty of time to pursue other interests.

In 1722, Zinzendorf married a countess named **Erdmuth Dorothea**. With a portion of his vast estate, Zinzendorf purchased land from his grandmother which included the town of Berthelsdorf. Then, in May 1722, he met a man from Moravia. His name was **Christian David**. This man had fled Moravia in search of a place where he and his fellow Moravians could worship the Lord freely. Zinzendorf offered his estate as a potential location where the Moravians might temporarily lodge.

**LOCATION OF HERRNHUT AND DRESDEN**

Christian David sent word to his fellow Moravians back home. Soon a number of families were on their way to Berthelsdorf. With Zinzendorf's permission, the Moravian refugees began building structures on the land for housing and worship. The Moravians soon named the new spot **Herrnhut**. Translated, this means, "on the watch for the Lord."

At first, Zinzendorf knew little about these Moravian Christians. But he was glad to provide a safe place for them. As he spent more time with them, he learned that these Moravian Christians had a rich history. These people maintained the Protestant legacy that dated back to John Hus. Hus was the great church reformer of the 14th century who was martyred for his faith. As with the man whose name they bore, these Hussites had encountered great persecution. Yet, for centuries, they endured. They buried Bibles in their gardens and held their church meetings in barns at midnight. They had preserved sacred records in birdhouses as well as in their cottage roofs. Finally, however, persecution at the hands of Roman Catholic civil leaders had reached such an intolerable level that they were forced to flee. The Moravians found a place of refuge on Zinzendorf's estate.

Over the next ten years, Herrnhut grew to house hundreds of Christians with similar ideals. Most of the community came from Moravia. But other Christians from a Lutheran and Reformed background heard about the community. They also wanted to join. Herrnhut was a unique community of spiritual devotion. Zinzendorf and the countess were excited to be part of a community dedicated to spiritual pursuits. But the first five years were marked by some spiritual immaturity. Some people came to the community for the wrong reasons. Some were divisive and unloving. It took time for the developing Moravian community to grow in love for one another. This should be no surprise. When sinners build a community together, there will be some pride, selfishness, and lack of love that must be repented of. In time, the Christians of Herrnhut grew in love and unity.

Herrnhut was unique in several ways. For one, the community gathered for worship every single day. Each day ended with a service of hymn singing. Thousands of hymns were produced by the Christians at Herrnhut. It was also a community dedicated to continual prayer. Starting on August 27, 1727, the Christians at Herrnhut began a pattern that would continue for one hundred years. For each hour of the day, someone was assigned to engage in intercessory prayer. The prayer warriors would gather weekly to meet and share letters and other news. These weekly meetings prepared the intercessors with content to bring to the Lord in prayer.

Herrnhut was not a community of perfect people. But it was a community centered on the unifying truth of Jesus Christ and His death and resurrection for sinners. The Moravians' zeal for the Lord would bear much fruit in the generations that followed.

## THE BEGINNING OF MORAVIAN MISSIONS

It shall be that I will gather all nations and tongues; and they shall come and see My glory. (Isa. 66:18)

Count Zinzendorf had long been committed to spreading the gospel. As a young man, the Order of the Grain of the Mustard Seed was evidence of his interest in missions. When the count was fifteen, he committed with a fellow friend to "do all in our power for the conversion of the heathen, especially for those for whom no one else cared, and by means of men whom God would provide." Now, the community of Herrnhut provided a path to do just that. The Moravians were ready to take the message of Jesus to other parts of the world. The first missionaries set out in 1732. Two men left for the small island of **St. Thomas** in the Caribbean. **Leonard Dober** and **David Nitschmann** said their goodbyes to the community on August

ISLAND OF ST. THOMAS

18, 1732. That night, before the missionaries departed, the community sang one hundred hymns together.

As this new missionary effort began, Zinzendorf and the Moravians committed themselves to certain principles. These included:
1. Instead of aiming at converting the whole nation (and transforming the culture) at least initially, they would look for individuals who were seeking the truth. In the past, kings and princes had taken an interest in the Christian message. This wasn't the case as much anymore. Now, a new strategy came into play. They would work to find individuals who were interested in the gospel. They would labor to convert these people before attempting a top-down discipleship of the nations.
2. They would speak directly of the life and death of Jesus Christ. Before speaking of the necessity of faith and repentance, it becomes necessary to teach first the work of God in salvation. This is the thing that men and women must believe in order to be saved.
3. They would not consider themselves above the native people as if they were superior to them. Instead, they would humble themselves and mix in with the people. They would pray with and work alongside those they ministered to.

Dober and Nitschmann found the work on St. Thomas difficult. Adjusting to the tropical climate was not easy. But the most significant challenges were spiritual in nature. They labored especially to teach the gospel to slaves. But conflict was rife on the island between the slave owners and slaves. Within four months, Nitschmann left the work and returned to his wife and children in Saxony. But Dober continued for nearly fifteen months with very little support. He tried to work as a house steward for the local governor and later as a supervisor on the plantations. But the black slaves considered him as one of the slaveowners. There was tremendous bitterness against the "Christian" slavers. These Huguenot, Dutch Reformed, and Lutheran whites were careful to avoid working the slaves on Sunday, the Lord's Day. However, they would not permit the slaves to marry. They killed the slaves for minor infractions. And they would not allow the slaves to meet together for any meetings (including church meetings). Thus, the only real witness Dober could provide the slaves came by way of one-on-one conversations. Most of the slaves were caught in a hopeless pattern of drunkenness and sexual sin.

Despite his many efforts, Dober only saw four or five people converted during his first two years of ministry. He was replaced by Frederick Martin in 1736. Using donations given to the mission work, Martin bought a small farm that came with slaves and used this as a means to teach the gospel to those who worked his farm. He educated the slaves' children and encouraged them to tithe their own money for the church's needs. Thus, the first black Christians formed a self-sustaining indigenous work. Martin didn't only minister to the slaves on his farm. With a smile and a shake of the hand, he made personal contact with every single black slave on the island.

In spite of attacks from a Dutch Reformed pastor named John Borm, Martin continued building the church, baptizing, and conducting marriages for the black slaves. Borm even had Martin arrested on trumped-up charges and thrown into prison in the castle, but this did not deter the ministry. His black converts would gather around the cell where Martin was confined, and he would preach to them through the bars.

When things could not get any worse, Count Zinzendorf finally intervened. He sailed to St. Thomas. On his arrival, he took immediate charge of the situation. He wrote to his wife of his actions, "I burst into the castle like thunder." He demanded that the governor release Frederick Martin and end all Christian persecution immediately. Then Zinzendorf divided the island into four sections and introduced three new members of the team to help Martin with the mission work. Count Zinzendorf's intervention on St. Thomas shows just how influential the count was among the Moravians.

Moravians continued to make their way across the Atlantic. Missions were established in Jamaica, Antigua, Barbados, St. Kitts, and Tobago. Another Moravian mission was launched far to the north in **Greenland** in 1733.

The Moravian work in Greenland became so well established that it survived until 1900. In that year, the church joined with the existing Danish Church. The geographical spread of Moravian missions continued into Suriname (on the northern coast of South America), South Africa, and Canada.

The dedication of the Moravians to the cause of missions was outstanding in the history of the Christian church. Their dedication to the cause of Christ's kingdom would inspire future missionaries for generations to come. The Moravians' earnest love for Christ, fanned by the flames of constant spiritual devotions at Herrnhut, resulted in a significant kingdom work that changed the world. Praise be to God for Moravian missions and the fruit it produced! ■

MORAVIAN SETTLEMENT IN GREENLAND

# PRAYER POINTS: GERMANY

> For they themselves declare concerning us what manner of entry we had to you, and how you turned to God from idols to serve the living and true God, and to wait for His Son from heaven, whom He raised from the dead, even Jesus who delivers us from the wrath to come. (1 Thess. 1:9-10)

- **Pray that the German people would turn from idols to serve God:** Like most nations in Europe, Germany has a rich Christian heritage. There was a time where the various native peoples of Germany turned from graven images and false gods to worship the one true God. But increasingly, as Germany departs from the faith, idol worship is on the rise. Often, these idols are secular idols like money, pleasure, and personal fulfillment. Yet idols do not provide true satisfaction. Depression and other mental illnesses are on the rise in Germany. In some cases, this results in such despair that people commit suicide. Pray that God would turn the hearts of the German people back to Him.

- **Pray for Gospel opportunities among immigrants:** People from other lands are moving to Germany in record numbers. Many from Middle Eastern and Asian nations are now living in Germany. Pray that God would open opportunities for Christians in Germany to reach these newly immigrated people groups with the gospel.

## Basic Facts about Germany (Federal Republic of Germany)

| | |
|---|---|
| Total population: | 83 million |
| Total area: | 137,000 square miles |
| Capital: | Berlin |
| Official language: | German |
| Primary religions: | Roman Catholic, Protestant Christian, Atheist, Agnostic |

BRISTOL, ENGLAND

# THE GREAT AWAKENING

**For thus says the High and Lofty One
Who inhabits eternity, whose name is Holy:
"I dwell in the high and holy place,
With him who has a contrite and humble spirit,
To revive the spirit of the humble,
And to revive the heart of the contrite ones."
(Isa. 57:15)**

In February 1739, on a cold day outside Bristol, England, **George Whitefield** preached in the open air for the first time. It was in a small region called **Kingswood**. The district was inhabited by many low-wage coalminers. Evangelist George Whitefield went from house to house, inviting the residents to gather and hear the preaching of the Word. On the first day he preached, Whitefield proclaimed the gospel to some two hundred people.

The next Wednesday, Whitefield preached again in Kingswood. This time, there were about 2,000 people present. Two days later, about 4,000 gathered. Then, on Sunday, Whitefield estimated he preached to over 10,000 people. He recounted, "The trees and hedges were full. All was hush when I began. The sun shone bright. God enabled me to preach for an hour with great power, and so loudly that all, I was told, could hear."

Whitefield's first time preaching in the open air was a massive success. His fellow evangelist, the Welshman Howell Harris, gave him the idea to try this. Harris had experienced many good opportunities by not limiting his preaching to the confines of a building.

From that point on, George Whitefield and his fellow evangelists would often preach under the blue sky. Enormous gatherings of people listening to preaching in the open air became a unique distinctive of this important period. Many call this time in church history the **Great Awakening**. A time of spiritual reviving swept over Great Britain, Ireland, and the American colonies. Men such as George

GEORGE WHITEFIELD (1714-1770)

**JOHN WESLEY (1703-1791)**

**CHARLES WESLEY (1707-1788)**

Whitefield (1714-1770), **John Wesley** (1703-1791) and his brother **Charles Wesley** (1707-1788), **Howell Harris** (1714-1773), and others traveled far and wide preaching the everlasting gospel.

Before we learn more about this Awakening, let's find out how these preachers were called to this work.

## THE HOLY CLUB

**Jesus answered and said to him, "Most assuredly, I say to you, unless one is born again, he cannot see the kingdom of God." (John 3:3)**

George Whitefield was born in 1714 in Gloucester, England. His father was an innkeeper named Thomas Whitefield. As with almost every other boy in England, George was baptized into and raised in the Church of England. This Christian upbringing was a blessing to him. But it was not until his college years that he experienced the new birth.

In the fall of 1732, Whitefield entered Pembroke College at Oxford. He began to dedicate himself to religious pursuits. He joined what was known as the Holy Club. This was a group of young people who were serious about religious disciplines. They fasted twice a week. They went to the local prison to visit inmates and minister to them. They diligently read their Bibles. And they were committed never to waste one minute of the day. Because they were so methodical, members of the Holy Club began to be called **Methodists**. It was a name given to club members by those who did not like the club. But the name stuck. The Methodist movement continues to this day in various churches and denominations.

George Whitefield met two other members of the Holy Club. Their names were John and Charles Wesley. Together, these three dedicated themselves to strict discipline. However, all three soon learned that their laborious exercises did not give them peace with God. Pursuing God zealously is a good thing (Rom. 12:11). But serving God doesn't make us right with God. We are made right with God by faith in Jesus Christ. We need the Holy Spirit to give us that new birth. Without the new birth, Jesus says, we cannot enter into God's kingdom (John 3:3).

## SPIRITUAL AWAKENING

But when the kindness and the love of God our Savior toward man appeared, not by works of righteousness which we have done, but according to His mercy He saved us, through the washing of regeneration and renewing of the Holy Spirit, whom He poured out on us abundantly through Jesus Christ our Savior, that having been justified by His grace we should become heirs according to the hope of eternal life. (Tit. 3:4-7)

Our works cannot save us. Whitefield realized this when he read a book by a man named **Henry Scougal** (1650-1678). The book was called *The Life of God in the Soul of Man*. At first, the book frightened Whitefield. He wrote, "God showed me that I must be born again, or be damned! I learned that a man may go to church, say prayers, receive the sacrament, and yet not be a Christian." Yet, through this book, Whitefield eventually realized he needed to

OXFORD UNIVERSITY

**JOHN WESLEY PREACHING TO A MASSIVE AUDIENCE IN CORNWALL**

trust Jesus. He needed to cast himself on God's mercy to be saved. His own works could never save him. Whitefield testified:

> God was pleased to remove the heavy load, to enable me to lay hold on his dear Son by a living faith. And by giving me the Spirit of adoption, to seal me, even to the day of everlasting redemption. O! with what joy—joy unspeakable—even joy that was full of and big with glory was my soul filled when the weight of sin went off. An abiding sense of the love of God broke in upon my disconsolate soul!

Suddenly, Whitefield became a new man. He read the Bible with a newfound joy. He prayed to God with great confidence. As a result of his salvation experience, he became a zealous evangelist. By the next year (1736), he was ordained to the ministry and began preaching frequently.

John Wesley and his brother Charles also experienced a spiritual awakening. Around the time Whitefield began preaching, John traveled to America. He was doing evangelistic work in the new colony of Georgia. On the long ocean voyage, John met a group of **Moravian** Christians. (In the previous chapter, we learned about the Moravians of **Herrnhut**.) John was impressed by the Moravians' faith and love. He watched as these people gladly took on any difficult or menial task that needed to be done aboard the ship.

Sometime during the Atlantic crossing, a tempestuous storm struck the ship. John Wesley and others on board panicked. Screams of fear arose from the ship. Wesley confessed, "I was afraid to die!" But there was one group that did not seem afraid. As the storm raged and the waves pummeled the ship, the Moravians didn't cry out in fear. Instead, they sang hymns of trust and praise to God. Amazed at their lack of fear, John desired to have that same faith in God.

In 1738, after returning to England, John did put all his trust in Jesus Christ. While visiting a church gathering at **Aldersgate Street**, London, he experienced a sense of confidence and assurance of salvation through Christ. A man was reading a portion of Martin Luther's commentary on Romans. It was the powerful, gospel words of Romans that gave assurance to John. He later wrote: "I felt my heart strangely warmed. I felt I did trust in Christ, Christ alone for salvation. And an assurance was given me that he had taken away my sins, even mine, and saved me from the law of sin and death."

Around the same time, John's brother Charles came to a similar confidence. On May 21, 1738, he gave up trying to save his own soul. He trusted in Christ alone to save him. In order to remember how Jesus had saved him, Charles wrote one of his greatest hymns, *And Can It Be*. Here are some words of that hymn:

> And can it be that I should gain
> An int'rest in the Savior's blood?
> Died He for me, who caused His pain?
> For me, who Him to death pursued?
> Amazing love! how can it be
> That Thou, my God, shouldst die for me?
>
> Amazing love! how can it be
> That Thou, my God, shouldst die for me!
>
> No condemnation now I dread;
> Jesus, and all in Him is mine!
> Alive in Him, my living Head,
> And clothed in righteousness divine,
> Bold I approach th'eternal throne,
> And claim the crown, through Christ my own.
>
> Amazing love! how can it be
> That Thou, my God, shouldst die for me!

Charles' gifts for poetry were evident. Eventually, he would write some 6,500 hymns. Many of those hymns continue to be sung by Christians today.

Whitefield and the Wesley brothers sensed a divine call to proclaim the gospel. And proclaim it they did! Through their combined efforts, millions would hear the gospel, and many were saved.

## THE BRITISH ISLES AWAKENED

> Will You not revive us again,
> That Your people may rejoice in You?
> Show us Your mercy, LORD,
> And grant us Your salvation. (Ps. 85:6-7)

Whitefield and the Wesleys traveled numerous times to the American colonies. Many of the most important events of this period happened in North America. However, the focus of this book is European history. For this reason, we will limit our attention to how the Great Awakening impacted the British Isles.

After preaching in Kingswood near Bristol, Whitefield went on to preach in London. He preached in a large open area called Moorfields. Then he preached in a second area near London. This second place was called Kennington Common. It is believed that about 30,000 gathered at Kennington Common to hear him preach. He returned to Moorfields and preached to about 20,000. Whitefield recounted, "Preached this morning at Moorfields to about twenty thousand. . . . My discourse was about two hours long. My heart was full of love, and people were so melted down on every side that the greatest scoffer must have confessed this was the finger of God."

Whitefield soon encouraged John and Charles to join in open-air preaching. At this time, preaching outside seemed strange. John Wesley was not comfortable with the idea at first. He confessed, "I could scarce reconcile myself at first to this strange way of preaching in the fields, . . . having been all my life . . . so tenacious of every point relating to decency and order, that I should have thought the saving of souls a sin if it had not been done in a church." But with some persuasion, both John and Charles joined in. Soon, massive crowds gathered to hear them preach as well.

In 1741, George Whitefield visited Scotland for a preaching tour. In July and August, he preached to audiences sometimes as large as 15,000. He stayed in Scotland for two weeks and preached to massive audiences every night of the week. Over a period of three months, Whitefield toured Scotland. He experienced similar opportunities in every town he visited. After he left Scotland, a fellow pastor wrote to Whitefield and described the changes taking place in the country.

> Religion in this city revives and flourishes.... New meetings for prayer and spiritual conference are happening everywhere. Religious conversation has banished slander and calumny from several tea-tables, and Christians are not ashamed to confess their Lord.

## OPPOSITION TO GOD'S WORD

**On the next Sabbath almost the whole city came together to hear the word of God. But when the Jews saw the multitudes, they were filled with envy; and contradicting and blaspheming, they opposed the things spoken by Paul. (Acts 13:44-45)**

God was doing a mighty work in saving many during this season. But not everyone who heard the Word received it. Wherever the Word of God is preached, some will oppose it. The situation was no different during the Great Awakening. As tens of thousands assembled to hear preaching, often a mob of violent and angry people formed as well.

For Whitefield, John Wesley, and Howell Harris, preaching could be physically dangerous. On numerous occasions, these men were violently attacked. In the case of Howell Harris, much of his preaching took place in Wales. In 1741, Harris visited the town of Bala and preached there. The local minister did not like Harris, so he opened a barrel of beer on the main street. He hoped to make the crowd drunk so they would assault Harris. As Harris attempted to preach, he was attacked by both men and women. He was beaten with fists and clubs.

God was merciful to protect Harris from death. On another occasion, he preached in London in a large building. A mob formed and broke into the assembly. In this case, the mob started beating people with sticks.

Another friend of Whitefield was a man named John Cennick. Cennick and Harris once visited the town of Swindon to preach. While there, they were assaulted in all different sorts of creative ways. Cennick recounted, "The mob fired guns over our heads, holding the muzzles so near to our faces that we were made as black as tinkers with the powder. We were not afraid but told them we were ready to lay down our lives."

In another place, John Cennick was preaching about the blood of Christ. An angry butcher shouted, "If he wants blood, I'll give him plenty." The butcher went back to his shop and filled a pail with blood. Then he returned to where Cennick was preaching. He tried to pour the entire pail of blood on the preacher. Thankfully, someone nearby stopped the butcher. Instead of drenching Cennick, the butcher found himself drenched in blood.

John and Charles Wesley were also attacked frequently. Charles wrote about one particularly challenging episode:

> I had just named my text from Isaiah (Isa.

40:1) when an army of rebels broke in on us.... They began in a most outrageous manner, threatening to murder the people. ...They broke the sconces, dashed the windows in pieces, tore away the shutters, benches, poor-box, and all but the stone walls...The longer they stayed the more they raged."

Preaching God's Word under such circumstances required courage. The Lord gave these men a spirit of boldness to keep preaching despite the danger.

## RESULTS OF THE GREAT AWAKENING

Countless additional stories could be told from this exceptional period of history. The testimonies we read above give us a window into what Christ was doing in His church at this time. Not everything that happened during the Great Awakening was perfect. Some preachers that participated in the revivals were not faithful to the Bible. Sometimes, people acted in a divisive way and claimed to be superior to other Christians because of what they learned. And some who claimed to be converted later did not continue in the faith. When the Holy Spirit moves in mighty ways, the forces of the evil one also come to distract, deceive, and divide.

Nevertheless, we must praise God for His power and mercy in saving sinners. No human being can know exactly how many were redeemed during the Great Awakening. Yet we must acknowledge the evident work of God in bringing about this time of spiritual awakening and renewal. ■

---

All the ends of the world
Shall remember and turn to the LORD,
And all the families of the nations
Shall worship before You.
For the kingdom is the LORD's,
And He rules over the nations. (Ps. 22:27-28)

---

# PRAYER POINTS

- **Praise God for His power to bring new life to sinners:** Let us praise God for His infinite power. He is able to raise dead sinners to life (Eph. 2:1-5). Let us acknowledge in our prayer that nothing is impossible with God. Let us thank Him for how He has brought the salvation of Jesus Christ to people in all different parts of the world.

- **Ask God for spiritual awakening in your local community:** Ask the Holy Spirit to come and bring spiritual life to your church and your local community. Pray that God would bring many to hear the Word of God preached at your local church. Ask the Lord to make people hungry for God. Pray also that the Lord would bless you and your family with the filling of the Holy Spirit in greater measure (Eph. 5:18-20).

OLNEY, ENGLAND

# JOHN NEWTON: GOD'S AMAZING GRACE TO A WRETCHED SINNER

For by grace you have been saved through faith, and that not of yourselves; it is the gift of God, not of works, lest anyone should boast. For we are His workmanship, created in Christ Jesus for good works, which God prepared beforehand that we should walk in them. (Eph. 2:8-10)

The words of Paul in Ephesians 2 remind every Christian of their spiritual journey. Once we were dead in our sins. We lived for sin, Satan, and self.

But God did not leave us in that condition. Because God loved us and because He is rich in mercy, He made us alive with Jesus! Then He seated us in heavenly places with Christ. From now into all eternity, God the Father will show us the "exceeding riches of His grace." We learn from Paul's inspired words that we are saved by God's grace. We aren't saved by any works of righteousness we do. We are saved by God's *mercy*. This is true of *every* Christian.

It is faith-building to read of saints from the past who were touched by the grace of God. It should lead every Christian to reflect on God's goodness to him or her. We find a powerful, remarkable, and memorable example of God's grace in the life of **John Newton** (1725-1807). Though he was once a blasphemer, idolater, torturer, and fornicator, God saved him. John Newton once lived for sin, Satan, and self. But because God was merciful, Newton became a servant of Jesus Christ. He became a living testimony of God's amazing grace to wretched sinners like you and me.

## LIFE AS A SAILOR

Those who go down to the sea in ships,
Who do business on great waters,
They see the works of the LORD,
And His wonders in the deep. (Ps. 107:23-24)

John Newton was born in London, England in 1725 to Christian parents. John's father, John Newton Sr., was a sea captain. Because of his occupation, Captain Newton did not spend

**JOHN NEWTON (1725-1807)**

much time with his son. He was usually traveling the seas on business. However, John was blessed to receive Christian instruction from his faithful mother. But when John was six years old, his mother died of tuberculosis.

John's father was often at sea, leaving John to the care of others. Occasionally, John would join his father on some sea voyages. Life at sea was not a healthy spiritual environment. As John grew older, he became increasingly rebellious and ungodly. In March 1744, when he was eighteen, John ran into a **press-gang** in Chatham. A press-gang was the name given to naval platoons which would come on land to force men into naval service. During this time in English history, it was lawful for young men to be forced into service in the Royal Navy. England's navy played an important role in the defense of the nation. At times, men like John Newton were forced to join the navy against their will. Now, Newton was required to serve for a time in the Royal Navy. His first service was aboard the HMS *Harwich*.

Newton's previous experience at sea gave him some advantages over other new naval recruits. But his dishonorable behavior soon got him into trouble. Newton was harsh toward others, prideful, and known for his speech laced with cursing and swearing. During his first year at sea, he longed to be in England. Before he was forced into naval service, he had set his heart on a young lady. The young woman's name was **Polly Catlett**. Naval tours at sea could last up to five years. Newton could not fathom being away from Polly for so long. Once, when the Harwich docked at Plymouth, Newton tried to desert. However, he was caught. As a result, he was flogged and stripped of his rank. Still, Newton was not humbled. He continued his reckless behavior. John later described his behavior at that time, "I was exceedingly vile. I not only sinned with a high hand myself but made it my study to tempt and seduce others upon every occasion."

**COAST OF GHANA, WEST AFRICA**

The captain became so fed up with John that he traded him to another ship. Newton became a crew member of the *Pegasus*. This was a trading ship that dealt in wares along the coast of West Africa. Newton did not last long on the *Pegasus* either. He eventually found himself in the service of a slave trader in Africa. The man's name was Amos Clow. The slave trade was a ruthless business. Often, Africans enslaved their fellow Africans and brought them to the coast. Then the enslaved Africans would be sold to European traders. Newton became a part of this cruel trade. Newton was already given over to many sins. But the evils of the slave trade only further corrupted his character. He fell into sexual sin and witchcraft.

Slave traders are not even kind to their own. John Newton found himself enslaved by his own employer, Amos Clow. Newton was brutally mistreated and almost starved to death by Amos. He now longed to escape and return to England. Newton sent letters back to England to his father. Providentially, the letters did make it back home. A ship was sent. The name of the ship was the *Greyhound*. It was captained by a man named Swanwick. The *Greyhound* eventually found John Newton. By this time, Newton had escaped the grips of Amos Clow. But Captain Swanwick was able to convince Newton to return with him to England.

The *Greyhound* continued its long journey of trading, now with Newton on board. Like the other captains, Captain Swanwick found Newton to be a very difficult character. Newton testified in later years of how wicked he was. "My life, when awake, was a course of the most horrid impiety and profaneness. I know not that I have ever met so daring a blasphemer. Not content with horrid oaths and imprecations, I daily invented new ones so that I was often seriously reproved by the captain."

In March 1748, a violent storm struck the *Greyhound* as it crossed the Atlantic Ocean. For days, the ship was tossed about. The ship was severely damaged. Many provisions were tossed overboard. For a time, it seemed that all hope was lost. Because Newton was such a blasphemer, the captain wondered whether this storm had come as God's judgment. Inspired by the Book of Jonah, Swanwick considered whether they should throw Newton overboard to calm the storm. Thankfully for Newton, the sailors never went through with this plan.

Something else very important in Newton's life happened during that storm. For the first time, John Newton prayed to God for mercy. The God whom Newton had so blasphemed was now the God to whom Newton prayed. This storm did bring a season of humble reflection to Newton's life.

God was merciful to the crew of the *Greyhound*. They safely landed in Ireland and began to repair and reprovision their ship. After the storm, Newton made a commitment to give his life to God. "I rose very early, was very particular and earnest in my private devotion, and with the greatest solemnity engaged myself to be the Lord's forever." Newton's life did begin to change. He still fell into many sins after this. But from this point on, his life was set on a different path.

## SEA CAPTAIN OF SLAVE SHIPS

This is a faithful saying and worthy of all acceptance, that Christ Jesus came into the world to save sinners, of whom I am chief. However, for this reason I obtained mercy, that in me first Jesus Christ might show all longsuffering, as a pattern to those who are going to believe on Him for everlasting life. (1 Tim. 1:15-16)

Newton returned home to England and

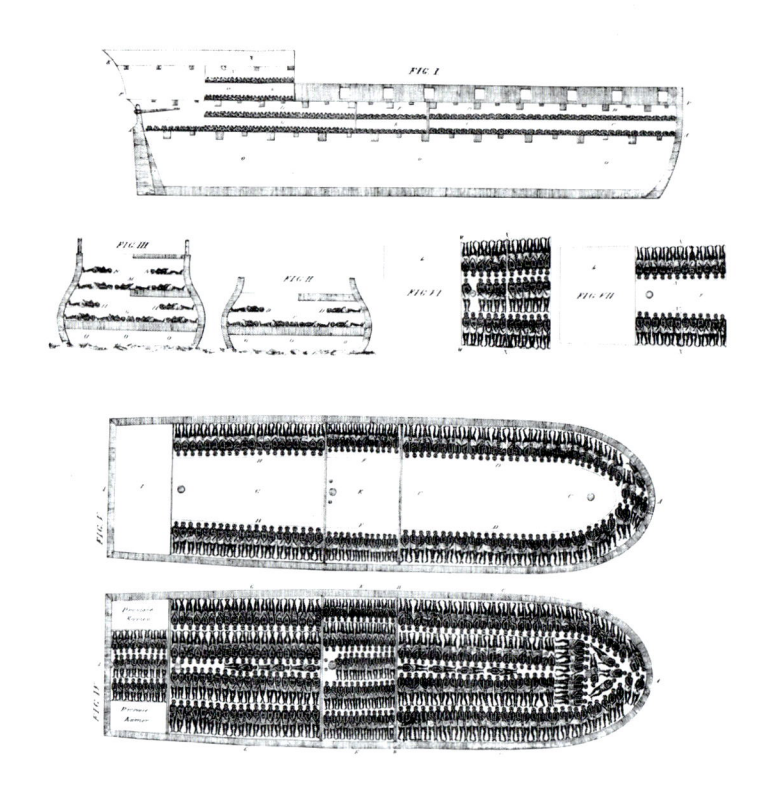

**DIAGRAM OF SLAVE SHIP SHOWING HUMAN "CARGO"**

looked for work. In 1750, his long-cherished desire to marry Polly Catlett was fulfilled. They were married February 11, 1750. Shortly after their wedding, John Newton found gainful employment as captain of the *Duke of Argyle*. This was no ordinary merchant ship, however. Newton would not be trading in physical goods. The *Duke of Argyle* was a slave-trading ship, and John was its captain.

Newton considered himself a Christian at this time in his life. Yet he did not see any conflict between his Christian faith and his profession as a slave-ship captain. How is this possible? Most Christians in John's day were blinded to the evils of the slave trade. The church needed to be awakened to this serious matter. Later in life, Newton's conscience would be awakened on this topic. But in this season of his life, he felt no pangs of conscience as a slave-trader. On board his ship, Newton spent time in Bible reading and prayer. On Sundays, he hosted a worship service for the sailors. He also studied numerous classic Christian writings.

After commanding the *Duke of Argyle*, Newton made numerous additional journeys between England, Africa, and the Americas. During this season, he witnessed the cruelty and evil of the slave trade up close. As he grew in his understanding of the Christian faith, he tried to treat the slaves in a more humane way. He tried to restrain his crew from inflicting harm on the slaves. But the trade itself, being such an evil practice, could not be made righteous. Newton found it hard to keep his men from acting in brutal and ungodly ways. Slave revolts on board were a common occurrence. Some violence and punishment was necessary to stop such rebellions. Once the slave ship reached the Caribbean or the American coast, slave families were routinely separated and sold to the highest payer.

Desiring to spend more time at home with his wife Polly, Newton ended his slave-trading career after many long voyages. He sought new employment on land.

## JOHN NEWTON CALLED TO MINISTRY

And I thank Christ Jesus our Lord who has enabled me, because He counted me faithful, putting me into the ministry, although I was formerly a blasphemer, a persecutor, and an insolent man; but I obtained mercy because I did it ignorantly in unbelief. And the grace of our Lord was exceedingly abundant, with faith and love which are in Christ Jesus. (1 Tim. 1:12-14)

John Newton secured a new job as the "sur-

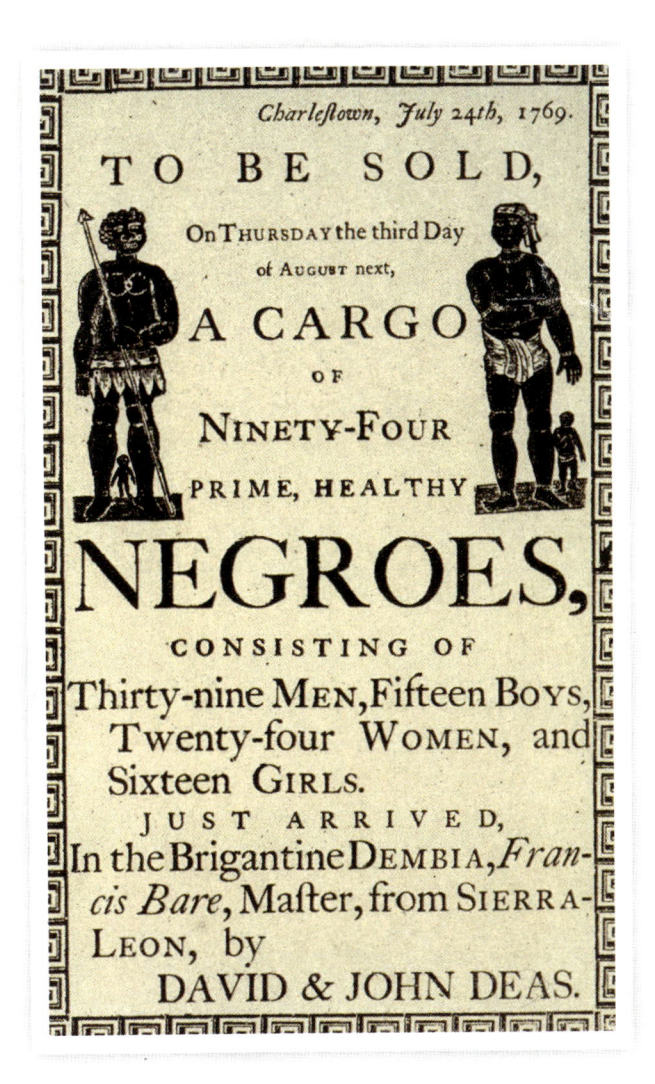

**ADVERTISEMENT IN CHARLESTON, SOUTH CAROLINA, 1769**

veyor of tides" in the city of Liverpool. This new job allowed him to be with his wife more often and still make enough money to provide for her. In 1755, he heard the famous revival preacher George Whitefield (1714-1770) for the first time. Newton was impressed by Whitefield's bold preaching and clear gospel message. Newton and his wife Polly joined in the Great Awakening.

At certain seasons of the year, Newton had additional time to rest and study. He spent much more time with Polly, but he also dedicated himself to the study of the Bible. Sometimes, he spent three hours a day reading God's Word in the original Hebrew and Greek languages.

By 1758, Newton sensed a call to pastoral ministry. He longed to preach the gospel he had found set forth so clearly in the pages of Scripture. The ministry of men like John Wesley and George Whitefield had brought a spiritual awakening to many, including John and Polly Newton.

The Holy Spirit was reshaping John into a new man. He was a man who loved Jesus Christ. He was a man who loved God's Word. He was a humble man. Newton understood how important it was to be humble if he wanted to become a shepherd of souls. He prayed:

> Lord, give me a humbling sense of my sins. Give me a humbling view of Your glory. Give me a humbling view of Your love. For surely nothing humbles like these. All my pride springs from ignorance.... May I be nothing in my own eyes. May I be willing and desirous to be the servant of all.

The Lord answered John's prayer. He became "as nothing" in his own eyes. Jesus Christ became everything for him.

Newton's pursuit of a pastoral calling was itself a humbling process. It took six years before he found an opportunity to serve as pastor. One obstacle was the fact that John lacked a formal ministerial education. Newton was largely self-taught. He read voraciously. But he did not have a degree from Oxford or Cambridge. There was another obstacle.

Many in the Church of England did not like the Methodist movement. They thought this new movement was dangerous. They believed the Methodists were too concerned about experience and feeling. The Methodist movement was given the name enthusiasm. An enthusiast was someone who supported the revivals taking place. To many in the Church of England, this was not a good thing. Newton

**PORT OF LIVERPOOL**

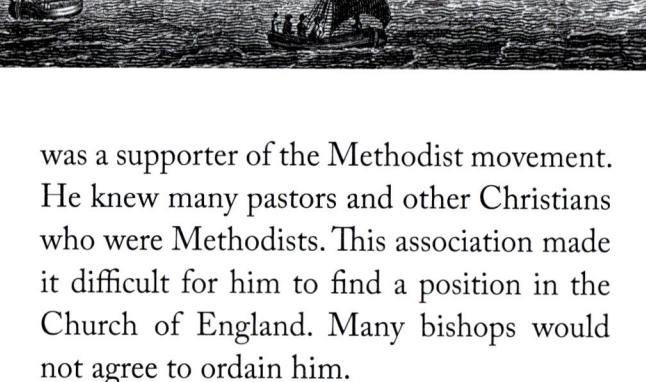

was a supporter of the Methodist movement. He knew many pastors and other Christians who were Methodists. This association made it difficult for him to find a position in the Church of England. Many bishops would not agree to ordain him.

But after six years, an opportunity opened. John was ordained a pastor at the parish church in **Olney**, England. This happened in 1764. Olney was a small town. Most of the members of the Olney Parish were poor. It was here that Newton set out to be a faithful minister of Jesus Christ. He preached the gospel. He visited God's people in their homes. He counseled those needing advice. He taught the Bible to children. He was a diligent pastor, often visiting three or four families a day. During his ministry, spiritual awakening came to Olney. Within three years, the number of regular church attenders increased from 200 to 600.

**LOCATION OF OLNEY, ENGLAND**

## THE HYMN "AMAZING GRACE"

When the kindness and the love of God our Savior toward man appeared, not by works of righteousness which we have done, but according to His mercy He saved us, through the washing of regeneration and renewing of the Holy Spirit, whom He poured out on us abundantly through Jesus Christ our Savior, that having been justified by His grace we should become heirs according to the hope of eternal life. (Tit. 3:4-7)

In 1767, John Newton met a man named **William Cowper** (1731-1800). William Cowper received training in law. He was planning to become a lawyer. But a series of mental breakdowns prevented him from entering the legal field. He attempted suicide three times. Out of concern for his life, his family sent him to a lunatic asylum. For two years, he was under the care of doctors. Then he was released.

After meeting William Cowper, Pastor Newton saw an opportunity for ministry. Cowper was drawing closer to the Lord, but he still struggled with anxiety, fear, doubt, worry, and sadness. In the 18th century, his condition was called **melancholy**. Today, it would be classified as **depression**. At times, Cowper seemed to be a committed believer. But at other times, he doubted that God loved him.

John Newton invited Cowper to live with him and Polly in Olney. This began a long and fruitful friendship between Newton and Cowper. For the rest of Cowper's life, Newton was a faithful friend, always seeking to encourage him. When Cowper had doubts, Newton reassured him. When Cowper gave way to despair, Newton reminded him of the life-giving truths of the gospel.

Cowper struggled with depression for the rest of his life. But he was a gifted writer. He employed these gifts to produce some of the most valuable hymns ever written. He wrote such hymns as *God Moves in a Mysterious Way* and *There is a Fountain Filled with Blood*. Recognizing Cowper's immense poetic gifts, John Newton encouraged him to write more hymns. Together, they began working on a hymn collection. It was eventually published as a hymnal in 1779. The title of the hymnal was *Olney Hymns*. Newton produced this collection because he knew how powerful music was as a teaching tool. He wrote hymns to teach and reinforce his preaching and teaching.

Of the two writers, William Cowper was the most poetically gifted. But Newton also produced some memorable hymns of his own. His most famous production is the hymn

WILLIAM COWPER (1731-1800)

*Amazing Grace*. He wrote it to accompany his sermon on New Year's Day, 1773. On that day, Newton preached on 1 Chronicles 17:16-17. In this passage, King David reflected on God's grace.

---

**Then King David went in and sat before the Lord; and he said: "Who am I, O Lord God? And what is my house, that You have brought me this far? And yet this was a small thing in Your sight, O God; and You have also spoken of Your servant's house for a great while to come, and have regarded me according to the rank of a man of high degree, O Lord God." (1 Chron. 17:16-17)**

---

To help explain the teaching of this sermon, Newton penned Amazing Grace. Here are the original words of the hymn:

> Amazing grace—how sweet the sound—
> That saved a wretch like me!
> I once was lost, but now am found—
> Was blind, but now I see.

'Twas grace that taught my heart to fear,
And grace my fears relieved;
How precious did that grace appear
The hour I first believed!

Thro' many dangers, toils and snares,
I have already come;
'Tis grace has brought me safe thus far,
And grace will lead me home.

And when this flesh and heart shall fail,
And mortal life shall cease,
I shall possess within the veil
A life of joy and peace.

The earth shall soon dissolve like snow,
The sun forbear to shine;
But God, who call'd me here below,
Will be forever mine.

For about fifty years, *Amazing Grace* was not a well-known hymn. It was published in *Olney Hymns*, but it was not popular. However, in the 1830s, it became a popular hymn in the revivals in the United States. A man named **William Walker** published a songbook titled *Southern Harmony* in 1835. In that songbook published in the American South, Walker took Newton's words and united them to a tune called New Britain. Since that time, Newton's words and that tune have become one. Later, in the 1850s, a new final verse replaced Newton's original fifth verse. This is the final verse most people now sing:

**VICARAGE IN OLNEY, ENGLAND (HOME OF PASTOR JOHN NEWTON)**

When we've been there ten thousand years,
Bright shining as the sun,
We've no less days to sing God's praise
Than when we've first begun.

No one knows who authored this final verse. But it likely came from African-American spiritual songs. These words had been sung by African slaves in the south for decades. This version from the 1850s became the standard version of *Amazing Grace*. Open up just about any hymnbook and you will find this version printed.

## GOD USES JOHN NEWTON TO COMBAT THE SLAVE TRADE

---

Though you offer Me burnt offerings and your grain offerings,
I will not accept them,
Nor will I regard your fattened peace offerings.
Take away from Me the noise of your songs,
For I will not hear the melody of your stringed instruments.
But let justice run down like water,
And righteousness like a mighty stream.
(Amos 5:22-24)

---

In 1779, John was given the opportunity to become pastor at a large church in London. The church's name was **St. Mary's Woolnoth**. It was at this congregation that Newton lived out his last years of pastoral ministry. City life was much different than the slower pace of country life in Olney. This new position in London opened new doors of opportunity for John. In his last decades of life, he used his testimony to combat the African slave trade.

In 1785, Newton became the spiritual mentor to a young man named **William Wilberforce** (1759-1833). He was a member of Parliament representing the town of Hull. Wilberforce became a Christian and sought Newton's advice. Wilberforce wondered, "Should I leave politics in order to follow Christ?"

Newton saw that Wilberforce was a gifted politician. He urged Wilberforce to remain

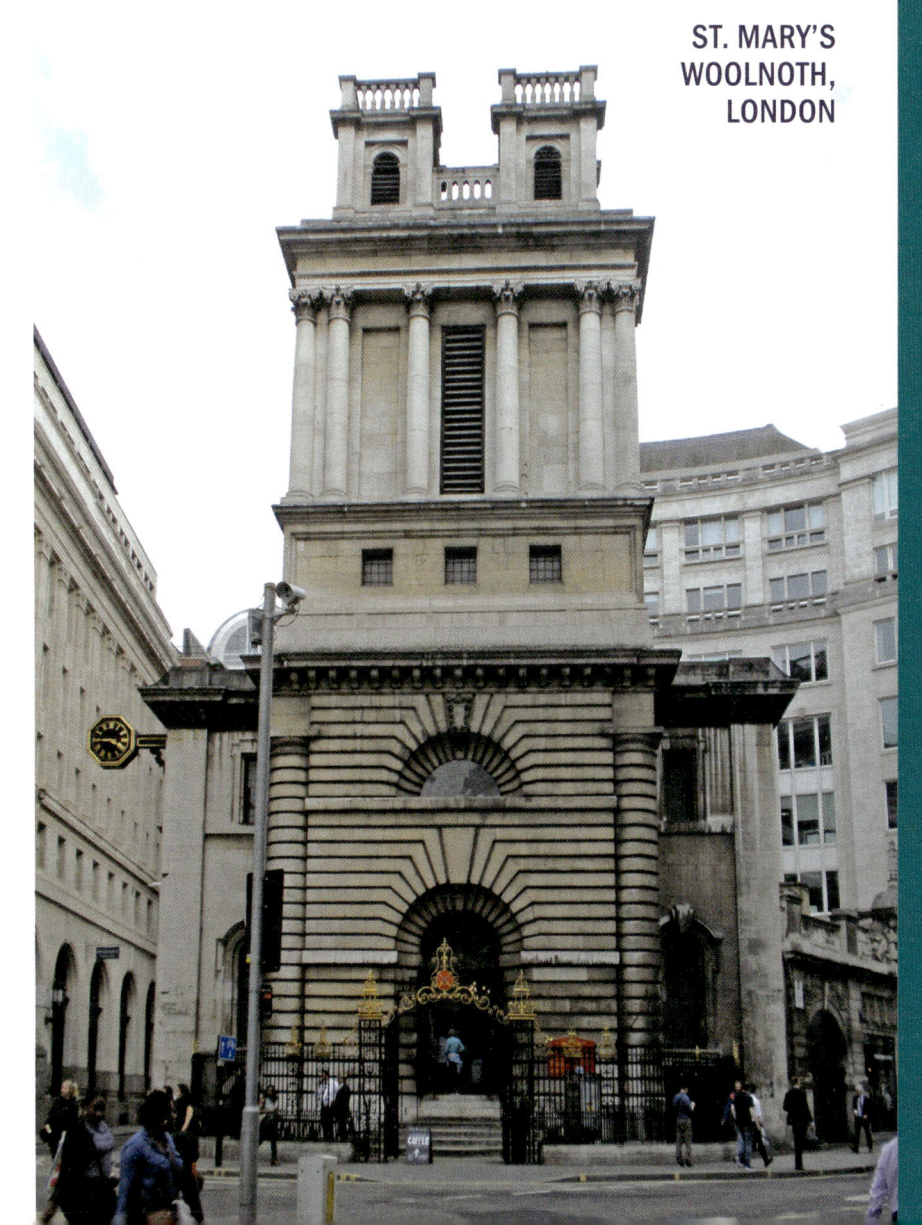

ST. MARY'S WOOLNOTH, LONDON

**WILLIAM WILBERFORCE (1759-1833)**

in Parliament and serve Jesus Christ there. Newton's wise counsel persuaded Wilberforce. He remained in his position as a **member of Parliament (MP)**. From that point on, Wilberforce worked for decades to see the slave trade abolished. But slavery was well ingrained in English society. Many benefited from the financial rewards. It was an uphill battle to see the slave trade ended. After a difficult defeat in Parliament, Newton wrote a letter to Wilberforce. He encouraged him to press on.

> You have acted nobly, Sir, in behalf of the poor Africans. I trust you will not lose your reward. But I believe the business is now transferred to a higher hand. If men will not redress their accumulated injuries, I believe the Lord will.... The Lord reigns. He has all hearts in his hands. He is carrying on his great designs in a straight line, and nothing can obstruct him.

In 1788, Newton published a small pamphlet titled *Thoughts on the African Slave Trade*. He recounted the many horrific evils he had witnessed firsthand in the slave trade. A copy of the booklet was sent to every member of Parliament. Newton's little book strengthened public support to end the slave trade. In the opening pages of the book, Newton wrote:

> I hope it always be a subject of humiliating reflection to me that I was once an active instrument in a business at which my heart now shudders. Yet, perhaps I am bound in conscience to take shame to myself by a public confession.

Newton went on to explain just how wicked the trade was.

> I know of no method of getting money, not even that of robbing for it upon the highway, which has so direct a tendency to efface the moral sense, to rob the heart of every gentle and humane disposition, and to harden like steel against all impressions of sensibility.

Here is what John Newton means. He saw that the effect of kidnapping, enslaving, abusing, and selling human beings was de-humanizing. It took away a man's sense of right and wrong. It made men brutal and uncaring.

On another occasion, Newton was called to give testimony in Parliament. His firsthand accounts were shocking to many. Many in England did not realize the extent of this evil.

It was Newton's support of Wilberforce, and his firsthand testimony to the nation, that helped bring about the end of the slave trade. In 1807, Parliament passed legislation to end the slave trade in the British Empire. Newton and Wilberforce had succeeded in their brave campaign.

## NEWTON'S FINAL YEARS

John Newton preached his final sermon at St. Mary's Woolnoth in 1806. Thereafter, he spent his last year at home in retirement. Visitors to Newton's home noticed that his memory was declining. But one visitor, a man named William Jay, saw that Newton still remembered the most important facts. Newton told Mr. Jay, "My memory is nearly gone. But I remember two things: That I am a great sinner, and that Christ is a great Savior."

On December 21, 1807, John Newton died in London. He was buried in that city, but his body was later moved to Olney, where he was buried with his wife Polly. Before he died, he planned what he wanted to have written on his gravestone. The inscription on his burial place in Olney reads:

> JOHN NEWTON
> ONCE AN INFIDEL AND LIBERTINE
> A SERVANT OF SLAVES IN AFRICA
> WAS
> BY THE RICH MERCY OF OUR LORD AND SAVIOR
> JESUS CHRIST
> PRESERVED, RESTORED, PARDONED
> AND APPOINTED TO PREACH THE FAITH
> HE HAD LONG LABORED TO DESTROY

This summarizes well the life of John Newton. God showed amazing grace to a wretched sinner. God used a wretched sinner like John Newton to glorify Himself and to bless the world. ■

## Basic Facts about England

*The United Kingdom consists of the nations of England, Wales, Scotland, and Northern Ireland. The facts below pertain to England, one of the countries within the UK.*

| Total population: | 56 million |
| --- | --- |
| Total area: | 50,000 square miles |
| Capital: | London |
| Official language: | English |
| Primary religions: | Protestant Christian, Atheist, Agnostic |

# PRAYER POINTS: ENGLAND

In this Prayer Points, we will pray for the churches of England.

- **Pray for the Church of England to return to God's Word:** The national church in England is called the Church of England. This national church has a rich heritage going back to the time of the Protestant Reformation. However, in recent decades, the Church of England has departed from biblical teaching in both its doctrine and its practice. There are some faithful pastors and church members within the Church of England. But the national church is in dire need of restoration and revival. Ask the Lord to cleanse all the churches in England of false doctrine and immoral practices.

- **Give thanks to God for faithful pastors:** Church attendance in England is a mere fraction of what it once was. As the nation has turned away from God, it has become increasingly difficult to minister to a people in rebellion against God. Give thanks to God for faithful pastors that keep on laboring in discipleship despite opposition.

- **Ask God to make the true churches in England to be bold in preaching, prayer, and evangelism:** As England becomes more hostile to Christianity, Christians may face additional opposition or persecution. There are recent news stories of street preachers in England being arrested for sharing the gospel. Pray that God's people in England would be faithful in proclaiming the truth, steadfast in prayer, and increasingly bold in sharing the truth with others.

UNIVERSITY OF CAMBRIDGE

# CHARLES SIMEON: PERSEVERANCE IN SUFFERING

*For you have need of endurance, so that after you have done the will of God, you may receive the promise. (Heb. 10:36)*

In the mid-1700s, the **University of Cambridge** was one of England's largest universities. Students from all over the world came to study at Cambridge. Graduates became lawyers, scientists, politicians, pastors, and professors. Cambridge was known for its successful graduates. But it was not known for its godly and humble students. Such was the testimony of a young man named **Charles Simeon** (1759-1836), who spent most of his life at Cambridge. While studying at Cambridge as a young man, Simeon came to saving faith in Jesus Christ. His life was radically changed. For the rest of his life, he would dedicate himself to pastoral ministry in the heart of Cambridge. But as we will see, this was not easy.

Charles Simeon was a man who was faithful year after year despite almost constant opposition. Many others would have given up. But Charles persevered. By faith, he endured.

Charles was born in 1759 into a rich family in Reading, England. His father was a wealthy attorney. At that time in England, everyone had some attachment to the church, but this did not mean that everyone was a true Christian. Simeon's family did not show much evidence of faith in Jesus. Because of this, Simeon knew little about Jesus Christ or the gospel.

Simeon's mother died when he was a young boy (around five or six years of age). After his mother's death, Simeon was sent to the premier boarding school in England. The name of this school is the **Royal College of Eton**. It was common at the time for well-to-do families to send their children away to boarding schools. At school, young men were expected to receive a thorough education. However, being surrounded by so many immature young men often had a disastrous effect upon the student's character.

Charles experienced the ugly consequences of sin at Eton. Behavior among the students was deplorable. Charles lived as a companion of many fools. Even though he had a father, at the school he did not have anyone that took the place of his father. No one discipled him. He was raised by harsh teachers and influenced by ungodly classmates. The environment at Eton was poisonous to a young man's soul. Sin was rampant. Charles later said that if he ever had a son, he would have rather seen his son dead than have him committed to schooling at Eton. That is how ungodly the environment was.

## SIMEON'S CONVERSION AT CAMBRIDGE

*For God so loved the world that He gave His only begotten Son, that whoever believes in Him should not perish but have everlasting life. For God did not send His Son into the world to condemn the world, but that the world through Him might be saved. (John 3:16-17)*

At age nineteen, Charles was sent to the University of Cambridge. And, by God's mercy, it was in his first four months at Cambridge that the Lord saved Simeon from his sins.

Chapel attendance was required of all stu-

307

ETON COLLEGE

dents at Cambridge, and there were many church buildings throughout town. Many people attended church, but many of them didn't understand or believe the gospel. Sadly, true faith in Jesus Christ was almost nonexistent. After Simeon was converted, he wrote that it was "three years before he met another believer in Cambridge." Even though attendance at chapel was required, the lives of many of these undergraduates was profligate and wasteful. Before he was converted, Charles joined others in drinking, partying, and other foolish behavior. He wrote after his conversion, "Never can I review my early life without the deepest shame and sorrow. My vanity, my folly, my wickedness, God alone knows."

If Charles didn't know a single Christian, how did he come to faith in Jesus Christ? No person shared the gospel directly with Charles. Instead, a direct encounter with God's Word gave him new life in Christ.

Since Charles was required to attend chapel services, he was also required to partake of communion. One day, he was informed that communion would take place in a few weeks. Simeon began to reflect upon his sins. He knew it was wrong to come to the Lord's Supper in an unworthy manner. He thought that before communion, he should try to behave better. He spent the following weeks trying to fix his behavior. But he still felt that he was unworthy to come to the table. What could he do with his sins? How would the debt be paid? Would he ever be worthy to come?

While reading a book on the Lord's Supper by Bishop Wilson, Charles encountered the truth of the gospel of Jesus Christ for the first time. In March 1779, he recounted what happened:

> In Passion Week, as I was reading Bishop Wilson *On the Lord's Supper*, I met with an

expression to this effect — "That the Jews knew what they did, when they transferred their sin to the head of their offering." The thought came into my mind, What, may I transfer all my guilt to another? Has God provided an Offering for me, that I may lay my sins on His head? Then, God willing, I will not bear them on my own soul one moment longer. Accordingly, I sought to lay my sins upon the sacred head of Jesus. And on the Wednesday I began to have a hope of mercy. On the Thursday that hope increased. On the Friday and Saturday it became more strong. And on the Sunday morning, Easter-day, April 4, I awoke early with those words upon my heart and lips, "Jesus Christ is risen to-day! Hallelujah! Hallelujah!" From that hour, peace flowed in rich abundance into my soul. And at the Lord's Table in our Chapel, I had the sweetest access to God through my blessed Savior.

This awakening in Charles' soul was no temporary change. His conversion brought about dramatic effects. The course of his life was changed forever. He changed how he used his time. He changed how he used his money. When he returned home to his family on vacation, he tried to gather everyone for family devotions. Never before had Charles cared about reading the Bible. His dramatic conversion shocked everyone in the Simeon family. In his private life, Charles began a strict discipline of personal prayer and meditation on God's Word.

**THE RIVER CAM, CAMBRIDGE, ENGLAND**

## SIMEON'S LABORS AT HOLY TRINITY CHURCH

For to this end we both labor and suffer reproach, because we trust in the living God, who is the Savior of all men, especially of those who believe. These things command and teach. (1 Tim. 4:10-11)

Charles grew in Christ day by day as he spent time in the Word and prayer. He desired to share what he learned with others. He wanted others to know Jesus Christ as well, so he decided to become a pastor.

Charles served first as a deacon in the Church of England. Then he was called to serve as the **vicar** of **Holy Trinity Church** in Cambridge in 1782. At the time, he was only twenty-three years old. Many members of Holy Trinity Church were not believers, and they did not want Simeon as a pastor. They wanted a man named Mr. Hammond appointed instead. But the congregation wasn't permitted to make this decision. In the Church of England, it was the bishop who decided who would be vicar.

At first, the people wanted nothing to do with Simeon. Most of the congregation rejected him. For about twelve years, Simeon endured many kinds of opposition from church

> **Vicar** ▪ In the Church of England, *vicar* is one title given to a priest who serves as the local pastor of a particular congregation.

**HOLY TRINITY CHURCH**

**LOCATION OF CAMBRIDGE, ENGLAND**

members. He also endured slander and abuse from the students at Cambridge University.

The congregation could not remove Charles from his role as their pastor. But they could make Charles' life very difficult. That is exactly what they did. The first thing the congregation did to oppose Simeon was to bar him from being the **afternoon lecturer**. The afternoon lecturer was responsible for leading the afternoon service. Members of the church did not allow Simeon to do this for over twelve years. Instead, that role went to Mr. Hammond (who himself opposed Simeon). This kind of divisive behavior is dishonoring to Jesus Christ. It is difficult for a church to survive long with this kind of division. However, despite the ungodly behavior of many in the church, Charles persevered.

Many members of the congregation held a key for different pews in the church. Those members who didn't like Charles locked their pews for Sunday morning service and did not attend. As a result, there were very few places to sit for those who did come to morning worship. Charles purchased chairs at his own expense and filled the aisles with seating for those who wanted to attend. Even then, some of the congregants threw his chairs onto the lawn of the church in between services.

For almost twelve years, Charles was largely unable to do any pastoral visitation. Why? Because most of his church members would not let him visit them.

Pastor Simeon tried to start an evening service since he was not allowed to lecture in the afternoons. But the churchwardens locked the doors so that he could not enter. Simeon even hired a locksmith to break in so that he could lead the service. However, after having to use a locksmith, Charles realized he would not win over members of the church in this way. Instead, he needed to keep on loving those who opposed him. He would win them over through faithful preaching, prayer, and loving service.

---

**Do not be overcome by evil, but overcome evil with good. (Rom. 12:21)**

---

Not only did he face opposition from his own congregation. He also endured years of mockery and ridicule from students in the university. It was common for university students who attended Holy Trinity Church to misbehave. To create a disruption, students would start "scraping." Students repeatedly dragged their shoes across the floor to express their boredom with the preacher. The students intended to distract the pastor and make it more difficult for him to preach. This was very dishonoring behavior.

Students also frequently insulted Pastor Simeon in the streets. Sometimes they threw things at him. Charles was always a man of

**HENRY MARTYN (1781-1812)**

clean, neat appearance. One day, as he walked the streets of Cambridge, he was pelted with dirt and rotten eggs.

Simeon was so shunned in those early years of ministry that almost no one on the streets of Cambridge would even look at him. On one occasion, while walking through Cambridge, a poor man looked at Simeon and smiled at him. Simeon was so deeply affected by that single smile that he hurried home. Upon returning home, he broke down in tears of gratitude that just one person had smiled at him!

How did Simeon handle all this opposition? Surely, he didn't handle it perfectly. Nor was he a perfect pastor either. He was known to have a short temper, and he confessed that sometimes he did not love those he preached to. As you might imagine, Simeon sometimes felt angry and frustrated by this mistreatment. But slowly, he learned the meaning and importance of what Paul wrote to Timothy.

> A servant of the Lord must not quarrel but be gentle to all, able to teach, patient, in humility correcting those who are in opposition, if God perhaps will grant them repentance, so that they may know the truth. (2 Tim. 2:24-25)

Over twelve years of ministry, Simeon slowly won many in his congregation by his faithful preaching of the Word. The Lord used him to bring many to saving faith in the Lord Jesus. God also used these afflictions to teach Pastor Simeon what it means to take up the cross and follow Jesus. Simeon wrote at a later time:

When I was an object of much contempt and derision in the university, I strolled forth one day, buffeted and afflicted with my little New Testament in my hand. I prayed earnestly to my God that he would comfort me with some cordial [medicine] from his Word, and that on opening the book I might find some text which would sustain me ... The first text which caught my eye was this:

"They found a man of Cyrene, Simon by name; him they compelled to bear his cross."

You know Simon is the same name as Simeon. What a word of instruction was here—what a blessed hint for my encouragement! To have the cross laid upon me, that I might bear it after Jesus—what a privilege! It was enough. Now I could leap and sing for joy as one whom Jesus was honoring with a participation in his sufferings.... I henceforth bound persecution as a wreath of glory around my brow!

This was an important lesson for Charles. He embraced the cross-shaped nature of the Christian life. He learned what it meant for him to take up his cross and follow in the footsteps of Jesus.

As the years passed, the situation become somewhat easier for Pastor Charles. He was loved and appreciated by most in the congregation. But this didn't mean the end of all suffering. For the rest of his life, Pastor Simeon endured opposition by those in Cambridge who hated the gospel of Jesus Christ. Because Charles was a gospel preacher, many did not like him or what he had to say.

But by the grace of God, Simeon endured. He persevered faithfully to the end. After fifty-four years of ministering in one church, he won many to Christ. During his lengthy pastoral ministry, he was responsible for training many young men for the ministry. Among those young men was the missionary **Henry Martyn** (1781-1812). Henry Martyn would one day become a missionary and Bible translator in India and Iran.

By the end of his ministry, Pastor Simeon preached through the entire Bible (creating a 21-volume commentary in the process). He also raised support for missions in other parts of the world. Simeon's gospel witness in Cambridge also spurred on a revival of faithful gospel preaching elsewhere in England.

Pastor Simeon died in 1836. By this time, He was known throughout England. About 1600 people in Cambridge attended his funeral services at the **King's College Chapel**. By enduring opposition and by persevering, Pastor Simeon won the admiration of tens of thousands of people. And more importantly, he did much for the kingdom of His Lord and Savior Jesus Christ. A friend once asked Simeon how he had endured such opposition during forty-nine years of ministry. Simeon replied:

My dear brother, we must not mind a little suffering for Christ's sake. When I am getting through a hedge, if my head and shoulders are safely through, I can bear the pricking of my legs. Let us rejoice in the

## Basic Facts about England

*The United Kingdom consists of the nations of England, Wales, Scotland, and Northern Ireland. The facts below pertain to England, one of the countries within the UK.*

| Total population: | 56 million |
| --- | --- |
| Total area: | 50,000 square miles |
| Capital: | London |
| Official language: | English |
| Primary religions: | Protestant Christian, Atheist, Agnostic |

**INTERIOR OF KING'S COLLEGE CHAPEL**

# PRAYER POINTS: PASTORS IN THE UNITED KINGDOM

In this Prayer Points, we will spend time praying for Christ's pastors laboring in the United Kingdom.

> Shepherd the flock of God which is among you, serving as overseers, not by compulsion but willingly, not for dishonest gain but eagerly; nor as being lords over those entrusted to you, but being examples to the flock; and when the Chief Shepherd appears, you will receive the crown of glory that does not fade away. (1 Pet. 5:2-4)

- **Pray for Pastors Who Are Faithful Examples to the Flock:** Ask the Lord to raise up faithful shepherds in the churches of the United Kingdom. Pray that these pastors would be Christlike examples to God's people.

- **Pray for Bold Pastors Who Preach the Word of God:** As it was in Charles Simeon's day, so it is still true today: faith comes through hearing the Word of Christ. Let us ask God to raise up bold pastors in the United Kingdom who will proclaim the whole counsel of God.

- **Pray for Pastors Who Endure:** Pastoral ministry is difficult. Pray that God would strengthen pastors who are laboring in the church. Pray that they would persevere, faithful to the end.

- **Pray for Your Pastors/Elders:** Also, take time to pray for your pastors and elders in your local church, wherever you may be reading this book. Pray the same things for them.

remembrance that our holy Head [Jesus Christ] has surmounted all His suffering and triumphed over death. Let us follow Him patiently; we shall soon be partakers of His victory.

Pastor Charles Simeon persevered faithful to the end. He followed in the footsteps of his suffering Savior. Hebrews 12 says:

> Therefore we also, since we are surrounded by so great a cloud of witnesses, let us lay aside every weight, and the sin which so easily ensnares us, and let us run with endurance the race that is set before us, looking unto Jesus, the author and finisher of our faith, who for the joy that was set before Him endured the cross, despising the shame, and has sat down at the right hand of the throne of God. For consider Him who endured such hostility from sinners against Himself, lest you become weary and discouraged in your souls. You have not yet resisted to bloodshed, striving against sin. (Heb. 12:1-4)

Let us then also run the race with endurance, always looking to Jesus, who is the author and the finisher of our faith! Amen. ∎

EDINBURGH, SCOTLAND

# BROWNLOW NORTH: EVANGELIST TO THE BRITISH ISLES

> But God forbid that I should boast except in the cross of our Lord Jesus Christ, by whom the world has been crucified to me, and I to the world. (Gal. 6:14)

As Saul of Tarsus journeyed on the road to Damascus, he was stopped in his tracks by the Lord Jesus Christ. By Christ's sovereign determination, Saul (or Paul) would no longer kill Christians. Instead, he would serve Jesus Christ. Paul would go on to preach the unsearchable riches of Christ to the world. And he would write thirteen books of the Bible.

But before that happened, Paul murdered Christians. He blasphemed Christ's name. To the early Christians who knew who he was, Paul seemed the most unlikely candidate to be an apostle of Jesus Christ. When Jesus told Ananias to go and baptize Paul, Ananias replied, "Lord, I have heard from many about this man, how much harm he has done to Your saints in Jerusalem. And here he has authority from the chief priests to bind all who call on Your name" (Acts 9:13-14). Ananias was surprised that the Lord Jesus would save a man such as Paul.

> Then, when Paul was first presented to the church, many did not believe that his conversion was real. When Paul preached in the synagogue, the people wondered at what had happened.

Then all who heard were amazed, and said, "Is this not he who destroyed those who called on this name in Jerusalem, and has come here for that purpose, so that he might bring them bound to the chief priests?" (Acts 9:21)

Jesus saved Paul and used Paul for His glory even though no one would have expected Paul to be used in such a way. God works in unexpected ways.

In this chapter, you will discover the life of a man who unexpectedly became a servant of Jesus Christ. In a similar way to Paul, few people who knew **Brownlow North** would have expected him to become such a gifted and faithful evangelist. For over four decades, Brownlow did not know God. He did not believe in Jesus Christ. He lived for himself.

But God was merciful. The Lord saved Brownlow when he was forty-four years old.

**BROWNLOW NORTH (1810-1875)**

Then Jesus sent him to preach the good news to the world. Through Brownlow North's faithful witness, hundreds of thousands of people heard the gospel in the British Isles. And many were saved. God was merciful to send these times of spiritual awakening.

## BROWNLOW'S LIFE APART FROM GOD

> At that time you were without Christ, being aliens from the commonwealth of Israel and strangers from the covenants of promise, having no hope and without God in the world. (Eph. 2:12)

Brownlow was born in 1810 in Chelsea, near London. His father was a pastor in the Church of England. Brownlow was faithfully brought up in a Christian home. His mother loved him dearly. She was faithful in praying for him daily and in teaching him God's Word. Sadly, Brownlow did not receive God's Word. Even from a young age, he was a rebellious young man. At age nine, he went to school at Eton. While there, he was a bad influence on all the other schoolboys. This grieved Brownlow's mother deeply. How she wished that Brownlow would turn to God!

In 1825, Brownlow experienced the grief of his father's death. He was just fifteen years old. After his time at Eton, Brownlow lived with his mother in **Cheltenham**. After school, his main pursuit in life was entertainment and pleasure. He loved to ride horses. He loved to dance. He enjoyed many games. For Brownlow, life was about pleasing self. He dedicated himself to the pursuit of his own interests.

While spending an extended period of time

CHELTENHAM, ENGLAND

ILLUSTRATION OF A HUNTER IN SCOTLAND

in Ireland, Brownlow caught the heart of a young lady named Grace Anne. Grace was the daughter of a pastor in Galway. In December 1828, Brownlow was married to Grace Anne. After getting married, Brownlow found it difficult to provide for his new family. As children came, expenses rose. Since Brownlow loved games and sports more than work, he turned to gambling to make money. This did not go well for him. With every loss, Brownlow found himself in a state of financial ruin. To escape his problems, he took his wife and children and left England. For a time, the family settled in France.

After a time, Brownlow and his family moved to Scotland. From that point on, Scotland would be their home. Year after year, Brownlow continued in pursuit of his own interests. Whenever he had free time, he would spend it riding his horse or hunting in the woods. He was a gifted outdoorsman. During these years, he did not know the Lord Jesus, but his religious upbringing would affect his heart at times.

One noteworthy event before Brownlow's conversion took place in 1839. One night, he was at dinner with friends at Huntly Lodge. **The Duchess of Gordon** was also at the dinner. She was a godly woman. While they ate, Brownlow turned to the duchess and asked, "Duchess, what should a man do who has often prayed to God and never been answered?" The duchess prayed silently for wisdom. Then she looked directly at Brownlow and answered his question. Quoting James 4:3, the Duchess said, "You ask, and receive not, because ye ask amiss, that ye may consume it upon your lusts." The Word of God pierced Brownlow's heart like a sword. He was quiet the rest of the evening.

Some time after this dinner, Brownlow was brought through a difficult time. One of his sons became dangerously ill. The Duchess of Gordon gave Brownlow a book to read to his son. This dangerous illness and the book Brownlow received were both used to awaken Brownlow to the things of God. After his son recovered, Brownlow decided he would become a minister. He went to Oxford for a degree. His goal was to become a pastor in the Church of England. In just three years, he finished these studies. He graduated from Oxford in 1842.

Brownlow prepared to take on a position in the church. But word about his past ways of life reached the bishop of Lincoln. As Brownlow was confronted by his past sins, he felt that it was not the right time to pursue the ministry, so he left this path.

As he reflected on this season later in life, Brownlow realized that he had been convicted about his sin, but he hadn't turned to Christ. Even though he had been convicted by God's law, he had not received God's mercy in Jesus Christ. He testified that during this time, "I never apprehended Christ. I never accepted Him as my sin-bearer and my righteousness." After a time, Brownlow's convictions wore off. Soon he went back to his old ways.

On Sundays, while many gathered to go to God's worship, Brownlow could be seen in the streets. He would pull his dog-cart behind him with a fishing rod and a basket. He was off to fish the entire day. The worship of God's people was of no interest to him. This was the general pattern of his life until God saved him when he was forty-four years old.

## BROWNLOW REDEEMED BY THE PRECIOUS BLOOD OF CHRIST

**Behold! The Lamb of God who takes away the sin of the world! (John 1:29)**

One night, in November 1854, everything in Brownlow's life began to change. Often in the years that followed, Brownlow would tell the story of his conversion. Here are his own words of what happened that night.

> In the month of November 1854, one night when I was sitting playing at cards, it pleased God to make me concerned about my soul. The instrument used was a sensation of sudden illness, which led me to think that I was going to die. I said to my son, "I am a dead man. Take me upstairs." As soon as this was done, I threw myself down on the bed. My first thought then was, "Now, what will my forty-four years of following the devices of my own heart profit me? In a few minutes I shall be in hell, and what good will all these things do me, for which I have sold my soul?" At that moment I felt constrained to pray, but it was merely the prayer of a coward, a cry for mercy. I was not sorry for what I had done. But I was afraid of the punishment of my sin. And yet still there was something trying to prevent me putting myself on my knees to call for mercy, and that was the presence of my maidservant in the room, lighting the fire.

Brownlow was afraid to cry out to God. He was embarrassed and was afraid of what the maid would think. But by God's grace, he did it anyway.

> By the grace of God, I did put myself on my knees before that girl, and I believe it was the turning-point with me.... By God's grace I was not prevented. I did pray, and though I am not what I should be, yet I am this day what I am, which at least is not what I was.

The next day, Brownlow announced to those in his house, "I am a changed man." He began writing letters to his friends to let them know what had happened. Many were amazed to hear about this change in his life. Had God really saved Brownlow and changed him? After forty-four years of sin, some doubted it. But the change was real.

Perhaps most joyful of all to receive this news was Brownlow's mother. In December 1854, Brownlow visited his mother for Christmas. He shared the good news of his faith in Christ with her. Her many prayers had been answered. The prodigal son had returned. Her son who was "dead and lost" was now "alive and found." Brownlow's mother exclaimed, "Brownlow, God is not only able to save you, but to make you more conspicuous for good than ever you were for evil!" She was right. God would use Brownlow for His glory and for the salvation of many. Brownlow is better remembered for his work as an evangelist for Christ than for his life of sin. Where sin abounded, grace abounded much more.

Now that he was saved, the priorities of Brownlow's life began to change. He loved to read God's Word. He found solace and comfort in prayer to his Heavenly Father. Even though he was a changed man, he still struggled with doubts and questions. He wondered whether God would really receive him since he had sinned so often against the Lord. Through the reading of Scripture and through prayer, Brownlow wrestled with these questions. In time, the consoling promises of God gave him assurance.

At times, Brownlow despaired for his own soul. But when he felt low, the word of Christ would come to him with particular force. Brownlow later testified:

> I was almost despairing. The only thing that kept my head above the water was the promise, "Him that cometh to me I will in no wise cast out." I repeated it again and again and prayed very earnestly, when the word came to me with such power, and with such a rebuke, "Believest thou that I am able to do this?" He was able, and I believed Him, and He did it.

One night, in distress, Brownlow turned to the Book of Romans and read chapter 3. There he found the words of Paul:

**For there is no difference; for all have sinned and fall short of the glory of God, being justified freely by His grace through the redemption that is in Christ Jesus. (Rom. 3:22-24)**

Brownlow recorded:

> With that passage came light into my soul. Striking my book with my hand, and springing from my chair, I cried, "If that scripture is true, I am a saved man! That is what I want. That is what God offers me. That is what I will have."

From that time on, Brownlow frequently shared the story of God's merciful redemption of his soul. In his many opportunities to preach in later years, he never tired of telling others what God had done for him.

Brownlow thought of himself like the man in Acts 4 who was over forty years of age when he was healed (Acts 4:22). Brownlow knew that he was just like that man. He had received spiritual life. This was an amazing miracle of God.

## BROWNLOW SHARES JESUS CHRIST WITH OTHERS

**Now the man from whom the demons had departed begged Him that he might be with Him. But Jesus sent him away, saying, "Return to your own house, and tell what great things God has done for you." And he went his way and proclaimed throughout the whole city what great things Jesus had done for him. (Luke 8:38-39)**

Brownlow loved the Lord Jesus who had redeemed him from sin. And having received such grace, Brownlow wanted others to know about the Lamb of God who takes away the sins of the world. The Lord began to provide numerous opportunities for him to share the good news. He began to distribute tracts and Bibles to the people around town. He did not always find it easy to share his faith. But the love of Christ constrained him to speak on numerous occasions.

An important opportunity occurred in November 1855. A woman who knew Brownlow asked him to go and speak comforting words to her dying niece. Brownlow felt this was God's will for him, so he went. He entered the home of the dying girl. He found that she was a Christian and would soon depart to be with her Lord. The girl urged Brownlow to instead go and speak to her father. She told Brownlow, "Oh, sir, never mind me. But say something through me to my father, for Father is a bad man."

Brownlow did just that. And within a short period of time, the girl's father repented and confessed Christ. Others in town heard the news about what had happened. Soon, many requested Brownlow to come and speak to their family members as well. The Lord blessed his words. Soon, he was holding a cottage meeting every night of the week. In some cases, over 200 people would gather to hear him. People were captured by Brownlow's honest, plain speech. The Spirit of God used his testimony and his proclamation of the Word to affect the souls of many.

Ministers throughout that region of Scotland learned of Brownlow's evangelistic efforts. Numerous pastors asked him to preach to their congregation. Brownlow's evangelism became

ILLUSTRATION OF DUNKELD CATHEDRAL, SCOTLAND

well known among the people. Yet there were still many who knew his past life. Not everyone accepted him. Some thought he had no right to preach since he had been such a wicked sinner for so long. One night, as Brownlow prepared to preach, someone approached him with a letter. The man said, "Here is a letter for you of great importance, and you are requested to read it before you preach tonight."

Brownlow promptly opened the letter and began to read. Contained in the letter were descriptions of his past sinful behavior. The letter concluded with these words: "How dare you, being conscious of the truth of all the above, pray and speak to the people this evening, when you are such a vile sinner?"

Such words would be very difficult to receive for anyone in Brownlow's position. But Brownlow used the opportunity to glorify God. He stepped into the pulpit and shared the letter with the congregation. He told the audience what it contained. Then he said:

> All that is here said is true, and it is a correct picture of the degraded sinner that I once was; and oh how wonderful must the grace be that could quicken and raise me up from such a death in trespasses and sins, and make me what I appear before you tonight, a vessel of mercy, one who knows that all his past sins have been cleansed away through the atoning blood of the Lamb of God. It is of His redeeming love that I have now to tell you, and to entreat any here who are not yet reconciled to God to come this night in faith to Jesus, that He may take their sins away and heal them.

Brownlow used his past sins, and God's merciful redemption, to call other sinners to faith in Christ. And many did come.

## TIMES OF SPIRITUAL REFRESHING

Repent therefore and be converted, that your sins may be blotted out, so that times of refreshing may come from the presence of the Lord, and that He may send Jesus Christ, who was preached to you before. (Acts 3:19-20)

Scotland witnessed a time of spiritual awakening in the 1840s. Many faithful preachers were used by God during that time. Among them, the most well-known is **William Chalmers Burns** (1815-1868). After his ministry in Scotland, Burns went to China and served as a missionary in that land. But twenty years after this, a time of spiritual lethargy followed. In God's mercy, the efforts of Brownlow North would be remarkably blessed. Through Brownlow and other faithful Christians, 1859

WILLIAM C. BURNS (1815-1868), SCOTTISH MISSIONARY TO CHINA

LONDONDERRY, NORTHERN IRELAND

and 1860 brought times of refreshing to Scotland.

As Brownlow became know all over Scotland, the **Free Church of Scotland**, of which Brownlow was a member, ordained him as an evangelist. It was evident to all that he had this calling from God. It was also important to Brownlow and to the church that this calling be formally recognized.

In 1859, Brownlow preached in Northern Ireland. The response to God's Word was momentous. It has been estimated that some 100,000 people joined the churches in Northern Ireland. In August of that year, Brownlow visited **Londonderry**. Newspapers estimated that 4,000 to 5,000 people gathered to hear him one Sunday. This gives the reader a sense of just how large the crowds were at times. Brownlow traveled throughout England and Scotland, speaking to large audiences.

Brownlow's preaching was characterized by earnestness, plain speech, and love for his hearers. He sincerely and ardently desired his hearers to be saved. One journalist, hearing Brownlow preach in 1857, recorded what he saw. Brownlow opened the service with a low and solemn voice. As he prayed, tears began to stream down his cheeks. Then, as he preached the Word, at times he would begin to cry again. As he detailed the sad condition of the sinner without God, he wept. Then, with intense passion, he called sinners to be made right with God through Jesus Christ. And with the most authentic smile, Brownlow would then describe his joy at knowing that some were being saved.

It was this bold, loving, authentic, faith-filled, and Scripture-saturated preaching that the Lord used to bring many to saving faith. It was the long-prayed-for mercy of God that visited the British Isles in those important years.

## LAST YEARS OF LABOR IN SCOTLAND

Brownlow's last years of ministry were especially focused on the large city of **Glasgow**, Scotland. There he preached frequently and visited with many who wished to speak with him. He was just as earnest in the pulpit as he was out of the pulpit. He spoke plainly, with love, to those who came asking for spiritual counsel. Having been converted at age forty-four, Brownlow was not a young man when he began his ministry. And as the years passed, he became physically weaker. He preached just as faithfully, but he was often not well physically. Sometimes he would preach when he was barely able to preach.

In October and November 1875, Brownlow became gravely ill. For ten days he lay in bed until he departed this life and went to be with the Lord. The date of his passing to glory was November 9, 1875. In his last days, Brownlow testified that he was at peace. He said, "I used to have a great terror of death, but that is quite gone from me; I have no fear of it now. I am resting on Christ."

Some might wonder at God's providence in Brownlow's life. Why didn't God save him when he was twelve or seventeen instead of forty-four? Couldn't Brownlow have been used for many more years for good? Of course, we can never question the wisdom of God. We can know with certainty that the Lord had a purpose in redeeming Brownlow when he was so old. It was in this way that Brownlow learned just how deep Christ's love is and how amazing God's grace is. It was Augustine who said, "The more desperate was my disease, the greater honor redounded to the Physician who cured me." That was Paul's testimony as well. He considered himself the chief of sinners. And yet, he says, "the grace of our Lord was exceedingly abundant" to him (1 Tim. 1:14). And so it was with David who testified that God "brought me out of a horrible pit, out of the miry clay, and set my feet upon a rock" (Ps. 40:2).

There are many lessons we can learn from Brownlow North's life.

First, no sinner is beyond God's mercy and power to save. For this reason, we should pray that God would save sinners, even those that appear most unlikely to come to him. Brownlow did not seem to be a likely candidate for salvation. But with God all things are possible. Let us learn to pray with more hope.

Second, may we learn to glorify God by sharing with others what He has done for our souls. Brownlow's faithful efforts at evangelism should encourage us to pray for our own opportunities to do the same. We can pray for the same love for Christ and the same love for lost souls. Not every Christian is called to preach to giant crowds. Not every Christian is gifted with Brownlow's particular gifts. But the Lord does call each of us to love our neighbor. And from the overflow of our own hearts, the Lord also calls us to speak of His goodness to others. ∎

**LOCATION OF GLASGOW AND EDINBURGH**

## Basic Facts about Scotland

| | |
|---|---|
| Total population: | 5.5 million |
| Total area: | 30,000 square miles |
| Capital: | Edinburgh |
| Official language: | English, Scots, Scottish Gaelic |
| Primary religions: | Protestant Christian, Atheist, Agnostic |

# PRAYER POINTS: SCOTLAND

- **Praise God for missionaries from Scotland:** The legacy of Scotland as a missionary-sending center goes all the way back to the time of Columba. But even in more recent centuries, numerous well-known missionaries have been Scottish. Scottish missionaries include David Livingstone, Mary Slessor, Robert Moffat, Eric Liddell, and others. God has graciously used many from this land to spread the good news of Jesus Christ all over the world. Give thanks to God for this heritage of faith.

- **Pray for repentance and freedom from idols:** Only about 50% of the population in Scotland profess any connection to Christianity. This number used to be much higher. As Scotland turns away from its Christian heritage, there has been a turning back to idols which cannot save. Alcohol and drug abuse are common in Scotland. Almost half of the children in Scotland are born to a father and mother who are not married. These sins have destructive effects on the people of Scotland. Pray that God would grant repentance and faith in Jesus to the Scottish people.

- **Pray for the Church of Scotland and other churches in Scotland:** The official Church of Scotland has a rich Protestant Christian heritage. During the time of the Reformation, the Church of Scotland became Protestant and Presbyterian. The church's beliefs and practices were reformed according to Scripture. But as the people of Scotland have departed from the faith, the official Church of Scotland has suffered greatly. Pray that God would revive this ailing church. Let us also pray for the many other churches in Scotland that are not part of this official church, that God would use them to advance the gospel.

HOUSES OF PARLIAMENT, WESTMINSTER, LONDON, ENGLAND

# CHARLES AND SUSANNAH SPURGEON: A SPIRITUAL HARVEST IN LONDON

How beautiful upon the mountains
Are the feet of him who brings good news,
Who proclaims peace,
Who brings glad tidings of good things,
Who proclaims salvation,
Who says to Zion,
"Your God reigns!" (Isa. 52:7)

It was the morning of Sunday, December 18, 1853. The **New Park Street Baptist Church** in London had a guest preacher. He was nineteen years old. His name was Charles Haddon Spurgeon. He was remarkably young, but his preaching had already earned him a reputation. He was called "the boy preacher of Waterbeach." Spurgeon had already spent two years pastoring a small congregation of believers in the English town of **Waterbeach**. The members of New Park Street were without a pastor, and Spurgeon was a candidate for that position.

Upon seeing the young man, many in the congregation were surprised. Was this the candidate they were to consider? Wasn't he far too young to preach?

But once Spurgeon began to preach, the believers at the church were astounded.

The young man ascended the pulpit and read his text:

Every good gift and every perfect gift is from above, and cometh down from the Father of lights, with whom is no variableness, neither shadow of turning. (Jas. 1:17 KJV)

Spurgeon was so young and yet so gifted at proclaiming the Word of God. He was a man

**CHARLES SPURGEON (1834-1892)**

uniquely gifted with expositing God's Word in a compelling way. Members of the congregation went home and invited their friends to attend the evening service.

That night, a much larger congregation gathered for the service. Spurgeon read his text for the evening message.

> These are they which were not defiled with women; for they are virgins. These are they which follow the Lamb whithersoever he goeth. These were redeemed from among men, being the firstfruits unto God and to the Lamb. And in their mouth was found no guile: for they are without fault before the throne of God. (Rev. 14:4-5 KJV)

Once again, the congregation of New Park Street were captured by the glory of God as Spurgeon proclaimed it. Though the believers in London knew little about Spurgeon, they were insistent that he should become their pastor. In April 1854, within a few months of his first sermon, Spurgeon was elected pastor and began his ministry there. He would stay in that post of service for almost forty years. He labored at New Park Street (later called the Metropolitan Tabernacle) until his death.

Charles was honored to fill such an important role, but he knew that he was only a young man. He wrote to the congregation upon accepting their invitation: "I ask you to remember me in prayer that I may realize the solemn responsibility of my trust. Remember my youth and inexperience, and pray that these may not hinder my usefulness."

## SPURGEON'S CONVERSION TO CHRIST

> And as Moses lifted up the serpent in the wilderness, even so must the Son of Man be lifted up, that whoever believes in Him should not perish but have eternal life. (John 3:14-15)

How did Spurgeon become a preacher? How did the Lord form this young man, at an early age, to be a pastor? To answer these questions, we must go back to the beginning of Spurgeon's life and to his conversion as a young man.

Charles was born in 1834 into a Christian household. His father and grandfather were both pastors. Charles was blessed with a faithful Christian upbringing in both his parents' and grandparents' home. From a very young age (four or five years old), Spurgeon would sit in his grandfather's study, poring over volumes of sermons and theology. He was a gifted reader and had a strong grasp of biblical doctrine.

But by his own confession, Charles had not experienced a saving conversion to Jesus Christ. He remained unconverted until December 1849, when he was fifteen years old. That month, an outbreak of fever in his school at Newmarket forced Spurgeon to go home for Christmas. He began his journey home to Colchester. On one Sunday morning, a fierce snowstorm forced him to stop in the closest chapel of worship he could find.

In a little Methodist chapel on that snowy day, Charles found about twelve to fifteen people gathered for worship. The minister who usually preached did not make it due to the snowstorm. Instead, another man filled the pulpit. Charles believed the man was a tailor or shoemaker. He was no professional preacher. But it was this man who proclaimed God's Word to the saving of Spurgeon's soul.

The man's text was from Isaiah:

> Look unto me, and be ye saved, all the ends of the earth:
> For I am God, and there is none else. (Isa. 45:22 KJV)

The preacher was plain spoken. He got right

to the point of the passage. Here is how Spurgeon recalled the message. The preacher said:

> This is a very simple text indeed. It says "Look." Now lookin' don't take a deal of pain. It aint liftin' your foot or your finger. It is just "Look." Well, a man needn't go to college to learn to look. You may be the biggest fool, and you can look. A man needn't be worth a thousand a year to look. Anyone can look. Even a child can look. But then the text says, "Look unto Me." Ay! Many of ye are lookin' to yourselves, but it's no use lookin' there. You'll never find any comfort in yourselves.... Jesus Christ says "Look unto Me." Look unto Me. I am sweatin' great drops of blood. Look unto Me. I am hangin' on the cross. Look unto Me. I am dead and buried. Look unto Me. I rise again. Look unto Me. I ascend to heaven.... O poor sinner, look unto Me! Look unto Me!

Then the preacher turned and looked directly at young Charles and said:

> Young man, you look very miserable! And you will always be miserable—miserable in life and miserable in death—if you don't obey my text. But if you obey now, this moment, you will be saved. Young man, look to Jesus Christ. Look! Look! Look! You have nothing to do but look and live!

The message struck Spurgeon's heart. He was feeling miserable. But by the power of God's Word and by the working of the Holy Spirit, Spurgeon found joy in Christ! The Holy Spirit awakened Charles to his lost condition and his need for a Savior. Spurgeon recounted, "There and then the cloud was gone, the darkness had rolled away." Now, Spurgeon believed in the Lord Jesus Christ. He looked to Jesus in faith, and he was saved.

Immediately after his conversion, Spurgeon was set on fire to serve the Lord. He diligently shared the gospel with everyone he met. He passed out tracts all over town. He joined a local Baptist congregation and was baptized.

Charles grew up in a Congregationalist home. Congregationalist churches practiced infant baptism. This meant that Charles was baptized as an infant in this church. But due to his newfound Baptist convictions, he believed the Bible taught that only professing believers were to be baptized. The local Baptist pastor gladly immersed Spurgeon in a nearby river. Charles remained a Baptist for the rest of his life. But he saw Congregationalists and Presbyterians as his brothers and sisters in the Lord, and he worked alongside them throughout his life. (Both Congregationalists and Presbyterians practice infant baptism, sometimes called household baptism. According to this practice, believing adults and their children are considered members of Christ's church by baptism.)

## THE BOY PREACHER

*Let no one despise your youth, but be an example to the believers in word, in conduct, in love, in spirit, in faith, in purity. (1 Tim. 4:12)*

Spurgeon took every opportunity available to share the gospel with others. His first occasion to preach came in a thatched-roof cottage. His audience was a few farmers and their wives. He preached from 1 Peter, taking the words: "Unto you therefore which believe He is precious." He was warmly received even though he was just seventeen years old.

Spurgeon's next opportunity for preaching took place in the small town of Waterbeach. There, he preached to a small assembly. After two Sundays, the congregation asked him to be their pastor. Spurgeon knew he was young, but he sensed the call of God to preach the Word.

SUSANNAH SPURGEON WITH HER TWO SONS

He accepted the offer of the Waterbeach congregation. For about two years, he preached there. Because of his youth, he was known as "the boy preacher of Waterbeach." After meeting an older man from New Park Street in London, Spurgeon was invited to proclaim God's Word there in December 1853. As we learned above, he was chosen as the new pastor of New Park Street Baptist Church.

The New Park Street Church seated over one thousand people. But attendance had dwindled to one or two hundred people. The church was without a pastor. This also diminished regular attendance. When Spurgeon took the pulpit, the congregation grew rapidly. Within months, the building was completely full. Spurgeon not only found his lifelong calling at New Park Street Baptist. He also found his wife.

## CHARLES AND SUSANNAH ARE MARRIED

He who finds a wife finds a good thing,
And obtains favor from the LORD. (Prov. 18:22)

The first night Spurgeon preached in London, there was a young lady named Susannah Thompson in the audience. That night, she listened to young Charles preach. She was not impressed with him at first. She wrote:

> I was not at all fascinated by the young orator's eloquence. . . . I was not spiritually minded enough to understand his earnest presentation of the Gospel. . . . the huge black satin stock, the long badly-trimmed hair and the blue pocket-handkerchief with the white spots . . . these attracted most of my attention, and, I fear, awakened some feelings of amusement.

Susannah's perception of Charles did not last. Shortly after becoming pastor, Charles presented Susannah with a gift. It was a copy of John Bunyan's *The Pilgrim's Progress*. Spurgeon addressed Susannah with a note in the front of the book:

> Miss Thompson
> with desires for her progress
> In the blessed pilgrimage
> From
> C. H. Spurgeon
> April 20, 1854

Their relationship blossomed through numerous conversations. Then, in August 1854, Spurgeon asked Susannah to marry him. She gave an enthusiastic "Yes!" In January 1856, their wedding took place. They would enjoy a happy, fruitful marriage all their days together. But it would not be without many trials. As we will see, both Charles and Susannah were racked with numerous and frequent health issues.

## REVIVAL AND TRIALS IN LONDON

> How then shall they call on Him in whom they have not believed? And how shall they believe in Him of whom they have not heard? And how shall they hear without a preacher? (Rom. 10:14)

Spurgeon's popularity in London exploded. Services in New Park Street Baptist attracted far more people than room allowed. Eventually, Spurgeon had to host additional services elsewhere. He held services for some 4,000 people in **Exeter Hall**. Much like the Great Awak-

**SPURGEON PREACHING AT SURREY GARDENS**

ening, thousands upon thousands were eager to hear the Word of God. Many people were hearing the gospel preached with clarity for the first time. The Lord saved many through the ministry of the Word.

But with great success also came bitter opposition. Because of Spurgeon's massive popularity, some believed he was a charlatan, out to make money for himself. This was not true. But negative press made Spurgeon look bad in the eyes of some. Horrible things were said about him that were not true. Nevertheless, this did not stop Spurgeon from preaching.

To encourage her husband, Susannah posted an important verse on a wall in their home:

---

**Blessed are you when they revile and persecute you, and say all kinds of evil against you falsely for My sake. Rejoice and be exceedingly glad, for great is your reward in heaven, for so they persecuted the prophets who were before you. (Matt. 5:11-12)**

---

Along with opposition, other trials came to Charles and Susannah as well. One of the most difficult events of Spurgeon's life took place on October 19, 1856. He had secured the use of an even larger facility than Exeter Hall. That night, a service was planned at the **Surrey Gardens Music Hall**. This building held about 10,000 people. Spurgeon began the service in prayer. But there were troublemakers present.

Someone in the crowd yelled "Fire!" Then another person cried out, "The galleries are falling!" Another exclaimed, "The whole place is collapsing!" This created a panic, and people began to rush out of the building. Some people jumped from the balconies. Others were trampled. In the process, seven people died. Twenty-eight other people were severely injured.

The service ended, and Spurgeon was taken to a side room. He was overcome with grief. Though he had done no wrong, the disaster at Surrey Gardens was again used by opponents to attack him. For weeks, Spurgeon fell into a deep depression. But in time, by God's grace, he recovered and resumed his preaching ministry. However, this event left a scar. Spurgeon would never forget it. From then on, he was always conscious of such dangers of overcrowding, particularly when the larger **Metropolitan Tabernacle** was built.

Despite significant trials such as the Surrey Gardens disaster, the Lord abundantly blessed Spurgeon's ministry. New Park Street Church grew rapidly. The number of converts was so large that Spurgeon tasked other assistants to visit these new Christians and hear their testimony of faith before they were brought into membership through baptism. Not only did Spurgeon's ministry flourish. This spiritual awakening spread to other ministers and congregations. Soon, other preachers also preached in Exeter Hall to thousands. Spurgeon testified:

> The times of refreshing from the presence of the Lord have at last dawned upon our land. Everywhere there are signs of aroused activity and increased earnestness. A spirit of prayer is visiting our churches.

## THE METROPOLITAN TABERNACLE AND OTHER MINISTRIES

---

**For My house shall be called a house of prayer for all nations. (Isa. 56:7)**

---

In 1861, a new church building was opened for worship. Now, the New Park Street Baptist Church was renamed the Metropolitan Tabernacle. This new church building was designed to seat a much larger audience. In some cases,

INTERIOR OF THE METROPOLITAN TABERNACLE

it was reported that up to 6,000 people could fit into the building at one time. The Metropolitan Tabernacle is still a functioning church today. If you visit London, you can visit it for worship on a Sunday!

On the first Sunday, as God's people gathered for worship, Spurgeon declared the purpose for which the building was constructed:

> I would propose that the subject of the ministry in this house, as long as this platform shall stand, and as long as this house shall be frequented by worshippers, shall be the person of Jesus Christ.

The Tabernacle became a hub for all different sorts of ministry activities. Many young men interested in preaching and pastoring came to Spurgeon. They desired to be mentored by Charles in order to be prepared for ministry. Spurgeon was eager to help. He founded a new educational institution called The **Pastor's College**. Here, for decades, men were trained for the ministry of the Word. Spurgeon's college was unique in that it required those who applied to already have experience in preaching. Spurgeon wanted to train only those who had experienced the call of God in their lives. Additionally, he and his fellow teachers wanted to see that the young men who came to the college had preaching gifts bestowed by God. Spurgeon was also busy publishing his sermons and editing a magazine. The title of the magazine was *The Sword and the Trowel*. The title was a reference to the Book of Nehemiah, chapter 4:

> Those who built on the wall, and those who carried burdens, loaded themselves so that with one hand they worked at construction, and with the other held a weapon. Every one of the builders had his sword girded at his side as he built. (Neh. 4:17-18)

The magazine's subtitle explained its connection to Nehemiah: "A record of combat with sin and labor for the Lord."

Another important ministry effort undertaken by the Tabernacle was an orphanage. It was established in central London near the church building. It came about as a very direct answer to prayer.

One night, at a prayer meeting in the summer of 1866, Spurgeon spoke to those at the meeting: "Dear friends, we are a huge church, and should be doing more for the Lord in this great city. I want us, tonight, to ask Him to send us some new work; and if we need money to carry it on, let us pray that the means also may be sent."

God answered the prayer a few days later. Spurgeon received a letter from a woman named Mrs. Hillyard. She desired to donate 20,000 British pounds to provide for orphan boys. In answer to the letter, Spurgeon visited Mrs. Hillyard. He thought so large a donation must have been a mistake. Pastor Charles took with him his deacon William Higgs. Upon arriving, Spurgeon told Mrs. Hillyard the purpose of his visit. "We have called, Madam, about the two hundred pounds that you mentioned in your letter."

Mrs. Hillyard replied, "Two hundred? I meant to write twenty thousand." She told Spurgeon that the large amount was no mistake. She wanted to donate 20,000 pounds, and she wanted to see it used for an orphanage. Since there was no orphanage yet established by the Tabernacle, Spurgeon recommended she donate to another existing orphanage. But Mrs. Hillyard was emphatic. The money was for an orphanage, and she wanted the Tabernacle to take it. And that is how the **Stockwell Orphanage** was founded by the Metropolitan Tabernacle.

## SUSANNAH'S MINISTRY

> As each one has received a gift, minister it to one another, as good stewards of the manifold grace of God. If anyone speaks, let him speak as the oracles of God. If anyone ministers, let him

**COVER PAGE OF *THE SWORD AND THE TROWEL***

do it as with the ability which God supplies, that in all things God may be glorified through Jesus Christ, to whom belong the glory and the dominion forever and ever. Amen. (1 Pet. 4:10-11)

In the late 1860s, both Charles and Susannah experienced frequent health challenges. Those challenges continued, in varying frequency, until the end of their lives. After Susannah gave birth to two boys, she suffered from various health issues. By the late 1860s, she was often confined to her home. For many Sundays, Susannah was not well enough to attend worship. This was a painful affliction, for she loved to hear her husband preach and to be in the assembly of the saints. Even though Susannah was often confined to her home, she wanted to be useful to the Lord's service in some way. In 1875, a new door of ministry opened for her.

Charles published a book containing lectures he delivered at the Pastor's College. The book was titled **Lectures to My Students**. The book was a treasure-house of wisdom drawn from Spurgeon's pastoral experience. Susannah read the book and commented to Charles, "I wish I could send a copy to every minister in England!"

Charles replied, "Then why not do it? How much will you give?"

Susannah counted up the money she had saved to give to some ministry. She found that she had enough to purchase one hundred copies of the book. This is how the idea of **Mrs. Spurgeon's Book Fund** was born. Susannah sent copies to poor pastors all over England. In reply, she received letters of gratitude from many pastors. It was clear she had found a need and a way to fulfill it.

Next, Susannah saved and collected money for another distribution. This time, she sent out her husband's commentary on the Psalms. This large set of writing on the Psalms is called *The Treasury of David*. Once again, the books were a great blessing to many pastors. Mrs. Spurgeon received letter after letter from pastors extremely grateful for such a gift. Many of them could hardly afford any books since they often lived on small incomes while caring for large families.

Within five months, Mrs. Spurgeon's Book Fund had distributed over 3,000 books. Susannah was overjoyed to hear what a blessing her ministry efforts were. Here is what she said:

> It is most touching to hear some tell with eloquence the effect the gift produced upon them. One is "not ashamed to say" he received the parcel with "tears of joy," wife and children standing around and rejoicing with him. Another, as soon as the wrappings fall from the precious volumes, praises God aloud and sings the Doxology with all his might; while a third, when his eyes light on the long-coveted "Treasury of David," "rushes from the room" that he may go alone and "pour out his full heart before his God."

The Book Fund continued to grow year after year. Eventually Mrs. Spurgeon, with her donors and helpers, sent books all over the world. The list of countries they reached include Patna, Bengal, Ceylon, Samoa, China, Jamaica, Russia, Canada, the Congo, Argentina, Spain, and more.

Susannah kept the Book Fund running even though she sometimes spent weeks in bed, unable to do anything. But when she was a bit stronger, she resumed her work. Her steadfast labors in writing letters, purchasing books, soliciting donations, and packaging books is an example of being busy about the work of the Lord even while suffering from poor health.

## CHARLES' LATER YEARS

Let Your work appear to Your servants,
And Your glory to their children.
And let the beauty of the LORD our God be upon us,
And establish the work of our hands for us;
Yes, establish the work of our hands. (Ps. 90:16-17)

With every passing year, Spurgeon's opportunities for ministry grew and grew. He received invitations to preach in the United States and Canada. However, he declined these invitations in order to focus his labors at home, to care for his wife, and to be a good steward of his own health. In later years, Charles suffered from frequent episodes of gout and other illnesses. During some months, he was so unwell that he was confined to bed, like his wife. In his later years of ministry, Charles was sometimes only able to preach six months out of the year. When he wasn't well enough to preach, his brother James Spurgeon often preached instead.

In order to recuperate from his frequent ailments, Charles traveled south for warmer weather, especially during the winter months. His favorite haven for rest and recovery was a town on the southern French coast. The name of the town was **Menton,** France. Even while Spurgeon rested in Menton, he was still busy writing letters and drafting books and articles. The years 1890 to 1892 were Spurgeon's most difficult years in terms of his health. He made frequent trips to Menton. He would return to England, but it wasn't long before he was on his way back to France once again.

On June 7, 1891, Charles Spurgeon preached his last sermon at the Metropolitan Tabernacle. Thereafter, he would be confined to home or on leave in Menton. On October 26 of that year, he and his wife went to Menton for the winter. It was his last trip, and he never returned to England. He spent his last months surrounded by his wife and friends in Menton. There, he completed a commentary on the Gospel of Matthew. Then, on January 31, 1892,

**METROPOLITAN TABERNACLE IN LONDON, ENGLAND**

# PRAYER POINTS: PASTORS IN THE UNITED KINGDOM

**Shepherd the flock of God which is among you, serving as overseers, not by compulsion but willingly, not for dishonest gain but eagerly; nor as being lords over those entrusted to you, but being examples to the flock; and when the Chief Shepherd appears, you will receive the crown of glory that does not fade away. (1 Pet. 5:2-4)**

In this Prayer Points, we will spend time praying for Christ's pastors laboring in the United Kingdom.

- **Pray for pastors who will be faithful examples to the flock:** Ask the Lord to raise up faithful shepherds in the churches of the United Kingdom. Pray that these pastors would be Christ-like examples to God's people.

- **Pray for bold pastors who preach the Word of God:** As it was in Spurgeon's day, so it is still true today: faith comes through hearing the Word of Christ. Let us ask God to raise up bold pastors in the United Kingdom who will proclaim the whole counsel of God.

- **Pray for pastors who will endure:** Pastoral ministry is difficult. Pray that God would strengthen pastors who are laboring in the church. Pray that they would persevere and remain faithful to the end.

- **Pray for your pastors/elders:** Take time to pray for the pastors and elders in your local church, wherever you may be reading this book. Pray the same things for them.

Spurgeon passed away. He was fifty-seven years old.

Spurgeon's body was brought back to England. Numerous funeral services followed as his prolific life was remembered with gratitude to God. Spurgeon was faithful to carry both the sword and trowel until the end of his life. He waged war against sin, and he labored faithfully for the Lord. Though he died, yet Charles still speaks. His sermons and books continue to be printed and distributed. And, thanks to Susannah's faithful and prayerful efforts, many pastors received nourishing resources to strengthen their ministry. As we remember their lives with gratitude, let us acknowledge them as God's blessing to England and to all the world. ∎

## Basic Facts about England

*The United Kingdom consists of the nations of England, Wales, Scotland, and Northern Ireland. The facts below pertain to England, one of the countries within the UK.*

| | |
|---|---|
| **Total population:** | 56 million |
| **Total area:** | 50,000 square miles |
| **Capital:** | London |
| **Official language:** | English |
| **Primary religions:** | Protestant Christian, Atheist, Agnostic |

MENTON, FRANCE

THREE CLIFFS BAY, WALES

# DR. MARTYN LLOYD-JONES: PREACHING THE WHOLE COUNSEL OF GOD

"For I have not shunned to declare to you the whole counsel of God." – the Apostle Paul (Acts 20:27)

Dr. Martyn Lloyd-Jones was a gifted medical doctor in London. By age twenty-one, he had graduated with his bachelor's in medicine and surgery from the distinguished program of St. **Bartholomew's Hospital,** London. Two years later, in 1923, Martyn earned a doctorate in medicine from London University. Dr. Lloyd-Jones was serving under another well-known physician by the name of **Sir Thomas Horder**. This connection was especially important because Sir Horder was the personal physician for King George V and the royal family.

Martyn's rapid progress in the medical profession opened many potential doors of opportunity. He was well-known at his young age as a gifted doctor. Sir James Patterson Ross, president of the Royal College of Surgeons, described Martyn as "one of the finest clinicians I have ever encountered." Had Martyn continued in the medical field, he likely would have been highly successful.

But the Lord had other plans for Martyn. In his mid-twenties, Dr. Lloyd-Jones sensed a call to preach the gospel of Jesus Christ. Christians all over the world are thankful the doctor heeded the call.

## MARTYN'S CALL TO THE MINISTRY

Martyn grew up in a Christian home in Wales. The country of Wales is part of the United Kingdom. It is a small country on the western side of the island of Great Britain. Martyn grew up in a Calvinistic Methodist church in Wales. As a child, he learned to speak both Welsh and English.

As Dr. Lloyd-Jones advanced in his medical profession, he sensed an emptiness about life. He saw that he could often bring healing to the physical bodies of his patients. But he

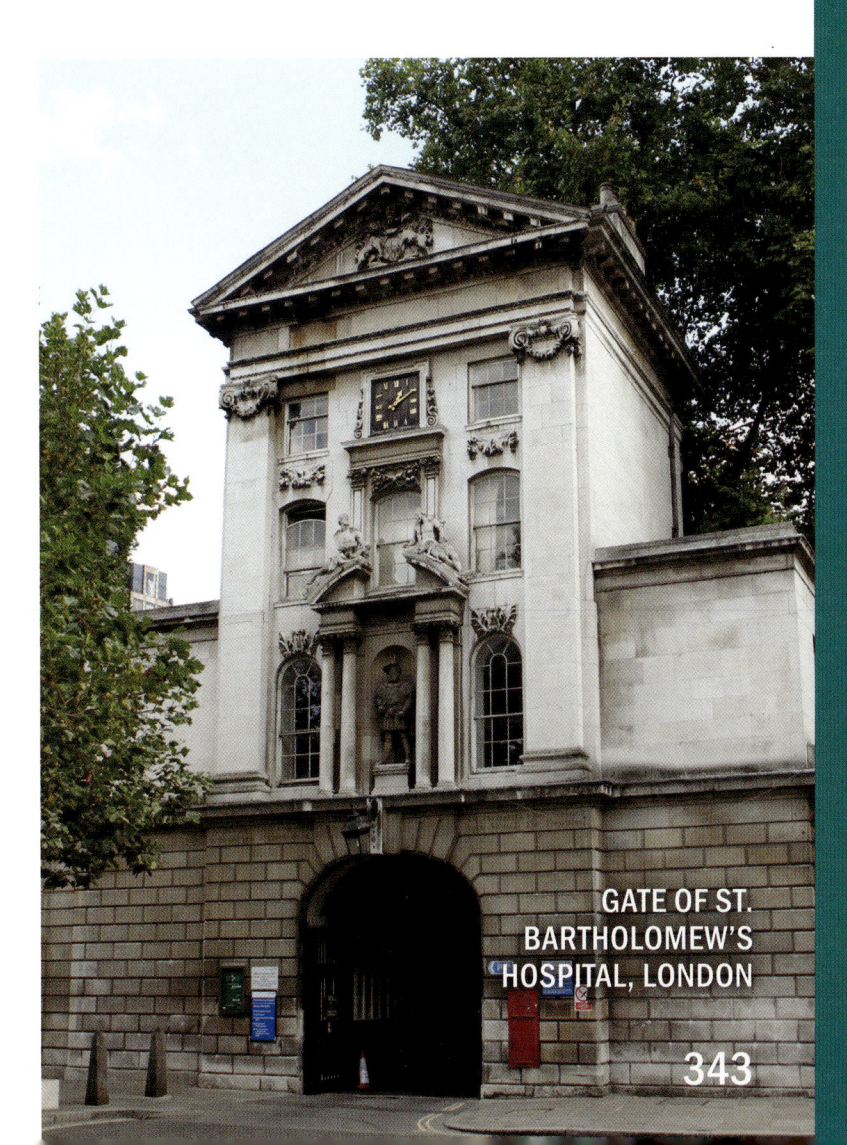

**GATE OF ST. BARTHOLOMEW'S HOSPITAL, LONDON**

realized this did not heal their souls. As a physician, he could not fix their more fundamental ailment: the reality of sin. After his patients were healed, they would just go back to their life of sin. The doctor was also sobered when his father died. Martyn was just twenty-two years old when this happened. Martyn had also lost his brother when he was eighteen. Sometime around these years, he was converted to faith in Jesus Christ. He testified:

> For many years I thought I was a Christian when in fact I was not. It was only later that I came to see that I had never been a Christian and became one.... What I needed was preaching that would convict me of sin ... But I never heard this. The preaching we had was always based on the assumption that we were all Christians.

In June 1926, Dr. Lloyd-Jones decided to leave the medical profession. He began seeking a pastoral call somewhere where he could preach the unsearchable riches of Christ found in the gospel. Dr. Lloyd-Jones had already gained recognition for his medical skills. His departure from the profession caused quite a stir. It surprised many that he would leave such a well-paying profession to preach. There wasn't much money to be made in preaching the Bible. But this didn't stop Dr. Lloyd-Jones from pursuing his plan. He was committed to the call he perceived was from God.

Another significant life-event happened in June 1926. That month, Martyn asked a young woman named **Bethan Phillips** to marry him. Bethan also was a gifted physician. But she willingly joined Martyn in a life of pastoral ministry. They were married in January 1927. Just a few weeks later, on February 1, 1927, Martyn accepted a pastoral call to **Aberavon**, Wales.

## MINISTRY IN ABERAVON

> For the word of God is living and powerful, and sharper than any two-edged sword, piercing even to the division of soul and spirit, and of joints and marrow, and is a discerner of the thoughts and intents of the heart. And there is no creature hidden from His sight, but all things are naked and open to the eyes of Him to whom we must give account. (Heb. 4:12-13)

Dr. Lloyd-Jones and his wife Bethan found Aberavon to be a community greatly in need of the gospel. Unemployment was high. Drunkenness was common. And many in the town lived in poverty. Not only was the town run down. The church Dr. Lloyd-Jones pastored was attended by very few people. The church's name was the Forward Movement Mission Hall.

Martyn was convinced that the ministry

**D. MARTYN LLOYD-JONES (1899-1981)**

PORT TALBOT, WALES (ABERAVON IS A COMMUNITY WITHIN PORT TALBOT)

of preaching and prayer was God's ordained means to build the church of Jesus Christ. He believed a ministry built around these two things was sufficient. But many in the church believed differently. Before the doctor's arrival, the church had attempted other approaches to bringing in new members. Evenings of musical performance were held in hopes that some in the community would begin attending the church. The church also had a drama society that would perform stage plays in the church.

Dr. Lloyd-Jones believed that the faithful preaching of the gospel was God's appointed means for saving sinners. Once he became pastor, he reorganized the ministries of the church. There were to be two Sunday services (11 AM and 6 PM), a prayer meeting on Mondays, and a mid-week meeting on Wednesdays. All other programs were suspended. Someone asked Dr. Lloyd-Jones what they should do with the wooden stage in the church hall. The stage had been used for the musical and dramatic performances. Being very practical, Dr. Lloyd-Jones replied, "You can heat the church with it." The committee didn't want to see the stage burned, so it was instead donated to a local YMCA. This is just one example of how committed Dr. Lloyd-Jones was to preaching and prayer above all.

The Lord was gracious to bless the doctor's preaching ministry. The church grew rapidly, and many were converted through the proclamation of the gospel. Preaching twice on Sundays, Dr. Lloyd-Jones usually dedicated one of his sermons to an evangelistic message. On his third Sunday as pastor, Martyn preached on Romans 6:23.

**For the wages of sin is death, but the gift of God is eternal life in Christ Jesus our Lord. (Rom. 6:23)**

Martyn preached to his listeners that God's gift of salvation in Jesus Christ is free. None of us deserve it. But God is merciful to all who call upon His name. Here is a portion of what he preached:

> It is a gift that is as open to the very worst man in Aberavon tonight as it is to the very

**FORWARD MOVEMENT MISSION HALL, WHERE LLOYD-JONES PASTORED**

best. For no one can ever get it because he deserves it. I have met men sometimes who have said to me that they know that they are beyond hope, that they have sunk so far into sin and iniquity that nothing can save them. My reply to them is just this, that the gifts of God are infinite gifts and that, were you ten times worse than you are already, God could still save you, and do so without realizing that his resources had been called upon at all. The most respectable sinner in Aberavon tonight has no more claim on it than the worst, and when you both avail yourselves of it you will be doing so on an equal footing. Hold on, my friends, all is not lost, no one is too bad—all are invited.

The Lord added to the number of the church those who were being saved. Church membership stood at 146 in 1926. By 1928, the church had increased to 196 members. In the year 1931, the Holy Spirit worked mightily. In that year alone, 135 people joined the membership of the church.

Dr. Lloyd-Jones' Spirit-blessed preaching didn't stay only in Aberavon. As word of his sermons spread, he received invitations to preach in many different parts of Great Britain. Between 1935-1937, Lloyd-Jones preached to thousands at a time in Great Britain and also in the United States.

In 1938, Dr. Lloyd-Jones was offered a new pastoral opportunity. Pastor **G. Campbell Morgan** (1863-1945), a minister in London, asked Lloyd-Jones to join him at a church called **Westminster Chapel**. Though Martyn and Bethan loved their church and home in Wales, they agreed to move to London and become part of Westminster Chapel.

## EARLY DAYS OF MINISTRY AT WESTMINSTER CHAPEL

I charge you therefore before God and the Lord Jesus Christ, who will judge the living and the

**G. CAMPBELL MORGAN IN 1907**

**WESTMINSTER CHAPEL, LONDON**

dead at His appearing and His kingdom: Preach the word! Be ready in season and out of season. Convince, rebuke, exhort, with all longsuffering and teaching. (2 Tim. 4:1-2)

---

Dr. Lloyd-Jones served as an assistant pastor at Westminster Chapel. From 1938 to 1943, he worked as an assistant to G. Campbell Morgan. The Chapel had a long history of ministry in London. The congregation was formed in 1840 and has continued to the present day. The church's current building was built in 1865 but has undergone significant repairs from time to time. Westminster Chapel is located just a short walk from the monarch's residence at Buckingham Palace. It was one of the largest churches in London at the time.

A year after Dr. Lloyd-Jones' arrival in London, a world war enveloped Europe. The year 1939 marks the beginning of what we call the **Second World War** (World War II, 1939-1945). During this war, Germany bombed London. These German bombings of the city are known as the **London Blitz**. The frequent bombings of London from 1940 to 1941 drove many out of the city. During this turbulent time, some 40,000 people died in the city. As you can imagine, going to church on Sundays was risky.

For some months, the congregation dwindled down to 100 or so, even though the Chapel could hold around 1,500 people. Most fled the city for safety in the countryside. But some remained in the city in the midst of constant danger. On many nights during the Blitz, the piercing wails of air raid sirens could be heard all over London. On Sunday, May 11, 1941, Dr. Lloyd-Jones was scheduled to preach the evening service at the Chapel. However, during the previous night, over 500 German planes had dropped bombs all over London. It was feared

**AFTERMATH OF AN AIR RAID IN LONDON, SEPTEMBER 9, 1940**

that the Chapel may have been destroyed. Many buildings were damaged including the Houses of Parliament, Westminster Abbey, and Westminster School. By morning, many streets were filled with the remnants of collapsed buildings.

However, Dr. Lloyd-Jones believed the church was intact. He returned from a visit to Oxford and made his way to the chapel. As he arrived by train in London, over 2,000 fires were burning all over the city. The doctor exited Paddington Station and asked a taxi driver to take him to Buckingham Gate. The driver replied, "I'm afraid, sir, you cannot get into Buckingham Gate."

"Why not?" the doctor asked.

"Oh, terrible bombing last night, everything flattened!"

Dr. Lloyd-Jones then said, "Look here, you get down in the direction of Victoria, and I will guide you."

The driver agreed and drove him to Victoria. Dr. Lloyd-Jones recounted the experience of that day:

> I was still absolutely certain that I would be preaching in this chapel. I will never forget it. We came round the corner from Palace Street into Castle Lane. I looked, and here was this old building standing as if there had not been a raid at all. I believe I am right in saying that two window-panes on the left side from the pulpit were cracked. And that was all that had happened. I preached here and took the service as usual.

Dr. Lloyd-Jones and G. Campbell Morgan continued their ministry throughout the Blitz. On some occasions, services were moved to another facility. But the church continued to meet even though the congregation was much smaller during the war years.

The war in Europe ended in 1945 with the surrender of Germany to the Allied Forces.

Despite the end of war, the Chapel's attendance was still significantly diminished. Many people had moved elsewhere and did not intend to return to London. Members of the congregation wondered how to rebuild the membership. Some suggested adding a choir or evening organ recitals to attract an audience. But Dr. Lloyd-Jones was immovable in his commitment to preaching. He knew that the proclamation of the gospel was sufficient to build up the church. In time, the church's attendance increased until the upper balconies were opened and filled.

## A MINISTRY OF EXPOSITORY PREACHING

> All Scripture is given by inspiration of God, and is profitable for doctrine, for reproof, for correction, for instruction in righteousness, that the man of God may be complete, thoroughly equipped for every good work. (2 Tim. 3:16-17)

From 1938 to 1968, Dr. Lloyd-Jones dedicated himself to the ministry of preaching, prayer, and shepherding at Westminster Chapel. What the doctor became most well-known for was his style of preaching. He brought back a form of preaching called **expository preaching**. This meant that he preached verse-by-verse through sections or books of the Bible, explaining the meaning of the passage and applying it to his listeners.

In 1952, Lloyd-Jones added a Friday evening preaching service. From 1952 to 1955, he preached a major series of messages called *Great Doctrines of the Bible*. In these messages, he taught the congregation the major doctrines of the Christian faith. He preached in a deep manner, but always spoke to the heart. After finishing this series, Dr. Lloyd-Jones embarked on his longest preaching series. For thirteen years (1955-1968), he preached through the Book of Romans. The series became so popular that Westminster Chapel was often full

SMOKE FROM BOMBS DROPPED ON LONDON DURING THE BLITZ

of eager listeners, ready for another dive into Paul's letter to the Romans. This was a remarkable work of God. While the majority of Londoners drank, partied, and enjoyed other amusements, thousands gathered to hear the Word of God preached on Friday nights.

On most Friday evenings, Lloyd-Jones would exposit just one verse at a time. He was deliberately slow in unpacking Romans verse by verse. He believed that every word of Scripture was worthy of careful consideration. As a result of his slow pace, Dr. Lloyd-Jones never finished preaching through Romans. Due to medical issues, he retired in 1968. After thirteen years, he had only made it as far as Romans 14:17.

> **For the kingdom of God is not eating and drinking, but righteousness and peace and joy in the Holy Spirit. (Rom. 14:17)**

Even though Lloyd-Jones did not finish Romans, he did preach through many other books of the Bible. He preached through the entire book of Ephesians in over 230 sermons. Many of the doctor's sermons are still available as audio recordings.

During Martyn's thirty years of ministry, Westminster Chapel grew and reached many people all over Great Britain and Europe. Dr. Lloyd-Jones received numerous invitations to preach elsewhere in Europe and in North America. The doctor's sermons were also published in book form and continue to enjoy a wide distribution all over the world.

Dr. Lloyd-Jones' ministry in Aberavon and London teaches us that God's Word is powerful. It also teaches us that the Holy Spirit works to save sinners through the preaching of the Bible. Christ's church is strengthened through the gifts of faithful preachers and shepherds. It is also strengthened by men and women of prayer who ask God to accomplish the mighty work of salvation in our midst. ■

## Basic Facts about Wales

*The United Kingdom consists of the nations of England, Wales, Scotland, and Northern Ireland. The facts below pertain to Wales, one of the countries within the UK.*

| Total population: | 3 million |
| --- | --- |
| Total area: | 8,000 square miles |
| Capital: | Cardiff |
| Official language: | English, Welsh |
| Primary religions: | Protestant Christian, Atheist, Agnostic |

TOWERS OF WESTMINSTER ABBEY, LONDON

## PRAYER POINTS: WALES

- **Give thanks to God for His great works in Wales:** Since the time of the Great Awakening, numerous revivals have occurred in Wales, including one within the lifetime of Dr. Martyn Lloyd-Jones in 1904. Let us thank the Lord for the power of the gospel at work in Wales in the past and God's work in the present.

- **Church attendance is dropping dramatically:** Among the countries that constitute the UK, Wales has the sharpest decline in church attendance. Operation World estimates overall church attendance is 7% of the population. For young people, the numbers are even lower. Only 3.5% of people thirty years old and younger attend church. Many churches in Wales are small, consisting sometimes of just twenty-five people. Pray that God would send times of refreshing to this spiritually barren land.

- **Pray for Christian families in Wales:** Ask the Lord to bless the discipleship work of Christian families in Wales. Pray that Christian parents would be faithful to teach God's Word to their children. It may be that another boy like Dr. Lloyd-Jones or a girl like Bethan Lloyd-Jones could arise within Wales and be a blessing to the church of Jesus in that land.

WINDMILLS IN THE NETHERLANDS

# DIET EMAN: FAITHFUL CHRISTIAN OF THE DUTCH RESISTANCE

---
He who dwells in the secret place of the Most High
Shall abide under the shadow of the Almighty.
I will say of the LORD, "He is my refuge and my fortress;
My God, in Him I will trust." (Ps. 91:1-2)
---

On the evening of May 9, 1940, Dutch men, women, and children all over Holland gathered around their radios at home. The voice of **Adolf Hitler** could be heard over the airwaves. Hitler, leader of the **Nazi Party** and **Führer** of Germany, had already conquered Austria and Poland. Other countries in Europe wondered, "Will we be next?" Many in Holland worried that soon their free country would be invaded and conquered by war-hungry Germany. Hitler assured the Dutch people that night that they had nothing to fear. Since the Netherlands had been neutral in World War I, Hitler promised he would respect Dutch neutrality.

Some in Holland went to bed that night hopeful that Hitler would keep his promise. But hours later, on May 10, the Dutch were awakened to the sound of aircraft, flak cannons, and machine-gun fire. The German army was invading. Hitler had lied to the Dutch. **Diet** (pronounced "deet") **Eman** (1920-2019), a twenty-year-old woman, woke up to the sound of battle. From her bedroom in The Hague, she could hear the planes overhead. From that day on, her life would never be the same.

**Queen Wilhelmina**, with the Dutch government, fled to England for safety. They carried with them the national treasury of the Dutch people so that it wouldn't fall into Hitler's hands. Five days later, on May 15, 1940, the Netherlands surrendered to Germany. The Dutch army was defeated. The great city of Rotterdam was pummeled by bombs, and much of the city was destroyed.

Before the surrender, on May 12, Diet wrote to the young man she planned to marry, **Hein Sietsma**. Hein was in the Dutch army, and Diet was concerned for his safety. Diet reminded Hein that they were safe in the hands of their Heavenly Father. She wrote:

> We're not afraid because you're in the Father's hands, where you're safe. We don't see him, but he is with us. He himself promised us that, and he will certainly do it in the hour of danger. . . . The Lord remains the same. He is the rock upon which we lean. He hears all our prayers and answers them in the way that he finds best for us.

Diet's faith, expressed in this letter to Hein, would carry her through many difficult and harrowing days. From the day Holland was invaded until the end of World War II, Diet would serve on the frontlines of the Dutch Resistance. And through it all, she held fast to her faith in Jesus Christ, her Lord and Savior.

## SERVING IN THE DUTCH RESISTANCE

---
And what more shall I say? For the time would fail me to tell of Gideon and Barak and Samson and Jephthah, also of David and Samuel and the prophets: who through faith subdued kingdoms,

353

THE CITY OF ROTTERDAM AFTER THE GERMAN BOMBING

worked righteousness, obtained promises, stopped the mouths of lions, quenched the violence of fire, escaped the edge of the sword, out of weakness were made strong, became valiant in battle, turned to flight the armies of the aliens. (Heb. 11:32-34)

After the Netherlands surrendered, the German army occupied the whole country. German soldiers walked the streets of The Hague where Diet lived. Dutch Christians began to debate how they should respond to this new situation. Was the Dutch government, in exile in England, their government still? Should they obey Queen Wilhelmina from afar? Or were they as Christians bound to submit to the Germans? Some believed that Romans 13 required them to submit to the new government imposed by Germany. Others believed they should resist the tyranny of the Nazis. As the Germans imposed more and more rules, Dutch Christians had to decide. Did they owe allegiance to Hitler? This was an important dividing line that divided families and churches.

The Dutch had enjoyed a long history of freedom. For centuries, the Netherlands was a nation enjoying much liberty. But that quickly changed as the Nazis began to rule with an iron fist. The Dutch were forbidden from listening to radio broadcasts from the BBC (British Broadcasting Corporation). The Germans were concerned that news from England would produce resistance among the Dutch. Then, the Nazis began confiscating everyone's radios. If the Dutch did not comply, they could be thrown in prison. The Nazis also demanded the Dutch to turn in gold and silver metals for the war effort.

Diet and other Christians with her believed the Nazis were evil. They believed that the Nazis were enemies who had no right to occupy Holland. Because they were at war with Germany, many of the Dutch Christians believed it was morally right—and was even their Christian obligation—to resist the Nazis. While not all Christians agreed that it was lawful to lie, others such as Diet believed lying to the enemy was the morally right thing to do. These Christians would point to the examples of the Hebrew midwives and Rahab, who both lied (Ex. 1:18-21; Josh. 2; Heb. 11:31). Because of this, many of the Dutch joined the resistance efforts. They would hide radios. They listened to the BBC voraciously for news about the war. And many protected their metals from confiscation.

As the months progressed, the Nazis began to persecute the Jews in Holland. Jews in Germany had already experienced persecution even before the war. But now, Hitler pressed his anti-Jewish policies in the Netherlands. Jews in Holland were rounded up and then sent away from Holland by train to prison camps in Holland, Poland, and Germany. Hitler believed that the Germans and other European races near Germany were the most highly-evolved human beings. Hitler believed the lie of evolution taught by **Charles Darwin** (1809-1882). In his book, *The Descent of Man*, Darwin taught that human beings were descended from primates. And he believed some races were superior to others. Lower races such as the Africans did not have as pure of blood as those of Germanic descent, Darwin taught. Hitler also believed the Jews were the very lowest form of humanity. He blamed the Jews for many hor-

MEMBERS OF THE DUTCH RESISTANCE

**RATION STAMPS**

rible things. Because of this, Hitler believed the Jews should be exterminated. German soldiers called the Jews many horrible names, including "lice" and "rat."

Christians now had a new challenge before them: would they protect the Jews from imprisonment and death? Some Christians, out of fear, refused to protect the Jews. They turned a blind eye to what was happening. But Diet, her dear friend Hein, and others believed that they had a duty to protect the Jews from Hitler's wicked plans. Diet wrote in her diary on July 21, 1942:

> The Jews are walking with their yellow stars on, are not allowed outside after 8 p.m., are not allowed to visit non-Jews, some streets are forbidden to them.... O God... let us, in the midst of all these things which drive us crazy, still remember that you are the ruler of everything and

**ADOLF HITLER SPEAKING IN THE REICHSTAG IN BERLIN**

that the punishment you will give them for these things will be more just than all things we think of to punish them. Please teach us Christians now to be true Christians and to put into practice what we confess, especially to these Jews. O Lord, make an end to all this, only you can do it. We know that you give strength according to our cross, but it is getting to be so very heavy, Lord.

As Jewish friends were summoned to the train stations to be sent to concentration camps, Diet and others began to find places to hide the Jews. Some were smuggled into the countryside to live on farms. Others stayed in the city, hiding inside apartments. Diet and her now-fiancé Hein would smuggle fake ID cards that could be used to protect the Jews with a false ID. Additionally, ration cards were stolen by the Dutch Resistance in order to get food for the Jews who were in hiding.

It was very dangerous to be a part of the Dutch Resistance. The Nazi police (known as the **Gestapo**) would arrest any resistance members they discovered. Often, Dutch Resistance members were executed for their clandestine actions. In order to protect themselves, Dutch Resistance fighters used false names and fake IDs to protect their real identity and place of residence. Diet went through several false names in her resistance work. Day after day, she rode her bike throughout the Netherlands delivering mail, fake IDs, and ration cards to Jews in hiding. At any time, she might be stopped and questioned by the Gestapo.

## DIET ARRESTED

And the LORD, He is the One who goes before you. He will be with you, He will not leave you nor forsake you; do not fear nor be dismayed." (Deut. 31:8)

One day, in the spring of 1943, Diet was in the town of Reinkenstraat. She met a woman in a city apartment. Diet soon discovered that this woman was secretly hosting twenty-seven Jews in her apartment. While this woman's provision for these Jews was admirable, it was considered foolish among the resistance to keep such a large number of Jews in the city. It was too easy for the Jews to be discovered by the Gestapo. If they were discovered, the Jews and their Dutch hosts would face severe penalties. Likely, every one of them would be shipped off to a concentration camp, perhaps never to return.

Diet warned the woman of how dangerous this situation was. The Jews made much noise, and their voices could be heard through the walls of nearby apartments. With the toilet flushing perhaps eighty to ninety times a day with so many guests, neighbors would quickly suspect something was not normal. Diet offered to help the woman find a new place for these Jews to live. Diet gave a false name to

**THE NETHERLANDS**

the woman to protect her identity. Diet called herself "Toos." Sometime later, the apartment was raided by the Gestapo. Among the papers in the apartment, the Gestapo found the name Toos in some of the woman's documents. Somehow, the Gestapo figured out the connection between Toos and Diet Eman. One evening, the Gestapo visited the Eman's house in The Hague.

Albert Eman, Diet's brother, sent her a message telling her not to return home. Diet worked at a bank in The Hague. But she knew that if she was to remain safe, she would have to leave The Hague and find a place to hide. She walked into her boss's office at the bank and said, "I have to go. See you after the war."

Diet fled to another city called Eindhoven. Meanwhile, her parents lied to the Gestapo about her whereabouts. For a few months, Diet worked as a housemaid in a Dutch home. The Bakker family gave her free lodging if she would work in the home. Diet lived in total isolation during this time. All the while, she longed to see her fiancé Hein. Diet and Hein sent letters back and forth, but they did not see each other for a long time.

On April 26, 1944, Hein was arrested by the Gestapo. He was discovered to have numerous stolen IDs and ration cards. Hein was taken to the prison camp at Amersfoort. Only a few weeks later, Diet was also arrested. The date was May 8, 1944. While sitting on a train, the Gestapo approached Diet and asked for her ID card. At this point, Diet went by the alias "Willie." Her fake ID said as much. But when the Germans examined the card, they realized that it was fake. Diet was escorted off the train and was held by six soldiers on the station platform to await questioning.

Diet was afraid the Gestapo would discover who she was and what she had been doing. Under her shirt, she had in her possession an envelope containing numerous fake IDs and ration cards. But now that she was surrounded by six soldiers, what could she do? While sitting on that train platform bench, Diet prayed silently to God. "Lord, if it's necessary, then we will give our lives, but if it is at all possible, grant that those six men give me half a minute so that I can get rid of this envelope."

What happened next, Diet said, was a miracle. One of the soldiers was wearing a nice, long, new raincoat. He began to show off its features to the other men. As they conversed, the six men near Diet were completely enthralled in the discussion about the man's new raincoat. Diet saw her opportunity. She quickly pulled the envelope out from her shirt and tossed it as far away from her as possible. God answered Diet's prayers. That particular issue was now gone. God in His providence had provided the distraction of that man's raincoat. It was just enough time to get rid of the incriminating envelope.

Nevertheless, with a false ID, Diet was still in trouble. She was taken to a prison near the coast of Holland. The prison was in Scheveningen. Two other Christian women, Corrie and Betsy ten Boom, were also being held there at the same time.

Prison life was very difficult. The food was disgusting. There was little space with so many prisoners jammed into one cell. There were no showers. Women in the prison frequently became ill. But at night, the sound of Allied planes was heard overhead. Dutch prisoners cheered because they knew the Allies were making progress against the Nazis. They longed for the day of liberation to come!

## VUGHT CONCENTRATION CAMP

The eternal God is your refuge,
And underneath are the everlasting arms;

**ALLIED SOLDIERS LAND ON OMAHA BEACH IN NORMANDY, JUNE 6, 1944**

---

He will thrust out the enemy from before you,
And will say, "Destroy!" (Deut. 33:27)

---

June 6, 1944 marked a turning point in World War II. Early in the morning on that day, thousands of Allied soldiers parachuted into the **Normandy** region of France. As the sun rose, thousands of sea vessels landed Allied soldiers on the beaches of Normandy. It was the largest amphibious (sea) invasion in world history. The Allied invasion of Europe had begun. It was a day marked by much bloodshed and suffering. But in God's providence, the Allies secured the beaches of Normandy. From that day on, the Allies continued to advance closer and closer to Berlin. Since that time, June 6 has been known as **D-Day**.

As a result of the invasion, the Germans began to evacuate the prison at **Scheveningen**. Diet and the other women were loaded onto trains and taken to a concentration camp in the southern region of the Netherlands. It was called the **Vught Concentration Camp**. Diet was housed with other women in Barracks #4. There she met Betsy and Corrie ten Boom. Diet was amazed by the steadfast faith of Betsy and Corrie in such appalling conditions. Betsy and Corrie led a daily Bible study for the women in the barracks. They prayed for the women. They also shared portions of the Bible with others. Women would hand scraps of the Bible back and forth, sharing the comforting, strengthening words of Scripture with one another.

Vught was very close to the border of Belgium. On certain days, the sound of artillery

**GATE OF VUGHT CONCENTRATION CAMP**

**CORRIE TEN BOOM (1892-1983)**

could be heard in the distance. General Patton's army was advancing against the Germans. Diet and the other women hoped that their day of liberation would soon come.

After some months of waiting, Diet was given a hearing before the Nazis in charge of the camp. At the hearing, Diet was to explain how she came into possession of a false ID. Because Diet's ID contained a fake name, Diet had to invent a complete fictional story if she wanted to convince the Nazis to set her free. For some weeks, Diet was anxious about the hearing. What if her true identity was discovered? What if the Nazis did not believe her story? But as the day came, the Lord comforted Diet with His promises from the Bible.

When Diet appeared before the soldiers to explain the ID, rather than being afraid, she recounted in her book that she actually felt pity for the men. She wrote:

I thought to myself, *You big shots think you can decide on my life, but I have news for you: you can't touch a hair on my head without the will of God my Father, because he is on my side.* The greatest miracle was that in the end I could actually feel pity for those men because they were so deluded: they thought they had the power, and really they had nothing. I will never forget it. And from that moment on, I've never really hated anymore. It all turned around when I sat there thinking what poor empty souls they were. I've always felt very strongly that when we do evil, we will have to give a final accounting for everything. And then I thought, *I would absolutely hate to be in your shoes, boys.*

After her hearing, Diet was released in August 1944. With the help of others, she eventually made it back to The Hague and was able to see her father and mother. Mr. and Mrs. Eman were overjoyed to see their daughter for the first time in a year. Though it was becoming clearer that the Germans would be defeated by the Allies, the war continued. It was still dangerous to do resistance work. But Diet threw her lot in with the Dutch Resistance once again and began her work of helping the Jews and others in the resistance.

Diet was also able to send letters to her fiancé Hein, who was still in prison. Diet received a letter from Hein dated October 12, 1944. Hein wrote:

> Darling, don't count on our seeing each other again soon. I have the feeling that it will take at least a year. But we are with friends altogether, and you will soon be in a free country. So we have many reasons to be optimistic. And here we see again that we do not decide our own lives. Even if we won't see each other again on earth, we will never be sorry for what we did, that we took this stand. And know, Diet, that of every last human being in this world, I loved you most. And it is still my great desire that we will become a happy family someday.

Diet longed for the day of reunion with Hein. She prayed daily for his safety and deliverance from prison.

## THE END OF THE WAR

Come, behold the works of the LORD,
Who has made desolations in the earth.
He makes wars cease to the end of the earth;
He breaks the bow and cuts the spear in two;
He burns the chariot in the fire.
Be still, and know that I am God;
I will be exalted among the nations,
I will be exalted in the earth!
The LORD of hosts is with us;
The God of Jacob is our refuge. (Ps. 46:8-11)

By April 1945, the end of war was in sight. The Germans were on the retreat. Allied forces pressed deeper into Germany. **Berlin,** the capital of Germany, was the intended destination. Soon, Hitler and the German war machine would come to an end.

British Spitfire planes flew

**ALLIED SOLDIERS IN THE NETHERLANDS, APRIL 1945**

DIET EMAN IN LATER YEARS

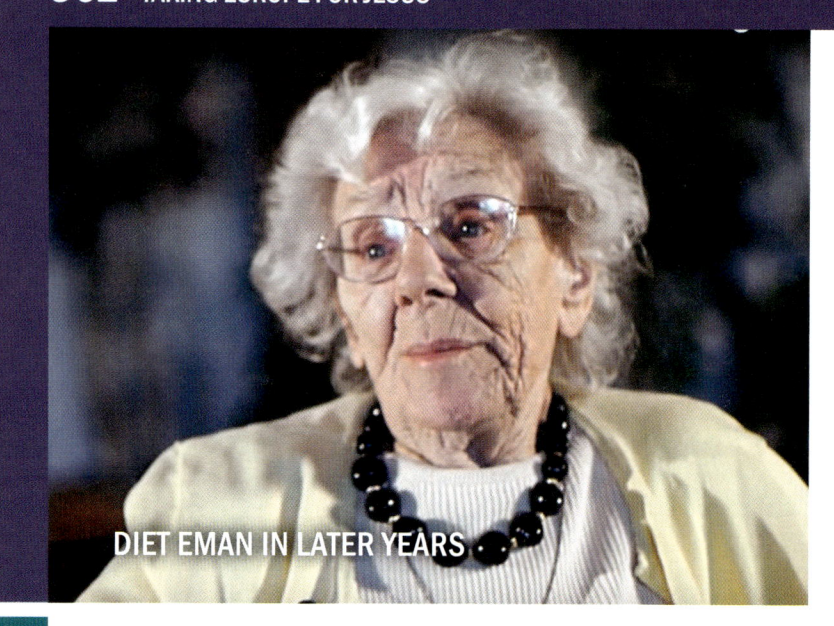

over the Netherlands, destroying German targets on the road. The Dutch had to be careful traveling from city to city lest the planes mistake them for Germans. On April 20, Diet had a special opportunity to contribute to the Allied war effort. She was walking near a field and spotted three German snipers hiding. Not far away, a group of Canadian tanks moved in. Diet ran to the front line of the tanks and spoke to the Canadians in English. She warned them of the snipers that were ahead and told the Canadians where to aim. Diet then sat on one of the tanks and joined the Canadian advance.

As the tanks got closer, Diet shouted out, "There they are! Do you see them?" The German snipers knew their cover was exposed. They immediately surrendered. It was a particularly satisfying day for Diet because April 20 happened to be Hitler's birthday. On that day in 1945, Diet saw that Hitler's empire was crumbling.

Then, on May 5, 1945, the Netherlands were fully liberated. Celebrations took place all over the country. The Lord had answered Diet's prayers. The Dutch were once again free. Now, Diet hoped that she would soon see Hein. Perhaps Hein would be released soon and return home. Then, after so many years of waiting, they would get married!

Sad news came in the form of a letter. It was from Hein's father Mr. Sietsma. Hein's father informed Diet that Hein had died in the prison camp of Dachau in January 1945. Diet was heartbroken. She prayed in her diary on June 7, "God, give me strength to go on from day to day, from hour to hour. Show me the way you want me to go." Diet struggled for a long time with hard questions. Why had God allowed this to happen? Why did Hein die so close to the end of the war? Why?

Diet did not know the answers to these questions. But she knew that she had to trust

## Basic Facts about the Netherlands

| Total population: | 17.5 million |
| Total area: | 16,000 square miles |
| Capital: | Amsterdam, The Hague (seat of government) |
| Official language: | Dutch |
| Primary religions: | Atheist, Agnostic |

# PRAYER POINTS: NETHERLANDS

- **Give thanks to God for a rich Protestant Christian heritage:** After the Protestant Reformation, the Netherlands became one of the most Protestant nations in Europe. It was here that the *Mayflower* Pilgrims lived for a time in the 1600s, seeking religious freedom from King James in England. For a time, a profession of Christianity was common among most citizens in the Netherlands.

- **Pray that God would awaken dead hearts:** Today, the Netherlands is among the most secular nations in Europe. Most in the Netherlands have turned their hearts away from God. Amsterdam, the capital, is among the most degraded cities in Europe. Most in the Netherlands profess to follow no religion, but they are slaves to sin. Pray that God would awaken dead hearts. Pray that the remaining churches in this land would stand fast and minister truth to a dying culture.

- **Pray for missionaries to the Netherlands:** The Netherlands once sent missionaries to other parts of the world. Now, this country needs missionaries to its own people! Pray that God would raise up and send faithful mission-minded Christians to the Netherlands. Ask the Lord to equip all Dutch Christians with a missionary mindset as well.

---

God's purposes. She also found comfort in the fact that Hein was now with the Lord. She wrote in her diary on June 14, "There is only one answer, and that gives me rest. Psalm 73:23-24: 'You have guided him with your eternal counsel and have now taken him into glory.'" Diet missed Hein deeply. But she knew that "to depart and be with Christ is far better" (see Phil. 1:23).

After the war, Diet left the Netherlands. She lived for a time in Venezuela working as a nurse for the Shell Oil Company. Later, she settled in **Grand Rapids**, Michigan. For a long time, Diet would not speak about her painful experiences during the war. But in 1994, she published a memoir of her life called *Things We Couldn't Say*. Her life story of faithfulness in difficulty has inspired Christians ever since to trust God, to serve Christ, to love their neighbor, and to resist evil. At the age of ninety-nine, Diet went to be with the Lord on September 3, 2019. ■

---

Do not fear any of those things which you are about to suffer. Indeed, the devil is about to throw some of you into prison, that you may be tested, and you will have tribulation ten days. Be faithful until death, and I will give you the crown of life. (Rev. 2:10)

# BIBLIOGRAPHY

Below is a list of works consulted in the research and writing of *Taking Europe for Jesus*.

Aitken, Jonathan, *John Newton: From Disgrace to Amazing Grace* (Crossway, 2007).

Audisio, Gabriel, *The Waldensian Dissent, c. 1170-c.1570*, trans. Claire Davison (Cambridge University Press, 1999).

Bede, *Ecclesiastical History of the English People*, trans. Leo Sherley-Price (Penguin, 1990).

Behr, John, *Irenaeus of Lyons: Identifying Christianity* (Oxford University Press, 2013).

Bellesheim, Alphons, *St. Columba and Iona: The Early History of the Christian Church in Scotland* (Eremitical Press, 1887).

Carr, Simonetta, *Irenaeus of Lyon* (Reformation Heritage Books, 2017).

Cook, Faith, *Lady Jane Grey: Nine Day Queen of England* (EP Books, 2004).

Dales, Douglas, *Alcuin: His Life and Legacy* (James Clarke & Co., 2012).

Dallimore, Arnold, *George Whitefield: The Life and Times of the Great Evangelist of the 18th Century Revival, Vol. 1* (Banner of Truth, 1970).

Dallimore, Arnold, *George Whitefield: The Life and Times of the Great Evangelist of the 18th Century Revival, Vol. 2* (Banner of Truth, 1980).

Dallimore, Arnold, *Spurgeon: A New Biography* (Banner of Truth, 1985).

Gonzalez, Justo L., *The Story of Christianity, Vol. 1: The Early Church to the Dawn of the Reformation* (Harper, 2010).

Gonzalez, Justo L., *The Story of Christianity, Vol. 2: The Reformation to the Present Day* (Harper, 2010).

Eman, Diet, *Things We Couldn't Say* (Eerdmans, 1994).

Eusebius, *The Church History*, trans. Paul L. Maier (Kregel, 2007).

Gordon, Bruce, *Calvin* (Yale University Press, 2009).

Holland, Tom, *Athelstan: The Making of England* (Allen Lane, 2016).

Hutton, J.E., *A History of Moravian Missions* (Moravian Publication Office, 1922).

Lahey, Stephen E, *John Wyclif* (Oxford University Press, 2009).

Lawson, Steven J., *The Bible Convictions of John Wycliffe* (Ligonier Ministries, 2021).

Lawson, Steven J., *The Passionate Preaching of Martyn Lloyd-Jones* (Ligonier Ministries, 2016).

MacCallum, Duncan, *The History of the Culdees; The Ancient Clergy of the British Isles, A.D. 177-1300* (Houlston and Stoneman, 1885).

Mandryk, Jason, *Operation World: The Definitive Prayer Guide to Every Nation*, 7th ed. (IVP, 2010).

Merkle, Benjamin, *The White Horse King: The Life of Alfred the Great* (Thomas Nelson, 2009).

Murray, Iain H., *D. Martyn Lloyd-Jones: The First Forty Years, 1899-1939* (Banner of Truth, 1982).

Murray, Iain H., *D. Martyn Lloyd-Jones: The Fight of Faith, 1939-1981* (Banner of Truth, 1990).

Needham, Nick, *2000 Years of Christ's Power, Vol. 1: The Age of the Early Church Fathers* (Christian Focus, 2016).

Needham, Nick, *2000 Years of Christ's Power, Vol. 2: The Middle Ages* (Christian Focus, 2016).

Needham, Nick, *2000 Years of Christ's Power, Vol. 3: Renaissance and Reformation* (Christian Focus, 2016).

Needham, Nick, *2000 Years of Christ's Power, Vol. 4: The Age of Religious Conflict* (Christian Focus, 2016).

Parker, G.H.W., *The Morning Star: Wycliffe and the Dawn of the Reformation* (Wipf and Stock, 2006).

Pasini, Cesare, *Ambrose of Milan: Deeds and Thoughts of a Bishop*, trans. Robert L. Grant (St. Pauls, 2013).

Potocek, Cyril J., *Saints Cyril and Methodius, Apostles of the Slavs* (P.J. Kennedy and Sons, 1941).

Price, Simon and Peter Thonemann, *The Birth of Classical Europe: A History from Troy to Augustine* (Viking, 2010).

Rex, Richard, *The Lollards* (Palgrave, 2002).

Rimbert, *Anskar: The Apostle of the North, translated from the Vita Anskarii*, trans. Charles H. Robinson (1921).

# BIBLIOGRAPHY

Ritchie, Bruce, *Columba: The Faith of an Island Soldier* (Christian Focus, 2019).

Schaff, David S., *John Huss: His Life, Teachings and Death After Five Hundred Years* (Charles Scribner's Sons, 1915).

Schaff, Philip, and David S. Schaff, *History of the Christian Church*, 8 volumes (Charles Scribner's Sons, 1910).

Sheats, R.A., *Pierre Viret: The Angel of the Reformation* (Zurich Publishing 2012).

Spurgeon, C.H., *Autobiography, Vol. 1: The Early Years* (Banner of Truth, 1962).

Spurgeon, C.H., *Autobiography, Vol. 2: The Full Harvest* (Banner of Truth, 1973).

Stuart, K. Moody, *Brownlow North: His Life and Work* (Banner of Truth, 2020).

Swanson, Kevin, *Epoch: The Rise and Fall of the West* (Generations, 2021).

Swanson, Kevin, *Taking the World for Jesus: The Remarkable Story of the Greatest Commission* (Master Books/Generations, 2017).

Tachiaos, Anthony-Emil N., *Cyril and Methodius of Thessalonica: The Acculturation of the Slavs* (St. Vladimir's Seminary Press, 2001).

Tracy, Joseph, *The Great Awakening: A History of the Revival of Religion in the Time of Whitefield and Edwards* (Banner of Truth, 2019).

Ward, Benedicta, *The Venerable Bede* (Cistercian Publications, 1998).

Weinlick, John R. *Count Zinzendorf: The Story of His Life and Leadership in the Renewed Moravian Church* (The Moravian Church in America, 1984).

Wylie, J.A. *The History of the Waldenses* (Cassell and Company, 1860).

# LIST OF IMAGES

All images, unless otherwise noted, are from iStock.com (Getty Images). The following are a list of exceptions.

## CHAPTER 1
1. Gulf Streams - Wikimedia Commons

## CHAPTER 2
1. The Roman Empire at its largest (AD 117) - Wikimedia Commons
2. Alexander the Great - Wikimedia Commons
3. Empire of Alexander the Great - Wikimedia Commons
4. Hannibal crossing the Alps - Wikimedia Commons

## CHAPTER 6
1. Pages from a Gnostic writing - Wikimedia Commons

## CHAPTER 7
1. Mosaic of Ambrose - Wikimedia Commons
2. Augustine and his mother Monica - Wikimedia Commons

## CHAPTER 8
1. Pelagius - Wikimedia Commons

## CHAPTER 9
1. Stained glass depiction of Patrick - Wikimedia Commons

## CHAPTER 10
1. A page from the *Book of Kells* displaying Jesus' genealogy from the Gospel of Luke - Wikimedia Commons
2. Statue of Aidan in Lindisfarne - Wikimedia Commons

## CHAPTER 11
1. Kingdoms of Great Britain around 600 - Wikimedia Commons
2. Helmet from the Anglo-Saxon period - Wikimedia Commons

## CHAPTER 12
1. St. Peter's Church, Monkwearmouth - Wikimedia Commons
2. Image of Bede writing his *History* - Wikimedia Commons

## CHAPTER 13
1. Coronation of Charlemagne - Wikimedia Commons
2. Medieval artwork depicting Alcuin - Wikimedia Commons
3. Illustration of Charlemagne - Wikimedia Commons
4. Charlemagne's conquests - Wikimedia Commons

## CHAPTER 14
1. Illustration of Anskar - Wikimedia Commons
2. Corbey Abbey - Wikimedia Commons
3. "Anskar's Cross" in Birka, Sweden - Wikimedia Commons
4. Hamburg, Germany in the 1100s - Wikimedia Commons

## CHAPTER 15
1. A text written in Cyrillic script, 13th century - Wikimedia Commons
2. Iconography of Ratislav - Wikimedia Commons
3. The Gospel of Mark using the Glagolitic alphabet - Wikimedia Commons
4. Sculpture of Cyril and Methodius - Wikimedia Commons

## CHAPTER 16
1. The Danelaw - Wikimedia Commons

## CHAPTER 17
1. King Athelstan - Wikimedia Commons
2. Statue of Aethelflaed with young Athelstan - Wikimedia Commons
3. Silver penny from the reign of Athelstan - Wikimedia Commons

## CHAPTER 18
1. Pope Innocent III - Wikimedia Commons
2. Illustration of the Albigensian Crusade - Wikimedia Commons

## CHAPTER 19
1. Statue of Peter Waldo, Worms, Germany - Wikimedia Commons
2. A picture of the Waldensians portrayed as witches - Wikimedia Commons
3. Waldensian church in Rome - Wikimedia Commons
4. King Francis I - Wikimedia Commons

## CHAPTER 20
1. Kublai Khan - Wikimedia Commons
2. Genghis Khan - Wikimedia Commons
3. Marco Polo - Wikimedia Commons
4. Spread of the Black Death - Wikimedia Commons

## CHAPTER 21
1. Illustration of Wycliffe sending out the Lollards - Wikimedia Commons
2. Beginning of the Gospel of John from a Wycliffe pocket translation - Wikimedia Commons
3. Modern-day Lutterworth, England - Wikimedia Commons

## CHAPTER 22
1. King Richard II - Wikimedia Commons
2. Reconstructed Bethlehem Chapel in Prague - Wikimedia Commons

3. Interior of the Bethlehem Chapel - Wikimedia Commons
4. John Huss at the Council of Constance - Wikimedia Commons

## CHAPTER 23
1. Illustration of Savonarola preaching - Wikimedia Commons
2. Lorenzo de Medici - Wikimedia Commons
3. Charles VIII - Wikimedia Commons
4. Savonarola executed - Wikimedia Commons

## CHAPTER 24
1. William Tyndale - Wikimedia Commons
2. King Henry VIII - Wikimedia Commons
3. Gaspard de Coligny - Wikimedia Commons
4. Catherine de Medici - Wikimedia Commons

## CHAPTER 25
1. Pierre Viret - Zurich Publishing, used by permission
2. Orbe, Switzerland - Wikimedia Commons
3. Jeanne d'Albret - Wikimedia Commons

## CHAPTER 26
1. Illustration of French Huguenots - Wikimedia Commons
2. King Henry IV - Wikimedia Commons
3. Huguenot church in Charleston, South Carolina - Wikimedia Commons

## CHAPTER 27
1. Lady Jane Grey - Wikimedia Commons
2. Edward VI - Wikimedia Commons
3. Thomas Cranmer - Wikimedia Commons
4. Mary I - Wikimedia Commons
5. The White Tower, within the Tower of London - Wikimedia Commons
6. The execution of Lady Jane Grey - Wikimedia Commons
7. Burning of Ridley and Latimer from *Foxe's Book of Martyrs* - Wikimedia Commons

## CHAPTER 28
1. Church in Gross-Hennersdorf - Wikimedia Commons
2. Herrnhut, center of the Moravian Church - Wikimedia Commons

## CHAPTER 29
1. George Whitefield - Wikimedia Commons
2. John Wesley - Wikimedia Commons
3. Charles Wesley - Wikimedia Commons

## CHAPTER 30
1. John Newton - Wikimedia Commons
2. Diagram of slave ship showing "human cargo" - Wikimedia Commons
3. Advertisement in Charleston, South Carolina, 1769 - Wikimedia Commons
4. William Cowper - Wikimedia Commons
5. St. Mary's Woolnoth, London - Wikimedia Commons

## CHAPTER 31
1. Henry Martyn - Wikimedia Commons

## CHAPTER 32
1. Brownlow North - Wikimedia Commons
2. Illustration of Dunkeld Cathedral, Scotland - Wikimedia Commons
3. William C. Burns - Wikimedia Commons

## CHAPTER 33
1. Charles Spurgeon - Wikimedia Commons
2. Susannah Spurgeon with her two sons - Wikimedia Commons
3. Spurgeon preaching at Surrey Gardens - Wikimedia Commons
4. Interior of the Metropolitan Tabernacle - Wikimedia Commons
5. Cover page of *The Sword and the Trowel* - Wikimedia Commons
6. Metropolitan Tabernacle in London, England - Wikimedia Commons

## CHAPTER 34
1. Gate of St. Bartholomew's Hospital, London - Wikimedia Commons
2. D. Martyn Lloyd-Jones - Wikimedia Commons
3. Forward Movement Mission Hall - Wikimedia Commons
4. G. Campbell Morgan - Wikimedia Commons
5. Westminster Chapel, London - Wikimedia Commons
6. Aftermath of an air raid in London, September 9, 1940 - Wikimedia Commons
7. Smoke from bombs dropped on London during the Blitz - Wikimedia Commons

## CHAPTER 35
1. The city of Rotterdam after the Germany Bombing - Wikimedia Commons
2. Members of the Dutch Resistance - Wikimedia Commons
3. Ration stamps - Wikimedia Commons
4. Adolf Hitler speaking in the Reichstag in Berlin - Wikimedia Commons
5. Allied soldiers land on Omaha Beach in Normandy, June 6, 1944 - Wikimedia Commons
6. Gate of Vught Concentration Camp - Wikimedia Commons
7. Corrie ten Boom - Wikimedia Commons
8. Allied soldiers in the Netherlands, April 1945 - Wikimedia Commons
9. Diet Eman in later years - Wikimedia Commons